INTRODUCING
DEATH *and* DYING

INTRODUCING
DEATH *and* DYING

READINGS AND EXERCISES

Thomas K. Carr

Associate Professor of Religious Studies and Philosophy
Mount Union College

PEARSON
Prentice Hall

Upper Saddle River, New Jersey 07458

Library of Congress Cataloging-in-Publication Data

Carr, Thomas K.
  Introducing death and dying: readings and exercises/Thomas K. Carr.
      p.   cm.
  Includes bibliographical references and index.
     ISBN 0-13-183103-8
    1. Death—Textbooks.   I. Title.

BD444.C365 2006
128'.5—dc22   2005047665

Editorial Director: Charlyce Jones-Owen
Assistant Editor: Wendy B. Yurash
Editorial Assistant: Carla Worner
Marketing Manager: Kara Kindstrom
Production Liaison: Joanne Hakim
Manufacturing Buyer: Christina Helder
Cover Art Director: Jayne Conte
Cover Design: Bruce Kenselaar
Manager, Cover Visual Research & Permissions: Karen Sanatar
Cover Photo: Getty Images, Inc.
Full-Service Project Management: Dennis Troutman/Stratford Publishing Services
Composition: Integra Software Services Pvt. Ltd.
Printer/Binder: Hamilton Printing Company

Credits and acknowledgments borrowed from other sources and reproduced, with permission, in this textbook appear on pages 359–362

Pearson Education LTD., London
Pearson Education Singapore, Pte. Ltd
Pearson Education, Canada, Ltd
Pearson Education—Japan
Pearson Education Australia PTY, Limited

Pearson Education North Asia Ltd
Pearson Educación de Mexico, S.A. de C.V.
Pearson Education Malaysia, Pte. Ltd
Pearson Education, Upper Saddle River, New Jersey

10 9 8 7 6 5 4 3 2 1
ISBN 0-13-183103-8

Contents

About the Author   ix
Acknowledgments   xi

PART I

The Meanings of Death
13

Introduction   **Why Study Death?**   1

Chapter 1   **Heavens and Hells**   13
   1. New Testament, *The Book of Revelation*   17
   2. St. Matthew, *The Gospel According to Matthew*   19
   3. Betty Eadie, *Embraced by the Light*   21
   4. Frank Tipler, *The Physics of Immortality*   27
   5. Karl Marx, *Religion, the Opium of the People*   31
   6. James Joyce, *Hell Is the Centre of Evils*   32
   7. Alice Turner, *Universalism*   34
     Small Group Exercises   38
     Practical Learning Component   38

Chapter 2   **Resurrection and Reincarnation**   39
   1. St. Paul, *First Letter to the Corinthians*   49
   2. A. N. Wilson, *Life After Death? A Fate Worse than Death*   52
   3. J. P. Moreland, *A Defense of the Resurrection of Jesus*   58
   4. Bishop John Shelby Spong, *Life After Death—This I Do Believe*   62
   5. John Bowker, *Death in Hinduism*   67
   6. Sogyal Rinpoche, *The Experiences of the Bardo*   74
   7. Brian Weiss, *Many Lives, Many Masters*   81

Small Group Exercises   85
Practical Learning Component   86

Chapter 3   **Death and Philosophy**   87

1. Plato, *Death as a Release from Prison*   92
2. Marcus Aurelius, *Mental Aids to a Happy Death*   99
3. Chuang Tzu, *Accepting Death*   101
4. Martin Heidegger, *Death Is Something Impending*   105
5. Bertrand Russell, *Do We Survive Death?*   107
   Small Group Exercises   111
   Practical Learning Component   112

PART II

The Practicalities of Dying
113

Chapter 4   **Being With the Dying**   113

1. Elisabeth Kübler-Ross, *Acceptance*   120
2. Marian Gentile, Maryanne Fello, *Hospice Care: A Concept Coming of Age*   126
3. Michael Christofer, *The Shadow Box*   135
4. Charles Meyer, *How to Be With the Dying*   139
5. Ira Byock, *Lessons from Michael*   150
6. Mitch Albom, *Tuesdays with Morrie*   165
   Small Group Exercises   168
   Practical Learning Component   168

Chapter 5   **Suicide**   169

1. Tom Beauchamp, *The Problem of Defining Suicide*   176
2. Joel Feinberg, *Whose Life Is It Anyway?*   181
3. Arthur Schopenhauer, *On Suicide*   187
4. St. Thomas Aquinas, *Whether It Is Lawful to Kill Oneself*   189
   Small Group Exercises   192
   Practical Learning Component   192

Chapter 6   **The Rights of the Dying**   193

1. Timothy Quill, *Death and Dignity: A Case of Individualized Decision Making*   202
2. Edmund Pellegrino, *Distortion of the Healing Relationship*   208
3. Hans Küng, *The Theological Controversy of Physician-Assisted Suicide*   212
4. Dan Brock, *When Is Patient Care Not Costworthy?*   216
5. John Harris, *The Value of Life*   222

Small Group Exercises 227
Practical Learning Component 228

Chapter 7 **Near-Death Experiences**   229
  1. Raymond Moody, *The Light Beyond* 237
  2. Allan Kellehear, *Non-Western Near-Death Experiences* 247
  3. Carol Zaleski, *NDEs as Symbolic Narratives* 260
  4. Susan Blackmore, *Near-Death Experiences: In or Out of the Body?* 269
  5. P. M. H. Atwater, *What Is Not Being Said about the
     Near-Death Experience* 280
  6. Dr. Kenneth Ring, *Interpretations of the NDE* 289
     Small Group Exercises 300
     Practical Learning Component 301

Chapter 8 **Preparing for Death**   302
  1. Elaine Landau, *Advance Directives for Health Care* 310
  2. Patricia Weenolsen, *Power over Pain* 316
  3. Kenneth J. Doka, *The Spiritual Needs of the Dying* 323
  4. Mr. David Kessler, *Spirituality and Death* 329
  5. Maggie Callanan and Patricia Kelley, *Final Gifts* 337
  6. Thomas Attig, *Relearning Our World* 349
  7. Elisabeth Kübler-Ross, *On Life and Living* 353
     Small Group Exercises 356
     Practical Learning Component 357

Copyright Acknowledgments 359
Glossary of End-of-Life Terms 363
Endnotes 365

About the Author

THOMAS K. CARR is currently associate professor and departmental chair of religious studies and philosophy at Mount Union College where his course, Death and Dying, is the most popular elective the college offers. He is a former research fellow in religious studies at Liverpool University in Liverpool, England. He holds the M.Phil. and D.Phil. degrees in theology and philosophy from the University of Oxford, England, along with the M.Div. degree from Princeton Theological Seminary. His B.A. in medicine is from Willamette University. He has served as a member of the Ethics Committee at Alliance Community Hospital and as a volunteer for Stark County Hospice, and is a member of the American Academy of Religion, the American Philosophical Association, and the Association for Death Education and Counseling. Dr. Carr has published widely on religious and philosophical subjects. His current research focuses on the connections between neurophysiology and religious experience. He lists his hobbies as reading, running, biking, the stock market, and spending time with his wife, Ina, and his two daughters, Natasha and Nadia.

Dr. Carr began his studies on the subject of death shortly after the passing of his mother from breast cancer (Laura Anne Kinsell Carr, 1936–1993). Serving as a caretaker of his mother in her last months, he became convinced that the experience of the approach of death is one of the most challenging, and most transformative, of all human experiences.

Dr. Carr is often in demand as a speaker and workshop leader on issues pertaining to death and dying. For booking information please contact him at carrtk@muc.edu.

Acknowledgments

The collection of readings here, their introductions, and the various group and practical learning exercises are largely a product of my collaboration over the past eight years with several hundred students who have taken my course in Death and Dying. Their insights, questions, responses, small group presentations, and critical course evaluations have all served to shape this material into its present form.

Credit should rightly be given to the former Dean of Mount Union College, David Watson, for allowing me in the spring of 1997 the right to teach Death and Dying for the first time. There was some concern that the class would not meet its entry requirements due to the dreary nature of the subject matter. Imagine our mutual surprise when eighty-seven students signed up for a class that was capped at twenty-five! It has remained ever since the most popular elective the College offers. Thanks are also due that Dean's successor, Richard Marriot, who graciously granted me a semester's leave from my teaching duties in order to finish the manuscript of this text.

An enormous amount of gratitude must be directed toward my lovely wife, Ina, for formatting much of the original manuscript, and for typing several of the readings when a scanning machine was not readily available. It will come as no surprise to those who know her that working on a book on "death" was not something to which she felt any degree of passionate commitment. Nevertheless, she persevered with the work at hand, enabling me to get the text to the publishers in time to celebrate the Christmas holidays.

I would like to thank the following reviewers for their comments and suggestions: Rev. Janet Fuller Carruthers, Hollins University; Gary Laderman, Emory University; Randal Cummings, California State University–Northridge; Douglas Shrader Jr., State University of New York–Oneonta; Ted A. Warfield, University of Notre Dame; Christine Perring, Dowling College; Barbara Darling-Smith, Wheaton College.

This book is dedicated to my father, Rev. Thomas H. Carr, for his unwavering affection and his enduring support. It also serves as a memorial to my mother, Laura Anne Carr, whose untimely death from breast cancer in the winter of 1993 prompted my conviction to further, in some small way, our understanding of death and the dying process.

Thomas K. Carr

INTRODUCING
DEATH and DYING

Introduction

-*-

Why Study Death?

Dying
Is an art, like everything else.
—SYLVIA PLATH

There are two surefire ways to stop an unwanted conversation with a stranger on a plane. One way is to proclaim with great pride to the person seated next to you that you are a professor of religion. And if that fails to dampen the chatter you mention that your favorite course is one on death and dying. There is no better way to send your seatmate back to her magazine or to staring out the window. "That's a rather morbid subject!" is one comment I have had. When I first took up my present position as a professor of philosophy at a small, midwestern liberal arts college, and word got out that I was teaching a course on death, three reporters from local newspapers came to the college to interview me. That is how "strange" the idea of death seems to some people.

There is an odd taboo placed on the talk of death in our American society. Along with politics and religion, death is one of those all too easily avoided subjects at dinner parties and family gatherings. Why is this so? Perhaps it is because the present generation has become deconditioned to the idea of death. A century ago, it would have been common for three, four, or even five generations to live together under the same roof. In such conditions, firsthand experiences with death would have been the norm. Children would have been expected to join their parents in the "death watch" at grandma's bedside as she passed on. By mid-century that began to change. Statistics show that by 1949, 50 percent of all deaths occurred not at home but in institutional settings—hospitals and nursing homes. This figure increased to 61 percent by 1959

1

and to 70 percent by 1979. Today, it is estimated that 80 percent of all deaths occur not in the secure setting where people have spent much of their lives, surrounded by family, friends, and treasured objects, but quite frequently alone and in the impersonal setting of clinical equipment monitored by strangers.[1] The removal of death from the home and family where it can potentially be a life-transforming event for all who witness it has prompted scholars Richard Dumont and Dennis Foss to ask,

> How is the modern American able to cope with his own death when the deaths he experiences are infrequent, highly impersonal, and viewed as virtually abnormal?[2]

    This trend of hiding death from the living, of keeping it "offstage,"[3] will likely continue into the future. As the number of elderly increases due to the increase in life expectancy, and the required mobility of many careers force younger generations to see their families less frequently, direct exposure to death and dying will become more and more rare. We simply are not as conditioned to experience and understand death as former generations were. As one textbook on death and dying puts it, "Modern-day Americans have been as repressed about death as the Victorians were about sex."[4]

Death and Dying Fact

In 1900, life expectancy from birth was about 46 for American females and 41 for American males. In 1990, these figures increased to 79 and 75. It is now estimated that by the year 2050, the average female will live to the age of 86, and the average male to the age of 80.

National Center for Health Statistics, 2001

THE DECONDITIONING OF DEATH

This deconditioning or "denial" of death has been furthered in our time by the unprecedented use of violence in film and on television. In earlier generations, death scenes were few, quickly shown, and relatively bloodless. A single gunshot or knife in the back was all it took to knock off the victim. Today, audiences are treated to extended scenes of torture, bloodletting, and compounded injury. This is partly driven by economics: thrillers featuring blood and gore have been big hits in recent years. And in the entertainment industry, a successful model is usually duplicated (consider the number of "Nightmare on Elm Street," "Halloween," and "Scream" movies). But it may also be a product of the increasing violence seen in real human society. A 1988 study concluded that by the age of 15, the average American teenager has not only seen 13,000 murders on television and in film, he or she has also been exposed to about the same number of deaths in the daily news as stories of war, famine, and holocaust are given first billing (undoubtedly these figures have increased since that study).[5]

Recent research has shown that frequent exposure to violence and death in the media serves to desensitize us to death and dying. Because the news, films, and television shows seldom portray the bitter realities of death—the grief, the existential questioning, the anger—they can cause the viewing public to feel that death is something dispassionate, that it has no *emotional* impact (either positive or negative). This in turn can lead to the idea that violence and death have no real consequences, that death is a kind of end in itself.

In 1997 two scholars at the University of Birmingham in England conducted a study of the influence of violence in film. While it concluded that violent films are not likely to incite violent behavior in those not predisposed to violence, they are at least partly responsible for increasing such behavior in those who are "at risk."[6] A British government report in 1998, citing the study, stated that "violent films may reinforce distorted perceptions about appropriate means of resolving conflict and responding to provocation."[7]

Whether or not violent films cause violence is not at issue here. What is at issue is the kind of numbness we may increasingly feel toward death from witnessing the amount of violence we see in our media. In May of 1999, a British teenager was sentenced to life in prison for setting his girlfriend on fire. The jury was told that he was inspired to the act by watching the Quentin Tarantino film, *Reservoir Dogs,* which had been aired the night before the murder on British television.[8] Six months later, the same film was shown again, and again disaster struck. This time, two teenage boys abducted a third boy, stripped him, tortured him for two hours, and finally killed him. They told the jury that they were simply acting out the infamous torture scene from the movie.[9]

What these and similar events from American society may be telling us is that death is no longer thought of as a life event filled with meaning, challenge, and potentially transformative power.

Death as a meaningful event is still very much with us, as was clearly evident in the tremendous outpouring of emotion at the deaths of Princess Diana and Mother Theresa in 1997 and John Kennedy Jr. in 1999. But death as a fictional event, death as *drama,* is too readily seen in the media portrayal of such tragedies as the 1993 raid on the Branch Davidian compound in Waco, Texas, the 1995 Oklahoma City bombings, and the 1999 killing spree at Columbine High School. While the "if it bleeds it leads" caricature of much of news programming may be sensationalist, there is evidence to suggest that the quantity of reported violence and the ways in which it is reported tend toward a "depersonalization" of death. As Robert Fulton and Greg Owen suggest, the media often "submerge the human meaning of death while depersonalizing the event further by sandwiching actual reports of loss of life between commercials or other mundane items."[10]

On October 9, 1995, a massive earthquake rocked the Pacific port city of Manzanillo, Mexico. It registered 7.9 on the Richter scale, and was responsible for over fifty deaths, 10,000 left homeless, and millions of dollars in structural damage. In quick response CNN sent a camera crew to the area in search of a human interest story. They immediately found one. Trapped inside a collapsed apartment building was a twelve-year-old girl named Emelia. As work crews struggled to free Emilia, the CNN camera crew positioned themselves inside the building, training their cameras on the young girl's pained and fearful face. For ten agonizing hours, the world stared transfixed as workers tried valiantly to remove the wall that had Emilia pinned down. But it soon became apparent that their efforts would be in vain. The quake had ruptured plumbing in the basement of the building and water was beginning to collect at the workers' feet. Soon it was up to their knees. Viewers agonized as little Emelia struggled to keep her head above water. A snorkel was brought in to help her breathe. Finally, after every possible effort was made, the workers said a prayer over Emelia as they watched the water rush over the top of her snorkel. After ten hours it was all over—and between commercials and brief news breaks, CNN had broadcast the whole ordeal to the world.

How often have we sat staring at televised news as the stories of plane crashes or terrorist bombings bring us the sights and sounds of real-life death? While we may be moved to tears of compassion, more than likely we are also beginning to develop a kind of spiritual callousness toward such scenes. The likely consequence of the death-voyeurism these media portrayals induce in us is an understanding of death as something not quite real. Recall the Saturday morning cartoons' depiction of death. Wile E. Coyote is blown to bits by his own bomb but returns in the next scene to chase the Road Runner again. Popeye drives a steamroller over Bluto who, flat as a pancake, walks off very much alive. Elmer Fudd sticks his face in front of a loaded rifle just as it goes off, stares at the camera blackfaced, and vows yet again to "catch that wascally wabbit!" In American society we are trained from an early age to think of death as something reversible, even trivial.

The language used to refer to death can be a key indicator of present attitudes toward death. Language mediates prevailing attitudes as they are brought to situations in the world around us that require a response. With this in mind, we can see that much of the language used for death in this country reveals an attitude of discomfort. For example, veterinarians do not "kill" pets, they "put them to sleep." Loved ones do not die, they "pass away" or are "laid to rest." When someone dies we enlist the help of a "funeral director," not a mortician or undertaker. Funeral directors sometimes refer to the room where the body is "laid out" for viewing as the "slumber room"—or "parlor," which is reminiscent of times when people died at home—and many of today's caskets are more comfortable than our own beds! Headstones read "R.I.P." (rest in peace), not simply "dead." Even the word "cemetery" is derived from the Greek *koimeterion,* which means "place for sleep." Cemeteries are given names such as "park," "garden," or "haven of rest." Walk into any card shop and go to the "recently departed" or "sympathy" section and you will find many examples of the use of pleasant language to conceal the often very unpleasant realities of death.

The military has made death-language into a kind of science. Soldiers killed in battle are often described as "KIAs" (killed in action) and as numbered among a "body count," while civilian deaths are called "casualties," or more darkly, "collateral damage." In this way, the real-life horrors of death in battle and the tragic consequences such death leaves in its wake are depersonalized, glossed over euphemistically in the effort to maintain public support for the military's "peace-keeping" missions abroad.

Metaphors and Euphemisms for Death

passed on, gone to heaven, gone home, breathed his/her last, succumbed, laid to rest, went to his/her eternal reward, went to meet his/her Maker, checked out, eternal rest, called home, was a goner, came to an end, bit the dust, kicked the bucket, left this world, rubbed out, snuffed, found everlasting peace, in the great beyond, no longer with us, on the other side, in the light, God took him/her, it was his/her time to go, asleep in Christ, dearly departed, with the angels in heaven, feeling no pain, cashed in his/her chips, crossed over the Jordan, translated into glory, returned to dust, a long sleep, resting in peace, out of his/her misery, ended it all, that was all he/she wrote, passed away, pushing up daisies.

The use of euphemisms and metaphors for death does not always indicate a denial of death. As is evident from the above list, there are many phrases used for death that convey religious meaning. While sometimes, no doubt, these are used merely by convention—that is, in an unfeeling or unbelieving sort of way—they can and often are used to symbolize an understanding of death of deep significance and conviction.

Another possible cause for what some call the "denial of death" in American society is the youth-oriented nature of American culture. When the primary marketing target of advertisers is seventeen to thirty-four years, when television prime-time offerings are dominated by twenty-something sitcoms, when Disney and teen horror films rank consistently high in box office ratings, when rap and pop stars become overnight millionaires with one hit song, there is clearly a youth-centered bias to popular culture.

The potential effect of this is to make the idea of aging, and of old age itself, something to be ashamed of or embarrassed about, something to be *denied*. Consider the proliferation and social acceptance of plastic surgery. Consider the prevalence on the market of rejuvenation diets and skin restoration products. Consider that a very high percentage of every healthcare dollar is spent on life prolongation in the face of terminal illness and injury. As one newspaper columnist said, "We're a society driven by living longer and better. . . . We're used to getting what we want . . . and most of us don't want to die."[11]

In 1998 I was asked by the Mount Union College summer programs director to teach an Elderhostel course. Elderhostel is a wonderful program that provides continuing education courses for senior citizens in a college setting. But it has one hard and fast rule that teachers are not allowed to break: there is to be no presentation of any topic related to death and dying. The next year I was invited to deliver a series of lectures on a topic of my choice to a local retirement community. Again, the same stricture was imposed: any topic *but* death and dying.

THE RISE OF "DEATH STUDIES"

David Stanard writes that in societies marked by an emphasis on individuality and uniqueness, death is normally attended by "a community-wide outpouring of grief for what is a genuine social loss."[12] American society, with its foundations in Puritanism and its stress upon the individual's uniqueness before God, is very much a society that values individual worth, achievement, and potential. We are a society that moves forward on the efforts of its pioneers, inventors, heroes, and leaders. It is little wonder then that when a person dies in the United States, it is often treated as a community event. An obituary is written up in the local paper, usually giving the times and places for the funeral, while funerals themselves are open to anyone and everyone who knew the deceased. When a favorite schoolteacher passes away, schoolchildren are led in a communal moment of silence. When military personnel are killed abroad, public buildings lower their flags to half-mast. And when someone of any fame dies, an entire day's broadcast on CNN or MSNBC is devoted to carrying the story, letting the whole nation participate in the grieving process. From the embroidered cloths of the AIDS Memorial Quilt to the engraved marble of the Vietnam Veterans Memorial, American society regularly practices forms of communal grief.

But if this fact lies at the heart of what makes American society unique, it becomes even more urgent that an awareness be developed of how we have become a society that tends to depersonalize, de-individualize, and even deny death and the dying process. As was stated eloquently by Mexican poet and philosopher Octavio Paz, "A civilization that denies death ends by denying life."[13] Denying death, treating it as "an obscenity to be avoided,"[14] tends to inhibit the sort of public grieving and sharing in loss that is necessary to the proper valuing of individuality in this country. It makes of it an object of ridicule, of shame. Anyone familiar with the controversies surrounding moments of silence in schools, the AIDS Memorial Quilt, and the Vietnam Veterans Memorial will know that public reminders of death and memorials for the dead are not always warmly welcomed in this country.

This is why the recent rise of "death studies" in American colleges and universities is such an encouraging sign. Sometimes called *thanatology* (literally, the study of *thanatos* or death), death studies refers to academic research on and the teaching of issues pertaining to death and the dying process. Death studies can be divided into five main types, each with its own set of subdisciplines.

1. Psychological Studies

- different types of grief
- techniques for coping with grief
- techniques for coping with terminal illness
- general attitudes toward death and dying
- attitudes toward death and dying among children
- issues related to aging and care of the elderly
- homicide
- suicide

2. Sociological Studies

- the statistics and demographics of mortality
- military objectives and the consequences of war
- comparative cultural attitudes toward death
- attitudes toward death in ancient cultures
- death in the media and entertainment industry
- various types of healthcare systems
- death education in schools
- the funeral industry
- homicide
- suicide

3. Literary and Aesthetic Studies

- death in literature
- death in art
- death in film
- death in theater
- death in mythology
- death in television programming

4. Philosophical Studies

- various teachings on death among the philosophers
- advanced directives, durable powers, living wills
- death and the meaning of life
- the problem of defining death
- the ethics of abortion
- the ethics of euthanasia
- the ethics of organ donation
- the ethics of capital punishment

5. Theological Studies

- Western religious concepts of life after death
- Eastern religious concepts of life after death
- the origins of belief in heaven and hell
- the role of faith in the grieving process
- secular concepts of immortality
- communicating with the dead
- near-death experiences
- death in religious art

People sometimes have adverse reactions to the idea that courses on death and dying are taught in our nation's colleges and universities. Some respond that death has no significant place in a higher education curriculum. They argue that the four (or more!) years a young person devotes to her or his college degree ought to be spent fostering experiences of life, not death; that courses should be upbeat, relevant to life in the world, preparatory for future careers in business, science, the arts, and so on. What possible currency could a focus on death have in such an economy as that? But others argue that death education is, in fact, an education in life. As Patrick Dean argues, "Only through an awareness of our lifelong losses and appreciation of our mortality are we free to be in the present, to live fully."[15]

Marie de Hennezel is a French psychologist on the staff of a palliative care unit—a medical unit that cares exclusively for dying patients—in a Paris hospital. In her 1997 book, *Intimate Death,* she writes,

> We hide death as if it were shameful and dirty. We see in it only horror, meaninglessness, useless struggle and suffering, an intolerable scandal, whereas it is our life's culmination, its crowning moment, and what gives it both sense and worth. It is . . . an immense mystery, a great question mark that we carry in our very marrow.[16]

If death is truly educative, if it is a "question" we carry with us throughout our lives, then it ought rightly to be a subject of academic study. Textbooks like this one, college and university courses on death and dying, organizations like the Association for Death Education and Counseling and the International Work Group on Death, Dying and Bereavement, and scholarly journals like *Death Studies* and *Omega: The Journal of Death and Dying* are all devoted to this very idea: that the study of death, however disruptive to our comfort level it may be, is potentially a gateway to a fuller understanding of life.

The tremendous growth of death education that has taken place in the last two decades can be attributed to a number of factors, including:

- the nuclear threat hanging over the world ever since Hiroshima and Nagasaki
- the aftermath of the Holocaust and other events of genocide
- the rise of fatal epidemics such as AIDS
- the "patients' rights" movement
- the increase of the elderly population
- the diminishing influence of religious belief in secular societies
- the increasing influence of nontraditional beliefs about death and the afterlife
- the increase of violence in film and on television
- the advancement of medical technology to prolong life
- the popularity of books written for a general audience on themes related to death and dying

This last influence merits attention here. Scarcely a month has gone by during the last three decades without a book related to death and dying appearing on *The New York Times* "bestseller list." The popularity of these books, some of which have sold millions of copies and been translated into numerous languages, has served to further the demand for death education. In their wake a generation has grown up with a set of readily accessible references to issues pertaining to, among other things, the dying process, grief, hospice care, palliative care, the rights of the terminally ill, and notions of the afterlife.

The book that almost single-handedly initiated the trend of offering death and dying courses in colleges across the country, is the 1969 publication, *On Death and Dying,* by Elisabeth Kübler-Ross. Dr. Kübler-Ross was then a teaching psychiatrist at the University of Chicago's Medical School and Hospital. Four years earlier, four students from Chicago Theological Seminary had approached her for help on an assignment. They required to write a paper on "crisis in human life," and considered death "the biggest crisis people face."[17] Dr. Kübler-Ross suggested that the students observe her interviewing several terminally ill patients at the hospital about what it was like to be dying. This experience led to an interdisciplinary seminar that soon caught on in popularity and eventually to her writing of the book. *On Death and Dying* is widely considered one of the most important psychological studies of the twentieth century. In the book, Dr. Kübler-Ross first identified the now-famous five stages of death which have been a staple of university psychology courses, hospital seminars, and even Hollywood films on the theme of death. The film *My Life,* starring Michael Keaton as a man who is dying of cancer, is one example of a film that explores how each of the five stages is lived out by someone facing death.

Two later books can also be considered landmark studies toward the advancement of death education in this country. The first is Dr. Raymond Moody's *Life After Life,* a study of near-death experiences (NDEs). Moody holds a Ph.D. in philosophy as well as an M.D. in psychiatry, a combination which gives him a unique perspective on life after death. First published in 1975, *Life After Life* allowed near-death experiences to come out of the closet. Selling over five million copies around the world, Moody's book single-handedly transformed the way a generation now views the afterlife. With countless other books written about the subject, with television documentaries and feature-length films, the NDE has entered the popular imagination like few other death-related phenomena have.

The second book is Sherwin Nuland's *How We Die: Reflections on Life's Final Chapter.* Though not as popular as either Kübler-Ross's *On Death and Dying* or Moody's *Life After Life,* Nuland's book won universal critical acclaim as well as the prestigious National Book Award. Oliver Sacks, the best-selling author of *Awakenings* and *The Man Who Mistook His Wife for a Hat,* said of the book, "As powerful and sensitive, and unsparing and unsentimental as anything I have ever read."[18] Dr. Nuland, a professor of medical history at Yale University as well as a full-time medical writer, describes in clear and compassionate prose both the psychological and physical processes of the dying experience. *How We Die* marks a transitional moment in American culture with respect to death: its frank discussion of the pain, challenges, and triumphs experienced by the dying, its critique (by a doctor!) of the technological hubris of much of modern medicine, and its eloquent philosophical discussion of the meaning of both life and death, mark a new willingness to discuss openly what were once considered taboos. As Dr. Nuland demonstrates, not only must this new conversation around death include practical emphasis upon patients' rights, comfort care, respect for the wishes of the dying, and the ethical tempering of medical technology, it must also include a more holistic emphasis upon the meaning and dignity of death and the dying process. At the close of his book, Dr. Nuland writes

> The dignity that we seek in dying must be found in the dignity with which we have lived our lives. *Ars moriendi is ars vivendi:* The art of dying is the art of living. The honesty and grace of the years of life that are ending is the real measure of how we die. It is not in the last weeks or days that we compose the message that will be remembered, but in all the decades that preceded them. Who has lived in dignity, dies in dignity.[19]

WHERE WE GO FROM HERE

What is clear as we move further into the new century is that the desensitization and denial of death and dying that our culture has been accustomed to can no longer be tolerated. In the wake of two world wars, the Holocaust, several genocides, the 9/11 terrorist bombings, and their aftermath of war, fear and hatred, forcing death into the sphere of the unreal is no longer an acceptable option. Death must be wrested from its hiding place and once again made to enter our awareness as an essential component of human experience. Fears and prejudices that inhibit our lifting the mask off death must be critically examined and evaluated. Open and honest discussion around the dying process must become the rule, not the exception. Elements for this transformation are already in place in our culture. What is needed now is the formal embrace by our educational institutions and medical establishments of death and dying as a necessary part of their respective curricula.

We are all social beings. This means among other things that, like every other aspect of our lives, our understandings and feelings about death originate in our participation in and commitment to the myriad of social relations that constitute our particular environments. What we as twenty-first-century Americans understand when we use the word "death" very likely differs from what twenty-first-century Chinese or twenty-first-century Palestinians understand when they use the word; even from what nineteenth-century or eighteenth-century Americans understood when they used the word. One primary reason for these differences is that the respective cultures, from which understandings and feelings are largely learned, are different: different in what they value or valued, in what they hold or held to be true. An essential part of death education, therefore, is the fostering of a personal values and assumptions critique to heighten awareness of any values and assumptions that prevent a compassionate, informed approach to death.

It is to this end that this book is dedicated. In the chapters that follow we will introduce a select number of quality readings on a wide variety of topics from various and sometimes competing perspectives. While favor is given to the Western cultural, philosophical, and religious traditions, voices from outside those traditions are also respectfully included. Together these readings are designed to educate students in the diversity of views, both recent and past, that have guided human understanding on the nature of death and the dying process. Examination of the assumptions and beliefs of others with respect to death will encourage the reader to examine critically her or his own assumptions and beliefs, and in so doing construct an integrative statement of the meaning, not only of death, but of life as well. What is more, such constructs may collectively serve to foster a larger synthesis of societal acceptance around this admittedly very difficult topic.

The text is divided into two main parts: "The Meanings of Death," a more theoretical collection of readings that examines the concept of death as it is represented by both

religious and philosophical traditions; and a more practical collection, "The Practicali-
ties of Dying," which looks at dying from psychological, ethical, and practical perspectives. Each reading selection is preceded by the editor's introductory comments and
followed by a variety of discussion questions. At the end of each chapter are suggestions
for small group exercises and and a practical learning component with additional activities that students might undertake, either individually or in small groups.

Chapter 1

⟋

Heavens and Hells

One short sleep past, we wake eternally,
And Death shall be no more; Death, thou shalt die.
—John Donne

HEAVEN

Heaven is ordinarily understood as a post-death abode of perfection and bliss; the dwelling place of God (or gods), along with other spiritual beings who have been found worthy, or who have been made worthy, to live with God eternally. The term, which has etymological relations to words meaning "sky" or "celestial sphere," is to be distinguished from both the earthly plane of space/time dimensionality, and the underworld abode of the damned. The latter, hell, is the reserve of spiritual beings whose earthly lives were judged to be lacking the qualities associated with sanctity. According to traditional Catholicism, there lies in between these two spiritual realms the domain of purgatory, a place for the temporary sojourn of souls who are destined for heaven but are not yet ready to receive its blessings in full. All three concepts received much and varied interpretation in all religious traditions as they developed over the centuries. In general, heaven is understood to be the highest good attainable by humans, hell the most punitive demerit, and purgatory the intermediate realm between the two. In more recent decades, and in keeping with recent developments in biblical hermeneutics and psychological theories, heaven, hell, and purgatory have all been subject to a more symbolic reading.

Heaven in the Western Religions

The Hebrew Bible annotates a development in the religious notion of heaven. The earliest strands of Jewish biblical tradition regard the heavenly sphere, that realm beyond the visible sky, as the dwelling place of Yahweh, from which Yahweh rules the earth, establishes its laws of behavior and religious devotion, and judges the day-to-day activities of humans. While a few select prophets were allowed to transcend life to that realm after death, it was not understood as the future dwelling place of ordinary believers. Rather, it was thought that all people, both the good and the transgressors of God's laws, would "sleep" eternally without reward or punishment in an underground region called "Sheol." In later strands of tradition, this view altered to include the idea of heaven as the postmortem resting place of those found to be righteous at the Day of Judgment, who would be miraculously "resurrected" or revivified in spiritual form to live eternally in the presence of God.

Christianity, born within the nexus of beliefs of later Judaism, along with those of certain post-Jewish apocalyptic sects, viewed heaven and its reward of the intellectually fulfilling *visio Dei* ("vision of God") as the hope of all true followers of Jesus Christ. "Heaven is the greatest good," writes Christian apologist and Boston College professor of philosophy Peter Kreeft. "It is the reason God banged out the Big Bang 18 billion years ago. Next to the idea of God, the idea of heaven is the greatest idea that has ever entered into the heart of man, woman or child" (1990: 3). Christian rhetoric portrays heaven as humanity's "true home," a relief from earthly trials, the righting of all injustices, the end of all pain and suffering, and the everlasting experience of perfect beauty, bliss, fellowship with others, and connection to God. Roman Catholic doctrine adds the teaching that all souls destined for heaven, but who are not yet pure enough to enter it, must pass time in "purgatory" where they will be cleansed through obedience and devotion.

Death and Dying Fact

The three major Western religions—Judaism, Christianity, and Islam—all began on the Asian continent. All three are monotheistic religions, which means they believe in and worship one God. All three are "religions of the book," meaning that they each possess a set of scriptures they consider divinely inspired. And each sets one day a week aside to worship God: Muslims worship on Fridays, Jews on Saturdays, and Christians on Sundays.

Islam, founded six centuries after the birth of Jesus and influenced strongly by the same Jewish matrix that gave Christianity its basic beliefs, views heaven as the unalterable reign of Allah's (God's) will, to which all faithful Muslims must go after death. Perhaps taking a cue from early Christian tradition, the Qur'an, Islam's bible, teaches that after death souls must pass certain tests, which for some may include a sojourn in hell, before entering into the blissful state of heaven. These tests are designed to evaluate the individual's understanding of the all-encompassing will of Allah as well as his or her devotion to the teachings of Mohammed, Islam's founding prophet.

Heaven in the East

Concepts of heaven vary considerably in the dominant Eastern religions of Hinduism and Buddhism. Hinduism's notion of heaven is especially pluriform, relying as it does on a variety of deity-centered devotional practices and beliefs. Some gods are thought to reward their devotees with a postmortem existence of bliss in a spiritual realm, while others are thought to mediate a more disintegrated existence after death where the individual soul becomes one with the ultimate ground of all existence. Buddhism's beliefs can generally be divided into two primary types: that heaven is a space-time dimension similar to our present one, reserved for the faithful, wherein all suffering ceases and a life of continual bliss and enlightenment is preserved; and that heaven (or more precisely, *Nirvana*) is the ultimate fulfillment of the teaching of *anatta,* or "non-self," by means of which the boundaries circumscribing the individual ego are shattered and a state of perfect emptiness obtained. Both traditions are in agreement, however, that the heavenly afterlife is one in which all forms of *dukha,* or "suffering," are minimized.

Both Hinduism and Buddhism agree that the final moments of life prior to bodily death are all-important to determining one's postmortem state. To be in a condition of enlightenment at the point of death, a mental state in which all earthly desires have ceased and perfect inner peace reigns, is the hope of every faithful Hindu and Buddhist. This state is the key that unlocks the gateway to eternal paradise. All those who die without benefit of such enlightenment are fated to be born again, or reincarnated, in another earthly life. The law of karma is thought to be operative here. Karma is like the spiritual baggage that is carried from one life to the next. Evil deeds accrue bad karma, which hinders one's attempts to reach enlightenment, and also dictates that the next life lived will be worse than the prior one. Good deeds, however, merit good karma, and so both facilitate enlightenment and the enjoyment of earthly delights in the next life.

CONCEPTS OF HELL, EAST AND WEST

Hell is traditionally defined in all religious traditions as the abode or state of being of souls that are damned to postmortem punishment. In the earliest forms of religion, hell is thought to be a gloomy subterranean realm where the souls of all unenlightened heathen reside eternally (the Greek *Hades*); a dark region in the nether world in which both good and evil souls exist as shadowy figures (the ancient Israelite *Sheol*); or a nebulous, postmortem existence on the face of the earth at the end of which souls eventually fade into nonexistence (as in certain North American Indian tribes). The view that hell is the punitive dwelling place of the damned after a Last Judgment, a place of suffering and torment, is a later development held commonly by the religions of Zoroastrianism, later Judaism, Christianity, and Islam.

The Christian view of hell, based on Jewish concepts, generally regards hell as the fiery domain of the devil and his evil angels, and a place of eternal damnation for those who have lived a life of sin and denial of God. This view was reinforced by the pre-scientific philosophizing of St. Augustine's *City of God,* and by the poetic presentations of Dante's *Inferno* and Milton's *Paradise Lost.* Some early Christian thinkers, such as Origen of Alexandria and Gregory of Nyssa, questioned the eternity of hell, insisting that God will extend mercy to all in time. The majority Christian view, however, teaches that hell is an eternal state of punishment for those who reject God's offer of salvation. In more recent times, some Christian theologians have come to question this view, forwarding the logic that eternal torment inflicted by divine decree is incompatible with the idea of God as infinite love, and that divine justice could never demand for finite human sin the infinite penalty of unending pain (cf. Hick 1994: 200–201). In 1995, the Anglican Church of England took the historic step of removing from the Book of Common Prayer all references to hell as a fiery realm of eternal torment, replacing them with the phrases "separation from God" and "annihilation" as indicative of the fate of the damned.

Death and Dying Fact

The Christian New Testament describes the punishment in hell as:

"everlasting punishment" (Mt. 25:46)
"a flaming fire" (2 Th. 1:8)
"everlasting fire" (Mt. 18:8)
"eternal fire" (Jude 7)
"the fire that will never be quenched" (Mk. 9:45)
"eternal destruction" (1The. 1:9)
"chains of darkness" (2 Pet. 2:4)
"everlasting chains" (Jude 6)
"a bottomless pit" (Rev. 9:2)
"the worm that never dies" (Mk. 9:46)
"the blackness of darkness forever" (Jude 13)
"the lake of fire and brimstone" (Rev. 20:10)

In Hinduism, it is believed that all actions have consequences and, in particular, that evil actions have evil consequences. Such evil consequences may include time spent between incarnations in one or more of the twenty-one hells located in and beneath the netherworld. However, Hinduism teaches that this consignment to various hells is not of ultimate significance. It is, rather, a preparatory exercise intended to correct bad habits in the hope that they will not be carried over into the next life. It is also believed that eventually all souls will reach a state of everlasting *nirvana,* or blissful union with the Ultimate, even though it may take many life periods to attain this.

By contrast, Buddhism denies the existence of both the individual soul and an Ultimate. Nevertheless, there exist in popular Buddhist mythologies multiple hells as realms of punishment and expiation after death. In certain ancient Buddhist traditions, there is described a judgment that takes place immediately after death: the virtuous are allowed to enter immediately into one of the Buddhist paradises, while sinners go to one of the many hells where they undergo a period of fixed punishment prior to their next rebirth. This time in hell can be shortened by the intercessions made on behalf of the departed by family and friends.

The concept of purgatory as an idea related to those of heaven and hell is of an intermediate state between our present existence and the eternal heavenly life. Purgatory has been developed within Roman Catholic theology as the next stage of life for those who die in a state of unconfessed sin. It is generally understood that most people fall into this category: they are destined by God's grace to enter heaven, but there remain too many imperfections for their immediate admittance. As the name implies, purgatory (Latin, *purgare,* "to make pure") exists to purify the soul from all that would hinder it from receiving the beatific vision of God in heaven. While purgatory is not understood to be a place of torment, it is a place of rigorous self-examination and discipline. It is also believed that friends and family should pray for their departed loved ones in purgatory, and that those prayers are efficacious in ensuring that the time in purgatory is spent wisely.

In the readings that follow, you will be introduced to the notions of heaven and hell by believers and nonbelievers alike. You will hear from theologians, philosophers, and scientists. Some will describe heaven or hell from the perspective of what they claim to be firsthand experience. Others will speak in the objective, detached manner of science. Together these readings ask us to consider an all-important question: What do we believe will happen to us, if anything, after we die?

---

1 New Testament, *The Book of Revelation*

The biblical book of Revelation is one of the most mysterious, and perhaps most misused, books of the Bible. Its author identifies himself simply as "John," a "servant of Jesus Christ" living in exile on the isle of Patmos, though tradition links the book with St. John, one of the disciples of Jesus. In Revelation, the author speaks of what has been revealed to him during certain ecstatic or mystical encounters with an angel of God. The language used to describe these experiences is symbolic, and often the meaning of the symbols is unclear. This has left the book vulnerable to those who would like to understand its strange and sometimes startling imagery as speaking about current or future events.

In the passage you are about to read, the author describes what has been revealed to him of the mystery of heaven. Much of the imagery used in this passage closely parallels that of the prophetic writings from the Hebrew Bible (Old Testament). The name of Jesus is never mentioned. Instead, at the center of heaven is the Jewish Messiah, the "heir to David's throne," the "Lamb who was slain." John speaks vividly of the glory of this Lamb, whose sacrificial slaughter was necessary to reconcile people all over the world to God. In the Jewish tradition, it is the Messiah who will judge all people after they die to determine whether or not they are worthy of a heavenly reward. In this passage you will read of a scroll which only the Lamb may open, and on which is written the final fate of earth and its inhabitants.

Then as I looked, I saw a door standing open in heaven, and the same voice I had heard before spoke to me with the sound of a mighty trumpet blast. The voice said, "Come up here, and I will show you what must happen after these things." And instantly I was in the Spirit, and I saw a throne in heaven and someone sitting on it! The one sitting on the throne was as brilliant as gemstones—jasper and carnelian. And the glow of an emerald circled his throne like a rainbow. Twenty-four thrones surrounded him, and twenty-four elders sat on them. They were all clothed in white and had gold crowns on their heads. And from the throne came flashes of lightning and the rumble of thunder. And in front of the throne were seven lampstands with burning flames. They are the seven spirits of God. In front of the throne was a shiny sea of glass, sparkling like crystal. In the center and around the throne were four living beings, each covered with eyes, front and back. The first of these living beings had the form of a lion; the second looked like an ox; the third had a human face; and the fourth had the form of an eagle with wings spread out as though in flight.

Each of these living beings had six wings, and their wings were covered with eyes, inside and out. Day after day and night after night they keep on saying, "Holy, holy, holy is the Lord God Almighty— the one who always was, who is, and who is still to come." Whenever the living beings give glory and honor and thanks to the one sitting on the throne, the one who lives forever and ever, the twenty-four elders fall down and worship the one who lives forever and ever. And they lay their crowns before the throne and say, "You are worthy, O Lord our God, to receive glory and honor and power. For you created everything, and it is for your pleasure that they exist and were created."

And I saw a scroll in the right hand of the one who was sitting on the throne. There was writing on the inside and the outside of the scroll, and it was sealed with seven seals. And I saw a strong angel, who shouted with a loud voice: "Who is worthy to break the seals on this scroll and unroll it?" But no one in heaven or on earth or under the earth was able to open the scroll and read it. Then I wept because no one could be found who was worthy to open the scroll and read it. But one of the twenty-four elders said to me, "Stop weeping! Look, the Lion of the tribe of Judah, the heir to David's throne, has conquered. He is worthy to open the scroll and break its seven seals."

I looked and I saw a Lamb that had been killed but was now standing between the throne and the four living beings and among the twenty-four elders. He had seven horns and seven eyes, which are the seven spirits of God that are sent out into every part of the earth. He stepped forward and took the scroll from the right hand of the one sitting on the throne. And as he took the scroll, the four living beings and the twenty-four elders fell down before the Lamb. Each one had a harp, and they held gold bowls filled with incense—the prayers of God's people! And they sang a new song with these words: "You are worthy to take the scroll and break its seals and open it. For you were killed, and your blood has ransomed people for God from every tribe and language and people and nation. And you have caused them to become God's Kingdom and his priests. And they will reign on the earth." Then I looked again, and I heard the singing of thousands and millions of angels around the throne and the living beings and the elders. And they sang in a mighty chorus: "The Lamb is worthy—the Lamb who was killed. He

is worthy to receive power and riches and wisdom and strength and honor and glory and blessing." And then I heard every creature in heaven and on earth and under the earth and in the sea. They also sang: "Blessing and honor and glory and power belong to the one sitting on the throne and to the Lamb forever and ever." And the four living beings said, "Amen!" And the twenty-four elders fell down and worshiped God and the Lamb.

Questions

1. What sort of picture of heaven is described here? What images come to mind as you read this passage?

2. This passage uses symbolic imagery to help us imagine certain religious ideas more vividly. Identify three such symbols, and describe what idea each might represent.

3. Is it the sort of heaven you would want to live in forever after you die? Why or why not?

---

2 St. Matthew, *The Gospel According to Matthew*

The gospel of Matthew from the Christian New Testament is commonly dated to the years 80–100 C.E., which places the book past the lifetimes of any possible eyewitness to the events it describes. It was most likely written by a disciple of one of the disciples of Jesus; someone who had, judging by the editorials that accompany the collected stories, a strong interest in emphasizing the Jewish nature of the teachings of Jesus. For example, out of respect for the Jewish prohibition against speaking the name of the almighty, Matthew refers to the "kingdom of heaven," not the "kingdom of God"; and in referring to Jesus, the "Son of God" becomes the "Son of Man."

The New Testament presents a varied picture as to what is required to enter into heaven after death. In different places it states that to avoid the pains of hell and spend eternity in the presence of God, one must:

- Believe that Jesus is the Son of God (John 3:16)
- Be humble, meek, peacemakers, and pure in heart (Matthew 5:3–10)
- Become like children, imitating their humility (Matthew 18:3, 4)
- Do good things and avoid doing bad things (2 Corinthians 5:10)

- Keep all the commandments (Mark 10:18)
- Be poor and destitute (Luke 16:19–24; Mark 10:25–30)
- Give to the poor and make restitution for wrongs done (Luke 19:8, 9)
- Repent of one's sins (Luke 15:7)

In this passage the author adds several other requirements to the list. Here the writer speaks, not of the Christian Christ, but of the Jewish Messiah, the "Son of Man," the Judge of all who is to come at the end of the age. Projecting ahead into the future, Matthew foresees a day when "all the nations"—not individuals—will be lined up and separated according to type: saints on the right and sinners on the left. And unlike traditional Christian teaching, it is not correct belief that determines the difference; it is correct social policy. Matthew's parable holds out the terrible warning that our neglect as a nation to stretch out a compassionate hand to support and comfort and plead for those in need is tantamount to ignoring the presence of Christ—a sin, according to the author, that deserves eternal punishment. Nor can we compensate for this ignorance by means of religious observance and devotion. For the knowledge of and devotion toward Christ, says Matthew, must always and only be mediated by a service towards those who are in need.

The striking passage, "As you did it to the least of these my brothers, you did it to me," puts a uniquely Christian spin on the parable, however. It entitles the reader to understand that the Messiah is not only coming in the future, but in a very real way is present with us here and now. The author of Matthew's gospel conveys the idea that Christ is present among us, in some mysterious way, in the poor, the infirmed, the prisoner, the outcast, and the socially disadvantaged.

"But when the Son of Man comes in his glory, and all the angels with him, then he will sit upon his glorious throne. All the nations will be gathered in his presence, and he will separate them as a shepherd separates the sheep from the goats. He will place the sheep at his right hand and the goats at his left. Then the King will say to those on the right, 'Come, you who are blessed by my Father, inherit the Kingdom prepared for you from the foundation of the world. For I was hungry, and you fed me. I was thirsty, and you gave me a drink. I was a stranger, and you invited me into your home. I was naked, and you gave me clothing. I was sick, and you cared for me. I was in prison, and you visited me.' Then these righteous ones will reply, 'Lord, when did we ever see you hungry and feed you? Or thirsty and give you something to drink? Or a stranger and show you hospitality? Or naked and give you clothing? When did we ever see you sick or in prison, and visit you?' And the King will tell them, 'I assure you, when you did it to one of the least of these my brothers and sisters, you were doing it to me!' Then the King will turn to those on the left and say, 'Away with you, you cursed ones, into the eternal fire prepared for the Devil and his demons! For I was hungry, and you didn't feed me. I was thirsty, and you didn't give me anything to drink. I was a stranger, and you didn't invite me into your home. I was naked, and you gave me no clothing. I was sick and in prison, and you didn't visit me.' Then they will reply, 'Lord, when did we ever see you hungry or thirsty or a stranger or naked or sick or in prison, and not help you?' And he will answer, 'I assure you, when you refused to help the least of these my brothers and sisters, you were refusing to help me.' And they will go away into eternal punishment, but the righteous will go into eternal life."

Questions

1. According to this passage, what is required to get into heaven?

2. Do you think this standard is fair? Why or why not?

3. If you were to set the standard for entrance into heaven, what would it be, and why?

---

3 Betty Eadie, *Embraced by the Light*

Of Native American and Scots-Irish parents, Betty Eadie was born in rural Nebraska and spent her early childhood on the Rosebud Indian Reservation in South Dakota. She was the seventh of ten children. When she was four, her parents separated, and she was placed in a Catholic boarding school along with six of her siblings.

In November of 1973, at the age of 31, Eadie experienced brief clinical death during routine surgery. She underwent a very detailed near-death experience ever recorded." Enlightened by her experience, Eadie turned to the study of psychology and philosophy. As part of that study, she volunteered her time with dying patients and their families, learning the various perspectives of others who, like her, had experienced near-death and recovered. She also participated in a near-death study with a local university. For nineteen years, Eadie shared the knowledge and message of her NDE with family and friends, and eventually began speaking publicly about it. In 1992 she was prompted to share her experience with the rest of the world. The result was the book *Embraced by the Light*.

The phenomenal success of *Embraced by the Light* stunned the publishing world. It went on to sell six million copies and stayed on *The New York Times* bestseller list in hardcover and paperback for more than two years, including more than a year in the #1 position. The worldwide attention and acclaim that followed its publication changed many lives. Study and therapy groups, inspired by the book's message of God's unconditional love, sprang up all over the world. Today *Embraced by the Light* stands as one of the best-selling books of the last decade.

Despite its immense popularity, *Embraced by the Light* remains on the fringes of the death and dying genre. It is rightly characterized as a work of "New Age" or paranormal psychology. The work centers on a conversation Eadie reportedly had with Jesus in heaven. Among the things she learned from Jesus during her NDE is that we are all evolving spirit-beings, and are meant to use our embodied state to grow spiritually. Before each new incarnation, we choose our future parents, our race and gender, even the physical condition of our bodies. In this way we can be sure that our circumstances will teach us what we need to know to progress in the spiritual life. According to *Embraced,* the spiritual life has one main goal: to enable us to love ourselves and each other more freely and generously. In the passage you are about to read, Betty summarizes much of what she learned from her interview with Jesus.

I saw a pinpoint of light in the distance. The black mass around me began to take on more of the shape of a tunnel, and I felt myself traveling through it at an even greater speed, rushing toward the light. I was instinctively attracted to it, although again, I felt that others might not be. As I approached it, I noticed the figure of a man standing in it, with the light radiating all around him. As I got closer the light became brilliant—brilliant beyond any description, far more brilliant than the sun—and I knew that no earthly eyes in their natural state could look upon this light without being destroyed. Only spiritual eyes could endure it—and appreciate it. As I drew closer I began to stand upright.

I saw that the light immediately around him was golden, as if his whole body had a golden halo around it, and I could see that the golden halo burst out from around him and spread into a brilliant, magnificent whiteness that extended out for some distance. I felt his light blending into mine, literally, and I felt my light being drawn to his. It was as if there were two lamps in a room, both shining, their light merging together. It's hard to tell where one light ends and the other begins; they just become one light. Although his light was much brighter than my own, I was aware that my light, too, illuminated us. And as our lights merged, I felt as if I had stepped into his countenance, and I felt an utter explosion of love.

It was the most unconditional love I have ever felt, and as I saw his arms open to receive me I went to him and received his complete embrace and said over and over, "I'm home. I'm home. I'm finally home." I felt his enormous spirit and knew that I had always been a part of him, that in reality I had never been away from him. And I knew that I was worthy to be with him, to embrace him. I knew that he was aware of all my sins and faults, but that they didn't matter right now. He just wanted to hold me and share his love with me, and I wanted to share mine with him.

There was no questioning who he was. I knew that he was my Savior, and friend, and God. He was Jesus Christ who had always loved me, even when I thought he hated me. He was life itself, love itself, and his love gave me a fullness of joy, even to overflowing. I knew that I had known him from the beginning, from long before my earth life, because my spirit *remembered* him.

All my life I had feared him, and I now saw—I *knew*—that he was my choicest friend. Gently, he opened his arms and let me stand back far enough to look into his eyes, and he said, "Your death was premature, it is not yet your time." No words ever spoken have penetrated me more than these. Until then, I had felt no purpose in life; I had simply ambled along looking for love and goodness but never really knowing if my actions were right. Now, within his words, I felt a mission, a purpose; I didn't know what it was, but I knew that my life on earth had not been meaningless.

It was not yet my time.

My time would come when my mission, my purpose, my *meaning* in this life was accomplished. I had a reason for existing on earth. But even though I understood this, my spirit rebelled. Did this mean I would have to go back? I said to him, "No, I can never leave you now."

He understood what I meant, and his love and acceptance for me never wavered. My thoughts raced on: "Is this Jesus, God, the being I feared all my life? He is nothing like what I had thought. He is filled with love."

Then questions began coming to my mind. I was still laboring under the teachings and beliefs of my childhood. His light now began to fill my mind, and my questions were answered even before I fully asked them. His light was knowledge. It had power to fill me with all truth. As I gained confidence and let the light flow into me, my questions came faster than I thought possible, and they were just as quickly answered. And the answers were absolute and complete. In my fears, I had misinterpreted death, had expected something that was not so. The grave was never intended for the spirit—only for the body. I felt no judgment for having been mistaken. There was just a feeling that a simple, living truth had replaced my error. I understood that he was the Son of God, though he himself was also a God and that he had been chosen from before the creation of the world to be our Savior. I understood, or rather, I *remembered,* his role as creator of the earth. His mission was to come into the world to teach love. This knowledge was more like remembering. Things were coming back to me from long before my life on earth, things that had been purposely blocked from me by a "veil" of forgetfulness at my birth.

As more questions bubbled out of me, I became aware of his sense of humor. Almost laughing, he suggested that I slow down, that I could know all I desired. But I wanted to know *everything,* from beginning to end. My curiosity had always been a torment to my parents and husband— and sometimes to me—but now it was a blessing, and I was thrilled with the freedom of learning. I was being taught by the master teacher! My comprehension was such that I could understand volumes in an instant. It was as if I could look at a

book and comprehend it at a glance—as though I could just sit back while the book revealed itself to me in every detail, forward and backward, inside and out, every nuance and possible suggestion. All in an instant. As I comprehended one thing, more questions and answers would come to me, all building on each other, and interacting as if all truth were intrinsically connected. The word "omniscient" had never been more meaningful to me. Knowledge permeated me. In a sense it became me, and I was amazed at my ability to comprehend the mysteries of the universe simply by reflecting on them.

I wanted to know why there were so many churches in the world. Why didn't God give us only one church, one pure religion? The answer came to me with the purest of understanding. Each of us, I was told, is at a different level of spiritual development and understanding. Each person is therefore prepared for a different level of spiritual knowledge. All religions upon the earth are necessary because there are people who need what they teach.

People in one religion may not have a complete understanding of the Lord's gospel and never will have while in that religion. But that religion is used as a stepping stone to further knowledge. Each church fulfills spiritual needs that perhaps others cannot fill. No one church can fulfill everybody's needs at every level. As an individual raises his level of understanding about God and his own eternal progress, he might feel discontented with the teachings of his present church and seek a different philosophy or religion to fill that void. When this occurs he has reached another level of understanding and will long for further truth and knowledge, and for another opportunity to grow. And at every step of the way, these new opportunities to learn will be given.

Having received this knowledge, I knew that we have no right to criticize any church or religion in any way. They are all precious and important in his sight. Very special people with important missions have been placed in all countries, in all religions, in every station of life, that they might touch others. There is a fullness of the gospel, but most people will not attain it here. In order to grasp this truth, we need to listen to the Spirit and let go of our egos.

I wanted to learn the purpose of life on the earth. Why are we here? As I basked in the love of Jesus Christ, I couldn't imagine why any spirit would voluntarily leave this wonderful paradise and all it offered—worlds to explore and ideas to create and knowledge to gain. Why would anyone want to come here? In answer, I *remembered* the creation of the earth. I actually experienced it as if it were being reenacted before my eyes. This was important. Jesus wanted me to internalize this knowledge. He wanted me to know how I felt when the creation occurred. And the only way to do that was for me to view it again and feel what I had felt before.

All people as spirits in the pre-mortal world took part in the creation of the earth. We were thrilled to be part of it. We were with God, and we knew that he created us, that we were his very own children. He was pleased with our development and was filled with absolute love for each one of us. Also, Jesus Christ was there. I understood, to my surprise, that Jesus was a separate being from God, with his own divine purpose, and I knew that God was our mutual Father. My Protestant upbringing had taught me that God the Father and Jesus Christ were one being. As we all assembled, the Father explained that coming to earth for a time would further our spiritual growth. Each spirit who was to come to earth assisted in planning the conditions on earth, including the laws of mortality which would govern us. These included the laws of physics as we know them, the limitations of our bodies, and spiritual powers that we would be able to access. We assisted God in the development of plants and animal life that would be here. Everything was created of spirit matter before it was created physically—solar systems, suns, moons, stars, planets, life upon the planets, mountains, rivers, seas, etc. I saw this process, and then, to further understand it, I was told by the Savior that the spirit creation could be compared to one of our photographic prints; the spirit creation would be like a sharp, brilliant print, and the earth would be like its dark negative. This earth is only a shadow of the beauty and glory of its spirit creation, but it is what we needed for our growth. It was important that I understand that we all assisted in creating our conditions here.

Many times the creative thoughts we have in this life are the result of unseen inspiration. Many of our important inventions and even technological developments were first created in the spirit by spirit prodigies. Then individuals on earth received the inspiration to create these inventions here. I understood that there is a vital, dynamic link between the spirit world and mortality, and that we need the spirits on the other side for our progression. I also saw that they are *very* happy to assist us in any way they can.

I saw that in the pre-mortal world we knew about and even chose our missions in life. I understood that our stations in life are based upon the objectives of those missions. Through divine knowledge we knew what many of our tests and experiences would be, and we prepared accordingly. We bonded with others—family members and friends—to help us complete our missions. We needed their help. We came as volunteers, each eager to learn and experience all that God had created for us. I knew that each of us who made the decision to come here was a valiant spirit. Even the least developed among us here was strong and valiant there.

We were given agency to act for ourselves here. Our own actions determine the course of our lives, and we can alter or redirect our lives at any time. I understood that this was crucial; God made the promise that he wouldn't intervene in our lives *unless we asked him*. And then through his omniscient knowledge he would help us attain our righteous desires. We were grateful for this ability to express our free will and to exercise its power. This would allow each of us to obtain great joy or to choose that which will bring us sadness. The choice would be ours through our decisions.

I was actually relieved to find that the earth is not our natural home; that we did not originate here. I was gratified to see that the earth is only a temporary place for our schooling and that sin is not our true nature. Spiritually, we are at various degrees of light—which is knowledge—

and because of our divine, spiritual nature we are filled with the desire to do good. Our earthly selves, however, are constantly in opposition to our spirits. I saw how weak the flesh is. But it is persistent. Although our spirit bodies are full of light, truth, and love, they must battle constantly to overcome the flesh, and this strengthens them. Those who are truly developed will find a perfect harmony between their flesh and spirits, a harmony that will bless them with peace and give them the ability to help others.

As we learn to abide by the laws of this creation, we learn how to use those laws to our own good. We learn how to live in harmony with the creative powers around us. God has given us individual talents, some more and some less according to our needs. As we use these talents, we learn how to work with, and eventually understand, the laws and overcome the limitations of this life. By understanding these laws we are better able to serve those around us. Whatever we become here in mortality is meaningless unless it is done for the benefit of others. Our gifts and talents are given to us to help us serve. And in serving others we grow, spiritually.

Above all, I was shown that love is supreme. I saw that truly without love we are nothing. We are here to help each other, to care for each other, to understand, forgive, and serve one another. We are here to have love for every person born on earth. Their earthly form might be black, yellow, brown, handsome, ugly, thin, fat, wealthy, poor, intelligent, or ignorant, but we are not to judge by these appearances. Each spirit has the capacity to be filled with love and eternal energy. At the beginning, each possesses some degree of light and truth that can be more fully developed. We cannot measure these things. Only God knows the heart of man, and only God can judge perfectly. He knows our spirits; we see only temporary strengths and weaknesses. Because of our own limitations, we can seldom look into the heart of man.

I knew that anything we do to show love is worthwhile: a smile, a word of encouragement, a small act of sacrifice. We grow by these actions. Not all people are lovable, but when we find someone difficult for us to love, it is often because they remind us of something within ourselves that we don't like. I learned that we must love our enemies—let go of anger, hate, envy, bitterness, and the refusal to forgive. These things destroy the spirit. We will have to account for how we treat others.

Upon receiving the plan of creation, we sang in rejoicing and were filled with God's love. We were filled with joy as we saw the growth we would have here on earth and the joyous bonds we would create with each other.

Then we watched as the earth was created. We watched as our spirit brothers and sisters entered physical bodies for their turns upon the earth, each experiencing the pains and joys that would help them progress. I distinctly remember watching the American pioneers crossing the continent and rejoicing as they endured their difficult tasks and completed their missions. I knew that only those who needed that experience were placed there. I saw the angels rejoicing for those who endured their trials and succeeded and grieving for those who failed. I saw that some failed because of their own weaknesses, and some failed because of the weaknesses of others. I sensed that many of us who were not there would not have been up to the tasks, that we would have made lousy pioneers, and we would have been the cause of more suffering for others. Likewise, some of the pioneers and people from other eras could not have endured the trials of today. We are where we need to be.

As all of these things came to me, I understood the perfection of the plan. I saw that we all volunteered for our positions and stations in the world, and that each of us is receiving more help, than we know. I saw the unconditional love of God, beyond any earthly love, radiating from him to all his children. I saw the angels standing near us, waiting to assist us, rejoicing in our accomplishments and joys. But above all, I saw Christ, the Creator and Savior of the earth, my friend, and the closest friend any of us can have. I seemed to melt with joy as I was held in his arms and comforted—home at last. I would give all in my power, all that I ever was, to be filled with that love again—to be embraced in the arms of his eternal light.

Questions

1. According to Ms. Eadie, why are there so many different religions?
2. Ms. Eadie claims that "in the premortal world we knew about and even chose our missions in life." What does she mean in saying this? Do you agree or disagree, and why?
3. What does Ms. Eadie mean when she says, "Love is supreme"? What is your response to this claim (and its related claims)?

4 Frank Tipler, *The Physics of Immortality*

Frank Tipler is professor of mathematical physics at Tulane University. He is the coauthor, along with John Barrow, of the highly acclaimed *The Anthropic Cosmological Principle*. His many articles have appeared in various scientific magazines and journals. A student of the famous Cambridge physicist Stephen Hawking, and a devoted scholar of relativity theory, Tipler is unique in seeking to combine the findings of theoretical physics with traditional religious notions from the Judeo-Christian tradition.

In his best-selling book, *The Physics of Immortality* (1994), Tipler outlines the three main principles of what he calls his "Omega Point Theory."

First, Tipler affirms and argues for the anthropic principle in its sharpest form: that life and intelligent life are not only necessary within our universe (the "anthropic principle"), but can in no way disappear after their emergence. Rather, intelligent life is destined to pervade and dominate the entire universe (the "final anthropic principle").

The second principle is the assumption that the expansion of the universe, the history of which according to cosmological theory began with a Big Bang about 15 billion years ago, will not continue indefinitely, but instead will enter into a phase of contraction under the influence of gravitation. This will finally end in a Big Crunch, a collapse of the matter of the universe within small space. The expansion of the universe, then, neither continues in "open" form into a steadily growing space, nor "flat"—according to the opinion of most contemporary cosmologists—in the state of an equilibrium of expansion and gravitation, but "closed" with a collapse of matter at its end. It is only in this model of the universe that there is a final point of its history, the Omega point.

Tipler's third presupposition is that the energy available in the universe is unlimited. Therefore, our universe will not end in a state of maximal entropy, but possibly in a state of eternal life, which Tipler defines as "maximal information processing." According to Tipler, the essential quality of life is "information." On its path towards the Omega point, life has to pervade and finally dominate the entire material universe. The Omega point itself, however, will be a place of maximal accumulation of information, and therefore it will be immanent as well as transcendent with relation to each point in space-time. Therefore, the Omega point will have the properties of personality, omnipresence, omniscience, omnipotence, and eternity.

It is in this way that Tipler demonstrates that physics, without any recourse to religious doctrine, can show not only that there is a God (the "Omega point"), but also that heaven exists, and that it is our fate to enjoy eternal life in it after death. Moreover, he argues that "the typical American theologian/religious studies professor has never seriously thought about the resurrection of the dead," and that "it is left to physicists" to undertake such a study.

Tipler's description of "resurrection," however, quickly departs from traditional theological description. In short, Tipler argues that at some point in the future, a super-evolved, computer-like Mind—"Omega point"—will have the power, and presumably the desire, to reconstruct and revivify all the dead, and place them in a kind of earthly paradise. Eventually, we will all unite ourselves with this Mind in what will be the climax of all religious teaching and experience. In the following passage, Tipler describes what this "cyberspace heaven" will be like. He even answers the question his students often ask, "Will there be sex in heaven?"

As discussed in Chapter IX, if information is stored in the brain of the resurrection body, there is a limit of 1,000 years of subjective experience, because a brain can only code a mere 10^{15} bits. Even if this limit is overruled by the Omega Point by storing information elsewhere, we run into a more fundamental limit owing to the fact that any living being even roughly similar to a member of our species is formed to have experiences in a rather limited environment: the collection of all environments which now exist in the visible universe. From the human perspective, this collection is extremely large: the environment of the everyday human world, the collection of all biospheres which have ever existed or will exist on the Earth, the center of the Sun, the center of a neutron star, the center of a black hole. Wide as this range of current environments is, nevertheless it is finite, and an immortal human could experience (and recall, if the 1,000-year limit is overruled) them all in far less than a mere $10^{10^{123}}$ years, a blink of an eye to an immortal being. As I pointed out in Chapter IX, enjoying new experiences forever—having a literal infinity of new experiences—will ultimately require being uploaded into the highest level of implementation of life near the Omega Point. I have given reasons above why I expect our resurrected selves to be given eventually the option of such uploading. Since as a consequence of this uploading we should become superhuman, I cannot imagine what life as such a superbeing would be like. So I shall not try to describe such a life. There will be two types of afterlife: a life in a resurrected human body, followed by a literally infinite life as part of the universal mind (for those humans who choose to be uploaded). These two types of afterlife are closely analogous to the two types of afterlife—the messianic age and the world to come—distinguished by the medieval Jewish rabbis, particularly

Maimonides. (I shall discuss the Jewish view in Chapter XI.) Maimonides got into trouble with his contemporary rabbis by concentrating too much on the unimaginable world to come. I shall avoid this by concentrating all my description on the Omega Point equivalent of the messianic age, which is life in a world close to our current world, but without the drawbacks. This is what most people are interested in, anyway. It's enough to know we shall all eventually have the option of the world to come, if and when we want it. It would be appropriate to regard both the present life and the early afterlife as a kindergarten class for the world to come.

My students—mainly young unmarried males—often ask me, "Will there be sex in heaven?" This is a perfectly reasonable question in Islamic eschatology, so I shall consider it. Since the utility of the Omega Point is increased by the increase of utility of the simulated creatures, and since some people desire sex, the answer has to be yes, sex will be available to those who wish it. This consequence of αγάπη is in sharp contrast with the picture of Heaven painted by academic theologians, who seem to think that only intellectual pleasures will be permitted people in the afterlife. The sensual pleasures will exist in the afterlife because nonascetic people wish them to, and each individual counts equally. A man like Aquinas who had no interest in sex will not experience it, but people who do desire it will experience it.

However, the problems which sex generates in our present life will not occur in the afterlife. The difficulties which humans currently have in finding a love partner are due to the fact that the sex/marriage market is a barter market, characterized by long search times and high transaction costs. This problem will not exist for the resurrected humans, since the Omega Point can match people: the Omega Point should be able to calculate which among all possible people would be the best mate for a given person, and simulate him in the same environment as her. The Omega Point, not the simulated humans, pays the transaction and information costs. To put it more dramatically (for unmarried males), it would be possible for each male to be matched not merely with the most beautiful woman in the world, not merely with the most beautiful woman who has ever lived, but to be matched with the most beautiful woman whose existence is logically possible. Because of the mutability of the appearance of the resurrection body, it would be easy to ensure that said male is also the most handsome (or desirable) man to this most beautiful woman (provided the man has spent sufficient time in Purgatory to correct personality defects). It is necessary that this requirement be satisfied, since from the viewpoint of the Omega Point the wishes of men and women count equally.

It is instructive to compute the psychological impact of the most beautiful woman on a man (the calculation is the same if we reverse the sexes). According to the Fechner-Weber Law, one of the most well-tested laws of experimental psychology, a response is proportional to the logarithm of the stimulus. That is, the psychological impact on a man of meeting the woman who is to him the most beautiful woman in the world is roughly nine times the impact of meeting any woman in the top 10%, since there are roughly one billion women in the world ($[\log 10^{10^{10}}]/[\log 10^{10}]=9$). To compute a lower bound on the psychological impact of meeting the most beautiful woman whose existence is logically possible, let us suppose that beauty is entirely genetic. I pointed out above that there are about 10^{10^6} genetically distinct possible women. Assuming the validity of the Fechner-Weber Law at large stimulus, the relative psychological impact of meeting the most beautiful of these is thus $[\log 10^{10^{10^6}}]/[\log 10^{10^{10^9}}]$ = 100,000 times the impact of meeting the most beautiful woman in the world. Including personality in addition to surface appearance makes the impact even greater, but even without this inclusion the impact is already greater than the human nervous system can stand. (The resurrection body could be modified to stand it.) I've gone through this calculation to illustrate dramatically one crucial point: the principle of nonsatiation will not hold for the resurrected humans. The finiteness of human beings means that their desires are necessarily finite, and hence it is possible for the Omega Point to satisfy them.

For example, about two thirds of adult humans experience at some point in their lives an intense passion for a member of the opposite sex which is not reciprocated: this is the phenomenon of unrequited love. The Omega Point has the power to turn this passion into requited love in the afterlife.

Let me illustrate the richness of experience available in the afterlife by analyzing "elbow room." It would be possible for the Omega Point to simulate an entire visible universe for the personal use of each and every resurrected human. ("In my Father's house are many mansions . . . " [John 14:2, KJVJ].) The required computer capacity is not measurably greater than that required to simulate all possible visible universes. ($10^{10^{123}} \times 10^{10^{45}} = 10^{10^{123}}$; remember that exponents *add,* so that $10^{123} \times 10^{45} = 10^{123}$). Each private visible universe could also be simulated to contain 10^{10} separate planet Earths, each a copy of the present Earth, or the Earth as it was at a different time in the past. (There are about 10^{20} stars in the visible universe, so replacing a mere 10^{10} solar systems in a visible universe would be a minor modification.) This is more Earths than a single human could explore before exhausting his/her memory storage capacity of 10^{15} bits, to say nothing of the memories stored while visiting other humans in *their* private universes. (Once again, the principle of nonsatiation will not apply in the afterlife.)

The literature on Christian speculations about the details of life after death is enormous, so I shall not undertake a detailed comparison of the various Christian pictures with the Omega Point cyberspace Heaven. The best available modern discussion of the Christian speculations is *Heaven: A History* by Colleen McDannell and Bernhard Lang. My overall impression is that, as a general rule, Christians grossly underestimate the pleasures that will be available in Heaven. They greatly underestimate what a Being with literally infinite power can do. The two examples I have given above involving sex and elbow room illustrate what He/She can in fact do.

The early twentieth-century Christian Heaven often pictured the resurrected dead singing praises to God for an eternity. Leaving aside the obvious fact that no omnipotent God—certainly not the Omega Point—would have any interest in such songs, human beings would find such an afterlife excruciatingly boring. The American historian Barbara Tuchman pointed out that, when the German army invaded Belgium and France in 1914, the German soldiers would sing patriotic songs as they marched, when they halted the march for a rest, and just before going to sleep after the day's march. Those soldiers who managed to survive the entire war remember the endless singing as the worst torment of the invasion.

Questions

1. Does Tipler's description of heaven sound attractive to you? Why or why not?

2. How does Tipler's "Omega Point" (God) solve the problems of "unrequited love" and the "boredom" associated with "singing praises to God for eternity"?

3. Whom do you believe is better equipped to talk about God in our day and age: physicists, who use the tools of science, or theologians, who rely on faith? Explain your answer.

5 Karl Marx, *Religion, the Opium of the People*

How do we account for religion—its origin, its development, and its persistence—in modern society? This is a question that has occupied many people in a variety of fields for quite a long time. At one point, the answers were framed in purely theological and religious terms, assuming the truth of Christian revelations and proceeding from there.

But through the eighteenth and nineteenth centuries, a more "naturalistic" approach developed. One person who attempted to examine religion from an objective, scientific perspective was political philosopher and founding father of communism, Karl Marx (1818–1883). According to Marx, religion is an expression of the "dialectical" interaction between material realities—such as our neighborhoods, where we work, our families—and economic injustices. This is another way of saying that religion is an invention bred by the need to help people cope with the inequalities in life. As such, it is used by those in power to make the powerless feel better about being poor and exploited. If the oppressed classes can look forward to heaven, they are less likely to complain about the unfair conditions they live under. This is the origin of his comment that religion is the "opium of the people"—long a rallying cry for atheists. Though impressed by some of the teachings of Jesus about the poor, Marx railed against Christianity's insistence that life in this world is unreal compared to life in the next, and that suffering is always for our benefit (making us stronger in our faith). Marx held the position that suffering reflected serious societal injustices that must be remedied by means of revolution and class struggle. The religious teaching that one must endure suffering in order to grow in faith, Marx thought, only perpetuates suffering by making people complacent when they should be actively striving to overcome the corruptions of society.

Though himself a German Jew, Marx turned against both Judaism and Christianity as sources of delusion and inhibitors of societal progress. In the well-known passage below, taken from his 1844 essay, "Contribution to the Critique of Hegel's *Philosophy of Right*," Marx delivers his famed definition of religion as "the opium of the people." At the same time, Marx expresses a very profound insight: that the teaching of religion about the sufferings of this world, even though it tends to gloss over those sufferings in the hope of a better life in the world to come, indicates a genuine sensitivity on the part of religious writers to the fact that ordinary societal life is not at all satisfactory. In this way, writes Marx, religious belief in a heavenly life is "a protest against real suffering." But what now must take place is not greater faith on the part of the sufferers, but a radical transformation of belief in a heavenly afterlife into a strategic plan to change real-life circumstances.

For Germany, the *criticism of religion* has been largely completed; and the criticism of religion is the premise of all criticism.

The *profane* existence of error is compromised once its *celestial oratio pro aris et focis* has been refuted. Man, who has found in the fantastic reality of heaven, where he sought a supernatural being, only his own reflection, will no longer be tempted to find only the *semblance* of himself—a non-human being—where he seeks and must seek his true reality.

The basis of irreligious criticism is this: *man makes religion*; religion does not make man. Religion is indeed man's self-consciousness and self-awareness so long as he has not found himself or has lost himself again. But *man* is not an abstract being, squatting outside the world. Man is *the human world*, the state, society. This state, this society, produce religion which is an *inverted world consciousness*, because they are an *inverted world*. Religion is the general theory of this world, its encyclopedic compendium, its logic in popular form, its spiritual *point d'honneur,* its enthusiasm, its moral sanction, its solemn complement, its general basis of consolation and justification. It is *the fantastic realization* of the *human being* inasmuch as the human being possesses no true reality. The struggle against religion is, therefore, indirectly a struggle against that world whose spiritual *aroma* is religion.

Religious suffering is at the same time an *expression* of real suffering and a *protest* against real suffering. Religion is the sigh of the oppressed creature, the sentiment of a heartless world, and the soul of soulless conditions. It is the *opium* of the people.

The abolition of religion as the *illusory* happiness of men is a demand for their *real* happiness. The call to abandon their illusions about their condition is a *call to abandon a condition which requires illusions.* The criticism of religion is, therefore, *the embryonic criticism of this vale of tears* of which religion is the *halo.*

Criticism has plucked the imaginary flowers from the chain, not in order that man shall bear the chain without caprice or consolation but so that he shall cast off the chain and pluck the living flower. The criticism of religion disillusions man so that he will think, act, and fashion his reality as a man who has lost his illusions and regained his reason; so that he will revolve about himself as his own true sun. Religion is only the illusory sun about which man revolves so long as he does not revolve about himself.

It is the *task of history,* therefore, once the *other-world of truth* has vanished, to establish the *truth of this world.* The immediate *task of philosophy,* which is in the service of history, is to unmask human self-alienation in its *secular form* now that it has been unmasked in its *sacred form.* Thus the criticism of heaven is transformed into the criticism of earth, the *criticism of religion* into the *criticism of law,* and the *criticism of theology* into the *criticism of politics.*

Questions

1. Does Marx make a valid point, that religion is "the opium of the people"? Why or why not?

2. Do some critical thinking around Marx's claim that "man makes religion; religion does not make man." What is he saying here? Do you agree with him? Why or why not?

3. What do you think Marx meant when he said, "Thus the criticism of heaven is transformed into the criticism of earth . . . "?

---

6 James Joyce, "Hell Is the Centre of Evils"

Few writers have so profoundly influenced the course of literature as the Irish poet and novelist James Joyce (1882–1940). Since 1922, the year of the publication of *Ulysses* (considered by many literary critics to be the most important novel of the twentieth century), Joyce has been acknowledged as the supreme innovator of modern fiction.

In his *Portrait of an Artist as a Young Man* (1916), Joyce portrays a young teenager who is torn between his allegiance to an inherited and culturally enforced Catholicism, on the one hand, and his desire for the grand freedom of spirit and expression attained by the artist on the other. In the end, the artist wins the day; but not before the boy undergoes one last attempt to live as a sincere believer. The passage below is taken from a sermon preached by the local priest on the eternal torments of hell. It was this sermon that, at least for the moment, convinced Joyce's protagonist, Stephen Daedalus, to remain loyal to the teachings of the Church.

It had been a debate in the time of Dante and Thomas Aquinas—the thirteenth and early fourteenth centuries—as to whether the pains experienced by the damned in hell were inter-mittent or constant. If they were constant, it was argued, then it would seem possible for the sufferer to get used to the pain, and therefore cease to experience it as pain. But if they were intermittent, so as to continually renew the painful sensations, it would give the damned soul something to look forward to—the next reprieve—and therefore provide a source of joy. Since hell is a place of eternal torment, and since there can never be any joy in hell, some other solu-tion had to be imagined. The dilemma was solved, therefore, by assuming that hell contains a variety of different types of torture which can be changed instantly whenever the sufferer appears to be getting used to one of them. Listing the types of torture found in hell thus became a kind of literary device used by priests and pastors who, from their Sunday pulpits, wished to persuade their audience to repent of their sins. This is what happened to Joyce's hero, Stephen Daedalus, upon hearing the sermon you are about to read. But much to the priest's dismay, Daedalus' repentance did not hold. Shortly thereafter, he abandoned the Catholic faith and adopted a moral code more in keeping with that of an artist.

Hell is the centre of evils and, as you know, things are more intense at their centres than at their remotest points. There are no contraries or admixtures of any kind to temper or soften in the least the pains of hell. Nay, things which are good in themselves become evil in hell. Company, elsewhere a source of comfort to the afflicted, will be there a continual torment: knowledge, so much longed for as the chief good of the intellect, will there be hated worse than ignorance: light, so much coveted by all creatures from the lord of creation down to the humblest plant in the forest, will be loathed intensely. In this life our sorrows are either not very long or not very great because nature either overcomes them by habits or puts an end to them by sinking under their weight. But in hell the tor-ments cannot be overcome by habit, for while they are of terrible intensity they are at the same time of continual variety, each pain, so to speak, taking fire from another and re-endowing that which has enkindled it with a still fiercer flame. Nor can nature escape from these intense and various tortures by succumbing to them for the soul is sustained and maintained in evil so that its suffering may be the greater. Boundless extension of torment, incredible intensity of suffering, unceas-ing variety of torture—this is what the divine majesty, so outraged by sinners, demands; this is what the holiness of heaven, slighted and set aside for the lust-ful and low pleasures of the corrupt flesh, requires; this is what the blood of the innocent Lamb of God, shed for the redemption of sinners, trampled upon by the vilest of the vile, insists upon.

Last and crowning torture of all the tortures of that awful place is the eternity of hell. Eternity! O, dread and dire word. Eternity! What mind of man can under-stand it? And remember, it is an eternity of pain. Even though the pains of hell were not so terrible as they are, yet they would become infinite, as they are destined to last for ever. But while they are everlasting they are at the same time, as you know, intolerably intense, unbearably extensive. To bear even the sting of an insect for all eternity would be a dreadful torment. What must it be, then, to bear the manifold tortures of hell for ever? For ever! For all eternity! Not for a year or for an age but for ever.

Questions

1. Describe your reaction to this description of hell.
2. In 1995, the Church of England declared that the traditional notion of "hell," with flames and devils and fiery pitchforks, is just a myth; that the real "hell" is here on earth. Do you agree, or disagree, and why?
3. If Christianity were to abandon all its talk of hell, would it be more or less effective as a religion, and why?

7 Alice Turner, *Universalism*

Universalism is the name commonly given to the belief that there will be universal redemption beyond death for every living creature, both the moral and the immoral; that all who enter eternity in a state of rebellion against God will eventually find reconciliation and peace. While there are varieties of Universalism, all forms teach that the character of God is animated primarily by benevolence and grace rather than justice; that the will of every person, however rebellious, can be overruled and subdued by this character.

In its Christian form, Universalism was first taught in the third century by the theologian and philosopher, Origen of Alexandria. Origen taught that all fallen beings who do not repent in this world are destined to pass through prolonged chastisement in the world to come. In the end, however, through their sufferings and the instruction of superior spirits all rebellious spirits, not excluding the Devil and his angels, will undergo a change and will ultimately be allowed entrance into heaven.

Though Origen's views were condemned by the Council of Constantinople in 543 C.E., the teaching continued to appear in certain sections of the Church for many centuries. At the Reformation the group known as Anabaptists adopted a universalist view of salvation, forcing John Calvin, the Protestant reformer, to write a condemning tract in response. In the middle of the eighteenth century a new impulse was given to the doctrine by the philosopher Otinger, and later by his more famous countryman, the theologian Schleiermacher, underscoring the necessity of universalism on the basis of an optimistic humanism rather than philosophical logic. The doctrine received a considerable boost when in 1879 F. W. Farrar published his book *Eternal Hope* and preached universalism from the famed pulpit of Westminster Abbey in London. It soon became the creed of a popular movement known as Modern Optimism.

Universalism came to America in 1770 when itinerant preacher and lapsed Calvinist John Murray began to espouse throughout the colonies the idea that "if Christ died for all, then all will be saved." Together with his Baptist colleague, Elhanan Winchester, Murray held the first Universalist Convocation in 1790 in Philadelphia, which was attended by over one hundred followers. By the 1820s, there were several active Universalist churches in New England. The philosopher Ralph Waldo Emerson was a member of one such church in Boston. Eventually these churches grew to become denominational institutions, the two largest of which—the American Unitarian Association and the Universalist Church of America—merged in 1960 to form the Unitarian Universalist Association. There are also large numbers in all mainline Christian denominations who either proclaim the doctrine openly or hold it as a matter of private belief.

The doctrinal basis of Universalism is understood to be required by certain manifestations of the being and character of God. It is argued, for example, that if the essential nature of God is Love, and if love is defined as a benevolence that cannot inflict pain or suffering except for an end consistent with that benevolence, then all suffering, including the torments of hell, is remedial and must have in view the reformation and restoration of the sinner. Moreover, it is argued on the basis of God's omnipotence that there is nothing that would hinder God from fulfilling the purpose of creation. Since the purpose of creation is to exist in full communion with God, there should be nothing, not even sin, that can stand in the way of God bringing that purpose about.

In Alice Turner's richly illustrated 1993 book, *The History of Hell,* the longtime fiction editor for *Playboy* magazine surveys the myriad forms hell has taken in the West. In her book, Turner traces the evolution of hell's topography and terrors, retelling old stories of the underworld and working her way through to the hellish visions of Christianity. Turner admits that these days, "Hell has become something of an embarrassment." This is perhaps why she closes her book with an essay on "Universalism." Turner suggests that if one cannot hope that all people will eventually be saved, then there is something wrong with one's heart. Others would counter that if the notion of hell is abandoned, the reward of heaven is cheapened; that to abandon hell is to discount the infinite cost God suffered on the cross to ensure the possibility of salvation. So in the end, perhaps, hell remains a "mystery"; or at least a very uncomfortable dilemma!

The late nineteenth century was also seeking to dispense with Hell inside the Christian fold, though not without a fierce struggle. Ever since Origen had first speculated about eventual forgiveness for all, the concept of universal salvation had lurked in the background of Christianity, sternly repudiated by both Protestant and Catholic hierarchies but never entirely vanquished. At the time of the Enlightenment, deviant theories were openly discussed for the first time in 1,500 years. The Romantic view of God as Love, familiar to us now but something of a novelty one hundred and fifty years ago, demanded a new look at damnation.

One of the first men to proclaim the doctrine of universal salvation, in about 1750, was the Englishman James Relly (c. 1720–1778), at first a Baptist follower of the notorious George Whitefield, whose fire-breathing revivalism gave pause even to Jonathan Edwards. Relly was apparently still more dismayed by it. He abandoned Whitefield for John Wesley's more moderate Methodism, but soon moved further to the left, eventually repudiating orthodox Calvinism—which would, at this point, include most English denominations except, perhaps, the Quakers—to become an itinerant preacher whose message was, "If Christ died for all, then all will be saved."

One of Relly's converts was the Calvinist John Murray (1741–1815), who arrived in Good Luck, New Jersey, in 1770, and began immediately to preach universal salvation all over the northeast colonies. His Baptist colleague, Elhanan Winchester (1751–1797), founded the Universal Baptist Church in 1781. By 1790, conversion had proceeded to the point where a Universalist Convocation was held in Philadelphia, and by the 1820s the church was securely established in America.

Early Universalists held to the orthodox views of whichever Protestant denomination they professed on all subjects except eternal torment. Like the early English deists, they believed in Hell, but regarded a sojourn there as temporary and corrective. Murray argued that God's goodness forbade anything more punitive, and also—following Origen, whether or not he knew it—that men would retain free will in Hell and could there repent, which they surely would, considering the horrors therein. But the influential leader Hosea Ballou (1771–1852), though no more educated than his predecessors, had a thoughtful and intellectual bent; he had read the deists and believed in reason, and he admired Thomas Jefferson and Ethan Allen. He began to face squarely the theological difficulties of the universalist position: If God's nature guarantees salvation, and man's nature is such that he will eventually choose good, what is the meaning of Christ's sacrifice? Why would one need to believe in his deity or his resurrection? Why is a Trinity needed? What meaning can be given to the Fall of Man or Original Sin? Most of all, if there is no everlasting Hell, what is there to be "saved" from?

Ballou concluded, radically, that none of the orthodox theological baggage was necessary: the Crucifixion guaranteed salvation from a doom that, since its time, no longer existed. He went from disbelief in eternal torment to disbelief in Hell altogether, which caused consternation leading to schism in his own church. Universalists

shifted back and forth along this ground, moving toward transitory punishment in the late nineteenth century—it was known as "restoration"—then away from it toward Ballou's extreme position in the twentieth, by which time many Universalists had stopped believing in any afterlife.

Universalism prospered, however, establishing its own schools—the American public school system owes much to Universalist Horace Mann—and universities. It handled the Darwin crisis of the 1860s much better than rival Christian denominations and generally established itself as pro-science. And pro-business, too: P. T. Barnum, the impresario and circus master, was a prominent Universalist, which did not prevent him from proclaiming that a sucker was born every minute. In the twentieth century, deciding that true religion is "universal" in all senses of the word, the Universalists reached out to the other great world religions. In 1960, the Universalist Church of America was consolidated with the American Unitarian Association.

But in the nineteenth century, when tempers ran hot among the orthodox, the doctrine of universal salvation, especially when even a temporary Hell was doubted, was attacked from all sides on precisely the grounds Ballou had identified. To put God in the position of having to save all men, even the worst sinners, seemed immoral and blasphemous, and, as Armenian free-will proponents pointed out, just as deterministic as Calvinism. To deny the reality of Hell, and thus the vital importance of the Crucifixion, was to abandon Christianity altogether. This was mere "humanism," anathema to many people by no means as restricted in their views as America's late-twentieth-century fundamentalists.

Most American theological seminaries were either founded or already operating in the nineteenth century, and a look through the dusty shelves of their old library collections is an education in the fervor of the argument. Some Victorian titles from Emory in Atlanta, founded by Methodists in 1836, include *A History of Opinion on the Scriptural Doctrine of Retribution* (1878), *Everlasting Punishment and Eternal Life* (1879), *Everlasting Punishment* (1880), *What Is of Faith as to Everlasting Punishment* (1880), *What Is the Truth as to Everlasting Punishment?* (1881), *The Endless Future: The Probable Connection between Human Probation and the Endless Universe That Is to Be* ("The author prefers to publish this book anonymously. Truth, not notoriety, is his aim and inspiration." 1885), *Doom Eternal* (1887), *Future Retribution: Viewed in the Light of Reason and Revelation* (1887), *God's Mercy in Punishment* (1890), *Future Retribution* (1892), and so on, on both sides of the debate. As many of these tracts were written by the British as by Americans, and many of the authors were not clergymen but simply outspoken Victorians with strong convictions.

The right wing was determined, however. Pope Leo XIII issued a bull in 1879 affirming an eternal Hell and the existence of the Devil, and Catholic intellectuals were expected to toe the line. Conventional Victorian parents presented their children with Bunyan's books or with *The Sight of Hell,* a best-seller by the Reverend Joseph Furniss, in which damned souls shrieked in dungeons:

The little child is in the red-hot oven. Hear how it screams to come out; see how it turns and twists itself about in the fire. It beats its head against the roof of the oven. It stamps its little feet on the floor . . . God was very good to this little child. Very likely God saw it would get worse and worse and never repent, and so it would have been punished more severely in Hell. So God in his mercy called it out of the world in early childhood.

Convention won the battle but not the war. Most Christian denominations still affirm belief in an eternal Hell, but only Catholic traditionalists and Protestant fundamentalists put much emphasis on it. Hell has become something of an embarrassment, and a bishop who resorts to threats of damnation is quickly roasted in the popular press. Privately, most people who believe in an afterlife seem to take a loose Universalist position, either the modern one or the older corrective one.

Publicly, no other Christian denomination has yet taken the step of the Unitarian-Universalists who ringingly proclaim, in near-Emersonian prose:

The doctrine of an eternal hell we unqualifiedly reject, as the foulest imputation upon the character of God possible to be conceived, and as something which would render happiness in heaven itself impossible, since no beings whose hearts were not stone, would be happy anywhere knowing that half the human family, including many of their own loved ones, were in torments. Instead of such a dark and God-dishonoring doctrine, we believe that the future existence will be one ruled by Eternal Justice and Love, that he whom in this world we call "our Father" will be no less a Father to all his human children in the world to come, and that the world will be so planned as not only to bring eternal good to all who have done well here, but also to offer eternal hope to such as have done ill here.

Questions

1. According to Turner, on what grounds was the teaching of Universalism attacked by more orthodox believers?

2. Do you think that divine justice requires there to be eternal punishment for those who do evil during their lifetimes? Why or why not?

3. Can you suggest other ways for God's justice to be expressed than a hellish torment for eternity? If so, what might these be? If not, why not?

Small Group Exercises

1. In your small group, brainstorm what you would want heaven to be like if such a thing exists:
   • Describe in detail what it looks like
   • Make a list of things you would want to do there
   • Make a list of the questions you would want to ask God in heaven

2. Consider the various objections raised by Karl Marx to the Christian notion of heaven. Create counterarguments to these objections.

3. Debate among your group whether there is a hell, and whether it is a necessary component to contemporary religious belief. Consider the following questions:
   • Is hell necessary to motivate people to live good lives?
   • If it could be proved that there is no hell, would people stop being religious?
   • Can the eternal torments of hell be replaced by an alternative form of punishment (annihilation, separation, isolation) without "cheapening" the notion of God's justice?

Practical Learning Component

1. Visit a pastor of a Christian church, a rabbi of a Jewish synagogue, and an imam of an Islamic mosque, and ask about their views of heaven and hell. Compare and contrast their answers.

2. Locate the nearest Unitarian Universalist church and attend a worship service. Compare and contrast this to worship services you are familiar with. Arrange an interview with the pastor of the church and ask him or her what Universalism teaches about heaven and hell.

3. Arrange a phone conference with a trained theologian from a nearby university or college. Ask her or him about heaven and hell.

Chapter 2

—

Resurrection and Reincarnation

Death is not extinguishing the light;
it is putting out the lamp because dawn has come.
—RABINDRANATH TAGORE

RESURRECTION

The word *resurrection* (Latin, to rise again, from *re-* + *surgere,* to rise) means the rising again from the dead, the resumption of life in all its fullness following the death of the body. All three of the world's Semitic religions—Judaism, Christianity, and Islam—teach that everyone, whether saved or unsaved, will in some form live again eternally following biological death. Belief in the resurrection has been a dynamic, motivating force in human history, both for good and for evil. On the one hand, it gave strength to martyrs forced to suffer terrible torture and death for their beliefs; on the other hand, it incited the tragic events of 9/11, along with the current rash of suicidal bombings that plague the Middle East and elsewhere.

The subject of the resurrection, however, remains a point of distinction among these three traditions of faith. Judaism teaches that the body, and only the body, will rise again at some point in the future: on the day the awaited Messiah appears in Jerusalem. Since Judaism rejects the notion of an immortal soul, the form the resurrected life takes after death is exclusively a material one. Only the body is raised from death, its atoms, scattered as a result of decomposition, miraculously knit back together by God. This teaching is known as *revivification* and as such is a unique form of resurrection. Islam, by contrast, teaches that the body is to be discarded after death, nevermore to be seen or used by the soul. Resurrection in Islam is singularly a spiritual matter. Following the death of the body, the soul or seat of consciousness will be questioned as to its beliefs regarding Allah and Mohammed. Those passing this exam will be rewarded with a heavenly life of bliss. The body, however, is left to its earthly fate and will never be seen or used again.

Resurrection of the Body

Christianity occupies a middle position between these two competing views of resurrection. In contrast to Judaism's physical resurrection and Islam's spiritual resurrection, Christianity teaches that both body and soul are resurrected or brought back to life again after death. In the Christian formulation, at death the human soul departs from its mortal body and immediately comes before the judgment seat of God; the body remains behind on the earth. The bodies of the dead, however, will only remain in the earth until the Last Day, or Day of Judgment, at which time an angel of God will descend from heaven to call all back to life. At that instant, all departed souls will be reunited with their re-created bodies. As the apostle Paul put it, "Then the trumpet will sound, and the dead will be raised imperishable" (1 Cor. 15:52).

It should be pointed out that questions around the exact nature and possibility of the bodily resurrection are very much modern ones. As a study by Caroline Walker Bynum illustrates,* medieval Christendom consistently attributed both to the resurrection of Jesus and the general resurrection the reviving of the flesh as it was before death. Popular Christianity as it came to be ratified in church doctrine held that, while death manages to disintegrate bodies by various means, God shall triumph in the end by reintegrating them to wholeness. The recurring concern in medieval Christianity, writes Walker Bynum, was not whether the body is resurrected, but rather how the body, when it rises again in glory, can be reassembled entire and identical to the earthly body. Believers wanted to know how a body that had undergone normal decomposition in the grave could be the same body reconstituted in heaven; and in the worst case, how a body mutilated by a violent death could be resurrected whole and unblemished. The dominant metaphors of the time used in sermons and devotional pamphlets are of death dismembering and devouring bodies, and then being forced by God to regurgitate them. Paintings from the period show animals at the general resurrection restoring to their owners human limbs they had consumed. This theme of death chewing and swallowing human flesh, and then being forced to vomit it back up again, seems to have provided for a largely illiterate populace the imaginative material needed to support the doctrine of bodily resurrection.

There was further debate among early Christian theologians as to what kind of body would be raised at the day of judgment. It was believed that, whatever form this body would take, it would be quite unlike the body we presently possess. While it may share

*From *Resurrection of the Body in Western Christianity, 200–1336,* by Caroline Walker Bynum, 1995, New York: Columbia University Press.

enough of the same physical features and characteristics to make us recognizable as the unique persons we are, it would qualitatively surpass this present form of flesh in a number of significant ways. According to St. Thomas Aquinas, bodies of the redeemed after the resurrection will possess four principal qualities*:

1. *Impassibility:* this will render them incapable of pain or suffering; resurrected bodies will be free from all desire for food (hence no hunger), sexual pleasure (hence no lust) and sleep (hence no weariness); they will suffer no disease or injury;
2. *Brightness:* they will shine in luminescence as if a light were inside them; the degree of this brightness will depend on the degree of holiness attained during the lifetime;
3. *Agility:* this will give them the ability, as quick as thought, to move from one end of creation to another; there is also an enhanced agility of cognition where all doubt is removed, all questions are answered, and where communication takes place without incomprehension or misunderstanding;
4. *Subtility:* the substance of these resurrected bodies will no longer be biological but spiritual; this will enable them, for example, to pass through material substances and perform other seemingly miraculous feats.

The bodies of the unredeemed, however, will possess four traits in opposition to their redeemed counterparts. Those destined for a hellish eternity, according to Aquinas, will occupy bodies that are*:

1. *Dark:* there will be no internal light of glory, but instead a frightening darkness, emanating an aura of fear and contempt;
2. *Passible:* their bodies will be capable of suffering tremendous amounts of pain without ever being fully consoled;
3. *Heavy:* there will be a certain sluggishness to their actions and thoughts; uncoordination will mark their movements and confusing obscurity their thoughts;
4. *Carnal:* as purely physical beings they will be enslaved to the desires of flesh, living in ceaseless hunger, unquenchable lust, and insomniacal weariness.

The Resurrection of Jesus

Christianity pins its hopes for the bodily resurrection of the redeemed on the bodily resurrection of Jesus Christ: "If there is no resurrection of the dead, then Christ has not been raised; and if Christ has not been raised, then our proclamation has been in vain and your faith has been in vain" (1 Cor. 15:13–14).

*From *The Catechism of the Summa Theologica of St. Thomas Aquinas,* by Thomas Pegues, (trans., ed.), 1993, Fort Collins, CO: Roman Catholic Books.

Theologically speaking, the resurrection of Jesus represents his entrance into the condition of "glory," a state free from suffering and guilt and a reward for a life lived in perfect devotion to God. The resurrection of Jesus is not considered to be meritorious of human salvation in the same way that the death of Jesus was. Rather it is taught in Christianity that the resurrection of Jesus is a sign that the redemption has already taken place. Moreover, Jesus' rising again is considered by Christians to be the symbol of humanity's spiritual resurrection from a life of sin, and the exemplar and pledge of humanity's future resurrection, which is its greatest hope.

The resurrection of Jesus is based on the belief that Jesus of Nazareth was raised from the dead on the third day following his crucifixion and that through his conquering of death all believers will subsequently share in his victory over "sin, sickness, death, and the devil." The celebration of this event—or, more formally, the Feast of the Resurrection—is the most sacred festival celebrated by the Christian Church. According to the New Testament accounts, certain women disciples went to the tomb where the body of Jesus had been laid after his death on the cross, and found it empty. Later, various disciples claimed to have seen Jesus alive in Jerusalem. Other accounts in the New Testament place the resurrected Jesus in the region of Galilee.

Critical study of the New Testament texts depicting the resurrection of Jesus have, in recent years, brought the historical reliability of these accounts into question. First, there is no account of a post-death appearance of Jesus in the Gospel of Mark, considered by

---

Death and Dying Fact

In recent years, many films have portrayed in symbolic form a Christlike martyrdom and resurrection. Among these are:

- *Cool Hand Luke*
- *King Kong*
- *One Flew Over the Cuckoo's Nest*
- *Babette's Feast*
- *Dead Poets Society*
- *Jesus of Montreal*
- *Twelve Monkeys*
- *The Truman Show*
- *The Cell*
- *Braveheart*
- *Dead Man Walking*
- *Iron Giant*
- *The Matrix*

nearly all scholars to be the earliest of the four New Testament Gospels. Some scholars have taken this to imply that the accounts found in Matthew, Luke, and John at least partially display legendary overtones. Second, scholars of the first-century Roman occupation of Palestine tell us that it would have been very unlikely for the body of a crucified criminal to be allowed the decency of a tomb burial. More likely, Jesus' body was burned in Gehenna, a garbage dump located outside the city gates of Jerusalem where crucified bodies were frequently burned after death. And third, there are stories in classical literature of great heroes coming back to life again after death. Julius Caesar and Alexander the Great were both said to have met this fate. It is concluded, then, that the resurrection of Jesus is but one more example of this genre.

Based on these observations, some modern theologians have made attempts to reconstruct the resurrection of Jesus in a way more in keeping with the results of critical scholarship. Dutch theologian Edward Schillebeeckx, for example, has argued that what took place between the death of Jesus and the church's proclamation that He had risen from the dead was a kind of intellectual conversion rather than anything miraculous. In Schillebeeckx's account, the early Christians reflected on Jesus' life and teachings and concluded that He must have been saved from death even if they had no empirical evidence to warrant that claim. More recently, Bishop John Shelby Spong has speculated that a long while after the crucifixion the first disciples of Jesus had some kind of spiritual vision of Jesus very much alive and with God, and that this vision invigorated their missionary activity.

Other theologians, however, have countered this trend toward reconstruction of the resurrection narratives with several pieces of evidence of their own. For example, they point to a passage recorded by the apostle Paul in his First Letter to the Corinthians (chapter 15) in which a series of post-death appearances of Jesus are listed. This passage begins, significantly, with a brief doctrinal statement—"that Christ died for our sins according to the Scriptures, and that he was buried, and that he was raised on the third day according to the Scriptures"—which may have been part of a hymn sung by the first Christians. Since Paul states that this tradition, including the hymn, is something that he had "received" from an earlier source, and since the Letter itself is dated to about 55 C.E., this list of appearances would represent the earliest testimony to the belief that Jesus rose from the dead. The attachment of a mature doctrinal formulation adds weight to this argument. This then places testimony to the resurrection in or around the year 40 C.E., very close to the date of the crucifixion itself and certainly within the lifetimes of key eyewitnesses.

Moreover, the claim to the validity of the New Testament resurrection accounts can also be defended with the "persecution argument": what else but an empirical encounter with the risen Jesus would have motivated those first-century Christians to openly preach his resurrection in the face of horrific torture and death which was inflicted on anyone making such a claim? In an age when Messianic movements rose and fell in each new generation, the movement which claimed the resurrection and Messiahship of Jesus only increased their numbers, and persevered through terrible hardships to build what would become, in the fourth century, the primary religion of the Roman empire. "We are forced to conclude," states New Testament scholar N. T. Wright, "that when the early Christians said that Jesus had been raised from the dead, and gave that as their reason for reshaping their beliefs about resurrection itself on the one hand and Messiahship on the other, they were using the language in its normal sense."[20]

REINCARNATION

Symbols of the death-and-rebirth cycle of reincarnation abound in ancient cultures. They are suggested by primordial images like the Ouroboros (the serpent whose tail is in its mouth) and the phoenix, the mythical bird that rises from the ashes of its own funeral pyre. They are recalled in ancient stories of the Hindus by the Dance of Shiva and the dreams of Vishnu, in the Sumerian descent of Inanna, and in the Egyptian imagery of the death and rebirth of Osiris.

The belief in reincarnation (Latin, rebirth; from *re* + *in* + *carnatus,* flesh, body), also called transmigration or metempsychosis, is the belief that the soul or spiritual essence of a person is reborn after death in one or more successive, bodily existences. These rebirths may be human, animal, or, in some instances, vegetable. While belief in reincarnation is most characteristic of Asian religions and philosophies, it also appears in the religious and philosophical thought of primitive religions, in some early forms of Middle Eastern religions (for example, Islamic Sufism and Jewish Cabbalism), and Gnosticism, as well as in such modern religious movements as Theosophy, New Age spirituality, and Scientology.

Reincarnation among the Religions

In primitive religions, belief in a transmigrating soul is common. The soul is frequently identified with one's breath. As such, it is viewed as capable of leaving the body through the mouth or nostrils and of being reborn, for example, as a bird, butterfly, or insect. The Venda of southern Africa believe that, when a person dies, the soul stays near the grave for a short time and then seeks a new resting place or another body—human, mammalian, or reptilian. Other cultures use this idea to explain family resemblances: the reason why a newborn might look like a departed relative is that the soul of the departed, residing for a time in the neighborhood, now inhabits the new life.

The major religions that hold a belief in reincarnation, however, are the Asian religions, especially Hinduism, Jainism, Buddhism, and Sikhism, the latter three of which arose as reformulations of Hinduism, which began in India around 1500 B.C.E. They all hold in common the doctrine of *karma* ("act"), the law of cause and effect, which states that what one does in this present life will have its effect in the next life. In Hinduism the process of birth and rebirth, i.e., transmigration of souls, is endless until one achieves *moksha,* or salvation, by realizing the truth that liberates: that the individual soul (*atman*) and the absolute soul (*Brahman*) are one. In embodying this truth through a life of self-sacrifice and world-renouncing asceticism, one can escape from the wheel of birth and rebirth (*samsara*).

Reflecting a belief in an absolute soul, Jainism holds that karma is affected in its quality or "weight" by the deeds that a person does. Karma is seen as a kind of spiritual "baggage" we carry with us from one life to the next. Good acts in this life mean the karma we take with us into the next language is light. Light karma adds buoyancy to our next birth and as such facilitates a happier, more spiritually productive life. Bad acts, however, weigh us down with heavy karma, and thus yield of necessity a life filled with great suffering and injustice. Jainism teaches, however, that even the heaviest karma can be lightened through the practice of religious disciplines—especially that of *ahimsa* ("nonviolence")—until the soul rises in its lightness to the place of liberated souls at the top of the universe and is free forever from the cycle of rebirth.

Although Buddhism denies the existence of an unchanging, substantial soul, it holds to a belief in the transmigration of the karma of souls. A complex of psychophysical elements and states changing from moment to moment, the soul with its five *skandhas* ("groups of elements")—body, sensations, perceptions, impulses, and consciousness—ceases to exist; but the karma of the deceased survives and becomes a *vijñana* ("germ of consciousness") in the womb of a mother. This vijñana is that aspect of the soul reincarnated in a new individual. By gaining a state of complete passiveness through discipline and meditation, one can leave the wheel of birth and rebirth and achieve *nirvana,* the perpetual state of the extinction of desires.

Sikhism teaches a doctrine of reincarnation based on the Hindu view, but in addition holds that after the Last Judgment, souls—which have been reincarnated in several existences—will be absorbed in God.

Reincarnation in the West

Among the ancient Greeks, Orphism held that a preexistent soul survives bodily death and is later reincarnated in a human or other mammalian body, eventually receiving release from the cycle of birth and death and regaining its former state of purity. The Greek pre-Socratic philosopher Heraclites taught that all existing things gain their being only in dialectical relationship to their opposite, so there exist both light and dark, hot and cold, smooth and rough, etc. Life itself, it would follow, can only exist where there is death; and thus where there is death there must also be life. Another pre-Socratic philosopher, the mathematician-mystic Pythagoras, taught that the soul was immortal and merely resides in the body as in a shell; therefore, it survives bodily death. His later teachings held that the soul goes through a series of rebirths. Between death and rebirth the soul rests and is purified in the Underworld. After the soul has completed this series of rebirths, it becomes so pure it can leave the transmigration or reincarnation cycle and enter into the bliss of heaven.

On the strength of a near-death experience he heard narrated by the great warrior, Er, the Greek philosopher Plato (in the fifth to fourth centuries B.C.E.) believed in an immortal soul that participates in frequent incarnations. In his magnum opus, *The Republic,* Plato described how between their incarnations souls select their parents, their bodies, and the kind of life they would lead in their next birth. Plato claimed the soul tends to become impure during these bodily inhabitations despite a minimal extant knowledge of its former lives. However, if through its transmigrations the soul continues doing good and eliminates its bodily impurities, it will eventually return to its pre-incarnate state. But if the soul refuses this salvation by clinging to the passions of its successive bodily existences, it will end up in Tartarus, a place of eternal damnation.

In the first century C.E. Greek and Roman writers expressed surprise that the Druids, a priestly caste of the Celts, believed in reincarnation. The Greek writer Diordus Siculus (c. 60 B.C.E.–30 C.E.) noted that the Druids believed "the souls of men are immortal, and that after a definite number of years they live a second life when the soul passes to another body." Even Julius Caesar wrote of the Celts that "They wish to inculcate this as one of their leading tenets, that souls do not become extinct, but pass after death from one body to another, and they think that men by this tenet are in a great degree stimulated to valor, the fear of death being disregarded."

There is little evidence of reincarnation among the early Hebrew people but it later became a part of the medieval teaching of mystical Jewish Cabbalism and the origins of Islamic Sufism. The idea of reincarnation was held among some early Christians, most notably those influenced by the philosophy of Neo-Platonism such as the third-century theologian Origen, the Christian Gnostics, Manicheans, and the Carthari. Origen's teaching of reincarnation, along with that of these latter groups, were denounced as heresy by orthodox Christian theologians in 533 C.E. at the Council of Constantinople.

It remains a matter of minor debate whether Jesus believed in reincarnation. The evidence suggesting Jesus believed in the idea is slim; on the contrary, He is consistently recorded as teaching the prospect of an eternal heavenly reward for a single life of devotion to God. But certain religious groups active in Jesus' day taught reincarnation, and Jesus is recorded as identifying his cousin, John the Baptist, with the long-deceased prophet Elijah (Matthew 17:12).

Evidence for Reincarnation

A 2001 Gallup poll revealed that 25 percent of American adults believe in reincarnation. The popularity of the notion may be due in part to the growing academic interest in reincarnation among professors at American universities and teaching hospitals. The leading figure in this trend is Dr. Ian Stevenson, director of personality studies at the University of Virginia, emeritus. Dr. Stevenson has devoted the last forty years to the scientific documentation of past-life memories of children from all over the world. He currently has over 3,000 cases in his files. In popular books such as *Old Souls: The Scientific Search for Proof of Past Lives* (1999) and *Children Who Remember Past Lives*

> ### Death and Dying Fact
>
> *Prominent people who believed in reincarnation:*
>
> Voltaire
> Benjamin Franklin
> Johann Wolfgang von Goethe
> William Wordsworth
> Richard Wagner
> Henry David Thoreau
> Walt Whitman
> Ralph Waldo Emerson
> Thomas Huxley
> Mark Twain
> Gustav Mahler
> Rudolf Steiner
> Henry Ford
> Carl Jung
> General George Patton

(1987), and in his more academic study, the four-volume *Cases of the Reincarnation Type,* Dr. Stevenson carefully outlines the empirical evidence which suggests reincarnation is a real possibility for what happens to us after we die.

What we learn from reincarnation researchers like Dr. Stevenson is that a number of people claim that the events from a past life are somehow affecting them in this life. Often the first hint of a past life people have is an inexplicable interest in a particular country, language, time period, historical event, etc. And often when presented with photographs or movie footage which relate to their past life, they might feel an emotional sense of connection, and even identify themselves, with what they are seeing.

Recurring dreams or nightmares are another common way people claim to be able to view their past lives. Past life dreams are usually of some dramatic or traumatic event, and therefore tend to be unpleasant. Dreams of this sort can vary between vague visions with a recurring theme to vivid dreams where other participants and contextual details are clearly recognized.

Phobias are another piece of evidence suggesting past lives. Some people have seemingly irrational fears from a young age of such things as water, flying, heights, closed spaces, open spaces, or loud noises. Occasionally, when trying to work through this problem under a fairly common form of therapy known as "regressive hypnosis," the person will state that the cause of their phobia seems to be an event from a time when they were someone else—and often the event is the cause of their death in that life.

Some people suffer from chronic health problems for which there seems to be no evident reason. Here again, when working through this issue under regressive hypnosis therapy, some people will state that the origin of their problem is a traumatic event from a past life. Surprisingly, once this discovery is made, the person's health concern will sometimes disappear.

Birthmarks are considered by some researchers using regressive hypnotherapy as possible evidence for genuine past lives. What the therapy appears to reveal is that serious, sometimes fatal, wounds received in a previous life appear as birthmarks in the present life. The birthmark seems to mark the spot on the body where the wound was received. For example, Dr. Stevenson writes of an Indian boy with an array of birthmarks on his chest who recalled being killed by a shotgun blast to the chest. Another boy in India remembers a past life in which several of his fingers were cut off by a fodder-chopping machine. This boy was born with mere stumps for fingers.[21]

Other pieces of evidence cited as proof for reincarnation include the *déjà vu* experience, that feeling that you have "been there, done that" even as you are doing something you have not done before. Some suggest that, in fact, you have been there and done that, but in a previous lifetime. There are also those seemingly inexplicable intuitions we have of other people we have only just met—a sense of dread, fear, or irrational attraction. One theory has it that these are people we knew in a previous lifetime and who have reincarnated along with us into this lifetime in order to continue the relationship. Finally, there is the phenomenon of the "child prodigy": a young child whose proficiency with languages, or abundance of musical or mathematical talent, cannot be accounted for in a single, short lifetime.

Reincarnation is not without its critics, of course. Many in Western nations reject the teaching as contrary either to common sense, to science, or to the teachings of religions like Judaism, Christianity, and Islam. Others raise certain logical contradictions inherent to the traditional forms of reincarnation doctrine. For example, if reincarnated souls only have two possible fates—to be reincarnated again in another body, or to be united to the divine in the bliss of *Nirvana*—then why is the population increasing? Surely we should see the world's population decreasing instead. Other questions raised include: why do we not more readily remember our past lives? And doesn't reincarnation, which teaches that we have many lives ahead of us in order to "get it right," promote laziness?

Such critical questions are answered by proponents of reincarnation in the following ways:

- The population increase we are now experiencing could be due to the souls of animals having evolved to such a degree that they are now being incarnated as humans (this would also explain the demise of certain animal populations).
- We do not always remember our past lives because memories are lost over time; just as we cannot remember much of our early childhood, it is even more difficult to remember events that took places before we were born.

- And the doctrine of karma—that our actions in previous lives will affect, negatively or positively, our present lives—ensures that we will still strive to be good people, and to grow spiritually in this life.

For many believers in reincarnation, the warrant for such commitment comes neither from evidence nor logical reasoning but from the emotional support a reincarnation worldview supplies. Many find in the teaching of multiple lives a sense of comfort when events in this life disappoint. One such person was Henry Ford, the famed automobile manufacturer (1863–1947). In a 1923 interview, Ford said,

> I adopted the theory of Reincarnation when I was twenty six. Religion offered nothing to the point. Even work could not give me complete satisfaction. Work is futile if we cannot utilize the experience we collect in one life in the next. When I discovered Reincarnation it was as if I had found a universal plan. I realized that there was a chance to work out my ideas. Time was no longer limited. I was no longer a slave to the hands of the clock. Genius is experience. Some seem to think that it is a gift or talent, but it is the fruit of long experience in many lives. Some are older souls than others, and so they know more. The discovery of Reincarnation put my mind at ease. If you preserve a record of this conversation, write it so that it puts men's minds at ease. I would like to communicate to others the calmness that the long view of life gives to us.[22]

In the following readings you will be introduced to the ideas of resurrection and reincarnation from a variety of perspectives. After reading a description of the general resurrection from the Christian New Testament, you will be engaged in a debate around the possibility of resurrection itself: an atheist explains why he thinks it does not happen, and a theist reasons that it does by arguing for the historical resurrection of Jesus Christ. Finally you will read how a prominent bishop in the Episcopal Church defines resurrection. On the subject of reincarnation, you will be introduced to the traditional teachings of Hinduism and Buddhism of this after-life scenario by a well-respected scholar of comparative religions. You will also read from a popular writing on the subject by an American proponent of reincarnation.

---

1 St. Paul, *First Letter to the Corinthians*

The First Letter of. Paul to the Corinthians is one of the earliest pieces of writing in the Christian New Testament. St. Paul had founded the church there around the year 50 c.e., and it is generally agreed that he wrote the letter to the church about six years later during his third missionary journey to the area. As was mentioned above, this date places St. Paul's testimony to the resurrection of Jesus in this chapter at least twenty years before the first Gospel account of the resurrection was written.

The Christian community at Corinth was not large, nor was it very cohesive. Many of its members fought amongst themselves over this or that doctrine, over this or that spiritual practice. This caused division in the struggling church as different factions rallied around whichever elder was believed to be teaching the truth. Moreover, as a Greek port city Corinth was filled with wandering philosophers who espoused a variety of new beliefs and religious practices. Some of these, apparently, had led members of the Corinthian church to doubt in the possibility of a resurrection from the dead. Since this is a tenet central to Christian belief, St. Paul made great efforts to convince the Corinthians that Jesus himself was raised from the dead, and that all who therefore died in the Christian faith could hold out the hope that the same would happen to them. In the passage that follows, St. Paul directly attacks the view of the philosophers that since there is no resurrection, there is no ultimate penalty for "sin," and so we are free to "eat, drink and be merry" (apparently some of the Corinthians were taking this all too literally, practicing forms of sexual impropriety that would make "even the pagans blush" [1 Cor. 5:1]). Paul's counterargument is to remind the Corinthians that Christian hope requires a belief in resurrection—that of Christ's first, and of their own second.

One of the interesting points of this passage is St. Paul's discussion of the sort of "body" one will have in the resurrection. He speaks of it as a kind of special "clothing" that is put on after death, once the "clothing" of the mortal body is discarded. While theologians have argued for centuries on the nature and substance of this spiritual embodiment, it remains in the end a mystery.

Now let me remind you, dear brothers and sisters, of the Good News I preached to you before. You welcomed it then and still do now, for your faith is built on this wonderful message. And it is this Good News that saves you if you firmly believe it—unless, of course, you believed something that was never true in the first place. I passed on to you what was most important and what had also been passed on to me—that Christ died for our sins, just as the Scriptures said. He was buried, and he was raised from the dead on the third day, as the Scriptures said. He was seen by Peter and then by the twelve apostles. After that, he was seen by more than five hundred of his followers at one time, most of whom are still alive, though some have died by now. Then he was seen by James and later by all the apostles. Last of all, I saw him, too, long after the others, as though I had been born at the wrong time. For I am the least of all the apostles, and I am not worthy to be called an apostle after the way I persecuted the church of God. But whatever I am now, it is all because God poured out his special favor on me—and not without results. For I have worked harder than all the other apostles, yet it was not I but God who was working through me by his grace. So it makes no difference whether I preach or they preach. The important thing is that you believed what we preached to you.

But tell me this—since we preach that Christ rose from the dead, why are some of you saying there will be no resurrection of the dead? For if there is no resurrection of the dead, then Christ has not been raised either. And if Christ was not raised, then all our preaching is useless, and your trust in God is useless. And we apostles would all be lying about God, for we have said that God raised Christ from the grave, but that can't be true if there is no resurrection of the dead. If there is no resurrection of the dead, then Christ has not been raised. And if Christ has not been raised, then your faith is useless, and you are still under condemnation for your sins. In that case, all who have died believing in Christ have perished! And if we have hope in Christ only for this life, we are the most miserable people in the world.

But the fact is that Christ has been raised from the dead. He has become the first of a great harvest of those who will be raised to life again. So you see, just as death came into the world through a man, Adam, now the resurrection from the dead has begun through another man, Christ. Everyone dies because all of us are related to Adam, the first man. But all who are related to Christ, the other man, will be given new life. But there is an order to this resurrection: Christ was raised first; then when Christ comes back, all his people will be raised. After that the end will come, when he will turn the Kingdom over to God the Father, having put down all enemies of every kind. For Christ must reign until he humbles all his enemies beneath his feet. And the last enemy to be destroyed is death. For the Scriptures say, "God has given him authority over all things." (Of course, when it says "authority over all things," it does not include God himself, who gave Christ his authority.) Then, when he has conquered all things, the Son will present himself to God, so that God, who gave his Son authority over all things, will be utterly supreme over everything everywhere. If the dead will not be raised, then what point is there in people being baptized for those who are dead? Why do it unless the dead will someday rise again? And why should we ourselves be continually risking our lives, facing death hour by hour? For I swear, dear brothers and sisters, I face death daily. This is as certain as my pride in what the Lord Jesus Christ has done in you. And what value was there in fighting wild beasts—those men of Ephesus—if there will be no resurrection from the dead? If there is no resurrection, "Let's feast and get drunk, for tomorrow we die!" Don't be fooled by those who say such things, for "bad company corrupts good character." Come to your senses and stop sinning. For to your shame I say that some of you don't even know God.

But someone may ask, "How will the dead be raised? What kind of bodies will they have?" What a foolish question! When you put a seed into the ground, it doesn't grow into a plant unless it dies first. And what you put in the ground is not the plant that will grow, but only a dry little seed of wheat or whatever it is you are planting. Then God gives it a new body—just the kind he wants it to have. A different kind of plant grows from each kind of seed. And just as there are different kinds of seeds and plants, so also there are different kinds of flesh—whether of humans, animals, birds, or fish. There are bodies in the heavens, and there are bodies on earth. The glory of the heavenly bodies is different from the beauty of the earthly bodies. The sun has one kind of glory, while the moon and stars each have another kind. And even the stars differ from each other in their beauty and brightness. It is the same way for the resurrection of the dead. Our earthly bodies, which die and decay, will be different when they are resurrected, for they will never die. Our bodies now disappoint us, but when they are raised, they will be full of glory. They are weak now, but when they are raised, they will be full of power. They are natural human bodies now, but when they are raised, they will be spiritual bodies. For just as there are natural bodies, so also there are spiritual bodies. The Scriptures tell us, "The first man, Adam, became a living person." But the last Adam—that is, Christ—is a life-giving Spirit. What came first was the natural body, then the spiritual body comes later. Adam, the first man, was made from the dust of the earth, while Christ, the second man, came from heaven. Every human being has an earthly body just like Adam's, but our heavenly bodies will be just like Christ's. Just as we are now like Adam, the man of the earth, so we will someday be like Christ, the man from heaven. What I am saying, dear brothers and sisters, is that flesh and blood cannot inherit the Kingdom of God. These perishable bodies of ours are not able to live forever.

But let me tell you a wonderful secret God has revealed to us. Not all of us will die, but we will all be transformed. It will happen in a moment, in the blinking of an eye, when the last trumpet is blown. For when the trumpet sounds, the Christians who have died will be raised with transformed bodies. And then we who are living will be transformed so that we will never die. For our perishable earthly bodies must be transformed into heavenly bodies that will never die. When this happens—when our perishable earthly bodies have been transformed into heavenly bodies that will never die—then at last the Scriptures will come true: "Death is swallowed up in victory. O death, where is your victory? O death, where is your sting?" For sin is the sting that results in death, and the law gives sin its power. How we thank God, who gives us victory over sin and death through Jesus Christ our Lord! So, my dear brothers and sisters, be strong and steady, always enthusiastic about the Lord's work, for you know that nothing you do for the Lord is ever useless.

Questions

1. On what grounds does Paul argue that the resurrection of Jesus really happened?

2. What is your reaction to Paul's claim that, "if Christ has not been raised, then . . . your faith is in vain"?

3. If there were no resurrection, no life after death, do you think that the only true philosophy of life would be that of "hedonism" (that life is made for pleasure alone)? Why or why not?

---

2 A. N. Wilson, *Life After Death? A Fate Worse Than Death*

A. N. Wilson was born in England in 1950. He was educated at Oxford University, and taught English literature there for several years. An accomplished journalist, he has written numerous articles for several of Great Britain's national newspapers, and currently serves as literary editor for the *London Evening Standard*. It is as a published author, however, that Wilson has made a name for himself. He has written several best-selling revisionist biographies of figures as varied as Leo Tolstoy, Hilaire Belloc, C. S. Lewis, and Jesus. His most controversial work, *Paul: The Mind of the Apostle,* caused a stir in Britain when it claimed that it was Paul, not Jesus, who is the rightful founder of Christianity, and that after Paul's death the religion went on to corrupt many of his teachings. Presently Wilson lives in Oxford and devotes the whole of his time to writing.

In his 1995 essay, "Life After Death? A Fate Worse Than Death," Wilson argues for the atheistic position that the idea of an immortal soul is a myth, and that therefore the ideas of heaven and hell are also myths. Wilson suggests that the traditional Christian concept of heaven, where an omnipotent God rewards those who have suffered innocently, is a "wholly abhorrent notion." Why would an all-powerful God who loves his creation, and should therefore be both willing and able to intervene on the part of the faithful, wait until after death to avenge their suffering?

This is only one of several arguments Wilson offers against the traditional idea of heaven and a heavenly reward that have been handed down by the Christian tradition. As you are reading, see how many others you can identify, and what counterarguments might be put against them.

To my way of thinking, life after death seems such a greedy idea, and such an ungrateful one, and one which is so likely to make us pass through this valley, which we are (many of us) agreed we shall only pass once, with such grudging hearts, such closed eyes. It was not only Jesus who came that we should have life and have it more abundantly. We all came for that purpose. Belief in personal immortality leads automatically to the sin of asceticism, with all its distrust of the body, and all the resultant misery which thereby inevitably ensues. . . .

When I was at school, we were still taught by the chaplain in our divinity classes that the concept of life after death was the only thing which could reconcile the idea of God's love with the fact of innocent suffering. He knew about innocent suffering, poor man, having been tortured for three years by the Japanese during the Second World War. At the time, it was the thought which caused one of those frequent adolescent abandonments of religious belief, and I now find it a wholly abhorrent notion. That there might be an omnipotent God, preparing for them that love him such good things as pass man's understanding, but waiting a little. . . . It is a horrible prospect. Imagine, if you or I were omnipotent, and we could remove the suffering of the starving, and the destitute and those wracked with the miseries of mental illness? Would we say "Let them wait until they get to Heaven"? Would we not see that the very idea of Heaven has provided Christians with the most wonderful excuse for not being Christians. How can anyone read the Gospel and think that slavery is compatible with the teaching of Jesus, who taught his disciples that they should become the slaves of all? And yet for 1800 years Christians hardly even thought about the matter. The slaves would go to Heaven the same as everyone else—or to hell—and it would all sort itself out in the wash.

I think that we can also see that the concept of Heaven is all tied up with the anthropocentric vision of the universe which has done such untold damage to our environment. We are here as stewards, because God put us here. That means that the earth is our plaything, that animals only exist for our sustenance, that we have every right to make as much mess and dirt and squalor here as we choose because it is ours, and, besides, it's not the only life we've got, so what does it matter; we're bound for heaven, and *après nous, le deluge.* It was only after human beings lost their belief in heaven that they began to take life on earth with the seriousness which it deserves, and to treat the earth, and our fellow-occupants of this mortal planet, with the affection and respect which they deserve.

In my experience, a Blakean idea of eternity can be restored to us if we discard and forget the myths of heaven and purgatory and hell, which are diseased, ugly ideas.

> He who binds to himself a joy
> Doth the wingèd life destroy.
> But he that kisseth the joy as it flies
> Lives in eternity's sunrise.

We should learn to kiss joy as it flies. The intolerable facts of death—the deaths of those whom we love—the deaths of the young who have not been given the chance to realise the full potential of their lives—these facts are not made more bearable by pretending that we shall see them again in some pearly palace, or, more horrible still, through the conversation of a spirit medium.

Anyone who has watched animals die must have come to the conclusion that in some ways they are better at accepting death than we are. Grief should be grief. It should be absolute. Rachel weeping for her children would not be comforted because they are not. There is no consolation in that, but at least one can be certain that it is true. We are not being paid off with a trivial placebo.

As Christianity gradually dismantles itself in the West—and it is only a matter of time before the same thing happens in Africa and the East where it is allegedly flourishing—we will come to understand how possible it might be to return to a truly noble vision of life, such as Spinoza taught in his philosophy and such as obtains in Ecclesiastes and Psalms. That has not happened yet in the West. We are not truly meditating upon life as Spinoza would want us to do. We are whistling in the dark to pretend that—it—that er, ahem—you know, does not happen.

Keep eating the muesli is not a substitute for our old immortality myths. It is a pathetic and undignified transmutation of them. The old believers taught that when we die we would go on forever. The new health freaks believe that before we die we shall go on forever: if only we lay off the booze and the fags and the polyunsaturates.

Wisdom can't be learnt until the fact of death is accepted and then, in the Spinoza manner, not run away from, but put out of our minds. We should take a leaf out of the cats' book. They are wiser than we. They know when to lie in the sun. They know when to play and to hunt and to make love. They know when to turn their faces to the wall and to die. If their legendary nine lives run out faster than the allotted span, their parents or lovers grieve as inconsolably as Rachel weeping for her children. Only time heals such wounds; what some would call nature. The wounds perhaps remain forever, but other things come to take their place—new hunting grounds, new lovers, new seasons. It is so, or it could be so with us.

Philip Larkin defined religion as:

That vast moth-eaten musical brocade
Created to pretend we never die . . .

He was a man who dreaded extinction
with a passion:

no sight, no sound,
No touch or taste or smell, nothing
to think with,
Nothing to love or link with,
The anaesthetic from which none
come round.

It is a thought with good literary
antecedents. Milton's Beelzebub asks:

For who would lose,
Though full of pain, this intellectual
being,
Those thoughts that wander through
eternity?

Even angels and archangels can dread
having "nothing to think with." I am certainly aware that one of the reasons I write
is a feeling that I wish to be immortal.
I lack the Blakean ability to delight in
essentially evanescent moments. I wish to
write them down, to stick them in some
mental photograph album.

It would be wiser to be like Jesus and
Socrates, and not to write: to trust one's
thoughts to conversation, to make one's
stories oral stories. The written word is
unquestionably one of the illusions with
which Western man has, particularly in
literature since Milton, disguised from
himself his own mortality.

I feel reasonably certain that cats do not
have such egotism. Thoughts presumably
pass through their heads as often as they
pass through mine. I do not say that these
thoughts are always as interesting as those
which wandered through eternity or
through the brain of John Milton—but
then, whose are? The point is, they pass,
and it is not a matter of regret to cats. This
must in part be because they do not anticipate death. Dostoyevsky, who should have
known, because he faced the firing squad,
says that knowing the hour of one's death,
the exact time of it, makes its terrors doubly worse. But surely the mere fact that we,
as human beings, can define to ourselves
our own mortality, can say that we know
that we shall die, and that this is the event
which we fear more than any other.

In the days when I knew Philip Larkin,
I used to think that there was a certain paradox here. I was still holding on by my fin-
ger-tips to Christian belief, and therefore
technically assented to a belief in the resurrection of the body and life everlasting.
But in my inner heart I did not really
believe in the resurrection of the body, not
really—not a reconstitution of my flesh as
resurrection flesh, not a rising up of my
bones as in the Epistles of Paul or the
paintings of Stanley Spencer in Cookham
Churchyard. Above all, as I had gradually
realised after my near-death experience, I
did not WANT immortality. I had no
innate dread of death, though like everyone I dread dying or the possible manner
of my dying. I simply did not wish to carry
on forever and ever. If I had been able to
state my wishes to the Almighty I should
have wished to put them in the words of
the Old Testament psalmist, that the days

of man were three score years and ten; I would have wanted to say that I was grateful for this; He really had no need to lay on that everlasting encore to assure me of his love or presence. For Larkin, however, who was incurably atheistic, the idea of mortality was unendurable and he would have done anything to make himself believe in some form of survival. That was why, rather to his annoyance, I used to question his lines about religion being "Created to pretend we never die." Surely the majority of religions, for whatever purpose they were created—if that is how they came into being—are only too ready to remind their adherents of the fact that they will die, quite often threatening them with horrible punishments thereafter if they do not, at all times and in all places, subscribe to the orthodoxies of faith and morals. And religion, whatever else it is, has been one very simple way of ritualising our knowledge of mortality. Jesus reminded his followers that not a sparrow falls to the ground unseen by its heavenly father. This is not an Animal Rights plea that sparrows should be granted the same status as human beings, or that after a major shoot of pigeon or grouse there should be state funerals or requiem masses. One of the implications of Jesus' saying, however, must be that we should conform our lives to those of other beings in the natural universe. We can spend the fortune of Solomon on fine raiment and still look no more beautiful than the flowers of the field; the earth provides us with sustenance in exactly the same way that it provides the beasts of the field with their food, even though we might be more ingenious in the cultivation, storage and preparation of food than the fowls of

the air and the fishes of the sea. The fact that God sees the fall of the sparrow does not mean that the sparrow should start to wail or rail against his mortality. It is a lesson in how to die. We should learn to die like sparrows.

There can be no more childish egotism, in my view, than in supposing that the universe has a creator who is constantly on the look-out, like some sadistic headmaster, for the way in which we behave or misbehave. At the end of term, the good children will be rewarded. The remainder will see him afterwards in his study. However sophisticated Christian theology becomes, its theories of the afterlife always boil down to this absurdist picture: of the First Cause, the source of all Life and Goodness, being perpetually engaged, sometimes with the assistance of a spy network of guardian angels, in assessing the condition of our souls. Those who have done sins, without repenting of them in time, will suffer eternally. The origins of this Dantean horror-story are to be found in the pages of the New Testament—with Jesus' stories of the division of the sheep and the goats, and his mentioning of the last judgment, when those who visited the sick and the imprisoned will be rewarded and those who neglected such works of charity will be punished. But he could not have supposed when he said such things, that a whole elaborate system of celestial rewards and infernal punishments would be concocted on the basis of these parables. It would be as literalist as to suppose that he genuinely thought true repentance was impossible until we had all undertaken a spell as swineherds; or that he was genuinely and literally a door, and Peter, James and John were in fact not human beings at all but sheep (like some of the holier desert fathers, at least one of whom developed the nether half of the sheep).

But to die as a sparrow dies, or as a cat dies, is to realise that we can leave our body behind, and our lives behind, like bathers hanging up their clothes in the locker before going into the swimming bath. It need not be horrific. In fact, it is something to rejoice over.

Larkin was a very popular poet. He was always complaining in his curmudgeonly way that he was popular, but it pleased him, and at the same time baffled him. Surely a man who expressed such strong views, who hated anywhere except Hull, (and wasn't very fond of that) who lived a life of such seclusion, and who hated women, blacks, most art—ought not to have been so popular. It worried him.

He was popular because he spoke to our condition. It is not of course religion which pretends we never die, it is the strange amalgam of superstitions and aspirations which possess the collective consciousness at this juncture of the late twentieth century. The health fads, the dread of nuclear war, the obsession with the wickedness of drink and cigarettes, are all part of the same weird view. My doctor, who has been looking after me for two or three years, is a conscientious man. All new patients in his practice undergo a test—blood-pressure, kidneys, and so forth. It would appear that when last heard of all my bodily functions were operative to the doctor's satisfaction. He then asked me how much I drank. I told him, roughly speaking truthfully, and he expressed a pained astonishment. He said that anyone who drank more than two glasses of wine PER WEEK was endangering their liver.

He then gave me a lecture about smoking cigarettes. Doubtless if he knew that I sometimes like to eat a fried breakfast he could have given me a lecture about that.

It was only a vivid and extreme example of an attitude of mind which emanated I suspect from the USA and which is now all but universal in the West. I happen to dread old age much more than I dread death, so that it does not particularly worry me that an indulgence in fried eggs, cigarettes or whisky might make my spell in the geriatric ward rather shorter than that of a more abstemious patient. But even in the geriatric ward you come across doctors and nurses who seem to have such a horror of the most obvious fact about human beings—that they are mortal—that they will do anything to preserve the life of their patients even though the kindest thing that could happen to them would be death. It is the kindest thing, in fact, which could happen to any of us, and without being morbid or suicidal in any way, I think we should all, if not positively looking forward to death, rejoice in the fact that life has perimeters. It does not go on forever, and nor should we wish it to go on forever. It would be a hell if it did.

We are physical beings and we inhabit a physical universe. If we discard the myths of self and soul and spirit, and recognise that all our life and sensation, all our capacity to think and to feel, are inextricably tied up with our bodies—if, in short, we see that we do not have bodies, we are bodies—then we might begin to realise what an extraordinary place we inhabit and what a mystery, in the true sense, life is. To be born, to grow up, to fall in love, to realise that by our actions, we can bring more human beings to life, and in watching them grow and develop, see the whole mystery re-enacted: is not all this wonderful? And to watch the changing seasons, and to find out more about the strange world of plants and fishes and beasts and birds with whom we share life on this planet—is that not wonderful too? And to realise the ingenuity of the human mind—which can produce the symphonies of Mozart, and the novels of Dostoyevsky and the canvases of Rembrandt and all the ingenious scientific discoveries of the twentieth century—is not that a humbling thought, when we realise that all human beings are made up of ingredients which could be bought for a pound or so at a chemist's shop—even Mozart, even Shakespeare. Is not that enough mystery, without your wishing to invent new mysteries of heaven and of hell? And is this life not rich, and varied and beautiful enough for you: or do you, like a greedy child, having stuffed its face with food, do you demand yet more? I

don't. Are you so obsessed with being you that you can't accept the fact of your own nonexistence? Can't you realise that the most deliriously happy moments in life have come when we have forgotten ourselves; and that, not only is it inconceivably unlikely that we should survive bodily death, it would be horrible if we did—a fate far worse than death itself.

Questions

1. Identify three arguments Wilson uses to try to persuade the reader that the idea of heaven is not a coherent idea. Do you find these arguments persuasive? Why or why not?
2. What possible counterarguments might be used against Wilson's arguments as listed in question 1?
3. What does Wilson mean when he writes, ". . . the very idea of Heaven has provided Christians with the most wonderful excuse for not being Christian"?

---

3 J. P. Moreland, *A Defense of the Resurrection of Jesus*

J. P. Moreland is a professor of philosophy at the Talbot School of Theology located on the campus of Biola University in southern California. Professor Moreland holds a doctorate in philosophy from the University of Southern California, and was twice awarded the coveted "Senior Class Professor of the Year" award by the graduating students of Biola. Biola University is a traditional Christian institution, and Moreland, as a convinced theist and Christian, upholds that standard. He is in frequent demand around the country as a speaker on the subject of Christian apologetics, and has engaged in public debate with many of the most famous living atheists. He has written a number of books, including *Christianity and the Nature of Science; Body and Soul: Human Nature and the Crisis in Ethics;* and *Scaling the Secular City.*

The passage you are about to read is part of a famous debate that took place in 1988 between Moreland and the atheistic philosopher Kai Nielson, from the University of Calgary in Canada. The debate, entitled "Does God Exist?", was later published under the same title along with several complementary articles.

In his opening statement, Professor Moreland lays out the traditional arguments for the existence of God, arguments that are foundational to the course of Western philosophy. There is the cosmological argument, which holds that if all things can be traced back to some prior cause, there must be, standing at the beginning of the long chain of cause and effect that structures the history of our universe, some First Cause—namely, God. And there is the design argument, which holds that the universe functions very much like a machine, having moving parts that all work in harmony with each other, and since all machines are made by some intelligent designer, the universe must also be made by a Designer—namely, God. But Moreland goes on to argue that one important proof that there is a God is that the Christian religion, which proclaims that God exists, is true in all its teachings and beliefs. And the way Moreland goes about proving that the Christian religion is true is by proving that the resurrection of Jesus from the dead—arguably the most central teaching of the Christian faith—really happened.

The second proposition that I would like to defend is that *Jesus of Nazareth is God's supreme revelation of Himself to mankind.* Among other things, this claim hinges upon the truthfulness of His resurrection from the dead. I want to argue that the historical evidence for Jesus' resurrection is strong and belief in His resurrection is reasonable. At least four lines of evidence can be used to defend the historicity of the resurrection.

First, *the time factor.* Let us consider the New Testament, not as an inspired book, though I believe it to be, but as a set of alleged historical sources about Jesus of Nazareth. We know He was most likely crucified in A.D. 33. All New Testament scholars date the Gospels within the lifetime of eyewitnesses of the life of Jesus, and the latest they can possibly be dated is toward the end of the first century, from A.D. 70 on. In recent years there has been a growing number of New Testament scholars who date the Gospels from A.D. 40 to A.D. 70, including the late W. F. Albright at Johns Hopkins, the dean of American archaeology. The bulk of the letters of the New Testament date from A.D. 48 to 64. This means that we have clear widespread testimony to a miracle-working, supernatural, resurrected Jesus no later than fifteen to twenty years after the events of His life.

In addition, the writings of the New Testament themselves contain statements, phrases, and hymns that are heavily Semitic and which translate easily back into Aramaic from Greek. These hymns are embedded in the epistles of the New Testament, and they existed prior to the New Testament because they are not spoken in characteristically Pauline language. As Martin Hengel argued, "These phrases and hymns present a miracle-working Jesus who rose from the dead and they can be dated within the first decade of Christianity after the death of Jesus." Further, there are good reasons for believing that the Acts account of the first preaching of the risen Jesus in Jerusalem just five weeks after His death is historically reliable.

All of this means that a clear, widespread picture of a miracle-working, supernatural Jesus who rose bodily from the dead existed within a few weeks after His death, and at the latest within the first decade of the spread of Christianity.

There was just not enough time for the facts of Jesus' life, death, and resurrection to be forgotten and replaced by a set of myths. A. N. Sherwin-White, a classical historian at the University of Oxford, has studied the rate at which myth replaced history in the ancient Near East. Sherwin-White argues, "Tests suggest that even two generations are too short a span to allow the mythical tendency to prevail over a hard historical core." There is then not enough time between the deeds of Jesus and our earliest sources to allow for a high degree of myth making.

Secondly, *the empty tomb*. A large number of New Testament scholars hold that the New Testament statements that Jesus' tomb was found empty three days after His death are historically reliable. They do so for several reasons.

First, archaeological discoveries have verified the accuracy of the description of Jesus' burial and tomb and the plausibility of its location. Archaeologists have discovered tombs just like the ones that are described in the Gospels, in just the place in Jerusalem where Jesus is said to have been buried.

Second, there were at least fifty tombs of holy men during the time of Jesus in Jerusalem that were sites of religious veneration. Thus, the location of Jesus' tomb would have been carefully noted by His followers in order to venerate Him after His death. But there is no evidence whatsoever that His tomb was ever a site of veneration. This is explained by the fact that His tomb was empty.

Third, the Gospel narratives of the discovery of the empty tomb bear attires of historicity. To Cite but one, the narratives tell us that women were the first to dis-

cover and witness the empty tomb. Given the low social status of women then and the fact that they were not allowed to give legal testimony, it is highly probable that women were in fact the first ones to see the risen Christ. A fabricated account of the empty tomb would have used men, certainly not women. In fact, when Paul cites the resurrection formula in First Corinthians used to evangelize unbelievers, he leaves the women out, no doubt to keep unbelievers from stumbling on a peripheral detail which was culturally insensitive. The women are left in the Gospel accounts, however, to preserve a record of *"wie es eigentlich gewesen ist,"* as it actually was, even though it was an embarrassment to them culturally.

Third, *the appearances of Jesus of Nazareth.* The historical evidence indicates that on separate occasions different individuals and groups, one group of at least five hundred persons, saw appearances of Jesus from the dead. Even one of the most skeptical New Testament scholars, the late Norman Perrin of the University of Chicago, has said, "The more we study the tradition with regard to the appearances, the firmer the rock begins to appear upon which they are based."

I personally know of no New Testament scholar who denies that several of Jesus' early followers at least had a life-changing experience they believed to have been an experience of the risen Jesus. Many who deny that it was a real resurrection interpret these reported experiences as subjective experiences or hallucinations. But two objections refute this explanation. First, the variety and number of people seeing the appearances makes hallucination unlikely. Second, hallucinations do not create completely new thoughts, but they put together old thoughts.

Let me explain. The resurrection picture of Jesus is so out of touch with what was already in existence in Judaism that it is hard to explain how they [Jesus' followers] would have used a resurrection to interpret hallucinating experiences. According to Jewish belief at that time, there was to be only one resurrection, all at once. No one would be raised by himself; everybody was to be raised together. Second, the general resurrection was at the end of the world; there was no resurrection in history before the end of the world. Third, the resurrection was conceived of in crude, reanimating terms where the body parts were reanimated on the skeleton. Fourth, visions of people who were translated to heaven or raised were never given to groups. And fifth, the Messiah, according to first-century Jewish religious belief, was not a suffering servant who died or rose from the dead.

The point is that if they had hallucinations, they would never have thought to interpret those hallucinations as a resurrection. Already available in their culture was a ready-made genre—namely, translations to heaven or resuscitations. The fact that they interpreted it as a resurrection is hard to explain in light of their cultural beliefs.

Finally, *the origination of the Christian church* implies a resurrection. Why did Christianity begin? Where did it come from? What motivation did the early church have for spreading Christianity? Christianity didn't come from the stork. Christianity was a unique new movement. Without the resurrection there is no adequate explanation for where it came from or how it got going.

For one thing, the church was not founded on loving your neighbor or doing good, but on spreading a message, the death and resurrection of the Son of God. But that message was so culturally unacceptable as to have little antecedent probability of success. If the early church was going to invent a message that would sell well and which was going to make them religious heroes, they did a horrible job. As one of the world's prominent New Testament scholars, Martin Hengel of Tübingen has put it, "To believe that the one pre-existent Son of the one true God, the mediator at creation and the redeemer of the world, had appeared in very recent times in out-of-the-way Galilee as a member of the obscure people of the Jews and even worse, had died the death of a common criminal on the cross, could only be regarded as a sign of madness."

The resurrection of Jesus offers the best explanation for the incredible success of the early church. Without the resurrection there would have been no early church. Furthermore, it explains how a large generation of Jewish people (remember, most of the early Christians were Jewish) would have been willing to risk the damnation of their own souls to hell and reject what had been sociologically embedded in their community for centuries; namely, the Law must be kept for salvation, sacrifices must be kept for salvation, the Sabbath must be kept, nontrinitarian monotheism, and there is only a political Messiah, not a dying and rising one. How does a group of people in a short time span, a society, disenfranchise themselves from that into which they had been culturally indoctrinated for centuries and risk the damnation of their own souls to hell to follow a carpenter from Nazareth? The most reasonable explanation is there was something about that man that caused this change. He was a miracle worker who rose from the dead.

The resurrection also explains the motivation and endurance of the early Christians. The early disciples experienced a life of pain, physical and social abuse, and martyrs' deaths for their message. What kept them going? The question is even more pressing in light of their state of betrayal, fear, and disillusionment just after Jesus' crucifixion. What changed them and motivated them? The resurrection.

So strong is this point that recently an orthodox Jewish rabbi, a Jewish scholar of New Testament in Frankfurt, Germany, Pinchas Lapide, was converted to belief in the resurrection on strictly historical evidence. And he has written a book defending its historicity. Lapide writes, "How was it possible that His disciples, who by no means excelled in intelligence, eloquence, or strength of faith, were able to begin their victorious march of conversion only *after* the shattering fiasco of Golgotha?"

Questions

1. Identify the various arguments Dr. Moreland uses to argue for the historical resurrection of Jesus from the dead.

2. For what reason, according to Dr. Moreland, would the early church's message that Jesus had risen from the dead be seen as "so culturally unacceptable as to have little antecedent probability of success"?

3. According to Dr. Moreland, why is it likely that the stories told about Jesus rising from the dead are not merely myths?

---

4 Bishop John Shelby Spong, *Life After Death—This I Do Believe*

Bishop John Shelby Spong was formerly the presiding bishop of Newark, New Jersey, for the Episcopal Church, a denomination closely affiliated with the Anglican Church of England. Bishop Spong has enjoyed a career filled with controversy, much of it thanks to his several best-selling books, such as *Rescuing the Bible from Fundamentalism, Living in Sin?*, and *Liberating the Gospels*. In an age when "pop spirituality" floods the marketplace, he has tapped into a healthy audience of people who are spiritually curious, yet unwilling to embrace traditional Christianity. His writings demonstrate a concerted effort to marry critical biblical scholarship and current trends in morality with traditional Christian symbols.

Bishop Spong refers to himself as "a believer in exile." He believes that the world into which Christianity was born was limited and provincial, particularly when viewed from the perspective of the progress in knowledge and technology made over the past two centuries. This makes any ideas or beliefs formulated in first-century Judea inadequate to our progressive minds and lives today. So Bishop Spong is "in exile" until Christianity is re-formed to discard all of its outdated and, according to him, false tenets. It is this theme the Bishop has pursued in his recent book, *Why Christianity Must Change or Die*.

The following essay is from Bishop Spong's 1994 book, *Resurrection: Myth or Reality?* Bishop Spong admits to a long-term scholarly interest in the study of the resurrection of Jesus, but finds the traditional view of that subject to be problematic. In this study, he turns to recent discussions of the nature of myth, and of the relationship between myth and religious belief. Against this background, the Bishop portrays the historical resurrection of Jesus as handed down to the Christian church through the ages in the form of mythology rather than history. Bishop Spong is quick to state that this does not necessarily rule out the historical veracity of the resurrection, but it does take attention away from the question, "Did the resurrection of Jesus really happen?" What actually happened, he asserts, is something that we, in the late twentieth century, can never fully recover. Too much legendary material has accrued around the event itself for us ever to be able to understand it as a "pure fact." Instead, he insists, the emphasis of the church should be placed upon the utter mystery of the life of Jesus, the meaning of his death, and on his continuing importance for the church as the one who reveals the way to God.

I do believe that death is not the end of our lives. But I do not know how to talk about that. I have no words, I possess no concepts. I am reduced to silence before this ultimate mystery. But if someone were to ask me Job's ancient and searching question, "If a man (or woman) dies, will he (she) live again?" my answer would be "Yes." That is my conviction. That is what I believe. Yet there is so much about the traditional content of heaven and hell that I do not believe, that I can speak negatively far more easily than I can speak positively.

I do not believe in life after death as a method of behavior control. I have no interest in the reward/punishment aspect of the afterlife. In the honesty of one's heart of hearts, the person whose life is noble only for the sake of gaining the ultimate reward of heaven is immediately guilty of being self-serving. If one acts one way and not another only to get a reward, one's life becomes insufferably shallow and petty. I would not be drawn to anyone or to any religious system that approached life in such a way. I recall the hymn that says: "I love thee Lord, but not because I hope for heaven thereby, Nor yet for fear that loving not, I might forever die." This hymn speeds to a higher good than that of the selfish person seeking a reward. It is my hope that Christianity will shed its reward and punishment motifs as a clear aberration in our understanding of the Gospels and as simply unworthy of the Lord we claim to serve.

I hope, too, that the church will someday reject the behavior control business as a blind and alien path that we have traveled in ignorance. The business of the church is to love people into life. When we confuse that and begin to think that our job is to judge one another, out of some self-imposed standard of righteousness, we have then, in my opinion, misread the whole message of the Gospel. To make moral pronouncements and to judge human life has become the favorite indoor sport of institutional Christianity, but it has never been of the essence of the Gospel. So I dismiss heaven as a place of reward, and I dismiss hell as a place of punishment. I find neither definition either believable or appealing.

Life after death must mean more than that. Talking about heaven is, for me, like talking about the resurrection. I no longer need to describe it. In this volume I have written about the resurrection of Jesus. I have dismissed many of the later-written details of Easter as legends, but I continue to cling to the core experience that inspired that legend. When I come to describe what actually happened on the first Easter, I find that I can talk about the effects that Easter had, the power it produced, the changes it wrought, the context in which it was experienced, and the results it created. But the moment itself? About that I discover that I am reduced to a profound, reverential silence. That moment was beyond time and space and, therefore, beyond the capacity of our language to capture or of our minds to understand. One has only to stand before that transcendent moment, containing that which the church has called the resurrection of Jesus, and there utter only a simple yes or no. In that silence I speak my yes, and then I seek to live into the power of that resurrection in my life. In a similar fashion my years of study on the issues of life after death have given me no words with which to discuss the idea. For Jesus it seemed to mean something like communion with God. It meant being in touch with something that transcended all of one's human categories, including a transcendence of the self that one is. It meant having one's eyes opened to see dimensions of life not normally seen and to have one's ears open to hear melodies and harmonies not normally heard.

This means that now I no longer look for God or for ultimate meaning in some distant place beyond this world. I rather seek these realities in every moment and in every relationship. For me the transcendence of God is no longer something different from the immanence of God. Transcendence is always a dimension of the immanent. The immanent is the point of entry; the transcendent is the infinite depth capable of being discerned behind any moment, beyond any point of entry.

For me heaven is an invitation into life, which, when explored deeply enough, when lived fully enough, when engaged significantly enough, is a way of passing into transcendence. In this way finite moments slip into being infinite, timeless moments. I also believe that human life can be lived so deeply, that love can be experienced so powerfully, that incarnation in fact occurs again and again. God is not a heavenly man, an external force, or a judging parent. God is the creating spirit that calls order out of chaos. God is the life force that emerges first into consciousness, then into self-consciousness, and now into self-transcendence, and ultimately into we know not what. God is the love that creates wholeness, the Being at the depths of our being, the Source from which all life comes.

This is the God that I see in Jesus of Nazareth, and so I affirm that this life is the life of God being lived among us. His was a life not finally bound by human limits. When those whose fear of God's presence was so total that they struck back to kill him, they finally were forced to discover that all they actually did was to free the meaning of his life from the boundaries of finitude and to make him timeless, eternal, and ever-present. When the eyes of Simon finally saw the meaning of Jesus' life, when the ears of Simon finally heard the music of Jesus' life, then he stared across that invisible but ever-so-real barrier that separated time from timelessness, finitude from infinity, human spirit from Holy Spirit, and he saw Jesus inside the meaning of God.

How does one talk about that? Only symbolically, I assure you. First there was the ecstatic negative proclamation, "Death cannot contain him!" In time the ecstasy of that claim was turned into human stories about tombs being empty, stones being rolled away to allow the divine exit, grave clothes being placed so as to suggest that he rose out of them, and startled women conversing with him in the garden.

Next there was the ecstatic positive proclamation, "We have seen the Lord!" In time the ecstasy of that claim was also turned into human stories about heavenly apparitions that appeared inside sealed space, during a meal in Emmaus, by the Sea of Galilee, or in the upper room. To quell the doubts and to answer the questions, details were added. So we are told that Jesus ate a piece of broiled fish, that he spoke to them to interpret the Scriptures, that he invited the physical inspection of his wounds, and that he commissioned them to be his agents in all the world. It was not long before that transcendent moment in which meaning broke into the consciousness of those still living inside this world, meaning that was beyond this world, had been turned by human beings into a concrete fact of history, complete with magical details.

Such a transformation might be sustained in a premodern age of faith, but that kind of magic and sleight of hand will never survive in our contemporary world, where miracle and the supernatural are both suspect. If we insist that Easter's truth must be carried inside such a literal framework, we doom Easter's truth to the death of irrelevance. Yet to talk about ultimate moments is something that human beings must do, and to explain human experiences is a compelling human need. We need not apologize for that. We do need to apologize for the arrogance of those human beings who insist that we reduce all transcendent reality to an explanation, using literalized human words, and then claim ultimacy not for the experience but for the explanation. We do need to apologize for the human assumption that when we have explained something in understandable human language, we have established the objectivity of our explanation as the bearer of ultimate truth.

Because Jesus was the name given to a life of ultimate, transcendent meaning that emerged in a Jewish context, Jewish concepts were inevitably the first line of human explanation. We see the influences of the feast of Tabernacles and the feast of Passover. We see the interpretative power of such Jewish concepts as prophet/martyr, atoning sacrifice, suffering servant, and son of man. There was nothing any more literal about these explanations than there was about the narratives of empty tombs or apparitions. The former was an intellectual attempt to explain. The latter was a legendary attempt to understand. The truth of Easter lies beyond both of these interpretive efforts.

So also does life after death get twisted and tangled in the words used to convey it, and in the power that is thought to derive from it. I want to move beyond the pious sentimentality used in times of crises even by those who do not believe in God. I want to move beyond the immature assurances with which an adult consoles a child who has lost either a pet or a parent to death. I want to move beyond the institutional tactics of behavior control, of reward and punishment, that finally issued in the practice of the sale of indulgences, primarily on the Catholic side of Christianity, and the manipulation of human fear by extolling the punishing power of divine wrath, primarily on the Protestant side of Christianity. I do not want either the promise of heaven or the fear of hell to manipulate any person into doing anything. That may well be a proper function of society, of the laws that govern the social order, of civic awards and public praise on one side and civil fines and even penal incarceration on the other. But that is not the role of God, the vocation of the Christian church, or the function of heaven.

Life is finite. At least in every individual expression of that life, it is finite. It comes into existence at a particular moment. It lives out, more or less, its appointed span of days. It passes out of existence, and the elements that once coalesced to form that life return to the primal soup to be reformed as part of another entity. My affirmation is that only those creatures who have developed self-consciousness can, within their span of days, commune with that which is beyond our limits. When we commune with the limitless, the eternal, the ultimately real one, we share in those aspects of that reality with which our hearts and minds are bound. If one does that completely enough it could well be

said of that one that his life had been incorporated into God at the moment of his death. If Jesus of Nazareth provided us with the means by which we can walk on his path into the same destiny, then it is easy to understand why some would claim that they heard him say, "I am the way, the truth, and the life. No one comes to the Father but by me"; or "I am the resurrection and the life, he [she] who believes in me, though he [she] die yet shall he [she] live."

So I stand before this portrait of God painted by Jesus of Nazareth and interpreted by the church. I recognize the legends, the accretions, the context of that ancient world which had the task of transforming the inbreeding reality into human words. I probe all of those elements until I get beyond them to the experience that produced them. Here words fail me. Silence engulfs me. I peer beyond the limits in which my life is lived, and I say my prayerful yes . . .

> Yes to Jesus—my primary window into
>   God;
>
> Yes to resurrection—which asserts that
>   the essence of
> Jesus is the essence of a living God;
>
> Yes to life after death—because one
>   who has entered a
> relationship with God has entered the
>   timelessness of God.

These three yeses coalesce into being the defining experience of my life. Out of these affirmations I will live, I will love, and I will enter life deeply. I will scale life's heights and explore its depths. I will seek truth without fear, and when I find it, I will act on it regardless of the cost. I will never rank peace above justice or the unity of an institution ahead of the integrity of that institution. Those are just other ways of being faithless to the primary defining "yes" that lies at the center of who I am.

I will never again seek to speculate on the nature of life after death, the definition of heaven, or the arguments for or against its reality. Those books on life after death that I read in my earlier life will remain in a row on a shelf in my library. I will not open them again. I will treasure those persons with whom my life is emotionally bound today, and I will enjoy the expanding privileges of their friendship. When they die, I will grieve at the loss that my life will experience. I will not speculate on how, if, or in what form I might see them again. That is not my business. My business is to live now, to love now, and to be now. As I give my life, my love, and myself away now, I hope that others can be called into deeper life, greater love, fuller being, and that by expanding each other, we enter the infinity of what Paul Tillich called "the eternal now." To live it, not to explain it, is my task and, I believe, the task of the Christ in this world and therefore the task of that group of people who dare to call themselves the body of Christ.

So let us live, my brothers and sisters. Let us even eat, drink, and be merry, not because tomorrow we shall die but because today we are alive and it is our vocation to be alive—to be alive to God, alive to each other, alive to ourselves.

"Choose ye this day whom you will serve!" As for me and my house we will serve the crucified/risen one, who said, "I have come that you might have life and that you might have it ABUNDANTLY," and I will live in expectant hope that where he is there will I someday be. That is quite enough for me.

Shalom.

Questions

1. In your own words, what is Bishop Spong's view of the resurrection of Jesus?

2. Do you agree with Bishop Spong's interpretation of the resurrection of Jesus? Why or why not?

3. What does Bishop Spong suggest would happen to the Christian faith if it turns out the Jesus was not resurrected from the dead? Do you agree with Bishop Spong when he argues that, without the resurrection, we can still view Jesus as "the essence of a living God"? Why or why not?

---

5 John Bowker, *Death in Hinduism*

John Bowker attained international attention as a young scholar when, in 1972, he delivered the Wilde Lectures at the University of Oxford. The lectures were subsequently published under the title *The Sense of God.* In this widely acclaimed work, the author tackles the age-old philosophical question, "If God cannot be seen or heard, how and when did the idea of God ever arise in human consciousness?" Bowker holds a teaching fellowship at Cambridge University in England, and two adjunct professorships at American universities—North Carolina State and the University of Pennsylvania.

In this passage taken from Bowker's 1991 book, *The Meanings of Death,* Bowker outlines the beliefs unique to Hinduism concerning death. Following are terms that Bowker introduces as essential to understanding the Hindu, and hence the Eastern, view of death:

- *Brahman:* the Absolute, the Divine Principle of the Universe, God
- *Atman:* the spark of the Divine Principle that resides in each of us
- *Prakrti:* all non-*Atman;* the physical, material form of existence
- *Jiva:* the temporal expression of *Atman* as individual character and personality
- *Buddhi:* the mental attitude of detachment from the world and its events
- *Dharma:* religious duty; the requirements necessary to attain salvation
- *Nirvana:* perfect oneness with *Brahman,* total peace, inner quietude
- *Karma:* spiritual law that rewards good deeds and punishes bad deeds
- *Samsara:* reincarnation, a return to the earth after death in another form
- *Maya:* illusion, material reality, falsehood, the world of change and death
- *Moksha:* salvation, liberation of *Atman* through spiritual training

One of the essential differences between an Eastern view of death and a traditional Western view is that in the religions of the West, it is expected that the soul will face a "day of judgment" in which all its thoughts, words and deeds will be measured against God's standards of justice and holiness. The bodiless soul will stand before the tribunal of God with its eternal fate hanging in the balance. In the East, however, there is no day of judgment, and hence no once-and-for-all banishment either to a heaven of bliss or a hell of torment. Instead, judgment is seen as being rendered as soon as an act is committed in the form of personal karma, and the salvation one hopes for—the peaceful bliss of Nirvana—is thought to be attained only by the effort of countless lifetimes, countless "incarnations," until one finally "gets it right." For this reason, some commentators consider the Eastern view of judgment superior to the Western view. It seems fairer, they say, to give an individual soul many chances to succeed, rather than a single chance. Others, however, note that the prospect of many lives ahead of one serves only to encourage procrastination. Why do the hard work required of salvation in this life, they argue, if one can put it off to the next incarnation?

Hinduism is the map of how to live appropriately: it is the description and the evocation of the ways in which to live, in whatever circumstances one finds oneself, in order to move towards (and perhaps attain) the goal.

This theme is central to the Bhagavad Gita, The Song of the Lord, the sacred text of greatest importance to most Hindus. Hindu scripture is made up of two parts, Sruti (texts recording revelation heard by the *risis* of old and transmitted orally) and Smriti (the "remembered" texts, which may be attached to Sruti texts, but may also extend them). Thus the main components of Hindu scripture are the four Vedas (mainly chants, hymns and songs), the Brahmanas attached to the Vedas (mainly concerned with the rituals to which the Vedic chants, etc., belong), and the Aranyakas and the Upanishads (recording and expressing the search for knowledge, insight and understanding). The Gita is closest in content and concern to the Upanishads, but it is not a part of them. It is a text which occurs within the long epic, the Mahabharata. It was regarded early as having spiritual authority, at least formally in the sense that it was regarded as one of the three texts or group of texts which required commentary—the others being the Upanishads and the Vedanta Sutras of Badarayana. These three form the *prasthana-traya* which are the basis of those interpretations of the Indian tradition which are known as Vedanta, the "end of the Vedas." Among these, the Gita occupies the central place in the formation of Indian life. As a Hindu put it in *Worlds of Faith:* "Our Holy Book is the Gita; and if you read it, and if you can understand it, you'll find the answer to all of your questions. The only question is, whether you can understand what is written there" (p. 131).

So the Gita is in any case a wise point at which to begin in attempting to understand the Hindu religion. But in the case of death, it is particularly important because the fundamental issue in the Gita of *dharma* is focused on death. In the Mahabharata, the story is told of a war between two branches of the Kaurava family, the hundred sons of Dhritarashtra, led by the eldest brother, Duryodhana, and on the other side, their cousins, the Pandavas, led by their eldest brother, Yudhishthira. Yudhishthira, who has been cheated and wronged by Duryodhana, goes to the limit to avoid war, but Duryodhana militantly refuses his overtures, even to the extent of defying the manifestation (*avatara,* or incarnation) of the god Vishnu in the form of Krishna: offered the choice of his army or of Krishna

alone, Duryodhana chose his army. But Yudhishthira's younger brother, Arjuna, offered the same choice, chose Krishna, who agrees to serve as his charioteer. At this point—the moment when the Gita begins—Arjuna has a crisis of conscience, and refuses to fight. In the second of two accounts of this crisis, Arjuna says that he cannot bring himself to kill his revered teachers and members of his own family.

The main part of the Gita is made up of Krishna's response to Arjuna's paralysis. There is an initial response in ch. ii, parts of which are then unpacked or extended to tie in with the rest of the Gita. In the initial response, Krishna (somewhat like Weiss' de Sade, p. 9, but for utterly different reasons) argues that Arjuna is giving a false importance to death, because the selves which are embodied are eternal and cannot therefore die when the body dies:

> The Blessed Lord said: ... Those who are truly wise do not mourn for the dead any more than they do for the living. Never was there a time when I did not exist—or you or these princes; nor will there be a time when any of us shall cease to be hereafter. Just as embodied selves [*dehin*] pass through childhood, youth and old age in their bodies, so too there is a passing [at death] to another body. (ii.12)

The argument of Krishna then follows that, if the embodied selves which are the true person (in contrast to the material constituents which are transient) cannot be affected by contingent accidents or even by death, then Arjuna should not hesitate to fight:

> Fight, then, son of Bharata. Whoever thinks that the embodied self can be the one who kills, or can be killed, has no sound understanding. It does not kill nor can it be killed. It is not born, it does not die . . . It is not killed when the body is killed . . . As a person throws away his clothes when they are worn out and puts on other new ones, so does the embodied self cast off its old bodies and enters new ones. Weapons cannot cut it, nor can fire burn it. Water does not make it wet, nor does the wind dry it. It cannot be cut or burned or made wet or dried. It is undying, flowing everywhere, stable, unmoved, eternal . . . And just as the death of all that is born is certain, so is the birth of that which has known death. Therefore, since this is something that no one can prevent, it should not be a cause of grief for you. (ii.18ff.)

To these arguments, Krishna then adds three further considerations. The first is that, since Arjuna is a warrior, he must fulfill the dharma of being a warrior: he must act in the ways laid down as being appropriate for a warrior, since otherwise he will create a far greater disorder than the relatively small episode of death: "Give thought to your duty (*dharma*) then you will have no reason to hesitate. . . . But if you will not engage in this battle which your duty requires, then by discarding both duty and honour, you will bring evil on yourself" (ii.33).

But the fulfillment of *svadharma* (his own *dharma*) is not a matter of setting sails

and drifting before the wind. It requires appropriation by acts of intention and will: "The essence of the soul [*buddhi*, concentrated mental attitude] is single-minded resolution" (ii.41). So the second point that Krishna adds is that action according to *dharma* must be cultivated, but without attachment to, or concern about, the consequences. Thus, if it is his *dharma* to be a warrior, he must indeed be that, but without getting preoccupied in an evaluation of that activity in terms of its immediate results: "Work alone is your proper business, and not the fruits of it. Do not allow the fruit of your works to be the motive, but on the other hand, do not seek to avoid acting altogether. Stand fast in Yoga, giving up all attachment" (ii.47f.). In practice, this involves drawing in one's senses as a tortoise withdraws into its shell.

There is clearly an inconsistency in the Gita at this point, because, despite this emphasis on non-attachment, Krishna has been advancing arguments which depend on consequences for their appeal: thus a war justly fought in accordance with one's *dharma* "opens the door to heaven" (ii.32); not to fight would break up the *dharma* of society on which order depends; and if he does not fight, he will lose face and be accused of cowardice (ii.34). But these arguments can be understood as examples of what is known in Eastern religions as *upaya-kausilya,* skill in means: a teacher will use arguments that will ultimately be transcended, because the pupil is at a level of understanding which requires such preliminary instruction in order to make that transcendental move. The overall picture of the Gita is not in doubt (which is not to say that it is not open to diverse and conflicting interpretation, as we shall see): reflection of a well-informed and well-intended kind (*samkhya,* not here in its technical sense of a school of Indian philosophy) leads to the realisation of the distinction between the true self (*atman*) and all that is not self (*prakrti),* the correct mental attitude (*buddhi*) which leads to this realisation involves non-attachment to all or anything that happens; however, disciplined effort and striving to be yoked to *buddhi* is entirely necessary; and this is the meaning of yoga in the Gita (not, as is sometimes supposed, yoked to, or united with, God), as in ii.39.

The point of that argument is then unfolded in the third of Krishna's additional points: the true objective is to become so detached from the transient appearances in the world that the self is no longer bound to this or any other world by its desires for things (including states) within the worlds of appearance. This is to realise that one's self is undying, eternal, immortal. To realise this and to attain this condition of wisdom is to attain *brahman:*

> Whoever forsakes all objects of desire and goes about without cravings or possessiveness or self-preoccupation becomes serene [*santi*]. This is the state of *brahman* [*brahmi stitih*], Partha. Whoever achieves it is not deceived. Maintaining this state even in his last hour, he attains to the *nirvana* which is *brahman.* (ii.71f.)

The earliest meaning of *brahman* seems to have been connected with "power", and especially with the power inherent in the words and chants of the Rig-Veda, as

Gonda (1950) has argued. In the Upanishads, attempts are made to determine what that power essentially is. Although the Upanishads can be read as suggesting that Brahman is the Absolute source of all manifestation, the unproduced Producer of all that is, a less partisan reading indicates that there are several candidates for understanding what *brahman* is: speech, mind, breath, space, sight, and so on, as well as the Absolute source. Equally, the meaning of *brahman* was not fixed by the time of the Mahabharata, where it refers to time, seasons, fire, even the god Prajapati. In the Gita, *brahman* may refer to Krishna himself (vi.28, x.12, xiii.12, 62), or to the Veda (vi.44), or to the offering in the ritual. But in this passage (ii.72) and elsewhere, *brahman* is the state experienced in liberation, both in this life and after-death. Thus it cannot be absorption into the Absolute, since consciousness of this state continues. Equally, the attainment of *brahman-nirvana* after death is not cessation, but rather the state in which the freed self abides eternally.

Thus *nirvana* is not at all like the Buddhist *nibbana/nirvana* (to be discussed later). At death, according to the Gita, the freed selves go to be with Krishna, and are in the same state of being as he is, but remain distinct from him. Nirvana is the state of happiness and peace of one who is eternally with Krishna. Far from it being "the blowing out of a candle," the Gita describes the condition of the yogin as being like "a candle flame away from a draught which does not flicker" (vi.19).

But what of the unfreed self, the one who remains attached and entangled in appearance? The self remains immutable but is reborn repeatedly, until it finds its way to liberation—and the Gita exists to indicate the paths to follow. In moral life a law exists which is as impersonal and inevitable in the consistency of its outcomes as gravity. It is the law of *karma*, *Karma* means both action and the consequence of action. According to the Gita, as we have already seen, the way to overcome the accumulation of bad *karma* is not to withdraw from all life and action, but to engage in appropriate action without attachment. Otherwise, the long continuation of rebirth (*samsara*) will continue.

In this way, the Gita contains all the main elements of the Hindu scheme of the self and its salvation. Can one say, then, that the Gita is the Hindu understanding of death? Clearly not, because the Gita itself is open to very different interpretations. Thus although the Gita seems to envisage the final state as a relation with Krishna, and not as a union with Brahman understood as the Absolute and undifferentiated source of all appearance, that other interpretation nevertheless appears in both ancient (such as the philosopher Sankara) and modern (such as Zaehner) guise.

This understanding of reality and appearance is known as Advaita, or nondualism. In this understanding, Brahman lies behind all appearance as its source, bringing things into appearance through *maya*. Maya is frequently translated as "illusion," and that translation does at least make the point that what presents itself to observation is not Brahman itself. Brahman is the guarantor of all appearance, subsisting beneath it and able to be discerned through it. *Maya* is thus the capacity of Brahman to bring all forms of

appearance into their manifest being. Those forms include the forms of appearance which can rightly be called theistic (that is, the gods and goddesses, of which Vishnu is an example), but in this perspective the gods are clearly subordinate to Brahman; thus the ultimate state cannot be union with Krishna, unless one sees that Krishna/Vishnu is one of the outer forms of appearance which is a consequence of Brahman and that Brahman is the Truth underlying them—and *maya* may also mean exactly that, the outward form of manifestation. In this perspective, the worlds of *maya* and *prakrti* are worlds of movement and change—hence the extreme importance of the dance in the Hindu religion. As such they are characterised by action (*karma*), and they are in a constant process of change. That necessarily involves death. The changeless is Brahman alone, and only Brahman is deathless.

In this understanding of the Gita, Brahman is present within the human appearance as *atman*, as the real and continuing identity persisting through the transient appearance of human form—"indestructible (alone) is That—know this—by which this whole universe was spun" (Gita ii.17). But insofar as the self attaches its desire to the transient manifestations of appearance, it projects itself as *jiva*. Jiva is the temporal projection of *atman*, and the more it gets entangled in the world of sense and appearance, the more it forgets its source (and liberation) in *atman* and identifies itself increasingly with this complex but nevertheless transient human form. *Atman* can therefore be considered under two aspects, the one in its true nature as the unchanging, unchangeable

Brahman, but the other in its attachment to the world of sense and change:

> Verily, this self [atman], the seers declare, wanders here on earth in every body [from body to body] unaffected, as it seems, by the light or the dark fruits of action. . . . As an enjoyer of righteous work he covers himself with a veil made of qualities, but he remains fixed, yea, he remains fixed. They said, Bhagavan, if you thus indicate the greatness of this self, then there is that other, different, one also called self, who, affected by the bright or dark fruits of action, enters a good or an evil womb, so that his course is downward or upward and he wanders about, affected by the pairs [of opposites like pleasure and pain]. (Maitri Up. ii-7, iii-1)

In a famous image, the two truths of *atman* (its independence, as Brahman, from transience; and its transience from form to form as it makes itself dependent on appearance) are seen as two birds sitting on a single branch:

> Two birds, companions [who are] always united, cling to the self-same tree. Of these two the one eats the sweet fruit, and the other looks on without eating. (Svet. Up. iv. 6)

While *atman* remains attached to *maya*, to the worlds of manifestation, it continues as *jiva-bhuta*, as living self. And the word "continues" is correct, because the *jiva*, so long as it remains attached to the objects of its experience, will necessarily reappear, or be reborn, in countless new forms of appearance. That must be so,

because the true self, Brahman, is deathless, and cannot be destroyed. Therefore, in a continuing flow of rebirth (*samsara*), the jiva will reappear. Traditionally, the self may be reborn as many as 84,000,000 times, perhaps as an animal or perhaps as a divine being, sometimes in heaven, sometimes in hell:

> Desire-Anger-Greed: this is the triple gate of hell, destruction of the self [*atman*]: therefore avoid these three. When once a man is freed from these three gates of darkness, then can he work for [his] self's salvation, thence tread the highest way. (Gita xvi. 21f.)

None of the states of rebirth, however long enduring, is permanent. Release from the endless chain of rebirth (*samsara*) is possible. But how to attain it? The Gita states (xvi. 24) that the guidance is already supplied in the *Sastras*, the post-Vedic compilations which gather together "the rules of the road," and which are therefore known, most usually as *Dharmasastra*. The following of *dharma* is the *sine qua non*; and indeed, Arjuna's *first* objection to fighting against his own kinsmen rested on this ground: the quickest way to hell (to a rebirth in that uncomfortable condition) is to disrupt the obligations within a family—and if, as in this case, the disruption involves *killing* members of the family, then other members of the family *already dead* may be precipitated into hell, because their successors are no longer alive to keep them afloat in a better circumstance by the appropriate sacrifices. Just as hazardous, the boundaries of caste would be confused, which makes the following of *dharma* impossible. (Caste is the formalisation of *dharma,* in the sense that it marks the boundaries within which particular life-ways can be pursued appropriately. The four original groups, Brahmans, Kshatriyas, Vaisyas and Sudras, were more divisions of occupation, but from those four classes, the multiplicity of castes eventually derived.)

What, then, determines whether one's rebirth is in a higher or lower outcome? Ultimately, it is *karma.* We have already encountered *karma* as action, but it is also action with the implication of consequence. Every action throws forward its long shadow of subsequent effect: what we are is a consequence of what we have done (or failed to do) in the past—not as a matter of crude reward or punishment, but as a simple matter of consequence. *Karma* is an impersonal law of the universe, much as gravity is. By that impersonal law of consequence, what we do now will create the circumstance that the *jiva* will inhabit at some future date—not necessarily in this birth, but in some

future form beyond rebirth. A person's basic character is thus the accumulated integration of good and evil actions in past lives which are now manifested in this present circumstance, which in turn is setting forward further consequence in the indefinite future horizon of rebirth.

Questions

1. What evidence can you think of that might support the idea of *Samsara*? What evidence can you think of that might argue against the idea of *Samsara*?

2. Put into your own words Bowker's description of *buddhi.* What do you think of this ideal?

3. Read again the passage from the *Gita* cited in Bowker's text: "Desire—Anger—Greed: this is the triple gate of hell, destruction of the self [*atman*]: therefore avoid these three". What sort of life would this be if one were to live this out fully? Is such a life possible? Why or why not?

---

6 Sogyal Rinpoche, *The Experiences of the Bardo*

A small but growing number of psychiatrists around the world have experimented in recent years with a therapeutic technique known as "regressive hypnotherapy." In this form of therapy, the patient is placed in a deep, hypnotic trance, and through the use of hypnotic suggestion, is aided in the recall of traumatic or otherwise influential memories. While not representing the mainstream use of this technique, a few practitioners claim to have used regressive hypnotherapy to uncover memories in their patients of former lives. Dr. Joel Whitton, for example, discovered that often patients suffering from phobias were able to remember events from past lives that may have contributed to their illness. Dr. Edith Fiore uses past-life regressive therapy in her clinical practice to treat eating disorders.

One of the ideas that past-life regressive hypnotherapy has underscored among these Western practitioners is the Eastern idea of the *bardo.* The bardo, which literally means "the between," refers in Tibetan Buddhism to a realm where the spirit-mind resides following its bodily death and prior to its rebirth in the next life. While in the bardo, the individual learns what went wrong in the previous life, and what needs to change in order to make the next life better. Past-life hypnotherapists claim to be able to help their patients recall their previous bardo experiences in order to uncover the innate wisdom that has been accumulated over successive lifetimes.

The person who is arguably most responsible for bringing the Tibetan notion of the bardo to the attention of the West is Buddhist lecturer and writer Sogyal Rinpoche. Born in Kham in Eastern Tibet, Sogyal Rinpoche is believed to be the incarnation of Lerab Lingpa Tertön Sogyal, a teacher to the thirteenth Dalai Lama. In 1971, Rinpoche went to England where he studied comparative religion at Cambridge University. He went on to study with several of the most revered Buddhist teachers of our time.

Sogyal Rinpoche is author of several books on Tibetan Buddhism aimed at Western readers, including his most popular work, *The Tibetan Book of Living and Dying,* which itself is based on an eighth-century Buddhist classic, *The Tibetan Book of the Dead.* Over 1.6 million copies of Rinpoche's book have been sold, in twenty-seven languages and fifty-four countries. It is widely used in college courses and by healthcare professionals. In 1993, Rinpoche founded the Spiritual Care Program which, under his guidance, aims to bring the teaching of this book to professional and trained volunteer caregivers who work in end-of-life care.

In *The Tibetan Book of Living and Dying,* Rinpoche describes the bardo as a multifaceted experience, a series of stages we must pass through before our next birth. In the following passage, Rinpoche summarizes the teachings of *The Tibetan Book of the Dead* on the *bardo of becoming,* the final stage in the bardo process. He allows a glimpse of what is thought to take place there. Rinpoche describes in detail the heart of the bardo of becoming experience: the "life-review," a concept which links the idea of the bardo with the Roman Catholic notion of purgatory.

The Experiences of the Bardo

During the first weeks of the bardo, we have the impression that we are a man or woman, just as in our previous life. We do not realize that we are dead. We return home to meet our family and loved ones. We try to talk to them, to touch them on the shoulder. But they do not reply, or even show they are aware we are there. As hard as we try, nothing can make them notice us. We watch, powerless, as they weep or sit stunned and heartbroken over our death. Fruitlessly we try to make use of our belongings. Our place is no longer laid at table, and arrangements are being made to dispose of our possessions. We feel angry, hurt, and frustrated, "like a fish," says

The Tibetan Book of the Dead, "writhing in hot sand."

If we are very attached to our body, we may even try, in vain, to reenter or hover around it. In extreme cases the mental body can linger near its possessions or body for weeks or even years. And still it may not dawn on us we are dead. It is only when we see that we cast no shadow, make no reflection in the mirror, no footprints on the ground, that finally we realize. And the sheer shock of recognizing we have died can be enough to make us faint away.

In the bardo of becoming we relive all the experiences of our past life, reviewing minute details long lost to memory, and revisiting places, the masters say, "where we did no more than spit on the ground."

Every seven days we are compelled to go through the experience of death once again, with all its suffering. If our death was peaceful, that peaceful state of mind is repeated; if it was tormented, however, that torment is repeated too. And remember that this is with a consciousness seven times more intense than that of life, and that in the fleeting period of the bardo of becoming, all the negative karma of previous lives is returning, in a fiercely concentrated and deranging way.

Our restless, solitary wandering through the bardo world is as frantic as a nightmare, and just as in a dream, we believe we have a physical body and that we really exist. Yet all the experiences of this bardo arise only from our mind, created by our karma and habits returning.

The winds of the elements return, and as Tulku Urgyen Rinpoche says, "One hears loud sounds caused by the four elements of earth, water, fire, and wind. There is the sound of an avalanche continuously falling behind one, the sound of a great rushing river, the sound of a huge blazing mass of fire like a volcano, and the sound of a great storm." Trying to escape them in the terrifying darkness, it is said that three different abysses, white, red, and black, "deep and dreadful," open up in front of us. These, *The Tibetan Book of the Dead* tells us, are our own anger, desire, and ignorance. We are assailed by freezing downpours, hailstorms of pus and blood; haunted by the sound of disembodied, menacing cries; hounded by flesh-eating demons and carnivorous beasts.

We are swept along relentlessly by the wind of karma, unable to hold onto any ground. *The Tibetan Book of the Dead* says: "At this time, the great tornado of karma, terrifying, unbearable, whirling fiercely, will drive you from behind." Consumed by fear, blown to and fro like dandelion seeds in the wind, we roam, helpless, through the gloom of the bardo. Tormented by hunger and thirst, we seek refuge here and there. Our mind's perceptions change every moment, projecting us, "like out of a catapult," says *The Tibetan Book of the Dead,* into alternate states of sorrow or joy. Into our minds comes the longing for a physical body, and yet we fail to find one, which plunges us into further suffering.

The whole landscape and environment is molded by our karma, just as the bardo world can be peopled by the nightmarish images of our own delusions. If our habitual conduct in life was positive, our perception and experience in the bardo will be mixed with bliss and happiness; and if our lives were harmful or hurtful to others, our experiences in the bardo will be ones of pain, grief, and fear. So, it was said in Tibet, fishermen, butchers, and hunters are attacked by monstrous versions of their former victims.

Some who have studied the near-death experience in detail, and especially the "life-review" that is one of its common features, have asked themselves: How could we possibly imagine the horror of the bardo experiences of a drug baron, a dictator, or a Nazi torturer? The "life-review" seems to suggest that, after death, we can experience *all* the suffering for which we were both directly and indirectly responsible.

The Duration of the Bardo of Becoming

The whole of the bardo of becoming has an average duration of forty-nine days, and a minimum length of one week. But it varies, just as now some people live to be a hundred years old, and others die in their youth. Some can even get stuck in the bardo, to become spirits or ghosts. Dudjom Rinpoche used to explain that during the first twenty-one days of the bardo, you still have a strong impression of your previous life, and this is therefore the most important period for the living to be able to help a dead person. After that, your future life slowly takes shape and becomes the dominant influence.

We have to wait in the bardo until we can make a karmic connection with our future parents. I sometimes think of the bardo as something like a transit lounge, in which you can wait for up to forty-nine days before transferring to the next life. But there are two special cases who don't have to wait in the intermediate state, because the intensity of the power of their karma sweeps them immediately on to their next rebirth. The first are those who have lived extremely beneficial and positive lives, and so trained their minds in spiritual practice that the force of their realization carries them directly into a good rebirth. The second case are those whose lives have been negative and harmful; they travel swiftly down to their next birth, wherever that might be.

Judgment

Some accounts of the bardo describe a judgment scene, a kind of life-review similar to the post-mortem judgment found in many of the world's cultures. Your good conscience, a white guardian angel, acts as your defense counsel, recounting the beneficial things you have done, while your bad conscience, a black demon, submits the case for the prosecution. Good and bad are totaled up as white and black pebbles. The "Lord of Death," who presides, then consults the mirror of karma and makes his judgment.

I feel that in this judgment scene there are some interesting parallels with the life-review of the near-death experience. *Ultimately all judgment takes place within our own mind. We are the judge and the judged.* "It is interesting to note," said Raymond Moody, "that the judgment in the cases I studied came not from the being of light, who seemed to love and accept these people anyway, but rather from within the individual being judged."

A woman who went through a near-death experience told Kenneth Ring: "You are shown your life—and you do the judging. . . . You are judging yourself. You have been forgiven all your sins, but are you able to forgive yourself for not doing the things you should have done, and some little cheating things that maybe you've done in life? Can you forgive yourself? This is the judgment."

The judgment scene also shows that what really counts, in the final analysis, is the motivation behind our every action, and that there is no escaping the effects of our past actions, words, and thoughts, and the imprints and habits they have stamped us with. It means that we are entirely responsible, not only for this life, but for our future lives as well.

The Power of the Mind

As our mind is so light, mobile, and vulnerable in the bardo, whatever thoughts arise, good or bad, have tremendous power and influence. Without a physical body to ground us, thoughts actually become reality. Imagine the sharp grief and anger we might feel on seeing a funeral service performed carelessly on our behalf, or greedy relatives squabbling over our possessions, or friends we loved deeply, and thought had loved us, talking about us in a sneering or hurtful or simply condescending way. Such a situation could be very dangerous, because our reaction, in its violence, could drive us directly toward an unfortunate rebirth.

The overwhelming power of thought, then, is the key issue in the bardo of becoming. This crucial moment finds us completely exposed to whatever habits and tendencies we have allowed to grow and dominate our lives. If you don't check those habits and tendencies now in life, and prevent them from seizing hold of your mind, then in the bardo of becoming you will be their helpless victim, buffeted to and fro by their power. The slightest irritation, for example, in the bardo of becoming can have a devastating effect, and that is why traditionally the person reading *The Tibetan Book of the Dead* had to be someone with whom you had a good connection; if not, the very sound of his or her voice could infuriate you, with the most disastrous consequences.

The teachings give us many descriptions of the rawness of the mind in the bardo of becoming; the most striking of these says that our mind in this bardo is like a flaming red-hot iron bar that can be bent in whichever way you want until it cools, when whatever form it finds itself in rapidly solidifies. In just the same way, it is said, a single positive thought in this bardo can lead directly to enlightenment, and a single negative reaction can plunge you into the most prolonged and extreme suffering. *The Tibetan Book of the Dead* could not warn us more strongly:

> *Now is the time which is the borderline between going up and going down; now is the time when by slipping into laziness even for a moment you will endure constant suffering: now is the time when by concentrating for an instant you will enjoy constant happiness. Focus your mind single-mindedly; strive to prolong the results of good karma!*

The Tibetan Book of the Dead tries to awaken any connection with spiritual practice the dead person may have had, and it encourages us: to give up attachment to people and possessions, to abandon yearning for a body, not to give in to desire or anger, to cultivate kindness rather than hostility, and not even to contemplate negative actions. It reminds the dead person there is no need to fear: On the one hand, it tells them that the terrifying bardo figures are nothing more than their own deluded projections and by nature empty; and on the other hand, that they themselves have only "a mental body of habitual tendencies," and are therefore empty too. "So emptiness cannot harm emptiness."

The shifting and precarious nature of the bardo of becoming can also be the source of many opportunities for liberation, and the susceptibility of mind in this bardo can be turned to our advantage. All we have to do is remember one instruction; all it needs is for one positive thought to spring into our mind. If we can recall any teaching that has inspired us to the nature of mind, if we have even one good inclination toward practice, or a deep connection with a spiritual practice, then that alone can free us.

In the bardo of becoming, the buddha realms do not appear spontaneously as they do in the bardo of dharmata. Just by remembering them, however, you can transfer yourself there directly by the power of your mind, and proceed toward enlightenment. It is said that if you can invoke a buddha, he will immediately appear before you. But remember, even though the possibilities are limitless, we must have at least some, if not total, control over our mind in this bardo; and this is extremely difficult, because the mind here is so vulnerable, fragmented, and restless.

So in this bardo, whenever you can suddenly retrieve your awareness, even for a moment, immediately recall your connection with spiritual practice, remember your master or Buddha, and invoke them with all your strength. If in life you have developed the natural reflex of praying whenever things become difficult or critical, or slip beyond your control, then instantly you will be able to invoke or call to mind an enlightened being, such as Buddha or Padmasambhava, Tara or

Avalokiteshvara, Christ or the Virgin Mary. If you are able to invoke them fervently with one-pointed devotion, and with all your heart, then through the power of their blessing, your mind will be liberated into the space of their wisdom mind. Prayer in this life may seem sometimes to bring little result, but its effects in the bardo are unprecedentedly powerful.

Yet the description that I have given you of the bardo shows the sheer difficulty of focusing the mind at this juncture, if we have had no previous training. Think how almost impossible it is to remember something like a prayer in a dream or nightmare, how impotent and powerless we feel in them; in the bardo of becoming it is just as hard, if not harder, to collect our thoughts at all. This is why the watch word of *The Tibetan Book of the Dead,* repeated over and over again, is: "Do not be distracted." As it points out:

> This is the dividing line where buddhas and sentient beings are separated . . .
>
> "In an instant they are separated, in an instant complete enlightenment."

Rebirth

As, in the bardo of becoming, the time for rebirth gets closer, you crave more and more for the support of a material body, and you search for any one that might be available in which to be reborn. Different signs will begin to appear, warning you of the realm in which you are likely to take rebirth. Lights of various colors shine from the six realms of existence, and you will feel drawn toward one or another, depending on the negative emotion that is predominant in your mind. Once you have been drawn into one of these lights, it is very difficult to turn back.

Then images and visions will arise, linked to the different realms. As you become more familiar with the teachings, you will become more alert to what they really mean. The signs vary slightly according to different teachings. Some say that if you are to be reborn as a god, you will have a vision of entering a heavenly palace with many stories. If you are to be reborn as a demigod, you will feel you are amidst spinning circular weapons of fire, or going onto a battlefield. If you are to be reborn as an animal, you find yourself in a cave, a hole in the ground, or a nest made of straw. If you have a vision of a tree stump, a deep forest, or a woven cloth, you are to be reborn as a hungry ghost. And if you are to be reborn in hell, you will feel you are being led, powerless, into a black pit, down a black road, into a somber land with black or red houses, or toward a city of iron.

There are many other signs, such as the way in which your gaze or movement is aligned, which indicate the realm for which you are heading. If you are to be reborn in a god or human realm, your gaze will be directed upward; if in an animal realm, you will look straight ahead, as do birds; and if in a hungry ghost or hell realm, you will look downward, as though you were diving.

If any of these signs appear, you should be on guard not to fall into any of these unfortunate rebirths.

At the same time, you will have an intense desire and longing for certain realms, and you are drawn toward them all

too instinctively. The teachings warn us that at this point there is a great danger that out of your avid eagerness to be reborn, you will rush to any place at all that seems to offer some security. If your desire is frustrated, the anger that arises will of itself bring the bardo abruptly to an end, as you are swept into your next rebirth by the current of that negative emotion. And so, as you can see, your future rebirth is directly determined by desire, anger, and ignorance.

Imagine that you run toward a place of refuge, simply to escape the onslaught of the bardo experiences. Then, terrified to leave, you might become attached and take on a new birth, no matter where, just in order to have one. You might even, *The Tibetan Book of the Dead* explains, become confused and mistake a good birthplace for a bad one, or a bad one for a good one. Or hear the voices of your loved ones calling you, or seductive singing, and follow these, only to find yourself being lured down into the lower realms.

You must take great care not to enter blindly into one of these undesirable realms. Yet what is wonderful is that the instant you become aware of what is happening to you, you can actually begin to influence and change your destiny.

Swept along by the wind of karma, you will then arrive at a place where your future parents are making love. Seeing them, you become emotionally drawn in; and because of past karmic connections, you begin spontaneously to feel strong attachment or aversion. Attraction and desire for the mother and aversion or jealousy for the father will result in your being born as a male child, and the reverse a female. But if you succumb to such strong passions, not only will you be reborn, but that very emotion may draw you into birth in a lower realm.

Questions

1. How does Sogyal Rinpoche describe the bardo of becoming? What is your response to this description?

2. What lessons are we meant to learn in the bardo? What specifically do you think you would learn about your life as it has been lived thus far?

3. Why does Sogyal Rinpoche say that, "the watchword of *The Tibetan Book of the Dead* . . . is 'Do not be distracted'"? How might one apply this teaching to our everyday existence?

---

7 Brian Weiss, *Many Lives, Many Masters*

Brian Weiss, M.D., is a psychiatrist educated at Columbia University and Yale Medical School, and trained in the Freudian school of psychoanalysis. He was therefore very skeptical when one of his patients, a young woman named Catherine, during a session of regressive hypnotic therapy began recounting information she had apparently learned in previous lifetimes. Catherine had come to Dr. Weiss complaining of various phobias, neuroses, and nightmares, all seemingly linked to traumatic childhood experiences. Dr. Weiss used hypnosis as a way of exploring these traumas in the hope that the conditions Catherine was suffering from would disappear. But despite a successful recall of painful childhood episodes, Catherine's symptoms failed to dissipate. It was only when, in a deep hypnotic trance, Catherine began to recall experiences from previous lives that her present troubles began to clear up. It seemed that certain anxious moments in former lives—drowning, fatal illness, rape, war—were linked to many of her present pathologies. Reliving those traumas through hypnotherapy enabled Catherine to understand the connection, and therefore to overcome her problems. The bad dreams, the anxiety attacks, and the difficulties in relationships all ceased.

Dr. Weiss was at first uncertain whether or not to believe that Catherine had indeed lived past lives. Her detailed recall of historical events, settings, geography, manner of dress, and so on, could hardly be explained in any other way. But he remained unconvinced until one day, Catherine began recounting what she apparently had learned in between her previous lives. According to Dr. Weiss's testimony, Catherine was able to reproduce lessons learned from "the Masters"—wise spiritual beings who inhabit the spiritual realm we visit between each new incarnation. In one of these lessons, which you are about to read, the Masters gave Catherine a specific message for Dr. Weiss. It was a message that completely obliterated his skepticism. From that point on, Dr. Weiss became a believer in the reality of reincarnation.

Dr. Weiss's experience with Catherine has since been confirmed by studies conducted by psychologist Edith Fiore. In her book *You Have Been Here Before* (1991), Dr. Fiore narrates the healing work she has performed using regressive hypnotherapy on patients suffering from a variety of psychosomatic illnesses. In a deep hypnotic trance, one man tortured by insomnia recalled a life as a marshal in a western town. In another study, a sexually frigid woman remembered a tragic life as a slave girl. A man suffering from an inexplicable fear of heights was able to recall a violent death from a fall during the Middle Ages. In each of these cases, the patient achieved relief from their problems through hypnosis despite the failure of more conventional methods of treatment.

"I see a square white house with a sandy road in front. People on horses are going back and forth." Catherine was speaking in her usual dreamy whisper. "There are trees . . . a plantation, a big house with a bunch of smaller houses, like slave houses. It's very hot. It's in the South . . . Virginia?" She thought the date was 1873. She was a child.

"There are horses and lots of crops . . . corn, tobacco." She and the other servants ate in a kitchen of the big house. She was black, and her name was Abby. She felt a foreboding, and her body tensed. The main house was on fire, and she watched it burn down. I progressed her fifteen years in time to 1888.

"I'm wearing an old dress, cleaning a mirror on the second floor of a house, a brick house with windows . . . with lots of panes. The mirror is wavy, not straight, and it has knobs on the end. The man who owns the house is named James Manson. He has a funny coat with three buttons and a big black collar. He has a beard. . . . I don't recognize him (as someone in Catherine's present lifetime). He treats me well. I live in a house on the property. I clean the rooms. There is a schoolhouse on the property, but I'm not allowed in the school. I make butter, too!"

Catherine was whispering slowly, using very simple terms and paying great attention to detail. Over the next five minutes, I learned how to make butter. Abby's knowledge of churning butter was new to Catherine, too. I moved her ahead in time.

"I am with somebody, but I don't think we are married. We sleep together . . . but we don't always live together. I feel okay about him, but nothing special. I don't see any children. There are apple trees and ducks. Other people are in the distance. I'm picking apples. Something is making my eyes itch." Catherine was grimacing with her eyes closed. "It's the smoke. The wind is blowing it this way . . . the smoke from burning wood. They're burning up wooden barrels." She was coughing now. "It happens a lot. They're making the inside of the barrels black . . . tar . . . to waterproof."

After the excitement of last week's session, I was eager to reach the in-between state again. We had already spent ninety minutes exploring her lifetime as a servant. I had learned about bedspreads, butter, and barrels; I was hungry for a more spiritual lesson. Forsaking my patience, I advanced her to her death.

"It's hard to breathe. My chest hurts so much." Catherine was gasping, in obvious pain. "My heart hurts; it's beating fast. I'm so cold . . . my body's shaking." Catherine began to shiver. "People are in the room, giving me leaves to drink (a tea). It smells funny. They're rubbing a liniment on my chest. Fever . . . but I feel very cold." She quietly died. Floating up to the ceiling, she could see her body in the bed, a small, shriveled woman in her sixties. She was just floating, waiting for someone to come and help her. She became aware of a light, feeling herself drawn toward it. The light was becoming brighter, and more luminous. We waited in silence as minutes slowly passed. Suddenly she was in another lifetime, thousands of years before Abby.

Catherine was softly whispering, "I see lots of garlic, hanging in an open room. I can *smell* it. It is believed to kill many evils in the blood and to cleanse the body, but you must take it every day. The garlic is outside too, on top of a garden. Other herbs are there . . . figs, dates, and other herbs. These plants help you. My mother is buying garlic and the other herbs. Somebody in the house is sick. These are strange roots. Sometimes you just keep them in your mouth, or ears, or other openings. You just keep them in.

"I see an old man with a beard. He's one of the healers in the village. He tells you what to do. There is some type of . . . plague . . . killing the people. They're not embalming because they're afraid of the disease. People are just buried. The people are unhappy about this. They feel the soul cannot pass on this way (contrary to Catherine's after-death reports). But so many have died. The cattle are dying, too. Water . . . floods . . . people are sick because of the floods. (She apparently just realized this bit of epidemiology.) I also have some disease from the water. It makes your stomach hurt. The disease is of the bowel and stomach. You lose so much water from the body. I'm by the water to bring more back, but that's what is killing us. I bring the water back. I see my mother and brothers. My father has already died. My brothers are very sick."

I paused before progressing her in time. I was fascinated by the way her conceptions of death and the afterlife changed so much from lifetime to lifetime. And yet her *experience* of death itself was so uniform, so similar, every time. A conscious part of her would leave the body around the moment of death,

floating above and then being drawn to a wonderful, energizing light. She would then wait for someone to come and help her. The soul automatically passed on. Embalming, burial rituals, or any other procedure after death had nothing to do with it. It was automatic, no preparation necessary, like walking through a just-opened door.

"The land is barren and dry. . . . I see no mountains around here, just land, very flat and dry. One of my brothers has died. I'm feeling better, but the pain is still there." However, she did not live much longer. "I'm lying on a pallet with some type of covering." She was very ill, and no amount of garlic or other herbs could prevent her death. Soon she was floating above her body, drawn to the familiar light. She waited patiently for someone to come to her.

Her head began to roll slowly from side to side, as if she were scanning some scene. Her voice was again husky and loud.

"They tell me there are many gods, for God is in each of us."

I recognized the voice from the in-between-lives state by its huskiness as well as by the decidedly spiritual tone of the message. What she said next left me breathless, pulling the air from my lungs.

"Your father is here, and your son, who is a small child. Your father says you will know him because his name is Avrom and your daughter is named after him. Also, his death was due to his heart. Your son's heart was also important, for it was backward, like a chicken's. He made a great sacrifice for you out of his love. His soul is very advanced. . . . His death satisfied his parents' debts. Also he wanted to show you that medicine could only go so far, that its scope is very limited."

Catherine stopped speaking, and I sat in an awed silence as my numbed mind tried to sort things out. The room felt icy cold.

Catherine knew very little about my personal life. On my desk I had a baby picture of my daughter, grinning happily with her two bottom baby teeth in an otherwise empty mouth. My son's picture was next to it. Otherwise Catherine knew virtually nothing about my family or my personal history. I had been well schooled in traditional psychotherapeutic techniques. The therapist was supposed to be a tabula rasa, a blank tablet upon which the patient could project her own feelings, thoughts, and attitudes. These then could be analyzed by the therapist, enlarging the arena of the patient's mind. I had kept this therapeutic distance with Catherine. She really knew me only as a psychiatrist, nothing of my past or of my private life. I had never even displayed my diplomas in the office.

The greatest tragedy in my life had been the unexpected death of our firstborn son, Adam, who was only twenty-three days old when he died, early in 1971. About ten days after we had brought him home from the hospital, he had developed respiratory problems and projectile vomiting. The diagnosis was extremely difficult to make. "Total anomalous pulmonary venous drainage with an atrial septal defect," we were told. "It occurs once in approximately every ten million births." The pulmonary veins, which were supposed to bring oxygenated blood back to the heart, were incorrectly routed, entering the heart on the wrong side. It was as if his heart were turned around, *backward*. Extremely, extremely rare.

Heroic open-heart surgery could not save Adam, who died several days later. We mourned for months, our hopes and dreams dashed. Our son, Jordan, was born a year later, a grateful balm for our wounds.

At the time of Adam's death, I had been wavering about my earlier choice of psychiatry as a career. I was enjoying my internship in internal medicine, and I had been offered a residency position in medicine. After Adam's death, I firmly decided that I would make psychiatry my profession. I was angry that modern medicine, with all of its advanced skills and technology, could not save my son, this simple, tiny baby.

My father had been in excellent health until he experienced a massive heart attack early in 1979, at the age of sixty-one. He survived the initial attack, but his heart wall had been irretrievably damaged, and he died three days later. This was about nine months before Catherine's first appointment.

My father had been a religious man, more ritualistic than spiritual. His Hebrew name, Avrom, suited him better than the English, Alvin. Four months after his death, our daughter, Amy, was born, and she was named after him.

Here, in 1982, in my quiet, darkened office, a deafening cascade of hidden, secret truths was pouring upon me. I was swimming in a spiritual sea, and I loved the water. My arms were gooseflesh. Catherine could not possibly know this information. There was no place even to look it up. My father's *Hebrew* name, that I had a son who died in infancy from a one-in-ten-million heart defect, my brooding about medicine, my father's death, and my daughter's naming—it was too much, too specific, too true. This unsophisticated laboratory technician was a conduit for transcendental knowledge. And if she could reveal these truths, what else was there? I needed to know more.

"Who," I sputtered, "who is there? Who tells you these things?"

"The Masters," she whispered, "the Master Spirits tell me. They tell me I have lived eighty-six times in physical state."

Catherine's breathing slowed, and her head stopped rolling from side to side. She was resting. I wanted to go on, but the implications of what she had said were distracting me. Did she really have eighty-six previous lifetimes? And what about "the Masters"? Could it be? Could our lives be guided by spirits who have no physical bodies but who seem to possess great knowledge? Are there steps on the way to God? Was this real? I found it difficult to doubt, in view of what she had just revealed, yet I still struggled to believe. I was overcoming years of alternative programming. But in my head and my heart and my gut, I knew she was right. She was revealing truths.

And what about my father and my son? In a sense, they were still alive; they had never really died. They were talking to me, years after their burials, and proving it by providing specific, very secret informa-tion. And since all that was true, was my son as advanced spiritually as Catherine had said? Did he indeed agree to be born to us and then die twenty-three days later in order to help us with our karmic debts and, in addition, to teach me about medicine and humankind, to nudge me back to psychiatry? I was very heartened by these thoughts. Beneath my chill, I felt a great love stirring, a strong feeling of oneness and connection with the heavens and the earth. I had missed my father and my son. It was good to hear from them again.

Questions

1. Does this story told by Dr. Weiss convince you of the reality of reincarnation? Why or why not? Illustrate your answer with references to the passage you read.

2. What implications does Catherine's story have for how we should be living our lives? What implications does it have for how we should view those people whom we love, our family and friends; and those with whom we have problems and struggles?

3. Assume for the moment that reincarnation is real, and that there are "Master Spirits" that we will meet as we move from one life to the next. What one question would you like them, in their wisdom, to answer for you?

Small Group Exercises

1. In your small group, debate the merits of and drawbacks to the ideas of resurrection and reincarnation.
   a. Draw up a list of pros and cons for each.
   b. Stage a debate between two teams; one side arguing for resurrection and the other side arguing for reincarnation.

2. Consider the various objections raised by A. N. Wilson in his article, "Life After Death?" in your small group.

    a. Make a list of his objections and their supporting arguments.

    b. Come up with your own counterarguments to Wilson's objections.

    c. Present these to the class and then ask the class to vote on the issue.

3. Watch several films that depict the death and resurrection of Jesus as a real event. Such films include *King of Kings, The Greatest Story Ever Told, Jesus of Nazareth, The Last Temptation of Christ,* and *Jesus of Montreal.* Then watch several of the films that portray a Christlike martyrdom and resurrection in symbolic form (see the suggested list earlier in the text). Discuss similarities and differences between the two types of portrayals.

Practical Learning Component

1. Interview a psychologist who uses "regressive hypnotherapy." A list of such professionals in your area can be obtained from the website of the International Association for Regression Research and Therapies. Ask him or her about the technique, how effective it is, and whether its use has ever uncovered any evidence of past lives.

2. Interview a pastor or priest on the idea of resurrection. Ask critical questions about the basis on which this belief is justified. Then interview someone familiar with Jewish teachings on resurrection (or "revivification") and ask the same kinds of questions. Compare and contrast their answers. This can also be done with someone familiar with Islamic teachings on resurrection.

3. Visit your local cemetery. Take an overview of the statuary there: the various tombstones, mausoleums, etc. Identify the many symbols used to represent the resurrection. Compare these with symbols typically used for the resurrection in Christian churches and cathedrals.

Chapter 3

~~~~

Death and Philosophy

The difficulty, my friends, is not in avoiding death, but in avoiding unrighteousness; for that runs faster than death.

—SOCRATES

DEATH AMONG THE CLASSICAL PHILOSOPHERS

Though they cast their analytical gaze upon a wide variety of phenomena, ancient Greek and Roman philosophers were not all that interested in asking questions about death. Between the rapid rise and fall of nation-states, the ravages of disease, and the high incidence of child mortality, ancient intellectuals may have seen too much of death to want to give their attention to it as a speculative problem. Nevertheless, there exists an important body of thanatological literature from classical times that bears discussion here.

Collectively, the range of thinking on the subject of death from such philosophers as Plato, Aristotle, Epicurus, and Marcus Aurelius is truly astounding. On the one hand, there is the intensely abstract thinking of the pre-Socratic writer, Heraclites. Heraclites' musings on the interdependent nature of opposites lead him to draw no distinction between morality and immortality, life and death, life on earth and life among the saints. Whether we are alive above ground or dead below, he says, we are always and everywhere part of the continuous and cyclical flux of nature (*Fragments* 26, 36, 62). On the other hand, we have Plato's very practical and detailed recollection of the near-death experience of the mythological hero-warrior Er (*Republic* X). In this graphic account we hear of Er's trip to heaven, his meeting with various deities to learn of the nature of human fate, and his crossing the river *Lethe,* the river of "forgetfulness."

In between these two extremes we find a small but influential body of death literature that is highly psychological in nature, with strong moral and religious overtones.

One of the common arguments among the classical philosophers is the idea that death is not something to be feared. Socrates argued that death is either a "dreamless sleep," in which case we have nothing to fear since we will not be conscious; or it is an endless conversation with interesting people, in which case it is a "great blessing" (*Apology* 40). Plato himself considered death to be the highest moment in any human's life, the whole of which is but a *meletei nekron,* a "rehearsal for death" (*Phaedo* 61). A century after Plato, Epicurus argued that death is literally no-thing, a non-event, and as such is rightly not to be feared:

> Get used to believing that death is nothing to us. For all good and bad consists in sense experience, and death is the privation of sense experience. Hence a correct knowledge of the fact that death is nothing to us makes the mortality of life a matter for contentment, not by adding a limitless time [to life] but by removing the longing for immortality. For there is nothing fearful in life for one who has grasped that there is nothing fearful in the absence of life. Thus, he is a fool who says that he fears death not because it will be painful when present but because it is painful when it is still to come. For that which while present causes no distress causes unnecessary pain when merely anticipated. So death, the most frightening of bad things, is nothing to us; since when we exist death is not yet present, and when death is present, we do not exist. Therefore it is relevant neither to the living nor the dead, since it does not affect the former, and the latter do not exist.

> *Letter to Menoeceus*

Marcus Aurelius, second century Roman emperor, moralist, and Stoic philosopher, echoes the sentiments of Epicurus that death, as a non-experience, is not to be feared. His "Writings to Himself," commonly called *Meditations,* are a remarkable set of personal reflections and aphorisms written for Aurelius' own edification during his long career of public service. His opinions in central philosophical questions are very much similar to those of Epictetus (c. 55–135 C.E.), the founder of late-Stoicism. Epictetus' two basic principles for a good and happy life were: endure the fate that life brings you, and abstain from sensual pleasures. He stressed that inner freedom is to be attained through submission to divine providence, and rigorous detachment from everything not in our power. In similar fashion, as Marcus Aurelius meditates on the nature of death he counsels endurance, self-abnegation, and resignation to one's fate:

> Time is like a river made up of the events which happen, and a violent stream; for as soon as a thing has been seen, it is carried away, and another comes in its place, and this will be carried away too.

If any god told you that you shall die tomorrow, or certainly on the day after to-morrow, you would not care much whether it was on the third day or on the next, unless you had a very degraded spirit for how small is the difference? So think it no great thing to die after as many years as you can count rather than tomorrow.

Think continually how many physicians are dead after often fretting over the sick; and how many astrologers after predicting with great pretensions the deaths of others; and how many philosophers after endless discourses on death or immortality; how many heroes after killing thousands; and how many tyrants who have used their power over men's lives with terrible insolence as if they were immortal; and how many cities are entirely dead, so to speak, Helice and Pompeii and Herculaneum, and innumerable others. Add to the total all whom you have known, one after another. One man after burying another has been laid out dead, and another buries him: and all this in a short time. To conclude, always observe how ephemeral and worthless human things are, and what was yesterday a little mucus to-morrow will be a mummy or ashes. Pass then through this little space of time in the way of nature, and end your journey in contentment, just as an olive falls off when it is ripe, blessing nature who produced it, and thanking the tree on which it grew.

Be like the cliff against which the waves continually break, but which stands firm and tames the fury of the water around it.

The Meditations

DEATH AMONG THE MODERN PHILOSOPHERS

Philosophers within the modern Anglo-American stream of philosophy, represented by such thinkers as Ludwig Wittgenstein, William James, and Hilary Putnam, have issued very little work on the subject of death. The one possible exception to this is Bertrand Russell's argument in his collection of essays, *Why I Am Not a Christian,* against the possibility of life after death. Russell argues that human life as we experience it is exclusively a function of the brain, and since the brain dies at death, human life is therefore also extinguished at death. But there is no further discussion on the topic.

This moratorium, so to speak, on the philosophical analysis of our mortal state is not found among the leading continental philosophers, however, by whom human mortality is treated with the utmost seriousness. Søren Kierkegaard, Friedrich Nietzsche, Martin Heidegger, Jean-Paul Sartre, and Albert Camus have all woven the subject of death into their respective philosophies.

The first modern philosopher to tackle the subject of death in depth was the eighteenth-century German and predecessor of the modern existentialists, Arthur Schopenhauer. A darkly pessimistic thinker, Schopenhauer felt that the philosophical consideration of death was something beneficial to the proper living of life. Life's sufferings and frustrations may lead some to believe that suicide is a more attractive option; but Schopenhauer countered that there was enough pleasure in life—found primarily in art, friendship, travel, and other aesthetic experiences—to make it worth living. But it took the philosopher and his insistence on human mortality to demonstrate that the sufferings of life are merely manifestations of our own thinking, and as such can be eradicated simply by exercising the will in remembrance of the shortness of life and its inevitable demise. This would be a theme taken up by the several existentialists who supported Schopenhauer's insistence that our willed "existence" precedes, and has priority over, any eternal "essence" we may or may not possess.

Foremost among the existentialists for giving the concept of death a central role is Martin Heidegger, the early-twentieth-century German philosopher. Heidegger writes abstractly about the nature of the human condition in general, and about death in particular. The human, he says, is radically distinct from everything non-human. This distinction is expressed by saying that while other things *are,* only humans *exist.* "The being that exists is man," writes Heidegger. "Man alone exists. Rocks are, but they do not exist. Trees are, but they do not exist. Horses are, but they do not exist" (*The Way Back into the Ground of Metaphysics*). Even God and the angels, if they are at all, do not exist, according to Heidegger. For the human's way of existing, unlike that of spiritual, bodiless beings, is that of "being-there" in an unavoidable relationship with and toward the ever-changing material world. And unlike rocks and plants, humans are beings that are uniquely conscious of this relationship. Ultimately, this means that the human is caught up in the same evolutionary incompleteness that characterizes the essential nature of the world: the human is temporal, claims Heidegger, never complete, always "on the way."

The does not mean, however, that humanity is always moving toward completeness. There is no resolution of the human predicament, taught Heidegger. Instead humans are always moving toward dissolution, which culminates in the final extinction of death. But this final extinction can be anticipated, and in that anticipation *experienced,* as a kind of wholeness. As the ultimate end of life, death symbolizes the fulfillment of all human striving. Thus meaning in life is to be found, not in denying death, but in embracing our mortality as a kind of fate; in facing each day the reality of the inevitable "impossibility of being" that awaits us all. To this end Heidegger describes death as humanity's "ownmost possibility, non-relational, certain and as such indefinite, not to be outstripped" (*Being and Time*).

A more pessimistic rendering of the inevitability of death can be found in the writings of Heidegger's French contemporary, Jean-Paul Sartre. Sartre repudiates Heidegger's optimistic view that acceptance of one's own coming end makes possible a meaningful form of living. On the contrary, argues Sartre, death deprives life of the only kind of meaning that it might conceivably have had.

One of the problems with death, suggests Sartre, is that it tends to come unexpectedly. Even when it is forced upon us by natural causes at the end of a long life, one can never know this ahead of time and therefore one's own death can never be something anticipated. We can therefore never live meaningfully with death in view because of the knowledge we have that it can come at any time to terminate the very things in life that give our lives meaning. "If we must die," Sartre writes, "then our life has no meaning

---

Death and Dying Fact

Films that deal with the idea of death in a philosophical way include:

Beaches
Philadelphia
My Life
Schindler's List
The Doctor
The Plague
The Green Mile
Stepmom
My Girl
Iris
Leaving Las Vegas
The Theory of Flight
Marvin's Room
Jesus of Montreal
A Taste of Cherry
The Killing Fields
Empire of the Sun
Saving Private Ryan
Shadowlands
The Horseman on the Roof
The Girl on the Bridge
Mother and Son
It's a Wonderful Life
Whose Life Is It Anyway?
Three Colors: Blue
Longtime Companion
What Dreams May Come
Love and Death
Fanny and Alexander
Being There
Antonia's Line
Lorenzo's Oil
Flatliners

because its problems receive no solution and because the very meaning of the problems remains undetermined" (*Being and Nothingness*).

Perhaps the darkest rendering of human mortality by any philosopher is that of Sartre's younger countryman, Albert Camus. In his most famous work of philosophical commentary, Camus examines the myth of Sisyphus as a kind of parable of the human condition. Sisyphus is one who has been condemned by the gods for his deity-defying arrogance and pride. His punishment, it will be recalled, is to push a heavy boulder up a steep hill, and once at the top, to see it roll back down to the bottom. Sisyphus is then ordered to the bottom of the hill only to push the stone back up again in an eternal cycle of meaningless, unproductive labor. Sisyphus' predicament summarizes for Camus the essential frustration of human existence: we are all condemned to see our daily efforts ultimately come to nothing as mortality is forced upon us by death. But Camus goes one step further in stating that at the moment he reaches the top of the hill, Sisyphus becomes aware of his fate, is conscious of the futility of his efforts, and recognizes that he is powerless to do anything about it.

Camus applies this to the human situation, and considers whether suicide might not be the most reasonable option. When Camus rules that out, he projects onto Sisyphus a resignation that symbolizes the universal surrender of humanity to its mortal fate. Camus admits this is indeed a tragic condition, but he also postulates the possibility of human happiness in the very act of resignation itself. There is a kind of dignity, he implies, in putting one's shoulder to the stone, even if one is fully conscious that at the end of the day, one's efforts to roll it up the hill will come to nothing. "The struggle itself toward the heights is enough to fill a man's heart," writes Camus. "One must imagine Sisyphus happy" (*The Myth of Sisyphus*).

In the readings to follow you will get a taste of how philosophers like these, from the ancients to the moderns, have approached the subject of death. In recent years the study of death has been dominated by either sociologists or psychologists. It thus serves a helpful contrast to get a feeling for how philosophers brought their keen intellects to bear on the idea of human mortality.

---

1 Plato, *Death as a Release from Prison*

Along with his mentor, Socrates, Plato is usually considered the founding father of Western philosophy. Plato was born in 429 B.C.E. in Athens, Greece, the son of a prominent family that had long been involved in the city's politics. Extremely little is known to us of Plato's youth, but he was raised in the shadow of the great Peloponnesian War, and its influence may have been a factor in his decision to reject a political career and take up instead an apprenticeship under the nomadic, eccentric, and brilliant teacher, Socrates. The political assassination of Socrates in 399 B.C.E. turned Plato forever from political involvement, and he devoted his life instead to writing and teaching. In both professions he developed his famous dialectical style of pedagogy, where conversation rather than straightforward lecture is the medium through which ideas are to be conveyed. Plato also took the time to establish the West's first university, the Academy, where he taught until his own death in 348 B.C.E. In time, the Academy attracted the best and brightest students of Greece and became a major seat of European scholarship. Today, Plato's dialogues, along with his unique "Socratic method" of teaching, are considered among the highest points of Western intellectual achievement.

The passage you are about to read comes from Plato's *Phaedo* dialogue, which recounts the last moments of Socrates' life before he was forced by the State to drink the poisonous hemlock (a kind of "guilt-free" form of assassination!). Socrates is the main character here, and is seen interacting with several of his disciples, among whom is Plato himself. At issue in this passage is the astonishment the disciples of Socrates feel when they see that, far from being afraid of his impending death, Socrates is actually looking forward to it. He tells them that all his life as a philosopher has been aimed at this moment, preparing him for death. For this reason he calls "philosophy"—here, meaning a lifestyle devoted to a cultivation of the soul and mind—a *meletei nekron*, a "getting oneself ready for death." As you read make note of Plato's dualism, that the soul and the body are two distinct entities, with one being of greater importance than the other. According to Plato, the body is like a prison, trapping the angelic soul inside it. Death, therefore, is like a release. Death is that act whereby the soul is finally liberated, and is free to "return home."

"So tell Euenus this, Cebes: and wish him good-bye, and tell him, if he has any sense to follow quickly as he can. I shall be taking my departure today, it seems: for such is the Athenians' will."

"What a thing to advise Euenus to do, Socrates!" said Simmias. "I have often come across the man, and from what I have seen of him I should say that he will certainly not willingly take your advice."

"But is he not a philosopher?" asked Socrates.

"I believe so," said Simmias.

"Well, Euenus or any one who deserves to have anything to do with this business will be willing to do as I advise—though he will not, perhaps, commit suicide; for they say that that is wrong." As he said this, Socrates put his feet down on the ground and sat up, and remained in this position for the rest of the discussion.

Then Cebes asked him a question. "How do you mean, Socrates, that it is wrong to commit suicide, and yet that the philosopher would gladly follow one who was dying?"

"But surely, Cebes, you and Simmias have heard all about this when you have been with Philolaus?"

"Not very clearly, Socrates."

"Well, I myself am only speaking about it according to what I have heard: but what I have heard, I am quite ready to pass on. It is perhaps particularly appropriate that one who is about to make the journey to the next world should look fully into the matter, and tell stories about what we suppose to be the nature of our residence there. And after all, how else could we spend the time until sunset?"

"Well, Socrates, what are the real reasons for saying that it is not right to take one's life? To answer the question you asked just now. I did indeed go to hear Philolaus, when he lived among us, and many others, who said that one should not commit suicide, but I have never heard any clear arguments from anyone on the subject."

"Well, don't be despondent," he said, "and perhaps you will hear of some. And yet maybe it will seem surprising to you that while this alone of all things admits of no qualification, and it *never* happens (as with everything else) that death is preferable to life for man only on *some* occasions and in *some* cases, yet nevertheless—it seems surprising to you, perhaps—these human beings, for whom death is preferable, are *not* morally justified in doing themselves a good turn, but must wait for someone else to do it for them."

Cebes chuckled, and in his native dialect replied, "Goodness knows how that can be."

"Looked at in this way," said Socrates, "it might appear to be illogical. And yet it has, perhaps, some explanation. The story told about them *sub arcano* to the effect that we mortals are in a sort of prison, and that a man must not, apparently, free himself from it, or try to run away, seems to me a weighty argument and difficult to grasp; but the doctrine that gods are our guardians and that we men are one of the gods' possessions does seem to me to be a good one—don't you agree?"

"I do," said Cebes.

"Now if one of your possessions were to destroy itself, without your having indicated that you wanted it to perish, you would be annoyed with it, and if you could punish it, you would?"

"Certainly," he said.

"So perhaps in that case it is not unreasonable, the idea that one should refrain from bringing one's life to an end until God sends some necessity, such as the present one in my case."

"That is probably true," said Cebes. "But what you said just now, that the philosophers would readily agree to die, seems strange, Socrates, if what we have just agreed upon is true, that God is our guardian and we are his possessions. It is not reasonable that the wisest of men should, without demur, leave this tutelage, in which gods, the best of all possible guardians, watch over them. I don't suppose such a man imagines that he will do better when, free from their care, he has to look after himself. A fool might think that he should escape from his master—he might not realize that so far from trying to escape from the good master, he should stay with him as long as possible, and that it would be quite unreasonable to run away; but the man of sense would want, I imagine, always to remain with someone better than himself. And yet this seems to contradict what was said just now, if the wise are to dislike dying, and the foolish to delight in it."

At this Socrates seemed to me very pleased with Cebes' analysis, and looking at us he remarked, "Cebes is always hunting out arguments; he doesn't like immediately accepting just what anyone may say."

"Well, this time," said Simmias, "I too believe that there is something in what Cebes says. Why should men who are really wise try to escape from masters who are better than themselves and lightly and readily free themselves from them?

I believe that Cebes is aiming his argument at you, because you take it so lightly that you should be leaving us, and leaving also masters who, on your own admission, are good—I mean, the gods."

"Fair enough," he said. "I suppose you mean that I should defend myself against these arguments as though I were in court."

"Certainly." said Simmias.

"Well then," he said, "let me try to make my defense, and to convince you more than I did my judges. If I did not believe, Simmias and Cebes, that I shall go to other wise and good gods, and moreover to men now dead who are better than the men on earth, then indeed I should be wrong in not complaining at my death, but, as it is, you may be sure that I do hope to join a company of good men. I would not swear to this, but one thing I would maintain, as certain of it as I can be of anything—that I shall go to gods who are very good masters. So for this reason I grumble less: I have a strong hope that there is something left to those who have died, and a something (according to the old accounts) that is much better of the good than for the bad."

"Well, Socrates," said Simmias, "do you intend to depart keeping this idea to yourself, or would you share it with us? This benefit seems to me to belong to us also, and it will be your defense, too, if you convince us that what you say is true."

"I will try," he said. "But first let us enquire what it is that Crito, if I am not mistaken, has long been wanting to say."

"Only, Socrates," said Crito, "that the man who is going to give you the poison keeps on telling me that we should urge you to talk as little as possible. He says

they get warmer through talking, and the poison mustn't come into contact with anything warm; otherwise, those who let that happen sometimes have to drink the draught two or three times over."

"Never mind him," said Socrates. "He, for his part, can just prepare to give it to me twice, or, if need be, three times over."

"I knew it!" cried Crito. "But he has kept on worrying me."

"Forget him," he said. "I want to render my account to you as my judges now, showing that a man who has really spent his life in philosophy is naturally glad when he is on the point of dying, and hopeful that in the next world, when he is dead, he will enjoy great blessings. I will try to explain to you, Simmias and Cebes, how this could be so."

"It may be that the rest of mankind is not aware that those who apply themselves correctly to the pursuit of philosophy are in fact practicing nothing more nor less than dying and death. If this is so, it would indeed be strange that men who had throughout their lives sought precisely this, should grumble when it came—the very thing which they had, for so long, desired and rehearsed."

And Simmias laughed and said, "Well, Socrates, I was not in a mood for laughter just now, but you have certainly made me laugh. I think that most people, when they heard this, would consider your remarks most appropriate as applied to the philosophers—and our fellow-citizens, I think, would very much agree—saying that philosophers are, in very fact, more dead than alive, and adding that they are well aware that they deserve to be."

"And they would be right in what they said, Simmias, except for their claim to be aware of it all; for they are *not* aware *in what sense* the true philosophers are more dead than alive, or *in what sense* they deserve death, or *what sort* of death they deserve. Now let us discuss the matter between ourselves, forgetting all about those others. Do we think that death is something definite and real?"

"Certainly," replied Simmias.

"Surely we think of it as separation of the soul from the body?—and of being dead as the independent state of the body in separation from the soul, and the independent state of the soul in separation from the body? Surely death can hardly be anything else?"

"Quite correct," he said.

"Then follow closely, my friend, and see if you reach the same opinions as I hold; for through these, I think, we shall achieve a better understanding of the object of our enquiry. Now do you think that a philosopher should concern himself greatly with the so-called pleasures of, for example, food and drink?"

"Certainly not, Socrates," said Simmias.

"Or of love-making?"

"No."

"Or do you think that such a man holds in high esteem any of the other ways of attending to the body?—for example, buying fine cloaks and shoes—or any of the other forms of showing-off in connection with the body; do you think that the philosopher regards these pursuits as honorable, or as worthless—except in so far as he *has* to concern himself with them?"

"The true philosopher regards them as worthless, in my opinion," he said.

"Then the philosopher *qua* philosopher, it seems, does not concern himself with the body, but so far as he can separates himself from it, and concentrates upon the soul?"

"Yes."

"Then is it not clear, to begin with in such cases, that the philosopher far more than anyone else is freeing his soul, as much as possible, from association with the body?"

"It seems so."

"And the man who finds no pleasure in any of these things, and takes no part in them, for him, I suppose, the majority of men think that life is not worth living; he who pays no heed to the pleasures of the body seems already to border upon the state of death."

"What you say is very true."

"Now how about the acquisition of wisdom? Is the body a hindrance, or is it not, if you use it as an accessory in the search? What I mean is, do sight and hearing provide men with any true knowledge, or are even the poets always trying to tell us something like this, that nothing that we hear or see is accurate? And yet if these bodily senses are not accurate or reliable, the others are hardly likely to be—for all the others are inferior, I suppose, to these. Don't you think so?"

"I do indeed," he said.

"When, then, does the soul attain to truth?" he went on. "When it tries to investigate anything with the help of the body the body quite clearly deceives it."

"True."

"So it is only through reasoning, if at all, that any part of reality can be plainly understood?"

"Yes."

"And the soul reasons best, presumably, when none of these things worries her; neither hearing, nor sight, nor pain, nor any pleasure; when she is, so far as may be, alone and by herself, forgetting all about the body, and when she strives after truth having no more communication with the body nor contact with it than is absolutely necessary."

"That is so."

"So here again the philosopher's soul has no respect for the body, and shuns it, seeking rather to be independent of it?"

"It appears so."

"Well, now, what about things of this sort—do we say that there is such a thing as the Just Itself or not?"

"We certainly do."

"And a Beautiful and a Good also?"

"Certainly."

"Well, have you ever seen any thing of this sort with your eyes?"

"No, indeed," he said.

"Then have you ever grasped them with any other form of bodily perception? I am talking about everything, for example Tallness, Health, Strength, and, in fact, the real nature of *everything* else as well—what each thing really is: is the truth about them perceived by means of the body, or is it rather thus—whoever among us aims at fixing his mind most carefully on precisely on each thing *in and by itself*—whatever it may be that he is considering—he would come nearest to having knowledge of that thing?"

"That is the case."

"Then he would reach the purest truth in this procedure who approached each thing with the intellect itself alone, not bringing in sight to aid his thinking, nor dragging in any other sense to supplement his reason: he who should try to track down each item of reality, alone by itself, in its pure essence, by using pure thought, alone by *its self*—disregarding, so far as was possible, eyes and ears, and practically all the body, on the ground that it caused confusion, and whenever it played any part, would not allow the soul to acquire truth and wisdom; is not this the man, Simmias, who, if anyone, is likely to reach truth?"

"You are absolutely right, Socrates." said Simmias.

"And so," he said, "it follows from all these considerations that some such notion as this is bound to present itself to the genuine philosophers, and they are bound to talk like this to one another: 'It looks as though a sort of narrow path will bring us out on to the trail, because so long as we use the body as well as reason in our search, and our soul is tainted with that sort of blemish, we will never fully attain to what we want—namely, the truth. The body presents us with innumerable distractions, because of the necessity of looking after it; and again, if any illnesses assail it, they too hamper us in our pursuit of truth. The body fills us with emotions of love, desire and fear, with all kinds of phantasy and nonsense, so that in very truth it really doesn't give us a chance, as they say, ever to think of anything at all. In fact, wars and strife and battles are all due simply to the body and its desires. All wars take place because of the acquisition of property, and property we are compelled to acquire simply because of the body—we are slaves in its service; and so, for all these reasons, we have no time for philosophy.

And, lastly, even if we do get some time off from looking after it, and turn to some investigation, it keeps on turning up everywhere in our search, and causes disturbance and confusion, and thoroughly dumbfounds us, so that because of it we cannot catch a glimpse of truth; it really is proved to us that if we are ever going to have pure knowledge of anything, we must get rid of the body and survey things alone in themselves by means of the soul herself alone; *then,* it seems, we shall have our heart's desire, that of which we claim to be lovers, even wisdom—when we die, as the argument indicates, but not so long as we live. For if it is not possible to have pure knowledge of anything so long as we are with the body, then one of two things must be true: either it is nowhere possible to acquire knowledge, or only after death—for then, but not till then, the soul will be independent, free from the body. So long as we are alive, it seems likely that we shall come nearest to having knowledge if we do our utmost to have no contact or association with the body except in so far as is absolutely necessary, and do not infect ourselves with its nature, but purify ourselves of it, until God himself gives us final release; and if we are thus purified and freed from the foolishness of the body, we shall probably be in the company of the pure, and through our very selves come to have knowledge of all that is unsullied, that is, I suppose, of truth; for it is, perhaps, not lawful for the impure to attain to that which is pure."

"That is the sort of thing, Simmias, that all true lovers of learning are bound to say to each other, and the sort of view that they are bound to hold. Don't you agree?"

"Most certainly, Socrates."

"And so," said Socrates, "if all this is true, my friend, there is every hope that when a man has arrived at the destination to which I am journeying, he may there, if anywhere satisfactorily obtain what has, throughout our lives past, been the object of our great endeavors: so that I may make the journey now enjoined upon me with good hopes, as may anyone else who feels that his mind has been purified, as it were, and thereby duly prepared."

"That is so," said Simmias.

"And purification—isn't it just what it has long been said to be, according to the old accounts, the separation (so far as is possible) of the soul from the body, and the attempt to habituate her to collecting herself up and gathering herself together, away from the body, into herself—and to living, so far as is possible, both now and in the future, alone by herself, freeing herself from the body as though from bonds?"

"Quite so," he said.

"Then this is what is called death, a freeing or separation of soul from body?"

"Certainly," he said.

"And we say that the true philosophers in particular, or rather alone, are always eager to free her, and that this very thing is the philosopher's occupation, a freeing or separation of soul from body. Isn't that the case?"

"It seems to be."

"So, as I said to begin with, it would be absurd for a man who was training himself throughout his life to live as closely as possible to death to grumble when death came to him?"

"Absurd, of course."

Questions

1. What does Socrates (through Plato) mean when he says that "those who apply themselves . . . to the pursuit of philosophy are in fact practicing nothing more nor less than dying and death"; and that "true philosophers are more dead than alive"?

2. What does Socrates (through Plato) mean when he says, ". . . so long as we use the body as well as reason in our search, and our soul is tainted with that sort of blemish, we will never fully attain to what we want—namely, the truth"? Do you agree with this statement? Why or why not?

3. Besides philosophy, what other things might prove to be a sufficient *meletei nekron*?

---

2 Marcus Aurelius, *Mental Aids to a Happy Death*

Marcus Aurelius (121–180, c.e.) is regarded as one of the greatest emperors in Roman history. Aurelius ruled the vast empire from 161 to 180 c.e. He stands out as one of the greatest intellectual rulers in Western Civilization and is often lauded in modern literature as a paragon of humanistic virtue.

Aurelius was born in Rome and raised in a wealthy and politically prominent family. He was noticed by the Emperor Hadrian while he was still a child and was consequently given special educational privileges. At the age of seven Aurelius was given special permission to attend the priestly college of the Salii in Rome. It was here that he was taught by the greatest thinkers of the day, representing a variety of cultures, religions, and philosophies.

Aurelius was crowned emperor in the year 161. There were three great external conflicts which mark his reign, and he dealt with all of them effectively. He won a victory for the empire in 163 against the Parthians when they had invaded Armenia; he coped with a great plague that swept the whole empire; and he successfully pushed barbarians off Roman soil in the Marcomannic Wars. Aurelius was not free from crisis in his personal life either: his wife was notorious for sleeping around and his heir lacked all of the leadership skills for which Aurelius was famous.

Marcus Aurelius found the strength to deal with the many problems he faced through Stoic philosophy. These beliefs are expressed in his *Meditations,* his most famous work, where he exhibits the tensions he experienced between his position as emperor and his prevailing feeling of inadequacy. The twelve books that make up the set are the most introspective of any ancient philosophical writing—so much so that they may be called a diary. Aurelius was consoled in his writings by the fact that life is short and that the spirit, which is the only thing valuable about a person, in some ineluctable way survives death. In this passage he speaks to those who fear death, offering a series of mental attitudes—all expressive of Stoic "indifferentism"—which embrace death's naturalness and mystery.

Since you might depart this life at any time, govern your actions, words, and thoughts accordingly. Leaving the world of mankind is nothing to be afraid of, if the gods do exist, for they will do you no harm. If on the other hand they do not exist, or do not care about what happens in human affairs, why go on living in a universe without either gods or goodness? But they do exist, and they do care.

If you look carefully at dying for what it is in itself, and with the analysis of your reason you strip away all the images you associate with death, you will find it to be an entirely natural process. And anyone who fears a natural process is a mere child.

The longest-lived and shortest-lived of men lose equally when they die. All any man has to lose is only his present, since he cannot in fact lose what he does not own—neither his past nor what he anticipates for his future.

You embarked, you made the voyage, you have arrived at the far shore. Now step ashore. If you land in a new life, there will be gods enough for you . . . if you step into nothing, a condition without consciousness, you will still be free of the constraints of your earthly body, of pain and pleasure.

Death is like birth, another of nature's secrets, a synthesis formed of identical elements and a dissolution back into them again. This is not a thing for which a man should be ashamed, since it is in no way contrary to his natural state as a rational being.

Always recall how many physicians are now dead, after much knitting of brows over their patients; how many astrologers dead, after much portentous foretelling of other men's deaths as though they were consequential events; how many philosophers dead after endless debate on death and immortality; how many famed warriors dead, after killing such multitudes; how many tyrants dead after exercising their powers of life and death with monumental arrogance, as though themselves immortal; and how many cities are—if I may use the term so—also dead: Helike, Pompeii, Herculaneum, innumerable others.

Remember also all those you have known, one after another. One man closed a friend's eyes in death, and was then himself laid out on his bier. Then the friend who closed his eyes was buried by another—all of this within a short span of time. This is the whole of it; never overlook how ephemeral and worthless human things are. What was yesterday life-semen tomorrow will be mummy, or ashes. Therefore, journey through this small span of time in accord with nature, and come to your journey's end content, just as an olive falls, when ripe: praising earth which bore it and grateful to the tree on which it grew.

A commonplace yet still useful aid in facing death unafraid is to reflect on those we know who have clung long and tenaciously to life. How are they better off than those who died prematurely? All of them lie in their graves at last . . . even though they buried many during their long lives, they were finally buried themselves. On the whole, the difference between a long life and a short one is insignificant, especially considering how many tribulations there are, what sort of companions, and in how weak a body this life is laboriously lived. Do not, therefore, consider life a thing of much value. Look instead at the immensity of time already past, and the infinity still ahead. In this eternity, a baby born but three days ago and a Nestor who has lived past three generations are as one.

Make no distinction in doing your duty whether you are cold or warm, drowsy or sated with sleep, whether defamed or praised, or whether you are in process of dying, or of doing any other business. For the act of dying too is one of the acts of life, and it is sufficient even then to "make the best use of the moment."

To fear death is to fear either losing all sensation or finding a new, unfamiliar sensation. But if you no longer have any sensation, you will have no sensation of any evil either; likewise, if you should find new sensations, you will be a different kind of living being, but a living creature still.

Do not disdain death, but be content to accept it, since it too is one of the processes which nature ordains. For dissolution of life is part of nature, just as it is part of nature to be young and to be old; to grow up and to grow old; to grow first teeth, then beard, then grey hairs; to beget, to be pregnant, and to give birth; and to move through the rest of the natural functions which the seasons of your life bring. A reasoning man, therefore, will not be careless nor over-eager nor disdainful towards death, but will await it as one of nature's inevitable processes.

As you perform each act in your life, pause and ask yourself this: Is death to be dreaded because it would deprive you of this deed, this act?

No man is so fortunate that someone will not be at his deathbed welcoming the end which is befalling him. Even supposing that he is a serious and wise man, someone will be there at the last to say: "We can breathe freely again, now we are relieved of this disciplinarian! I can't actually say that he was hard on any one of us, but I knew that he was condemning us in his heart." So much for the serious and wise man. In the case of each of us, however, how numerous the reasons for so many to want to be quit of us! If you consider this when you are dying, you will depart the more easily.

Consider that in a little while you will be no one and nowhere, nor will anything you now see nor anyone who now lives still exist.

Questions

1. Describe three "aids in facing death" Marcus Aurelius says are invaluable if one wants to approach death without fear. Which of these would you find most helpful, and why?

2. Describe two metaphors Aurelius uses to define the dying process. Which of these two do you find most appropriate, and why?

3. Do you think Aurelius' more humanistic or secular approach to death is realistic? Is it attainable by the average person? Why or why not?

---

3 Chuang Tzu, *Accepting Death*

Chuang Tzu refers both to an historical person, and to a collection of writings attributed to this person's disciples. The writings are among the most stylistically variable of all philosophical writings. Short, discrete aphorisms of diamond-like density are placed alongside extended dialogues, parables, stories, real-life examples, images, and metaphors. While the range of topics is broad, they are subsumed under the general character of ethical consideration for how the good life should be lived.

Chuang Tzu probably lived some time in the fourth century B.C.E., but his dates are uncertain, as are the specific details of his life. His philosophy drove him to avoid all public action: he was, it is said, invited to become prime minister, but he declined so as to retain his freedom. Later Chinese philosophers condemned this attitude as irresponsible.

This condemnation notwithstanding, Chuang Tzu's writings express a deeply compassionate insight into human weaknesses and suffering, and a refreshing concern with the poor which is unusual in ancient texts. Like the Greek pre-Socratic philosopher Heraclites, Chuang Tzu accepted the experiential reality of constant change, and the empirical reality of physical death. Like most Chinese philosophers he did not believe in an afterlife, but like his more famous predecessor, Lou Tzu, he did hold to certain spiritual principles which govern the natural state of things and which therefore must be adhered to if one is to live well. These principles are summarized in the doctrine of *yin* and *yang:* the opposing forces of nature (dark/light, winter/summer, hot/cold, earth/air, etc.) which control all movement and change. These polarities find their resolution in the ultimate principle of unity, the *Tao,* or as it is translated in the reading below, "the Way."

According to Chuang Tzu, individuals can attain mystical unity with the Tao by achieving complete emptiness—a mental state free of anxiety or selfish desires. To this end, taught Chuang Tzu, people should abandon concern for fame, power, and wealth and follow a simple life. They should distrust ethical and political schemes and follow their instincts. Life should be enjoyed while it lasts, and death should not be feared. As you will read below, when Chuang Tzu's wife died, he was found by a friend banging on a tub and singing. His colleague questioned the propriety of this. "This is the Way [Tao] of things," Chuang Tzu replied. "If I went on sobbing and wailing, it would mean I don't understand the Way."

In the following teachings, aphorisms, and parables, the disciples of Chuang Tzu call the reader to abandon themselves to the Way and simply to accept what befalls them, even death, with equanimity and courage.

What do I mean by a True Man? If he had little, or had no recognition, there was no complaining. If he came to high station, he didn't put on airs. So he could make a mistake and not be disturbed, and he could get things right without being self-satisfied. He could climb high without fear, enter the water without getting soaked. He could breach the fire but not be burned. He knew how to climb to the heights and follow the Way itself.

The True Man of ancient times slept a dreamless sleep. Awake, he had no cares, no hungers. His breath arose from deep down, from his very heels. But the common man's breath comes barely out his throat; it's as if he were vomiting out his words. His cravings are strong, so his commitment to the Way is weak.

The True Man of ancient times knew this: not to love life, not to hate death. He came into life without rejoicing, left it without resisting. He didn't forget where he'd come from, didn't worry about where he'd end. He enjoyed what he received, and handed it back without a thought. He came in briskly, left briskly—and that was that . . .

Life and death are ordained by Heaven, just as the succession of night and day. That's the nature of things; we can't do anything about it.

The sage moves in a realm where things are stable and not constantly slipping away. So for him the end is as good as the beginning, and an early death is as good as reaching old age.

Master Yu became ill, and Ssu went to ask after him. "It's remarkable!" said Yu. "The maker of things has made me so crooked that my back sticks way up, and my chin has sunk to my navel. My insides are upside down, my shoulders are above my head, and my neckbone is like a spine pointing up to the sky! The yin and the yang seem all out of kilter."

But Yu didn't fuss about it; he was inwardly at ease. He hobbled over to a well and gazed at his reflection. "Oh my! What a crumpled thing I've been made into!" "Do you hate being in this condition?" asked Ssu. "Why, no! Why should I? The way things go, my left arm may end up as a rooster and I'll be watching for the dawn. Or maybe my left arm will end up as a crossbow, and I'll bring down a good roasting bird. Or maybe after a time my rear end will have turned into a pair of cartwheels, and my spirit into a horse, and I'd go for a ride. I'd never need a carriage again!

"I get something because the time has come, and I lose it when the time comes. I take whatever time brings, I don't sorrow; I don't celebrate. In the old days this was called 'getting free of the bonds.' Some people can't manage to get free, and they remain in bondage. Such is our fate, and such it ever was. So why hate it?"

Shortly afterward, Lai grew ill. He lay gasping, at the point of death. Gathered round him, weeping and bemoaning his fate, were his wife and children. Li came to ask after him. "Shoo!" he said to the family. "Get back! Let the change take its course."

Then he leaned comfortably against the door and chatted with Lai. "Isn't it a wonderful process," Li said, "this change we go through? What do you think you'll turn into? A rat's liver? A bug's arm? Where will you be taken?"

Lai replied, "A child obeys his father and mother, and goes where he is told. The yin and yang are more to us than father or mother! They are taking me to my death. Should I rebel? Anyway it's pointless to defy them or to blame them. This great ball of mud gave shape to me, kept me toiling in order to keep alive, gave me ease in my old age, and now will give me rest in death. If I think life is good, then I have to think death is, too."

Yen Hui said to Confucius, "When Meng-sun Ts'ai's mother died, he wailed but he didn't shed any tears. He didn't really grieve. In fact he didn't even put on a show of sorrow in conducting the funeral. In spite of that he has a reputation everywhere in the country for handling funerals well. How does a man gain such a reputation with nothing solid to support it? To me it's a puzzle."

Confucius said, "Meng-sun did whatever needed doing. He wasn't negligent, though it might look as if he were. He has unusual wisdom. He doesn't claim to know why there is life, or why there is death. He doesn't know whether to press ahead or lag behind. The fact that all things continually change leaves him waiting for the next change but not pretending to know what it will bring. Besides, once he has changed, how would he know he has? And if it seems he hasn't yet changed, how would he know if that's so? Even if something startles his body, it won't disturb his spirit. Like an alarming noise in the house at night, when dawn comes there's nothing there. Meng-sun alone is awake. He did wail at the funeral—why?—simply because that's what's done at funerals.

"You and I—maybe we're still asleep and dreaming. When I say 'I,' do I really know who 'I' is? You dream you're a bird and fly high into the sky; you dream you're a fish diving down into a pool. You tell me about it, but how do I know whether we are dreaming or are awake?

"There's no point in running to meet what comes. Better to just laugh, or even better than that, just go along. If you can be at ease about the changes, forget about them, then, though there's no map, you'll be on the right path."

Chuang Tzu was fishing in the P'u River when two officials came to him with this message from the king of Ch'u: "It is my desire that you should take up the weighty task of administering my realm."

Chuang Tzu didn't bother to turn his head, but just kept on fishing. He said, "I've heard there's a sacred tortoise in Ch'u, dead three thousand years. And I've heard the king keeps it wrapped in cloth in a case, and has it stored in the temple of his ancestors. Would that tortoise rather be dead and have its bones honored? Or would it rather be alive and dragging its tail in the mud?"

The officers replied: "It would rather be alive and dragging its tail in the mud."

Chuang Tzu said, "Go away! I'll drag my tail in the mud!"

Chuang Tzu's wife died, and Hui Tzu went to convey his condolences. Chuang Tzu was sitting, his legs sprawled out, pounding on a tub, and singing. "You lived with her, she brought up your children, you grew old together," said Hui Tzu. "It's bad enough not to weep at her death. But pounding on a tub? That's too much!"

"Wrong," said Chuang Tzu. "Do you think I didn't have any feelings when she died? But then I reflected, I went back to the very beginning, to the time before she was born, in fact to the time before she had a body, before she even had a spirit. In the Great Chaos there was a change, then another and another—and her spirit came into being. More change—and she had a body. Still more—she was born. So now there's been still another change—she's dead. It's like spring, summer, autumn, winter—change and transformation, the Way of things. Now she lies at peace in the Great Chamber. If I went on sobbing and wailing, it would mean I don't understand the Way and its transformations. But I stopped."

Lieh Tzu was traveling and stopped for a roadside meal. Under a bush he saw a hundred-year-old skull. He turned to it and said: "Only you and I know you aren't dead, and that you never lived. Are you satisfied? For that matter, am I?"

Chuang Tzu was dying and his disciples wanted to give him a grand burial. But Chuang said that all the ceremonial needs were already there: "Heaven and earth will be my outer and inner coffin, the sun and moon my pair of jade discs, the stars in their constellations will be my pearl jewels, the myriad things of this world will be my mourners. Nothing is lacking. What could you add?"

"Master, we are afraid if we simply leave you the crows and kites will eat you."

"True, but below ground, I'll be eaten by the ants and worms. You want to take from one to give to the other. Why so?"

Questions

1. Describe what is required to live a good life according to the teachings of Chuang Tzu. Think of one person you know who lives like this. In your opinion, is this person happy with his or her life? Why or why not?

2. Identify the one story or parable narrated in the reading that meant the most to you. Explain why.

3. Chuang Tzu was criticized by later Chinese philosophers as being socially irresponsible and a "fatalist" (simply accepting whatever comes without desire to change things). Would you agree with this criticism? Why or why not?

---

4 Martin Heidegger, *Death Is Something Impending*

Martin Heidegger is arguably Europe's, if not the world's, most influential twentieth-century philosopher. From his immense body of work have arisen numerous philosophical, literary, aesthetic, ethical, political, psychological, and, perhaps most abundantly, theological movements, each of which still commands a large following. Heidegger's influence has been dimmed somewhat in recent years by increased attention drawn to his one-year involvement with National Socialism when, in 1933, he was elected to the rectorship of the then-Nazi-governed University of Freiburg. Nazi affiliation was required for office and Heidegger complied. But most scholars find little in Heidegger's work to account for his brief flirtation with Nazism, and much that would caution against a commitment to any sort of totalitarian regime.

Traditionally, Heidegger is classified among philosophers as a preeminent member of the school of thought known as existentialism. Existentialism, as both a philosophical school and a literary movement, seeks to embrace the totality of concrete existence as the basis for any theory of reality, and tends to shun the more abstract generalizations which lie at the heart of traditional philosophy. The great motto of existentialism, coined by the Heidegger-influenced French writer Jean-Paul Sartre, is "existence precedes essence." This phrase has been taken to mean that to be fully human we must create our life's meaning and purpose for ourselves. Meaning is not something given to us by religion, philosophy, political systems, or even "Western Civilization," but rather is something that we are free to invent. We humans are truly free, say existentialists, to determine for ourselves what we value and hold to be true.

Heidegger, however, repudiated this interpretation of the phrase. It was integral to Heidegger's concept of human self-understanding that meaning is something that is already given to us by the world in which we live. We are, to use his famous phrase, "thrown into the world" at birth, and are from the start surrounded and therefore nurtured by meanings that condition and limit our thinking. As Heidegger famously declares, the essential nature of human existence is that of its "being-in-the-world." But he adds that we do possess the capacity to sort through those meanings, and to choose among them those that seem to make the most sense to us. Heidegger considers this sorting process the "existential duty" of each person, and a necessary part of becoming a mature adult.

Heidegger labels the mature adult *Dasein,* a German word which means something like the Buddhist phrase "right mindfulness"—a living consciously in the "here and now." *Dasein,* which can be loosely translated as "being there," is one who is fully aware of his or her predicament in the world as having been unwillingly "thrown" into it, and yet who fully takes responsibility for that predicament and so seeks to carve out a unique niche there.

According to Heidegger, if our birth is the event that forces the issue of our becoming a mature adult, a *Dasein,* in an already meaning-saturated world, then it is that other "event," death, that brings this issue to a climax. Heidegger contends, in agreement with other existentialists, that death is the most important "moment" in our lives. Death is what gives life its ultimacy, its passion, its desire to search for personally appropriate meaning. According to Heidegger, there is a sort of undercurrent of *Angst,* "anxiety," to all of life because of death. Deep down, we all know intuitively that life will not go on forever, and this creates anxiety, or a kind of death-colored experience of the present. This mostly unconscious awareness tends to be expressed in a variety of unhealthy ways—stress-related illnesses, for example, or sadness at the realization that one is getting older. But once we realize that death is an event "not to be outstripped" (that is, death is inescapable), and accept that death is "non-relational" (we all die alone), then we are able to take the limited nature of life as a unique challenge. The inevitability of death, says Heidegger, is like a wake-up call to us to develop a sense of meaning and value that is unique to us as individuals. For this reason, Heidegger calls death our "ownmost potentiality-for-Being."

Death is not something not yet present-at-hand, nor is it that which is ultimately still outstanding but which has been reduced to a minimum. *Death is something that stands before us—something impending.*

However, there is much that can impend for Dasein as Being-in-the-world. The character of impendence is not distinctive of death. On the contrary, this Interpretation could even lead us to suppose that death must be understood in the sense of some impending event encountered environmentally. For instance, a storm, the remodeling of the house, or the arrival of a friend, may be impending; and these are entities which are respectively present-at-hand, ready-to-hand, and there-with-us. The death which impends does not have this kind of Being.

But there may also be impending for Dasein a journey, for instance, or a disputation with Others, or the forgoing of something of a kind which Dasein itself can be—its own possibilities of Being, which are based on its Being with Others.

Death is a possibility-of-Being which Dasein itself has to take over in every case. With death, Dasein stands before itself in its ownmost potentiality-for-Being. This is a possibility in which the issue is nothing less than Dasein's Being-in-the-world. Its death is the possibility of no-longer being-able-to-be-there. If Dasein stands before itself as this possibility, it has been *fully* assigned to its ownmost potentiality-for-Being. When it stands before itself in this way, all its relations to any other Dasein have been undone. This ownmost non-relational possibility is at the same time the uttermost one.

As potentiality-for-Being, Dasein cannot outstrip the possibility of death.

Death is the possibility of the absolute impossibility of Dasein. Thus death reveals itself as that *possibility which is one's ownmost, which is non-relational, and which is not to be outstripped [unüberholbare]*. As such, death is something *distinctively* impending. Its existential possibility is based on the fact that Dasein is essentially disclosed to itself, and disclosed, indeed, as ahead-of-itself. This item in the structure of care has its most primordial concretion in Being-towards-death. As a phenomenon, Being-towards-the-end becomes plainer as Being towards that distinctive possibility of Dasein which we have characterized.

This ownmost possibility, however, non-relational and not to be outstripped, is not one which Dasein procures for itself subsequently and occasionally in the course of its Being. On the contrary, if Dasein exists, it has already been *thrown* into this possibility. Dasein does not, proximally and for the most part, have any explicit or even any theoretical knowledge of the fact that it has been delivered over to its death, and that death thus belongs to Being-in-the-world. Thrownness into death reveals itself to Dasein in a more primordial and impressive manner in that state-of-mind which we have called "anxiety." Anxiety in the face of death is anxiety in the face of that potentiality-for-Being which is one's ownmost, non-relational, and not to be outstripped. That in the face of which one has anxiety is Being-in-the-world itself. That about which one has this anxiety is simply Dasein's potentiality-for-Being. Anxiety in the face of death must not be confused with fear in the face of one's demise. This anxiety is not an accidental or random mood of "weakness" in some individual; but, as a basic state-of-mind of Dasein, it amounts to the disclosedness of the fact that Dasein exists as thrown Being *towards* its end. Thus the existential conception of "dying" is made clear as thrown Being towards its ownmost potentiality-for-Being, which is non-relational and not to be outstripped.

Questions

1. What do you think Heidegger means when he says that "death is something that stands before us—impending"?
2. What do you think it means to say that death is a present part of everyday experience? What everyday experiences are symbolic of death in this sense?
3. Do you agree or disagree with Heidegger that death is a) "non-relational" and b) "not to be outstripped," and why?

---

5 Bertrand Russell, *Do We Survive Death?*

Born into the British nobility in 1872, Bertrand Russell studied mathematics and philosophy at Cambridge University, and soon distinguished himself as an original and talented student. He later took a teaching position there, and began work on what would turn out to be a long list of major works in philosophy. His most influential contributions include his defense of logicism (the view that mathematics is in some important sense reducible to logic), and his theories of definite descriptions and logical atomism. Along with G. E. Moore, Russell is generally recognized as one of the founders of analytic philosophy. With Kurt Gödel, he is also regularly credited as being one of the two most important logicians of the twentieth century.

In 1908, Russell was elected Fellow of the British Royal Society, and in 1931 he became the third Earl Russell upon the death of his elder brother. He won the Order of Merit in 1949 and the Nobel Prize for Literature in 1950. These honors allowed him to travel broadly as a visiting lecturer, and during the 1950s he held temporary positions at the University of Chicago, UCLA, and Harvard.

Russell dedicated his life not only to academic scholarship and teaching, but also to social activism and educational reform. He was imprisoned twice for antiwar protests, and became founding president of the Campaign for Nuclear Disarmament. With his second wife, Dora, Russell opened an experimental primary school.

This brief essay is taken from Russell's 1957 collection of essays entitled *Why I Am Not a Christian,* which established him as a leading figure in the European and American secular humanist movement. In it Russell outlines several reasons why he answers the question "Do we survive death?" in the negative.

Before we can profitably discuss whether we shall continue to exist after death, it is well to be clear as to the sense in which a man is the same person as he was yesterday. Philosophers used to think that there were definite substances, the soul and the body, that each lasted on from day to day, that a soul, once created, continued to exist throughout all future time, whereas a body ceased temporarily from death till the resurrection of the body.

The part of this doctrine which concerns the present life is pretty certainly false. The matter of the body is continually changing by processes of nutriment and wastage. Even if it were not, atoms in physics are no longer supposed to have continuous existence; there is no sense in saying: this is the same atom as the one that existed a few minutes ago. The continuity of a human body is a matter of appearance and behavior, not of substance.

The same thing applies to the mind. We think and feel and act, but there is not, in addition to thoughts and feelings and actions, a bare entity, the mind or the soul, which does or suffers these occurrences. The mental continuity of a person is a continuity of habit and memory: there was yesterday one person whose feelings I can remember, and that person I regard as myself of yesterday; but, in fact, my self of yesterday was only certain mental occurrences which are now remembered and are regarded as part of the person who now recollects them. All that constitutes a person is a series of experiences connected by memory and by certain similarities of the sort we call habit.

If, therefore, we are to believe that a person survives death, we must believe that the memories and habits which constitute the person will continue to be exhibited in a new set of occurrences.

No one can prove that this will not happen. But it is easy to see that it is very unlikely. Our memories and habits are bound up with the structure of the brain, in much the same way in which a river is connected with the riverbed. The water in the river is always changing, but it keeps to the same course because previous rains have worn a channel. In like manner, previous events have worn a channel in the brain, and our thoughts flow along this channel. This is the cause of memory and mental habits. But the brain, as a structure, is dissolved at death, and memory therefore may be expected to be also dissolved. There is no more reason to think otherwise than to expect a river to persist in its old course after an earthquake has raised a mountain where a valley used to be.

All memory, and therefore (one may say) all minds, depend upon a property which is very noticeable in certain kinds of material structures but exists little if at all in other kinds. This is the property of forming habits as a result of frequent similar occurrences. For example: a bright light makes the pupils of the eyes contract; and if you repeatedly flash a light in a man's eyes and beat a gong at the same time, the gong alone will, in the end, cause his pupils to contract. This is a fact about the brain and nervous system— that is to say, about a certain material structure. It will be found that exactly similar facts explain our response to language and our use of it, our memories and the emotions they arouse, our moral or immoral habits of behavior, and indeed everything that constitutes our mental personality, except the part deter-

mined by heredity. The part determined by heredity is handed on to our posterity but cannot, in the individual, survive the disintegration of the body. Thus both the hereditary and the acquired parts of a personality are, so far as our experience goes, bound up with the characteristics of certain bodily structures. We all know that memory may be obliterated by an injury to the brain, that a virtuous person may be rendered vicious by encephalitis lethargica, and that a clever child can be turned into an idiot by lack of iodine. In view of such familiar facts, it seems scarcely probable that the mind survives the total destruction of brain structure which occurs at death.

It is not rational arguments but emotions that cause belief in a future life.

The most important of these emotions is fear of death, which is instinctive and biologically useful. If we genuinely and wholeheartedly believed in the future life, we should cease completely to fear death. The effects would be curious, and probably such as most of us would deplore. But our human and subhuman ancestors have fought and exterminated their enemies throughout many geological ages and have profited by courage; it is therefore an advantage to the victors in the struggle for life to be able, on occasion, to overcome the natural fear of death. Among animals and savages, instinctive pugnacity suffices for this purpose; but at a certain stage of development, as the Mohammedans first proved, belief in Paradise has considerable military value as reinforcing natural pugnacity. We should therefore admit that militarists are wise in encouraging the belief in immortality, always supposing that this belief does not become so profound as to produce indifference to the affairs of the world.

Another emotion which encourages the belief in survival is admiration of the excellence of man. As the Bishop of Birmingham says, "His mind is a far finer instrument than anything that had appeared earlier—he knows right and wrong. He can build Westminster Abbey. He can make an airplane. He can calculate the distance of the sun. . . . Shall, then, man at death perish utterly? Does that incomparable instrument, his mind, vanish when life ceases?"

The Bishop proceeds to argue that "the universe has been shaped and is governed by an intelligent purpose," and that it would have been unintelligent, having made man, to let him perish.

To this argument there are many answers. In the first place, it has been found, in the scientific investigation of nature, that the intrusion of moral or aesthetic values has always been an obstacle to discovery. It used to be thought that the heavenly bodies must move in circles because the circle is the most perfect curve, that species must be immutable because God would only create what was perfect and what therefore stood in no need of improvement, that it was useless to combat epidemics except by repentance because they were sent as a punishment for sin, and so on. It has been found, however, that, so far as we can discover, nature is indifferent to our values and can only be understood by ignoring our notions of good and bad. The Universe may have a purpose,

but nothing that we know suggests that, if so, this purpose has any similarity to ours.

Nor is there in this anything surprising. Dr. Barnes tells us that man "knows right and wrong." But, in fact, as anthropology shows, men's views of right and wrong have varied to such an extent that no single item has been permanent. We cannot say, therefore, that man knows right and wrong, but only that some men do. Which men? Nietzsche argued in favor of an ethic profoundly different from Christ's, and some powerful governments have accepted his teaching. If knowledge of right and wrong is to be an argument for immortality, we must first settle whether to believe Christ or Nietzsche, and then argue that Christians are immortal, but Hitler and Mussolini are not, or vice versa. The decision will obviously be made on the battlefield, not in the study. Those who have the best poison gas will have the ethic of the future and will therefore be the immortal ones.

Our feelings and beliefs on the subject of good and evil are, like everything else about us, natural facts, developed in the struggle for existence and not having any divine or supernatural origin. In one of Aesop's fables, a lion is shown pictures of huntsmen catching lions and remarks that, if he had painted them, they would have shown lions catching huntsmen. Man, says Dr. Barnes, is a fine fellow because he can make airplanes. A little while ago there was a popular song about the cleverness of flies in walking upside down on the ceiling, with the chorus: "Could Lloyd George do it? Could

Mr. Baldwin do it? Could Ramsay Mac do it? Why, no." On this basis a very telling argument could be constructed by a theologically-minded fly, which no doubt the other flies would find most convincing.

Moreover, it is only when we think abstractly that we have such a high opinion of man. Of men in the concrete, most of us think the vast majority very bad. Civilized states spend more than half their revenue on killing each other's citizens. Consider the long history of the activities inspired by moral fervor: human sacrifices, persecutions of heretics, witch-hunts, pogroms leading up to wholesale extermination by poison gases, which one at least of Dr. Barnes's episcopal colleagues must be supposed to favor, since he holds pacifism to be un-Christian. Are these abominations, and the ethical doctrines by which they are prompted, really evidence of an intelligent Creator? And can we really wish that the men who practiced them should live forever? The world in which we live can be understood as a result of muddle and accident; but if it is the outcome of deliberate purpose, the purpose must have been that of a fiend. For my part, I find accident a less painful and more plausible hypothesis.

Questions

1. Russell argues that personhood (what makes us individual persons, each with our own identity) is strictly tied to the body, the brain in particular. What analogy does he use to illustrate his point? Do you find this analogy to be accurate? Why or why not?

2. Explain Russell's comment, "It is not rational arguments but emotions that cause belief in a future life." Do you agree with him? Why or why not?

3. Russell raises the idea that humans must survive death simply because of human "excellence." How does Russell counter this argument? Do you find his counterarguments persuasive? Why or why not?

Small Group Exercises

1. In your small group, discuss the various reasons people fear death. Make a list of these and rank them according to how difficult you think they are to overcome. For each fear, come up with ways of coping with and minimizing its emotional impact.

2. Give your group the assignment of coming up with a "philosophy of life and living" based on Epicurus' idea that "when death comes, then we do not exist." Give this philosophy a name, and write out five primary doctrines of the philosophy. Identify two or three famous people that you think best represent the philosophy.

3. In your small group, prepare a public debate on the issue of life after death. Identify the strongest rational arguments for both sides. Present these to the class and then have the class vote on the issue.

Practical Learning Component

1. Interview members of the philosophy department in your college or university regarding their views of death. Ask such questions as:
   a. What does death mean to you?
   b. What do you think happens to us, if anything, after death?
   c. Would life have more or less meaning if we could live forever?

2. Make a survey of popular ads in magazines and newspapers and on television that mention death or dying in some way. Identify the various philosophies of death evident in these ads.

3. Watch several films that deal with death as a philosophical idea. You will find a list of such films in the introduction to this chapter. Make a list of the ideas of death portrayed in these films.

Chapter 4

Chapter 4

✦

Being With the Dying

When it comes time to die, be not like those whose hearts are
filled with the fear of death, so when their time comes they
weep and pray for a little more time to live their lives over
again in a different way. Sing your death song, and die like
a hero going home.

—MOHICAN CHIEF AUPUMUT

When I teach my Death and Dying class, I usually ask the students, "How many of
you have had firsthand experience with death? How many have spent time with a close
loved one as he or she was in the final stages of the dying process?" In a class of eighty
students, most of whom are under twenty-two years of age, maybe fifteen hands go up
at most. Not many, considering the size of the class and the topic being taught. The
truth is, until we reach a certain age (about forty), most of us only know death as
something that happens to others: neighbors who live down the street, relatives we
haven't seen for years, victims we hear about on television and read about in the newspaper. Death is not something that happens to us or to those we love. The miracles of
science, the institutionalization of the dying, and the neutral, objective stance of the
media all conspire to keep the pain and fear of death at arm's length.

Not all young people are so sheltered from death. I've had students who have seen
one or both parents die, who have buried siblings after car crashes, who have lost best
friends to suicide, and who are themselves, at an all-too-young age, suffering from
terminal cancer. But these are the exceptions: most young people today have simply
not had to deal directly with death. This lack of experience can create an unreadiness
psychologically to face the difficult inner struggles associated with the dying process.

Whether one is going through the process oneself, or is caring for a loved one going through the process, dying exacts a heavy psychological toll upon all involved. It unearths the darkest of fears and anxieties; it provokes the strongest feelings of anger; it can reduce the most independent of characters to a state of helplessness. It is therefore imperative that one develop an understanding of what kinds of mental and emotional issues can arise as a result of death's intrusion.

At the moment a terminal diagnosis is made, the patient is subject to a large set of potential problems and challenges. These can include grief in the wake of failed treatment, fears around the possibility of physical pain and discomfort, the loss of personal autonomy and the ability to care for oneself, changes to one's physical appearance, worries about mounting financial costs, concerns over loved ones to be left behind, and uncertainty about life after death. People cope with these challenges in various ways depending on their personalities, psychological profile, family and social patterns, and general environment.[23] For many, the comforts of religious faith become especially important during the time of dying. The teachings of a religion about postmortem rewards, and about the meaning and purpose of all events in life, even death, can bring a tremendous amount of support to those experiencing death and dying. For others, simply having friends and family near is enough to enable them to journey through the unknowns of death with courage. In either case, professional caregivers assert that finding appropriate avenues of emotional expression and resources of comfort and care is essential to coping with the realities of the dying process.

The aforementioned issues circumscribe a field of study known as the psychology of death and dying. Practitioners of this field involve themselves with such topics as psychosocial attitudes toward death, child and adult bereavement processes, the nature of doctor-patient communication around the terminal prognosis, coping mechanisms for grief, responding to unexpected losses (as in traffic accidents), the spirituality of the dying process, and methods of suicide prevention. Their findings are widely discussed in a variety of best-selling books, at popular conferences, in college classrooms around the world, and in several academic journals devoted to the subject.

DR. ELISABETH KÜBLER-ROSS

At the heart of the psychology of death and dying lies the study of the emotional and behavioral impact upon individuals of the knowledge of their immanent death, and the impact that knowledge has upon those who care for them. The person who is universally recognized as the founder of this field—it is more of a populist movement, really—and for developing its most famous theory, is an energetic psychiatrist from Switzerland, Elisabeth Kübler-Ross. Dr. Kübler-Ross was an assistant professor of psychiatry at Billings Hospital, University of Chicago, when she was approached by four divinity students from the university. In order to fulfill an assignment, the students needed to do research on a "human crisis situation" and wanted to know whether she might help them. Dr. Kübler-Ross told them that she had been wanting for some time to research the subject of death, and suggested that "there is no more important or universal crisis situation in life." So together they arranged to interview dying patients and their families at the hospital.

The year this research began was 1965. At that time, there was little open discussion of death in the United States, and patients' rights were relatively nonexistent. It is not surprising, therefore, that the doctors at Billings Hospital were initially opposed to Dr. Kübler-Ross's proposed project. They worried that getting dying patients to talk about their feelings might compromise their emotional state and therefore hinder any palliative treatment they were receiving. But Dr. Kübler-Ross persisted, and eventually she won the right to interview a single dying patient. Much to her and the doctors' surprise, the patient responded very positively to the interview. She expressed her thanks that someone, finally, was willing to listen to her talk about her fears and concerns. She became more cooperative with her doctors, and was able to reconcile her differences with several family members.

This small success led to subsequent interviews, first at Billings Hospital, then at other hospitals in the Chicago area. Over the next three years, Dr. Kübler-Ross, now working alone, met with hundreds of dying patients and with thousands of their family members around the subject of the dying process. In 1967, she began to teach a class entitled "Death and Dying" at the University of Chicago, which consisted primarily of open discussions between the students and patients of the hospital who had been diagnosed as terminal. In 1968 she began to formalize this research into a systematic theory that would come to be known as the "five stages of the dying process." Finally, in 1969, this theory was published by Simon and Schuster in the book that made Elisabeth Kübler-Ross a household name: *On Death and Dying.* The book went on to sell over three million copies, and single-handedly sparked a revolution in the way death and those who are dying are treated in the United States.

THE FIVE STAGES OF THE DYING PROCESS

Dr. Kübler-Ross's famous theory, which is now commonly taught as part of the required curriculum in psychology departments around the country, defines what it feels like to know that one is dying. It outlines and illustrates five stages the dying patient is likely to go through on the way toward death: denial, anger, bargaining, depression, and finally acceptance. While Dr. Kübler-Ross initially understood these stages to be experienced in sequential fashion—that is, the patient moves through each of the stages in progressive order, from denial to acceptance—she later recognized that each patient experiences them in a unique way: some only experience one or two of the stages; some skip over certain stages; and some can even experience the stages in reverse order.

The five stages of the dying process according to *On Death and Dying* can be described as follows:

- **Denial:** In this stage one cannot come to full terms with the fact that one is dying; one refuses to accept the diagnosis of the physician. Sometimes denial can take a more religious form where one believes against the medical establishment that one has been healed through prayer. Dr. Kübler-Ross insists that denial is a perfectly normal response to shocking news, and in most cases is temporary. It is the mind's way of allowing the reality of one's terminal condition to "sink in." The unfortunate part of denial is that while in this state, the patient is usually not able to do the important emotional and spiritual work that really should be done at this time. In the days and weeks that precede death, and before the patient progresses beyond being able to communicate, he or she should be putting closure on important relationships, asking for forgiveness from anyone he or she may have wronged, and seeking peace with his or her God. But when in denial, one feels no need to do any of these things. If one stays in denial to the end, these important tasks can sadly be left undone. It is essential, therefore, to work with someone in denial around what possible fears might lie behind the denial which keep the person from facing the reality of his or her death. Normally the two most prominent fears that face the dying person are the fear of being left alone and the fear of pain. Reassurance needs to be given, therefore, that he or she will not be left alone, and that any pain and discomfort associated with dying can and will be dealt with as much as possible.

- **Anger:** In this stage, the patient experiences rage at the prospect of death—"Why is this happening to me?"—and may lash out at anyone near enough to get in the way. Family, friends, doctors and nurses, even God, can serve as objects at which the patient's anger is directed. Dr. Kübler-Ross tells us that when it follows denial, anger is actually a healthy sign. It indicates the patient is now fully aware of the fact of his or her death, that he or she is no longer denying it. But the problem with anger is that, like denial, it can hinder the important work of closure that should be taking place at this time. An appropriate way to respond to someone in this stage is to help him or her to identify the fear and hurt that lie behind the anger so that there can be healing and a reorientation of attitude. Sometimes this healing only comes in the form of difficult reconciliation work between the patient and a friend or family member over long-held resentments. What is important to remember here is that this may be the last chance possible for this reconciliation to take place, and that therefore an attitude of openness and forgiveness is required.

- **Bargaining:** While not commonly experienced during the dying process, bargaining is one of the coping tools sometimes used by those who have a strong religious orientation. The "bargain" normally takes place between the dying patient and God as the patient promises to reform his or her life—for example, give up drinking or smoking, read the bible more, or enroll in seminary—in exchange for healing. Occasionally the bargain is made not for a complete healing, but simply to live until a certain date such as a child's wedding or a spouse's birthday. Kübler-Ross sees this stage as a healthy sign that the patient has retained a will to live; that life still has meaning enough to induce personal sacrifice. And usually the changes promised are positive ones: to become less self-indulgent, to take up new spiritual practices, to spend time caring for others, etc. But what sometimes happens to someone in this stage is that others ridicule the bargaining as "wishful thinking." The patient is put down for trying to manipulate God. A more appropriate response, suggests Kübler-Ross, is to encourage the patient to make those healthy changes in his or her life, even if the hoped-for healing never comes. If the person promises God to read the bible daily, for example, one can volunteer to read the bible aloud to the patient.

• **Depression:** This is the most common of the five stages, and the one most difficult to deal with. When the news of an incurable condition sinks in, there is an inevitable sadness that occurs as one contemplates the loss of one's own life, and the fate of the loved ones left behind. Dr. Kübler-Ross considers depression to be at the opposite end of the spectrum from denial: if denial means that one cannot face the reality of one's own death, then depression means that one is fully facing it, along with all the horrible experiences that come with that fact. Sometimes depression is mistreated as a superficial condition that can be alleviated simply through diversion and accelerated activity. But normally it is far more complex, and as such requires a thorough prognosis. Treating depression in terminal patients can include the use of pharmaceutical aids such as antidepressants, psychological counseling, and spiritual guidance. Sometimes simply sitting with the patient and listening to them can go a long way toward bringing a sense of peace.

• **Acceptance:** Not all terminal patients ever come to fully accept their condition, and so remain in one or more of the other stages in the dying process. And in some respects, none of us ever should expect this to happen; after all, an untimely death is one of life's greatest injustices. But for those who do come to a place of acceptance, the final days of life can be the most fruitful and fulfilling period for the patient. Acceptance should not be confused with resignation, states Kübler-Ross, for it is not a giving up or a surrender to the inevitable. It is not a "suicide wish." Rather, it is an active state of mind in which one chooses willfully to live in the full awareness of one's impending death, and to make the most of the short time available. Acceptance is often the background condition that allows a patient to put closure on significant relationships, to enjoy time with loved ones, and to make peace with God. In certain family systems, however, there can be the tendency to put down the patient for his or her acceptance; to put a "guilt trip" on the patient by claiming that he or she is abandoning the family; that his or her refusal to fight the disease is somehow an act of cowardice. But a healthier response is to simply come to accept the patient's acceptance, and to work on those issues that would hinder one from coming to the same state of mind.

THE WORK OF HOSPICE

The publication of *On Death and Dying* in 1969 began a revolution in the way dying patients were treated in hospitals and nursing homes. In the book, Dr. Kübler-Ross argues for allowing the dying to die at home, surrounded by family and friends instead of unknown medical personnel, and for giving the patient full autonomy in determining the medical care he or she would receive. Until this time such conditions would have been thought cruel treatment of the dying. Today, they are considered indispensable rights all humans possess.

At about the same time Kübler-Ross was publishing her landmark study, a revolution had already begun in England that called for the same changes to be made. In 1957, Dame Cicely Saunders established St. Christopher's Inpatient Hospice in London, an outpatient medical establishment that admitted only terminal patients. Dr. Saunders, a young physician previously trained as a nurse and a social worker, had pioneered the study of pain control in advanced cancer. She was the first to advocate the regular use of opioid analgesics given "by the clock" instead of waiting for the pain to return before administering the drugs. This now standard practice became the model for all other palliative care institutions around the world. Moreover, St. Christopher's was the first hospice to emphasize a multidisciplinary approach to caring for the dying, and careful attention to social, spiritual, and psychological suffering in patients and families.

The following definition of hospice is adapted from statements located on the websites of the Hospice Education Institute and the Hospice Foundation of America:

> Hospice is a special concept of care designed to provide comfort and support to patients and their families when a life-limiting illness no longer responds to cure-oriented treatments. Hospice care neither prolongs life nor hastens death. Hospice staff and volunteers offer a specialized knowledge of medical care, including pain management. The goal of hospice care is to improve the quality of a patient's last days by offering comfort and dignity. Hospice care is provided by a team-oriented group of specially trained professionals, volunteers and family members. Hospice addresses all symptoms of a disease, with a special emphasis on controlling a patient's pain and discomfort. Hospice deals with the emotional, social and spiritual impact of the disease on the patient and the patient's family and friends. Hospice offers a variety of bereavement and counseling services to families before and after a patient's death.

The word "hospice" comes from the Latin word *hospitium* meaning "guesthouse." It was originally used to describe a place of shelter for weary and sick travelers returning from religious pilgrimages. The first hospice in the United States was established in New Haven, Connecticut in 1974. Today there are more than 3,100 hospice programs in the United States caring for more than 600,000 terminal patients.

Death and Dying Fact

These are the most common misconceptions about the work of Hospice:[24]

Myth #1 *Hospice is a place.*
About 80 percent of hospice care takes place at home.

Myth #2 *Hospice is only for people with cancer.*
More than one-fifth of hospice patients nationwide have diagnoses other than cancer.

Myth #3 *Hospice is only for old people.*
Although the majority of hospice patients are older, hospices serve patients of all ages.

Myth #4 *Hospice is only for dying people.*
As a family-centered institution, hospice focuses as much on the grieving family as on the dying patient.

Myth #5 *Hospice can only help when family members are available to provide care.*
Recognizing that terminally ill people may live alone, many hospices coordinate community resources to make home care possible.

Myth #6 *Hospice is for people who don't need a high level of care.*
Most hospices employ experienced medical and nursing personnel skilled in state-of-the-art palliative care, offering advanced technologies to prevent or alleviate distressing symptoms.

Myth #7 *Hospice is only for people who can accept death.*
Many hospices welcome inquiries from families who are unsure about their needs and preferences. Hospice staff are readily available to discuss all options and to facilitate family decisions.

Myth #8 *Hospice care is expensive.*
Most people who use hospice are over 65 and are entitled to the Medicare Hospice Benefit. This benefit covers virtually all hospice services and requires little, if any, out-of-pocket cost.

Myth #9 *Hospice is not covered by managed care.*
Managed care programs are more and more frequently accepting hospice charges. Often a simple inquiry is all that is needed to gain at least partial coverage.

Myth #10 *Hospice is for when there is no hope.*
The gift of hospice is its capacity to help families see how much can be experienced at the end of life by making personal and spiritual connections. There is little focus on these in traditional hospital settings.

It should be stated that hospice is not a place; it is a system of caregiving for terminal patients and their families. Eighty percent of hospice care is provided in the home or at elderly care facilities. Moreover, hospice is not just about pain management. Though that is perhaps the most important part of what they do, it is but a small part of their overall care strategy. Each patient under hospice's care is assigned a team of caregivers, including doctors and nurses, but also including pastors, social workers, psychologists, even massage therapists and beauticians. Hospice is about caring for the whole person, not just the person's body.

In this chapter you will hear from Dr. Kübler-Ross as she outlines the fifth stage of the dying process, "acceptance," and two hospice nurses will introduce you to the unique organization and caring strategies of hospice. From a gifted playwright you will read a scene in which an intelligent, articulate young man, who is dying, is provoked by his ex-wife to express how he is feeling about his condition. To offer a more explicitly psychological approach, you will read of the very practical suggestions made by a hospice chaplain and what to do, not do, say and not say should you find yourself in the position of caring for someone you love who is dying. This chapter will close with two readings. First comes a passage from the writings of a hospice physician who describes his work with a family caring for a severely disabled young boy. It represents well the psychological approach even hospice physicians take with their patients. Be warned: this particular reading often moves students to tears. And finally, you will read from Mitch Albom's runaway bestseller, *Tuesdays with Morrie*, Albom's account of spending time with a beloved professor in his final days on earth.

---

1 Elisabeth Kübler-Ross, *Acceptance*

For those familiar with the field of death and dying, the name of Elisabeth Kübler-Ross hardly needs an introduction. Educated in medicine at the University of Zurich (1957) and psychiatry at the University of Colorado (1963), she is the author of the book which started a revival of interest in death studies in the late 1960s and established an international conversation on end-of-life issues. First published in 1969, Kübler-Ross's *On Death and Dying* sold over three million copies worldwide, establishing her as the foremost authority on the psychology of the dying process.

As mentioned previously, Dr. Kübler-Ross is famous for having identified the now well-known five stages of the dying process: denial, anger, bargaining, depression, and acceptance. The five stages can be characterized as follows:

- Denial: "No, not me!"
- Anger: "Why me?"
- Bargaining: "Yes, me . . . but . . . "
- Depression: "Yes, me, and it's not okay!"
- Acceptance: "Yes, me, and it's okay!"

Dr. Kübler-Ross came later in life to lament the use of the term "stage" for these five moments in the dying and bereavement processes. Not only do the stages mistakenly lead one to believe that the dying should progress smoothly from stage to stage, they also tend to mask some of the deeper, more mysterious movements that mark the experience as something that simply cannot be categorized in this way. Too often, she noted, healthcare workers use the five stages as quantifying criteria for discerning "where a patient is at," when what is really needed is reflective conversation and a deeper psychological assessment. Kübler-Ross warns that when the stages are used to categorize a patient—she is "in denial," or he is "depressed"—what can be missed are the more subtle complexities of emotion that that particular person may be capable of. Nevertheless, the theory remains a valid starting point for understanding what a dying person, and what those in grief, may be experiencing.

Following the publication of *On Death and Dying,* Dr. Kübler-Ross went on to write twenty more books on the subject of death, including *Death, the Final Stage of Growth* (1974), *Living with Death and Dying* (1981), *On Children and Death* (1985), *AIDS: The Ultimate Challenge* (1988), and the autobiographical *The Wheel of Life* (1997). Through her foundation, she established grief support centers in eight different countries. At one point she tried to establish a home for children suffering from AIDS near her farm, "Healing Waters," in rural Virginia but the local residents objected. Prior to being finished, the home was subject to an arson attack that destroyed it.

Kübler-Ross has been awarded over twenty-five honorary doctorates from major universities. Although universally recognized as the primary contributor to the current revolution in caregiving to the dying, Dr. Kübler-Ross is not without her critics. Some claim she borrowed freely from the previous work of others without recognizing her sources. Others point to the esoteric nature of her more recent work. At the Shanti Nilaya Institute in California which she founded, for example, Dr. Kübler-Ross promotes such occultic studies as communication with the dead and engaging the presence of "spirit-guides." But while her life and teachings may be controversial, her impact on the field of death studies in general, and on the individual perception of the dying process in particular, will always remain strong.

If a patient has had enough time (i.e., not a sudden, unexpected death) and has been given some help in working through the previously described stages, he will reach a stage during which he is neither depressed nor angry about his "fate." He will have been able to express his previous feelings, his envy for the living and the healthy, his anger at those who do not have to face their end so soon. He will have mourned the impending loss of so many meaningful people and places and he will contemplate his coming end with a certain degree of quiet expectation. He will be tired and, in most cases, quite weak. He will also have a need to doze off or to sleep often and in brief intervals, which is different from the need to sleep during the times of depression. This is not a sleep of avoidance or a period of rest to get relief from pain, discomfort, or itching. It is a gradually increasing need to extend the hours of sleep very similar to that of the newborn child but in reverse order. It is not a resigned and hopeless "giving up," a sense of "what's the use" or "I just cannot fight it any longer," though we hear such statements too. (They also indicate the beginning of the end of the struggle, but the latter are not indications of acceptance.)

Acceptance should not be mistaken for a happy stage. It is almost void of feelings. It is as if the pain had gone, the struggle is over, and there comes a time for "the final rest before the long journey" as one patient phrased it. This is also the time during which the family needs usually more help, understanding, and support than the patient himself. While the dying patient has found some peace and acceptance, his circle of interest diminishes. He wishes to be left alone or at least not stirred up by news and problems of the outside world. Visitors are often not desired and if they come, the patient is no longer in a talkative mood. He often requests limitation on the number of people and prefers short visits. This is the time when the television is off. Our communications then become more nonverbal than verbal. The patient may just make a gesture of the hand to invite us to sit down for a while. He may just hold our hand and ask us to sit in silence. Such moments of silence may be the most meaningful communications for people who are not uncomfortable in the presence of a dying person. We may together listen to the song of a bird from the outside. Our presence may just confirm that we are going to be around until the end. We may just let him know that it is all right to say nothing when the important things are taken care of and it is only a question of time until he can close his eyes forever. It may reassure him that he is not left alone when he is no longer talking and a pressure of the hand, a look, a leaning back in the pillows may say more than many "noisy" words.

A visit in the evening may lend itself best to such an encounter as it is the end of the day both for the visitor and the patient. It is the time when the hospital's page system does not interrupt such a moment, when the nurse does not come in to take the temperature, and the cleaning woman is not mopping the floor—it is this little private moment that can complete the day at the end of the rounds for the physician, when he is not interrupted by anyone. It takes just a little time but it is comforting for the patient to know that he is not forgotten when nothing else can be done for him. It is gratifying for the visitor as well, as it will show him that dying is not such a frightening, horrible thing that so many want to avoid.

There are a few patients who fight to the end, who struggle and keep a hope that makes it almost impossible to reach this stage of acceptance. They are the ones who will say one day, "I just cannot make it anymore," the day they stop fighting, the fight is over. In other words, the harder they struggle to avoid the inevitable death, the more they try to deny it, the more difficult it will be for them to reach this final stage of acceptance with peace and dignity. The family and staff may consider these patients tough and strong, they may encourage the fight for life to the end, and they may implicitly communicate that accepting one's end is regarded as a cowardly giving up, as a deceit or, worse yet, a rejection of the family.

How, then, do we know when a patient is giving up "too early" when we feel that a little fight on his part combined with the help of the medical profession could give him a chance to live longer? How can we differentiate this from the stage of acceptance, when our wish to prolong his life often contradicts his wish to rest and die in peace? If we are unable to differentiate these two stages we do more harm than good to our patients, we will be frustrated in our efforts, and will make his dying a painful last experience. The following case of Mrs. W. is a brief summary of such an event, where this differentiation was not made.

Mrs. W., a married fifty-eight-year-old woman, was hospitalized with a malignancy in her abdomen which gave her much pain and discomfort. She had been able to face her serious illness with courage and dignity. She complained very rarely and attempted to do as many things as possible by herself. She rejected any offer of help as long as she was able to do it herself and impressed the staff and her family by her cheerfulness and ability to face her impending death with equanimity.

Briefly after her last admission to the hospital she became suddenly depressed. The staff was puzzled about this change and asked for a psychiatric consultation. She was not in her room when we looked for her and a second visit a few hours later found her still absent. We finally found her in the hallway outside of the X-ray room where she lay uncomfortably and obviously in pain on a stretcher. A brief interview revealed that she had undergone two rather lengthy X-ray procedures and had to wait for other pictures to be taken. She was in great discomfort because of a sore on her back, had not had any food or drink for the past several hours, and most uncomfortable of all, needed to go to the bathroom urgently. She related all this in a whispering voice, describing herself as being "just numb from pain." I offered to carry her to the adjacent bathroom. She looked at me—for the first time smiling faintly—and said, "No, I am barefoot, I'd rather wait until I am back in my room. I can go there myself."

This brief remark showed us one of the patient's needs: to care for herself as long as possible, to keep her dignity and independence as long as it was possible. She was enraged that her endurance was tested to the point where she was ready to scream in public, where she was ready to let go of her bowel movements in a hallway, where she was on the verge of crying in front of strangers "who only did their duty."

When we talked with her a few days later under more favorable circumstances, it was obvious that she was increasingly tired and ready to die. She talked about her children briefly, about her husband who would be able to carry on without her. She felt strongly that her life, especially her marriage, had been a good and meaningful one and that there was little left that she could do. She asked to be allowed to die in peace, wished to be left alone—even asked for less involvement on the part of her husband. She said that the only reason that kept her still alive was her husband's inability to accept the fact that she had to die. She was angry at him for not facing it and for so desperately clinging on to something that she was willing and ready to give up. I translated to her that she wished to detach herself from this world and she nodded gratefully as I left her alone.

In the meantime, unbeknown to the patient and myself, the medical–surgical staff had a meeting which included the husband. While the surgeons believed that another surgical procedure could possibly prolong her life, the husband pleaded with them to do everything in their power to "turn the clock back." It was unacceptable to him to lose his wife. He could not comprehend that she did not have the need to be with him any longer. Her need to detach herself, to make dying easier, was interpreted by him as a rejection which was beyond his comprehension. There was no one there to explain to him that this was a natural process, a progress indeed, a sign perhaps that a dying person has found his peace and is preparing himself to face it alone.

The team decided to operate on the patient the following week. As soon as she was informed of the plans she weakened rapidly. Almost overnight she required double the dose of medication for her pains. She often asked for drugs the moment she was given an injection. She became restless and anxious, often calling for help. She was hardly the patient of a few days before; the dignified lady who could not go to the bathroom because she was not wearing slippers!

Such behavioral changes should make us alert. They are communications of our patients who try to tell us something. It is not always possible for a patient to openly reject a life-prolonging operation, in the face of a pleading, desperate husband and children who hope to have mother home once more. Last but not least, we should not underestimate the patient's own glimpse of hope for a cure in the face of impending death. As outlined earlier, it is not in human nature to accept the finality of death without leaving a door open for some hope. It is therefore not enough to listen only to the overt verbal communications of our patients.

Mrs. W. had clearly indicated that she wished to be left in peace. She was in much more pain and discomfort after the announcement of the planned surgery. Her anxiety increased as the day of the operation approached. It was not in our authority to cancel the operation. We merely communicated our strong reservations and felt sure that the patient would not tolerate the operation.

Mrs. W. did not have the strength to refuse the operation nor did she die before or during the procedure. She became grossly psychotic in the operating room, expressed ideas of persecution, screamed and carried on until she was returned to her room minutes before the planned surgery was to take place.

She was clearly delusional, had visual hallucinations and paranoid ideas. She looked frightened and bewildered and made no sense in her communications to the staff. Yet, in all this psychotic behavior, there was a degree of awareness and logic that remained impressive. As she was returned to her room, she asked to see me. When I entered the room the following day, she looked at her bewildered husband and then said, "Talk to this man and make him understand." She then turned her back to us, clearly indicating her need to be left alone. I had my first meeting with her husband, who was at a loss for words. He could not understand the "crazy" behavior of his wife who had always been such a dignified lady. It was hard for him to cope with her rapidly deteriorating physical illness, but incomprehensible what our "crazy dialogue" was all about.

Her husband said with tears in his eyes that he was totally puzzled by this unexpected change. He described his marriage as an extremely happy one and his wife's terminal illness as totally unacceptable. He had hopes that the operation would allow them once more to be "as close together as they had been" for the many happy years of their marriage. He was disturbed by his wife's detachment and even more so by her psychotic behavior.

When I asked him about the patient's needs, rather than his own, he sat in silence. He slowly began to realize that he never listened to her needs but took it for granted that they were the same. He could not comprehend that a patient reaches a point when death comes as a great relief, and that patients die easier if they are allowed and helped to detach themselves slowly from all the meaningful relationships in their life.

We had a long session together. As we talked, things slowly began to clear and came into focus. He gave much anecdotal material to confirm that she had tried to communicate her needs to him, but that he could not hear it because they were opposing his needs. Mr. W. felt obviously relieved when he left and rejected an offer to return with him to the patient's room. He felt more capable of talking with his wife frankly about the outcome of her illness and was almost glad that the operation had to be canceled because of her "resistance" as he called it. His reaction to her psychosis was, "My God, maybe she is stronger than all of us. She sure fooled us. She made it clear she did not want the operation. Maybe the psychosis was the only way out of it without dying before she was ready."

Mrs. W. confirmed a few days later that she was not able to die until she knew that her husband was willing to let go. She wanted him to share some of her feelings rather than "always pretend that I am going to be all right." Her husband did make an attempt to let her talk about it, though it came hard and he "regressed" many times. Once he clung to the hope for radiation, at another time he tried to put pressure on her to come home, promising to hire a private nurse for her care.

During the following two weeks he often came to talk about his wife and his hopes but also about her eventual death. Finally he came to accept the fact that she would become weaker and less able to share the many things that had been so meaningful in their life.

She recovered from her psychotic episode as soon as the operation was permanently canceled and her husband acknowledged the impending death and shared this with her. She had less pain and resumed her role of the dignified lady who continued to do as many things as her physical condition allowed. The medical staff became increasingly sensitive to the subtle expressions to which they responded tactfully, always keeping in mind her most important need: to live to the end with dignity.

Mrs. W. was representative of most of our dying patients, though she was the only one I have seen to resort to such an acute psychotic episode. I am sure that this was a defense, a desperate attempt to prevent a life-prolonging intervention which came too late.

As stated earlier, we have found that those patients do best who have been encouraged to express their rage, to cry in preparatory grief, and to express their fears and fantasies to someone who can quietly sit and listen. We should be aware of the monumental task which is required to achieve this stage of acceptance, leading towards a gradual separation (decathexis) where there is no longer a two-way communication.

We have found two ways of achieving this goal more easily. One kind of patient will achieve it with little if any help from the environment—except a silent understanding and no interference. This is the older patient who feels at the end of his life, who has worked and suffered, raised his children and completed his tasks. He will have found meaning in his life and has a sense of contentment when he looks back at his years of work.

Others, less fortunate ones, may reach a similar state of body and mind when they are given enough time to prepare for their death. They will need more help and understanding from the environment as they struggle through all the previously described stages. We have seen the majority of our patients die in the stage of acceptance, an existence without fear and despair. It is perhaps best compared with what Bettelheim describes about early infancy: "Indeed it was an age when nothing was asked of us and all that we wanted was given. Psychoanalysis views earliest infancy as a time of passivity, an age of primary narcissism when we experience the self as being all."

And so, maybe at the end of our days, when we have worked and given, enjoyed ourselves and suffered, we are going back to the stage that we started out with and the circle of life is closed.

Questions

1. What caused Mrs. W.'s husband to change his attitude about his wife's death from one of denial to one of acceptance?

2. Summarize what Dr. Kübler-Ross says about the end of life, and how it resembles the beginning of life.

3. What life lessons can be learned from the struggles displayed here by Mrs. W.'s husband?

------

2 Marian Gentile, Maryanne Fello, *Hospice Care: A Concept Coming of Age*

The term "hospice" (from the root of "hospitality") can be traced back to early Western Civilization when it was used to describe a place of shelter and rest for weary or sick travelers on long journeys. With time and the advance of medicine, birth and death were transplanted to a new and often intimidating environment: the modern hospital. In this setting family members were sometimes made to feel "in the way" as control of the patient's care rested not with them but with unknown health professionals.

While acknowledging the many benefits of modern medicine, a group of clergy, healthcare professionals, and social workers began wondering whether the advances in the technology of caring for the dying did not at the same deprive the dying process of its dignity. Out of these concerns, hospice care was born in the United States. In 1974 the United State's first hospice was established in New Haven, Connecticut, and the natural process of dying was returned to a more natural setting.

Hospice has experienced extraordinary growth since then, with more than 3,000 hospices established in the United States alone. While the hospice experience may not be for everyone, many who choose hospice find that participating in the caring for a loved one during the dying process is a rewarding experience never to be forgotten.

In the following article the authors, both hospice nurses, present an overview of the history, development, and design of the typical American hospice. Focus is placed on the interdisciplinary team which is the primary implement for the delivery of hospice care. Common clinical and management issues are discussed as well.

The Roots of Hospice

Even though its roots can be traced to the Middle Ages, the modern hospice program did not take shape until the mid-1960s. At that time the work of two remarkable physicians, Elisabeth Kübler-Ross and Dame Cicely Saunders, converged to bring the emotional and physical needs of the dying to the forefront.

In 1970, Kübler-Ross's landmark book, *On Death and Dying*, revolutionized the psychological approaches to patients with terminal illness. After several years of observation and actual interviews with the dying, Kübler-Ross created a theoretic framework describing the psychological stages of dying and pointed out to health care workers a sobering fact: as dying patients needed *more* attention and support, they were actually receiving *less*. Indeed, Kübler-Ross brought death and dying "out of the closet," making health care providers and society in general more aware that death is a part of life and a legitimate part of clinical care, and that with sensitivity and understanding it can be faced openly and honestly.

In 1967, while Kübler-Ross was working at the University of Chicago Hospital, a British physician, Cicely Saunders, MD, opened the doors of St. Christopher's Hospice in London. Trained as a nurse and social worker, she received her medical degree and set about her life's work to improve the care of the dying—and what better background? Some have called Saunders "a whole hospice team wrapped up in one person"!

Saunders' approach to the dying was first and foremost geared to achieving and maintaining comfort. Her approach to pain management has shaped the development of a pain control philosophy that has become a benchmark of hospice care.

Her model, prescribing an interdisciplinary team, communicating effectively, treating symptoms of terminal disease, including the patient *and* family, has been replicated in concept over 1,400 times in the United States today.

Hospice in the United States

In the early 1970s, as the work of Kübler-Ross and Saunders became known, individuals in the United States became eager to put their concepts into action. The United States programs, however similar in concept to the British world, were very different in design. The first US hospice, Hospice of Connecticut (New Haven) began to deliver care to the dying at home, since funding problems forced delays in the construction of a free-standing facility. After 6 years of delays an inpatient unit was christened in 1980 but its early years as a home care program left an indelible impression on the purposes and practices of the hospice staff and administrators. It provided the country with a new and different model of care for the dying, care focused primarily on patients at home.

As the hospice movement spread across the United States, programs took on various shapes and sizes. In most instances the shape of each hospice was determined by its genesis. For example, if a hospital felt that its commitment included the provision of terminal care, its hospice program would probably be a hospital-based hospice; if a group of active lay volunteers began a program, it might be a consortium model hospice. In all, there are at least six common program designs for hospice.

In an effort to more exactly define this concept, the National Hospice Organization (NHO) and the then Joint Commission of Accreditation of Hospitals (JCAH) developed standards of care to which hospice should adhere. Standards were developed in seven areas: (1) the patient and family as the unit of care, (2) interdisciplinary team services, (3) continuity of care, (4) home care services, (5) symptom control, (6) bereavement, and (7) quality assurance.

Most significant in the creation of uniformity of hospice programming was the addition of hospice to the Federal Medicare Program in 1982. Maintenance of a certification to deliver hospice care calls for rigid adherence to the standards developed. As we look toward the 1990s, many uncertainties still exist, may questions remain unanswered, such as

- What is the best model for delivery of hospice care?
- Will hospice in the United States face a dilemma as larger programs force out small, community programs?
- Will hospice care be assimilated into mainstream health care, or can it only stand alone?
- Will patients be *forced* to participate in hospice?
- What will be the impact of high technology on the dying process?

Criteria for Admission

Probably the most crucial element in the management of a hospice in today's society is the development of the program's admission criteria. Surely the kinds of support the hospice offers might be well received by any patient and family facing a major illness, but just when during that illness does a patient become eligible?

After years of developing a careful decision-making process, the authors' hospice has developed a fairly rigid set of three criteria for admission:

1. completion of all active, curative treatment
2. patient's awareness of diagnosis and prognosis
3. patient and family's clear understanding of the goals of hospice care.

Clearly these criteria bring to mind grey areas for questioning such as, "What if a patient is receiving palliative chemotherapy?" "What if a patient knows the diagnosis but not the prognosis?" "What if the family is divided about how the patient's illness should be treated?" And more recently, "What if the patient wants no life supports, but does want artificial hydration and nutrition?" These so-called grey areas demand that each patient's application for hospice care is reviewed in depth with the most important question: "Are the patient and family choosing supportive care for a terminal disease with the care delivered primarily in the home setting?"

Who Works in a Hospice Program?

In this age of nursing shortages across the country, the opportunity to work in a hospice setting still draws nurses. Why?

Two reasons come to mind. The first is the satisfaction of the work itself. To assist the patient and family during the dying process carries many rewards. Becoming involved after a family has been told "there is nothing more to be done" can restore the family's faith that it will not be abandoned even though curative medical treatment has been exhausted. Helping a family know what to expect, putting effective symptom management skills into practice, and supporting with effective counseling skills makes a hero of many nurses in the eyes of grateful families.

The second draw is the role of the nurse within the hospice team itself. Medical intervention takes a back seat to nursing intervention in terminal care. This fact thrusts the nurse into a primary role for both direct care and the coordination of the care provided by other members of the team. More will be said about that role later in the discussion of the interdisciplinary team.

The Interdisciplinary Team

The essence of hospice care is derived from the multifaceted and comprehensive approach of the hospice interdisciplinary team, whose members look for solutions to a patient's medical, psychosocial, and spiritual problems. The diversity of talent, cultural and ethnic backgrounds, life style, and educational background creates a blend that can sort out various problems to find the approach most suitable for that individual patient and family. A well-coordinated, confident group of hospice professionals can work together with everyone having equal say in most matters only if each team member is comfortable offering information from his or her experience and knowledge as well as listening to and accepting the differing contributions of others.

"Role blurring" (overlapping of duties of various professional disciplines) is acceptable and actually encouraged to some extent within hospice programs. Every team member has an area of expertise accompanied by some primary responsibilities but each also must have some knowledge of other disciplines and be sensitive to problems and needs not directly related to the particular area of expertise. A common example of role blurring is when a hospice nurse spends time with family members advising them on how to approach the children about an impending death. There is no need (and often, no time) to wait until the counselor can be called to talk or meet with the family. A well-trained, experienced, and sensitive hospice nurse can give meaningful and accurate information in this situation. However, the lines must be drawn when the problems require more specific expertise and that team member must defer to another member of the team. Furthermore, sharp distinctions must be made in some areas because of primary responsibility and liabilities (i.e., the patient's physician has the final decision in the ordering of medications, treatments, etc). Hospice personnel need to be cognizant of and comfortable with role blurring and to know their boundaries.

The Composition of the Interdisciplinary Team: The Members' Roles

The composition of the hospice team may vary from program to program depending on the model and whether the program is Medicare certified to provide hospice care. Typical members are discussed below.

Hospice nurse

Often the nucleus of a hospice team, the nurse may find herself or himself in the role of coordinating the care of most patients. Because the majority of hospice patients need some assistance with symptom management along with accompanying problems related to their physical care, the discipline of nursing is drawn on heavily by hospice care. It is the hospice nurse who is available 24 hours a day as needed

by patients and families; it is usually the nurse who has the most day-by-day contact with the families, who visits regularly and calls frequently to give added reassurance and guidance. Regardless of the setting, the nurses are the principal support to patients and their families.

Clinical competence coupled with sensitivity and kindness seem to be key ingredients in the practice of hospice nursing. Hospice nurses generally have a great deal of autonomy on the job which, in itself, means that they must have good decision making skills in addition to better than average communication abilities. The ability to communicate is demonstrated most keenly when a patient and family have chosen an avenue of treatment (or more often, nontreatment) that is contrary to the physician's plan. On the other hand, the hospice nurse may need to help a patient understand why no further treatment is advocated by the patent's physicians; the nurse must then employ gentle methods of reinforcing bad news. By staying open to communication from many directions, the hospice nurse can open up meaningful and useful dialogues not only for that patient and family but also for the community at large.

Hospice aide

Working closely with the hospice nurses, the home health aide is one of the most valuable members of the hospice team. Formally the home health aide's role is to help provide personal care and light housekeeping duties in the home. The home health aide is encouraged to provide the care in the way that is most satisfying to the family—either by working with the family member to help provide the care or by doing the care alone to allow the family a much needed rest. (It is important for some families to feel like they have "done it all" even when it drives them to the point of exhaustion.) By working *with* the family they give the family members some assistance and help lighten the load and still allow them to feel that they really have done it all.

Light housekeeping duties can be of great importance in some households. At times the primary caregiver is somewhat incapacitated or just plain tired. Having someone clean up last night's supper dishes or vacuum the carpets or launder a few loads of clothes can be supportive to a caregiver and an emotional boost as well.

Without question, however, the home health aide plays an important informal role. The aide's visits are generally longer than those of other members of the team (except the volunteer) and are geared to giving the caregiver a break. This may be the time the family relaxes just a bit more than usual and starts talking. Relationships between families and home health aides often become very intimate. Caregivers may derive their greatest support from the chance to talk over coffee with their friend, the home health aide. There is less professional distance obvious in these relationships. And, even though the relationships are encouraged, the aide must attempt to remain objective and not become enmeshed in family problems.

Counselor

The person looking most closely at families and family dynamics is the hospice counselor. The counselor's educational background is generally in the areas of psychology or social work. This specialized training is brought into practice in the usual ways of seeking out community resources, and finding help with financial, legal, and insurance issues. With hospice patients these problems take on exaggerated proportions because so much is happening at once in their lives. Sorting through these issues can bring about some peace of mind for the patient and caregivers but also permits insight into the more critical areas of the family system. Developing a relationship while working on the more tangible problems is a natural link into the more private (and thus guarded) family relationships. The crux of many of the difficulties for hospice families can be found within the family system. The counselor must employ special skills and sensitivity to help the families work through their issues. Most important, the counselor must sort through the details of the particular difficulty and offer options but allow the family to make the actual decision. This is a formidable task at times because many families have great difficulty making decisions or may be asking the counselor to rescue them. Developing skills that help people adapt to the crisis of terminal illness and all of its ramifications requires much emotional fortitude and keen perceptive talents on the part of the counselor.

Therapists

Physical therapists, occupational therapists, and speech therapists contribute in their own way to the enhancement of each day of life for a hospice patient. Physical therapists usually teach families transfer techniques, proper positioning, and maintenance exercises for the patients. Because rehabilitation is generally not feasible for the terminally ill patient, the emphasis is on maintaining strength and mobility as long as possible. In conjunction with this maintenance plan the occupational therapist evaluates the patient and the home setting for ways to continue a semblance of the patient's former activities of daily living. In both cases the emphasis is on maintaining function as long as possible and conserving energy so that remaining energy can be channeled into the patient's most important activities. Speech therapists emphasize communication and swallowing problems, both of which might be seen in the same patient (such as patients with brain tumor or amyotrophic lateral sclerosis [ALS]). Some hospice programs also include music and art therapists as part of the interdisciplinary team. Each of these therapists, using individual expertise, tries to enable patients to maximize their diminishing physical and communication abilities.

Nutritionist

Specializing in the nutritional aspects of terminal illness, the nutritionist counsels families on the special needs of these patients. The nutritionist focuses on understanding the meaning of food in each individual family system. Recognizing different ethnic and cultural views relating to food, the nutritionist attempts to help families look at these nutritional problems from their own perspective.

Families for whom food was the center of life and pleasure need to continue to work on feeding and nourishing their dying family member. For them the emphasis is on getting as much nourishment as possible into every bite while knowing that the patient's food intake will probably continue to decline. At the same time the nutritionist emphasizes that what is most important at this stage of life is to eat and *enjoy*—not just to eat for the sake of eating. Families need to be told that nutritional problems are commonplace and that it is not their failing if the patent continues to lose weight and has a poor appetite. No one says that more convincingly than the hospice nutritionist.

Medical director

A major force within the interdisciplinary team is the medical director. The medical director presents the physician's view within the hospice framework and then represents the hospice approach to the medical community whose members often are struggling with decisions related to terminal illness in other settings such as acute care. The medical director must possess expertise in clinical aspects of symptom management in order to help implement effective palliative care. The medical director plays a variety of parts. On one hand, the medical director may actually manage the care of some hospice patients or act as a consultant to the care in other cases. Acting as a teacher, the medical director works with the rest of the hospice staff and interdisciplinary team to understand the various disease processes and their clinical implications.

It is the hospice medical director who can most fully see the patient in the context of prior medical history and who, because of the physician's knowledge of the natural history of the disease process, will be instrumental in helping the team plan for the patient's medical care in the days ahead. The hospice medical director must display compassion and patience to the other team members while often acting as a stabilizing force within the group framework.

Chaplain

Spiritual care is an integral component of the hospice concept. Clergy serving as hospice chaplains form the most formal aspect of a hospice pastoral care program. All members of a hospice team must be able to attend to the spiritual needs of patients and families as questions and fears arise when death becomes more immanent. But the chaplain is a resource to both the staff, as staff persons address the spiritual concerns of patients and families, and the terminally ill patients and their families who are grappling with those life and death issues.

Chaplains represent faith and a link to God and eternity. They must be careful to help patients explore spiritual dimensions in a broad sense, not within one particular denomination or religious affiliation unless requested by the patient. Many of the patients to which hospice chaplains minister have been alienated from formal religion and now are feeling a need to reestablish themselves with their spiritual roots. Caution and sensitivity, along with a caring and loving nature, enable the chaplain to explore

areas sometimes unreachable by anyone else.

The hospice chaplain represents the religious community within the context of the interdisciplinary team and, in turn, represents the hospice program in the community. Chaplains not only work directly with patients and families but also may participate in staff and volunteer training and continuing education. Hospice chaplains participate regularly in interdisciplinary team meetings where each patient's medical, social, and spiritual picture is reviewed. And the chaplain's involvement continues into the bereavement period when spiritual care may be the most important ingredient in grief support.

Volunteers

Embracing the spirit of hospice care, the volunteers donate their time to hospice programs and the terminally ill patients the programs serve. It is doubtful that any other area of health care involves volunteers to the extent that hospices do. Many hospice programs could not continue to operate without their volunteer constituency and no program could be considered a full-service hospice without a strong volunteer component.

Volunteers are in a position to provide a tremendous contribution to the hospice program and to individual patients and families. Because expectations of the volunteers are naturally high it is vital that they are carefully selected and trained. Hospice programs gear their selection and training programs to their own needs with training usually comprised of 20 to 40 hours of lectures, group discussion, outside reading, and instruction on physical care including hands-on nursing care. Then the volunteers begin assisting the hospice staff, all the while becoming entrenched in the care of terminally ill patients and their families. At the same time it is important for staff to supervise volunteers and provide them with outlets for emotional support.

Every component of a hospice program might include volunteers from inpatient care to home care and bereavement care, but they also help with office duties, speaker's bureau work, and fundraising. Some serve on hospice boards and help formulate and enact policy changes. Each area has its own needs and calls upon many different kinds of talents.

The most common area of hospice volunteering is the home care setting. Volunteers in the home act in the capacity of a friend—one who knows how to care for a sick person. Most commonly the volunteer provides respite for the caregivers by affording them an opportunity to get out of the home during the volunteer's visit. Even if the caregivers do not choose to leave the home, they have a chance to rest or do other chores without having to be concerned with the patient's care. Other home care volunteer duties include light housekeeping, laundry, grocery shopping, meal preparation, errands, even babysitting to give caregivers more time with the patient.

Volunteers give an added dimension to the families and the programs they serve. Their perspective is one of kindness and caring, along with a belief in maintaining human dignity in the dying process. They give much of themselves and reap only the gratification that comes

from helping people in their darkest hour.

The Role of the Family in Hospice Care

In the early days of the hospice programming, many held the view that hospice staff was essential to do *for* the family, to be a substitute for the family in the care of the patient. Hospice, by its very nature, seemed to attract those helpers caught up with the notion of the "rescue fantasy." This, combined with an underestimation of what families are capable of doing, made for much over-functioning and early warning signs of staff burnout.

As staff members learned together about the nature of family systems and how best to be helpful, they realized that the primary role of the hospice nurse was to be an enabler. When staff members share their competence in caring with families, rather than taking over, families are able to feel as if *they* did everything they could until their loved one died. One of the highest compliments to hospice staff is the thank-you note that says, "You gave us what it took to be able to do it ourselves. . . . "

Pain Management

Probably the most valuable contribution to the health care system at large has been the development of the body of knowledge by hospice professionals regarding pain management. Even though only approximately 50% of hospice patients have moderate to severe pain problems, pain is often what patients and families fear most. Some of the most important pain management concepts follow:

- Chronic pain management requires regularly scheduled (not prn) delivery of appropriate analgesia *in advance of* the return of pain.
- Patients do *not* exhibit signs of drug addiction (i.e., drug-seeking behavior, ever-escalating dosages) when placed on appropriate pain management program.
- Various routes of administration (i.e., sublingual, rectal, oral) can be equally effective to the IV route when used in equianalgesic ratios.
- Morphine and its derivatives are by far the most useful drugs in the management of intractable pain.
- Knowledge of combinations of drugs such as narcotics with nonsteroidal anti-inflammatory drugs can be very effective for bone pain.

- Careful assessment of pain and all of its components is essential to developing an effective intervention.

Before dealing with some of the more complex psychological problems such as loss and grief, the hospice nurse must make a thorough evaluation of all symptoms, particularly pain. As Maslow suggested in his theory of human motivation, basic physiologic needs must be addressed and satisfied before higher order needs can be considered.

Questions

1. What are the essential differences between dying only under medical supervision, and dying under hospice care?
2. In your own words, what are the admission criteria for determining whether someone is a viable candidate for hospice?
3. What, according to the article, is the primary role of each member of the hospice care team?

---

3 Michael Christofer, *The Shadow Box*

Michael Cristofer is a Los Angeles playwright, screenwriter, and film director concerned with bringing meaningful issues of life and death to American audiences. His 1977 play, *The Shadow Box,* is one such example of his concern. Playing to enthusiastic audiences the year it debuted on Broadway, the play won Cristofer a Tony Award as well as a Pulitzer Prize. It has since become a staple in the offerings of college theater departments. Christofer went on after this success to write the screenplays for and direct several feature films such as *Original Sin, Gia,* and *The Witches of Eastwick.*

In the scene you are about to read, Brian, who has been diagnosed with a terminal illness, is surprised by the visit of his ex-wife, Beverly. Beverly is a brash character, speaking her mind, especially when she has been drinking (she had just been to a party before this scene). They meet up at Brian's cottage in the woods where he has gone to live out the last of his days with his lover, Mark. Beverly knows Brian is dying, and desires to find out how he is taking it. The answer Brian gives is one of the finest in thanatological literature, describing the sudden mood shifts, the freedom, and the fear that come with one's final days of life.

BEVERLY. Caro! Caro! You old fart! Vieni qua!

BRIAN. (*Delighted.*) Sweet Jesus! Beverly!

BEVERLY. My God, he even remembers my name! What a mind! (*She hugs and kisses him.*)

BRIAN. What a picture!

BEVERLY. (*Taking off her coat to show her dress and jewels.*) All my medals. All of them! I wore as many of them as I could fit.

BRIAN. Fantastic.

BEVERLY. Everything I could carry. I tried to get X-rays done but there wasn't time. Inside and out. I'll strip later and show you all of it.

BRIAN. (*Laughing.*) Good. Good. What a surprise! (*Another embrace.*) I'm so happy you've come. Where's Mark? Have you met him?

BEVERLY. Oh, yes. He's beautiful. A little cool, but I'm sure there's a heart in there somewhere.

BRIAN. Where is he?

BEVERLY. Well . . . he's gone.

BRIAN. What?

BEVERLY. It's my fault. I made a very sloppy entrance. I think he left in lieu of punching me in the mouth.

BRIAN. I don't believe it.

BEVERLY. It's true. But I do like him.

BRIAN. Good. So do I.

BEVERLY. (*insinuating.*) So I gather.

BRIAN. (*Cheerfully.*) Uh-uh. Careful.

BEVERLY. Is he any good?

BRIAN. Beverly!

BEVERLY. Well, what's it like?

BRIAN. "It"?

BEVERLY. Yes. Him, you, it . . . you know I'm a glutton for pornography. Tell me, quick.

BRIAN. (*Laughs.*) Oh, no.

BEVERLY. No?

BRIAN. No. And that's final. I refuse to discuss it.

BEVERLY. Brian, that's not fair. Here I am all damp in my panties and you're changing the subject. Now come on. Tell me all about it.

BRIAN. Absolutely not. I'm much too happy.

BEVERLY. Brian . . . I was married to you. I deserve an explanation. Isn't that what I'm supposed to say?

BRIAN. Yes, but you're too late. No excuses, no explanations. (*Singing.*) He is my sunshine, my only sunshine . . . He's the—pardon the expression—cream in my coffee—the milk in my tea—He will always be my necessity . . .

BEVERLY. Ah, but is he enough?

BRIAN. More than enough.

BEVERLY. Shucks.

BRIAN. (*Laughs.*) Sorry, but it's out of my hands. All of it. Some supreme logic has taken hold of my life. And in the absence of any refutable tomorrow, every insane thing I do today seems to make a great deal of sense.

BEVERLY. What the hell does that mean?

BRIAN. It means there are more important things in this world.

BEVERLY. More important than what?

BRIAN. More important than worrying about who is fucking whom.

BEVERLY. You *are* happy, aren't you?

BRIAN. Ecstatic. I'm even writing again.

BEVERLY. Oh, my God. You couldn't be that happy!

BRIAN. Why not?

BEVERLY. Brian, you're a terrible writer, and you know it.

BRIAN. So?

BEVERLY. Outside of that wonderful book of crossword puzzles, your greatest contribution to the literary world was your retirement.

BRIAN. (*Finishes the sentence with her.*) . . . was my retirement. Yes. Well, the literary world, such as it is, will have to brave the storm. Because I'm back.

BEVERLY. But why?

BRIAN. Pure and unadulterated masochism. No. It's just that when they told me I was on the way out . . . so to speak . . . I realized that there was a lot to do that I hadn't done yet. So I figured I better get off my ass and start working.

BEVERLY. Doing what?

BRIAN. Everything! Everything! Its amazing what you can accomplish. Two rotten novels, twenty-seven boring stories, several volumes of tortured verse—including twelve Italian sonnets and one epic investigation of the Firth of Forth Bridge . . .

BEVERLY. The what?

BRIAN. The bridge. The railroad bridge in Scotland. The one Hitchcock used in "The Thirty-Nine Steps." You remember. We saw the picture on our honeymoon.

BEVERLY. Oh, yes.

BRIAN. And I swore that one day I would do a poem about it. Well, I've done it.

BEVERLY. Thank God.

BRIAN. Yes. Four hundred stanzas—trochaic hexameters with rhymed couplets. (*He demonstrates the rhythm.*) *Da-da-da, Da-da-da, Da-da-da, Da-da-da, Da-da-da, Da-da-da, Da-da-da-Dee*! It's perfectly ghastly. But it's done. I've also completed nearly one hundred

and thirty-six epitaphs, the largest contribution to the Forest Lawn catalogue since Edna St. Vincent Millay, and I've also done four autobiographies.

BEVERLY. Four?!

BRIAN. Yes. Each one under a different name. There's a huge market for dying people right now. My agent assured me.

BEVERLY. I don't believe it.

BRIAN. It's true. And then we thought we'd give them each one of those insipid dirty titles—like 'Sex . . . And the Dying Man'!

BEVERLY. Or 'The Sensuous Corpse.'

BRIAN. Very good.

BEVERLY. (*Affectionately.*) You idiot. What else?

BRIAN. Not too much. For a while they were giving me this drug and my vision was doubled. I couldn't really see to write. So I started to paint.

BEVERLY. Paint?

BRIAN. Pictures. I did fourteen of them. Really extraordinary stuff. I was amazed. I mean, you know I can't draw a straight line. But with my vision all cockeyed—I could do a bowl of fruit that sent people screaming from the room.

BEVERLY. I can believe it. So now you're painting.

BRIAN. No, no. They changed the medication. Now all the fruit just looks like fruit again. But I did learn to drive.

BEVERLY. A car?

BRIAN. Yes.

BEVERLY. Good grief.

BRIAN. Not very well, but with a certain style and sufficient accuracy to keep myself alive—although that is beside the point, isn't it? Let's see, what else?

I've become a master at chess, bridge, poker, and mah-jongg, I finally bought a television set, I sold the house and everything that was in it, closed all bank accounts, got rid of all stocks, bonds, securities, everything.

BEVERLY. What did you do with the money?

BRIAN. I put it in a sock and buried it on Staten Island.

BEVERLY. You did, didn't you?

BRIAN. Almost. I gave back my American Express card, my BankAmericard— severed all my patriotic connections. I even closed my account at Bloomingdale's.

BEVERLY. This is serious.

BRIAN. You're damn right it is. I sleep only three hours a day, I never miss a dawn or a sunset, I say and do everything that comes into my head. I even sent letters to everyone I know and told them exactly what I think of them . . . just so none of the wrong people show up for the funeral. And finally . . . I went to Passaic, New Jersey.

BEVERLY. For God's sake, why?!

BRIAN. Because I had no desire to go there.

BEVERLY. Then why did you go?

BRIAN. Because I wanted to be absolutely *sure* I had no desire to go there.

BEVERLY. And now you know.

BRIAN. Yes. I spent two weeks at a Holiday Inn and had all my meals at Howard Johnson.

BEVERLY. Jesus! You've really gone the limit.

BRIAN. Believe me, Passaic is beyond the limit. Anyway, that's what I've been doing. Every day in every way, I get smaller and smaller. There's practically nothing left of me.

BEVERLY. You're disappearing before my very eyes.

BRIAN. Good. You see, the only way to beat this thing is to leave absolutely nothing behind. I don't want to leave anything unsaid, undone . . . not a word, not even a lonely, obscure, silly, worthless thought. I want it all used up. All of it. That's not too much to ask, is it?

BEVERLY. No.

BRIAN. That's what I thought. Then I can happily leap into my coffin and call it a day. Lie down, close my eyes, shut my mouth and disappear into eternity.

BEVERLY. As easy as that?

BRIAN. Like falling off a log. (BRIAN *laughs.* BEVERLY *laughs. And then the laughter slowly dies.* BEVERLY *goes to him, takes his hands, holds them for a moment, Long Pause.*) It shows. Doesn't it?

BEVERLY. You're shaking.

BRIAN. I can't help it. I'm scared to death.

BEVERLY. It's a lot to deal with.

BRIAN. No. Not really. It's a little thing. I mean, all this . . . this is easy. Pain, discomfort . . . that's all part of living. And I'm just as alive now as I ever was. And I *will* be alive right up to the last moment. *That's* the hard part, that last fraction of a second—when you know that the next fraction of a second— I can't seem to fit that moment into my life . . . You're absolutely alone facing an absolute unknown and there is absolutely nothing you can do about it . . . except give in. (*Pause.*)

BEVERLY. That's how I felt the first time I lost my virginity.

BRIAN. (*Laughs.*) How was it the second time?

BEVERLY. Much easier.

BRIAN. There. You see? The real trouble with dying is you only get to do it once. (BRIAN *drifts into the thoughts.*)

BEVERLY. (*Pulling him back.*) I brought you some champagne.

BRIAN. I'm sorry. I must be the most tedious person alive.

BEVERLY. As a matter of fact, you are. Thank God you won't be around much longer.

BRIAN. (*Looking at the champagne.*) I hope you don't think I'm going to pass away drunk. I intend to be cold sober.

BEVERLY. No. No. I thought we could break it on your ass and shove you off with a great bon voyage, confetti and streamers all over the grave.

BRIAN. (*Laughing.*) Perfect. Perfect. I've missed your foolishness.

BEVERLY. You hated my foolishness.

BRIAN. I never understood it.

BEVERLY. Neither did I. But it was the only way. The only way I knew.

BRIAN. Well, all these roads, they all go to Rome, as they say.

BEVERLY. Yes. But why is it I always seem to end up in Naples?

Questions

1. With reference to Elisabeth Kübler-Ross's five stages of dying, describe the response of Brian to Beverly's questioning about his impending death. Use examples from the text to support your answer.

2. What do you think Brian meant when he said, "Every day in every way I get smaller and smaller"?

3. What is your response to Brian's statement that, "That's the hard part, that last fraction of a second—when you know that the next fraction of a second . . . you're absolutely alone facing an absolute unknown and there is absolutely nothing you can do about it . . . except give in."?

---

4 Charles Meyer, *How to Be With the Dying*

Rev. Charles Meyer is an ordained Episcopal priest and serves concurrently as vice president of operations and director of pastoral care at St. David's Hospital in Austin, Texas. He also sits on the boards of the American Cancer Society and Friends of Hospice. Rev. Meyer has ministered to dying patients as a hospital chaplain and hospice caregiver for over twenty years, and is considered a national authority on end-of-life issues with five books in print on the subject.

Dealing daily with long-term illness and death, Mr. Meyer has a special interest in biomedical ethics. He has written and spoken nationally and internationally (London, Sydney, Rio de Janeiro) on hospital ethics committees, death and dying, grief and intimacy, assisted reproduction, and withdrawal of hydration and nutrition. His book *Surviving Death: A Practical Guide to Caring for the Dying and Bereaved* (1991), from which the following reading is taken, is in its second edition and received the Austin Violet Crown Award for best nonfiction. His newest book on the subject of death is *A Good Death: Challenges, Choices, and Care Options.*

As a member of the Texas Department of Mental Health and Mental Retardation Task Force on Life Sustaining Treatment, Rev. Meyer developed the department's guidelines for withdrawing artificial interventions, and has traveled around Texas assisting hospitals to establish ethics committees. He chaired the Texas Hospital Association Legislative Task Force on AIDS, and serves on several ethics committees in the Austin area.

His book titles indicate why he is known for his ability to combine difficult information with a sense of humor. They include *God's Laughter and Other Heresies; Fast, Funny and Forty;* and *The Gospel According to Bubba. His latest book is Twelve Smooth Stones—A Father Writes to His Daughter about Money, Sex, Spirituality, and Other Things That Really Matter.*

In the following passage from *Surviving Death,* from the chapter entitled, "How to Be With Dying Persons," Rev. Meyer gives us a practical, down-to-earth guide for those who one day will have to relate to a dying loved one—which is to say, all of us. He includes advice on what to say, and what not to say, to the patient. And he also gives a checklist of questions to ask your loved one to make sure they are fully prepared to die. Among those are questions about living wills and durable powers of attorney for healthcare. The first of these is a directive, signed by the patient while in a competent state (usually upon first entering the hospital for treatment), which orders the attending physician not to use any "extraordinary means" to resuscitate the patient should he or she go into cardiac arrest. The idea behind a living will, usually, is that since the patient is suffering from a terminal illness anyway, and since often such illnesses bring with them discomfort both physical and psychological, there is no real sense in prolonging life mechanically, even when it can be done. "Simply let nature take its course" is what the living will guarantees. And the durable power of attorney is the individual appointed by the patient—normally a relative or friend—to make decisions pertaining to healthcare should the patient become mentally incompetent or comatose.

We all are dying. There will come a time when each person reading these pages will not be alive. But there are some people who know they are dying before us. They have been diagnosed with a terminal illness, injured in an accident, or born with a congenital condition that guarantees a short lifespan. It is interesting that we treat these people differently than we treat each other. We treat them as though *they* are dying and *we* are not, as though death is a secret that must be guarded or a taboo that must be avoided at all costs.

Still, a part of us feels obligated to tell the secret and approach the taboo. We want to show our affection without being sad and teary. We want to ask what the person thinks and feels about dying without appearing to be intrusive or impolite.

We want to share our own fears and hopes without sounding morose or unrealistic. We want to be of help but we don't know how.

There is no "right" way to behave toward a dying person. There are, however, some general principles to remember that will enhance your effectiveness and make your time together more meaningful. Because each person is different, the information presented here can offer only general guidelines. Each person can then incorporate the suggestions into his or her own particular style and method of interacting with the dying person.

Contrary to popular literature and belief, there are no "stages" of dying. The Kübler-Ross categories are helpful for observing the different behaviors likely to be seen in people who are dying. But the denial, anger, bargaining, depression, and acceptance are not always in the sequence she describes. For instance, the patient's first reaction might be anger, but it might also be bargaining or acceptance, depending on a whole list of psychological and sociological variables affecting that person. Likewise, it is not unusual for a dying patient to show depression, denial, and acceptance—all in the course of a few days, or even hours.

Thus, to simplify matters, and to avoid the already overused "stages," we will divide the time frame of dealing with a dying person into three parts: *Before, During,* and *After,* and will explore separately what to do—and not do—during each time.

Before. In the time preceding the death of the patient, the most important thing to remember is *be there.*

Be there consistently, as often as the patient wants you there and as frequently as your own time schedule permits. When the person is initially diagnosed, or is initially hospitalized, friends flock around for the first two weeks. They bring flowers, they offer to run errands, they stop by the hospital room with somber expressions on their faces. Wondering what to say, they try to be cheerful, offering assurances that the sick person will be just fine, and avoiding any talk of death. Then they vanish.

Naturally, people do go on with their lives when a friend or family member is initially diagnosed. Babies need to be fed, kids taken to ballet class, spouses looked after, and personal needs met. But, for the patient, a sudden change has occurred that has radically rearranged his or her outlook

on life. Things that were extremely important before hearing the words "incurable," "comfort measures," or "attempt to slow the process down," are now of minor interest. Things that were taken for granted—personal projects, family relationships, friendships—are now of the highest value. The patient's life continues to go on, but with a very different perspective, and she or he may wish to share it with the very people who have suddenly disappeared.

The most common complaints, and the most poignant ones, from terminally ill patients involve isolation.

"The worst thing about this is the loneliness."

"Nobody will talk to me any more. I feel like I've done something wrong."

"Where are my friends? Where did they all go?"

"Why won't anyone listen to me talk about death?"

But being there consistently does not mean devoting every waking minute to the needs of the patient. It means continuing to go on with your own life just as everyone else does. However, unlike most everyone else, it also means continuing to maintain regular contact with the person. Whether the contact is in the form of a personal visit, a periodic phone call or letter or card, or a weekly game time or night out together (depending on the acuity of the illness), what is important is the certainty of a consistent, continuing relationship.

Most people, for whatever reason, will abandon the dying patient at some point. But to continue to stay in touch consistently with that patient reinforces the value of his or her life and indicates that you are not being scared off by the dying process. Maintaining contact on a regular basis will also, over a period of time, build the kind of relationship that will allow the patient to share with you thoughts, feelings, fears, wishes, dreams, and hopes that begin to surface as she or he comes to terms with dying. As that reality sets in, you, based on your regular contact, may be the person the patient feels most comfortable with to share ideas and opinions, or to make final plans.

It is important to remember, however, that you and your family still have obligations and duties to be maintained. You can, without feeling guilty, set limits on your involvement with the dying patient just as you would with anyone else. Everyone has realistic boundaries that preclude being at someone's beck and call every minute. Dying patients (just like the rest of us dying living folks) can understand that and appreciate the honesty. The object is to continue to go on with your life and also to maintain a consistent relationship of care, assistance and support with the patient throughout the entire course of the illness.

As you begin to spend time with the dying patient, from the initial diagnosis through the final breaths, be sure to *listen more than talk*. If you notice during the course of the conversation that all the words are coming from your mouth, something is wrong. Either you're not listening to what the patient is trying to say, you really don't want to hear about the pain and the death, or you're trying to cheer the patient up and avoid "unpleasant" topics, topics like the reality of dying.

It is important to *follow the patient's agenda* as you spend time in that room. Listen carefully for the clues dropped for you to follow: feelings of uncertainty as to the outcome of the illness ("I'm not sure I should bother with further treatment"); fear or apprehension about getting better ("I hope I live to see my hair grow back"); concerns about caring for the family now and later ("I wish I could be home to cook dinner tonight").

Most patients will let you know what they are willing to talk about and what they are not. It is not *required* that dying patients talk about their illness and death. Some will and some won't. What is required is that their friends listen to their agenda and follow it wherever it leads— from weather to whether or not they'll survive, from sports to life supports, from daily news to the latest news of their test results.

If, for whatever reason, dialogue is difficult, look around the room for clues about the person's family or friends or support system:

- Are there photographs? Who are the people? What are the relationships? Are there books lying near the bed? Ask about them.
- Are there religious materials in the room? Inquire about the person's religious background. How does he or she see God in this illness? What religious resources can be brought into the situation? Would the patient appreciate a visit from the clergy, Bible study or prayer group, or a bedside service of prayer, communion, sacrament of the sick, or baptism? Does the

person wish to go to church "one last time?"

- Is the room fairly vacant and bare? What does that mean? Does it mean the patient has no friends, does not want money wasted on flowers, or does not want to be reminded that she or he is ill?

Never say to the patient: "I know how you feel." The truth is, even if you have been through a similar illness or hospitalization, neither you nor anyone else *knows* how the patient feels. Likewise, do not bring in pamphlets or articles describing miracle cures or suggesting how to deal with pain and death. Such information is extremely unhelpful, angering, and depressing for the patient.

Whatever ideas come to mind as you talk with the dying patient/family always *ask* rather than *assume.* Something that might be extremely helpful for you in the situation might not be helpful at all for the patient. Your presumption about the meaning of something the patient has said, an object you see in the room, or about what you think the patient "should" be thinking or doing may be totally inaccurate. Check out any hunches you may have directly with the patient. When in doubt, *ask.*

As you listen to the patient, help him or her to clarify whether it is "death" or "dying" that is most problematic or fearful. Since, at some level of our being, we all know that death is inevitable, most people fear the process of dying much more than death. Concerns range from uncertainty regarding pain control and loss of physical and mental functions to the effect of the patient's disability on family members, both emotionally and financially.

- "Will I die with tubes running in and out of every orifice I've got and some I didn't start out with?"
- "Will I die with loss of bowel and bladder control and be infantilized?"
- "Will I die with brain cancer causing loss of control of my words and making me say things that are terrible to my loved ones?"
- "Will I die in excruciating pain?"
- "Will I die knowing I am dying, yet unable to do anything about it?"
- "Will I die not knowing my loving spouse of many years, but knowing the nurse who has taken care of me only a few days?"

Some patients, however, will be worried about the afterlife and will want to talk with someone about religious beliefs and practices.

- "What will happen to me after I'm dead?"
- "Where will I go?"
- "Will I see my family again? My children? My wife? My parents?"
- "What happens if I don't get into heaven?"

Thus, an extremely helpful resource to the patient and family can be their relationship to a religious congregation or member of the clergy. (This can also be disastrous, as will be discussed later.)

Does the patient have a religious affiliation? Is that group willing to be of help?

In some cases the congregation will supply money to help through difficult times. People from different church groups may volunteer to provide food, transportation, child-sitting service, or help with homework. They may even provide persons to stay a few hours during the day (or overnight) in the hospital room with the patient to give the family members a break from the intensity of the hospitalization and allow them to take care of the normal business details that inevitably pile up when someone is ill.

You will quickly find, however, that most people have no church, synagogue or clergy affiliation whatsoever. A recent Gallup poll found that fewer than 40 percent of Americans had any current such affiliation. In this case, many service organizations (for example, Lions, Kiwanis, Rotary, Eastern Star, Hospital Auxiliary) will provide the same service. Again, ask the patient or family about these suggestions before acting on them. It may be that they want no outside involvement at all. (In each of these situations, it is important to maintain an open attitude of offering real options that people can choose from rather than condescendingly making pointed suggestions. The task is to be sure that the needs and concerns of the patient/family are met, not that the helpers be paternalistically correct.)

Another organization that can be incredibly helpful throughout the course of the illness, the death of the patient, and the following period of bereavement with the family is Hospice. If there is a Hospice of some kind in your vicinity, check with the family or physician (most hospices require a physician's order) to see

about their involvement. Sometimes the Hospice is a building, or a place patients go to die. Often, it is a program, using a variety of community resources to enable the patient to die at home. Usually a trained volunteer is assigned to the patient to be a friendly support, a listener, a companion on the final journey. It is the job of the Hospice team to help patients live those final days as fully as they are able.

Medicare patients now have the option of signing in to the Medicare Hospice program. While normal Medicare reimburses 80 percent of reasonable costs, the Medicare Hospice program reimburses at 100 percent of such costs. But the focus of care becomes *palliative only.* This means that, once the determination is made that the patient is dying, care will be aimed at comfort only, not at aggressive treatment. Usually no more CAT scans or surgery will be done, no more blood or chemotherapy will be given, tubes may be withheld or withdrawn, and antibiotics will probably not be administered in case of infection. And, of course, the patient's "code status" (resuscitative status) will switch to DNR (Do Not Resuscitate).

Many patients and families are likely to choose this option as a reasonable alternative to aggressive, high-tech, high-cost dying. In any case, they will need caring, competent people around to help with these and other decisions.

At an appropriate time it is important to raise the issue of *death planning.* This need not be done with a morose tone or a sense of foreboding. Usually the patient will make a direct or indirect statement concerning "what will happen." At this or any other timely point, you can simply ask matter-of-factly, "Well, have you thought about any funeral plans?" Most patients are not shocked at this inquiry and, in fact, welcome the opportunity to talk about what arrangements they want and do not want.

In addition it is a good idea to check out other related areas:

- Do they have a legal, binding will?
- Do they have a durable power of attorney for healthcare in case they become incapacitated?
- Have they talked with a funeral director (and, even more importantly, with their family) and decided on the arrangements, casket of choice, type of service, hymns, and readings?
- Have they chosen someone to do the service?
- Do they want to be embalmed, viewed, cremated, buried? (All of these?)
- Have they made a decision regarding organ donations? Are they registered with The Living Bank or an Organ Procurement Agency so those wishes will be honored?
- Have they made a decision regarding extraordinary life support? Do they have a Living Will so that decision might be honored?
- Have they filled out a "Death Planning Record" indicating all of these decisions?

Finally, it is much easier for you to ask these questions of others if you have made your own plans for yourself. If you have

not faced these issues, you are probably not going to feel comfortable talking about them with the patient. In fact, you may not even hear the patient raise the issue due to your own hesitation or fear about it. If you really want to be helpful to dying persons, take the time to make your own plans, in writing, and to discuss them with your family. Then, as issues arise, you will be much better able—and willing—to face them with the patient.

During. During the actual time of the patient's dying, the most important thing you can do is, once again, *be there.* Be there as much as the patient and family want you there. A disinterested or less involved third party can often take care of the many small tasks that need to be done, such as making phone calls, canceling or making arrangements, and organizing meals and relatives. You can also provide small comforts to ease the pain of being at the bedside, both for the patient and the family: cold cloths for the forehead of the patient, wet washcloths gently passed over the mouth or tongue to provide moisture to the dry wheezing breath, pillows carefully placed, blankets or bright quilts to maintain warmth, fans to circulate air and ease breathing, favorite music gently playing in the background.

It is hard to overstate the indelible impression made on family members in this trying time. To be there with them, providing comfort for them and their loved one is both a privilege and a gift. Your presence will be remembered always, the small tasks you performed never forgotten. But being there also means knowing what to do while there, even modeling the appropriate behavior so the other persons present will learn from you what to do.

Most people have no idea what to do around dying persons. Although many courses in death and dying deal extensively with psychological reactions, seldom do they give concrete suggestions for being at the bedside. Simply put, the most helpful things to remember are to *touch and talk.*

Tactility (the sense of touch) and hearing are the last two senses to diminish as one dies. In fact, the more the other senses fade due to coma or medication, the more sensitive and acute touch and hearing become. Contrary to the opinion of some physicians and other healthcare practitioners, it is clear that even comatose or highly sedated patients can hear and feel touch. Many times, those persons working daily with dying patients have seen responses to particular voices, individual touches and special persons entering the room. Reactions range from a sense of panic to obvious relaxation, depending on which person arrives.

In addition, the comatose or sedated person loses a sense of body boundaries, forgetting or not being able to tell where the body ends and the bed begins. Thus it is extremely important to keep touching the patient. Stroke, caress, hold, pat, or do whatever feels natural to you. You will not only help establish those body boundaries internally but also will be adding comfort and security to a very uncomfortable and insecure situation.

Talking, at first, may be more difficult. We are used to talking *with* someone, sharing information back and forth, holding a conversation. With a comatose or sedated patient who is dying, this type of interaction is obviously not possible. More desirable in this situation is to give information to the dying patient. Often this will help to orient the patient to time, place, and date. It also helps to relieve some of the fear caused by hearing voices in the room but not knowing whose they are.

Caregivers are often the worst offenders in this area. They turn patients, give baths, take temperatures and blood pressures, change i.v.'s, and give medication (even through i.v. lines) without telling the comatose, dying patient what they are doing. It is important to remember that these patients can hear and feel touch, may experience an internal change due to the drug or bed positioning, and may be quite fearful of that change. Thus, it is extremely important for caregivers, visitors, family, clergy, housekeeping staff, and others to explain to the patient what is being done and by whom. From fluffing a pillow to changing the sheets, dying patients must be treated as though they were fully cognizant of their surroundings on the strong possibility that they very well are.

Let the patient know who is in the room. Encourage visitors to go to the bedside (and not stay plastered against the wall, gawking) and speak to the patient. Do not ask the patient questions since the patient can't respond. Tell him or her who is touching an arm or patting a shoulder. Remind the patient of the time and date. (Dates are often important to a dying patient in terms of birthdays, anniversaries, special times of the year.) Reminisce with dying persons, telling pleasant stories or funny incidents that occurred in their lives. (It really is okay to laugh around a deathbed.) Give information about who might be coming to visit and at what time. If a beloved brother or grandchild is arriving at three in the afternoon, the dying patient may wait to die until after that arrival. If it is a less than beloved family member, the patient may decide to die sooner. Caregivers working with dying patients have witnessed both occurrences.

While in the room do not talk about the patient in the past tense, as though already deceased, or in the third person, as though not present or nonexistent. This can be very upsetting for the patient who can hear but not respond to the conversation. The dying patient may think the visitors believe that he or she is already dead and thus disregarded. Continue, instead, to treat him or her as a whole, complete, sentient person deserving of respect and acknowledgment all the way up to the time of death.

A common occurrence, and one promoted by the daytime T.V. soap operas, is demanding that dying patients do tricks for their family and visitors. The scenario usually involves the tearful son or daughter coming in at the last minute from out of town, frantically rushing up to the bedside of the comatose patient and demanding in loud, sobbing tones: "Momma! If you can *hear* me, *squeeze* my hand!" Or ". . . *blink* an eye!" Or " . . . *wiggle* a toe!" Or " . . . *nod* your head!"

Remember that the patient is using every ounce of energy just to force air in and out of gurgling lungs and so cannot begin to perform these acts to please and reassure the visitor. Imagine yourself in the patient's position: you can hear the request and you very much want somehow to let this loved one know that you do hear, and understand that you are still alive and listening to their words. And yet it is all you can do to breathe or to remember to breathe, to gasp at times for air, to muster your strength to suck in one more shallow breath. You want desperately to "squeeze . . . blink . . . wiggle . . . or nod" and you just *can't* do it. Imagine how frustrating that would be for you and how disappointed you would feel that you had failed your loved one's last request.

Dying patients have enough to worry about and plenty of hard work to do without being asked to perform and respond in their final moments. Give them information, treat them with the dignity they deserve, and comfort them with touch and talk.

Throughout the length of the illness, and especially during the hours or minutes immediately preceding death, arrangements need to be made for the patient and family member, friend, spouse, or significant other to have *time alone*. Friends and family members frequently forget that a couple has spent twenty, thirty, or fifty years together and might like some personal, or even intimate moments to hold, to touch, to say things one last time before they part. The same need is often present for younger patients and their friends, as well as for infants and parents. Be sensitive to this need for time alone and offer to arrange for it.

Depending upon the religious belief system of the patient, *prayer* can be a meaningful way to comfort and support someone during the dying process. If the patient is lucid and responsive, first ask what she or he would like to pray about. Do not assume that you know what's important to the patient at that time.

A woman going in for a Hickman Catheter placement was asked if she wanted to have a prayer. When asked what she wanted to pray about, she replied, "my divorce," a subject she had not mentioned in the entire interview up to that time. Asking patients what they want to pray about is a powerful way to get at the most pressing concerns on their mind at that time.

Next, pay close attention to what is said, as you may be asked to offer it up in prayer. Then ask if the person would like to start or would prefer for you to begin. Gather others in the room around the bedside, touch the patient, tell the patient (if comatose) what you are doing together, and invite his or her participation with you. Keep it relatively short and also invite the persons gathered around the bed to offer their prayers or comments silently or aloud.

Many things may happen at the time of death. Usually the patient will wind down slowly, breathing ever more shallowly until the breath finally ceases. Facial contortions, muscle jerks, and skin color changes are not uncommon. Occasionally the contents of the lungs or stomach may be aspirated or vomited up, and loss of bladder and bowel control will result in urine and feces being excreted. Most of the time the death will be quiet and peaceful, aided and supported by all of the things you and others have done by being present there.

After. Following the death, whether immediately or long term, again the most important thing to remember is *be there.* Be attentive without being obtrusive. Be available to hold the survivors as they express their sorrow in the room. Escort them to a waiting area while the nurses remove tubes and prepare the body to be picked up. Help them make the phone call to the funeral home and to begin to make funeral and other arrangements for the coming few days of organized confusion. Offer to help pack up the room for or with them and help them remember to check the bedside table, closet, window sill, and under the bed for personal belongings.

While waiting for the funeral home, ask if you can help with phone calls or food arrangements, gently reminding survivors that they will need to eat to keep up their own strength in the coming days. Ask what they are tentatively planning to do for the next twenty-four hours. This question begins the process of thinking about the future and moving slowly beyond the painful present.

When the funeral home attendant arrives and people have said their goodbyes, there is frequently a reluctance on the part of the family to leave the hospital. It is very difficult, sad, and lonely to leave carrying the remnants of the illness and of the relationship in plastic bags.

Support the family in whatever makes them feel best. There is no need for them to hurry to leave the hospital. They can leave when they feel comfortable or when they gather the strength to do so. Be sure to escort them from the room to the car. The longest walk in the world is from the empty hospital room where a loved one has died to the car that is now filled only with fading flowers and plastic bags of memories.

Because many survivors become disoriented following a death, it is wise to assess their ability to drive. Offer to call a cab, to drive them home, or to follow them in your car if a family member or friend is not available to do so. Walk the survivor(s) into the empty house for the first time, or arrange for someone to be there when they arrive, to help them deal with the feelings and thoughts that will inevitably surface.

While the information here has focused primarily on hospitalized patients, the same suggestions apply when the patient is dying at home. The involvement of Hospice, the rising cost of (and lower reimbursement for) inpatient care, and the increasing availability of supportive home care services have combined to enable more and more persons to be at home for the final days of their lives.

Patients frequently want to die amidst the familiar surroundings of their own bedroom or den, maintaining closer contact with neighbors and friends, and having favorite pets at their side. Families, fearing they will be unable to adequately care for their loved one, or thinking they will always see the person dead in that room, usually want the patient to die in the emotionally neutral territory of the hospital. Thus, when the decision is made to die at home, both patient and family will need the constant support and encouragement of friends.

When the patient does die in the home, care must be taken to avoid the extremely unpleasant, though frequent, occurrence of having the EMS (Emergency Medical Services) arrive with lights, sirens, police cars, and fire trucks. In addition, EMS personnel will usually feel obligated to attempt to resuscitate the person, even though the person has been dead for some time.

Proper arrangements often can be made by first calling the physician and then notifying the funeral home. Since laws and practices vary widely from state to state, it is important for the family to check with the physician or Hospice program ahead of time to know how to avoid this potentially traumatizing scene for the family at the moment of death.

Whether the death occurs at home or in the hospital, as time goes by remember to *be there* by periodically checking in with the survivor. Friends, neighbors, and other family members will flock around (just as they did during the initial diagnosis) for about two weeks following the funeral. Then, as is to be expected, they leave and go on with their lives. You may be the *only* person who calls one month, three months, six months, or a year later *on the date of the death* to express your concern and to offer to stop by for coffee, take the person to lunch, and be available to listen. You may be the *only* person who is not afraid to call on holidays, birthdays, anniversaries, or other special times to show your support and risk having the person cry with you. You may be the *only* person who checks in periodically and is willing to hear the pain told and relived again and again.

As you maintain contact and continue to hear the survivor's struggle with grief, *do not demand* that the survivor hurry up and "get over it." Many persons, due to their own discomfort with death and sad feelings, will push the survivor to "get on with life" and "stop thinking about the past." They will say and do insensitive things, encouraging the grieving person to get rid of personal mementos of the deceased and to take on new commitments, relationships, and obligations so as to ignore the grief and accept the future.

Once again, you may be the *only* person who is not pushing the survivor to change, to date, to go out with people, to throw out clothes or take down pictures, to move and change jobs. You may be the only person who is willing to listen to the tears and loneliness, and even encourage their expression, two or three years after the event, with the same empathy you offered on the day of the death.

Questions

1. As you were reading Rev. Meyer's practical advice for caregivers at the time of dying and death, what struck you as important to remember?

2. Describe some of the advice Rev. Meyers gives that you think might be hard for you to do if you were actually with a dying loved one. What would hold you back from doing what is suggested in the article?

3. What other practical advice might you want to add to Rev. Meyer's list of suggestions?

---

5 Ira Byock, *Lessons from Michael*

Though Dr. Ira Byock took his original training in family medicine, he currently serves as a palliative care physician working for hospice and has been a long-time public advocate for improving care through the end of life. Dr. Byock is cofounder of Life's End Institute: Missoula Demonstration Project, Inc, a community-based research and quality improvement organization focused on end-of-life experience and care. He was formerly research professor of philosophy and faculty member at the Practical Ethics Center at the University of Montana, currently he is director of palliative medicine at Dartmouth Hitchcock Medical Center and professor of anesthesiology, and community and family medicine at Dartmouth Medical School.

Nationally, Dr. Byock directs the Promoting Excellence in End-of-Life Care national grant and technical assistance program of The Robert Wood Johnson Foundation. Dr. Byock serves on a number of association boards of directors including the National Health Council, and currently serves on public policy committees of the National Hospice and Palliative Care Organization and the National Coalition for Cancer Survivorship. He is a past president of the American Academy of Hospice and Palliative Medicine (1997), and recipient of the Academy's Distinguished Service Award in 2002. He received the National Hospice and Palliative Care Organization prestigious Person of the Year award (1995), and the National Coalition for Cancer Survivorship's Natalie Davis Springarn Writers Award (2000).

Dr. Byock is a skillful debater and has participated in discussions of ethical issues related to end-of-life care on innumerable radio and television broadcasts, including *One on One with John McLaughlin, The Jim Lehrer News Hour, Talk of the Nation,* and National Public Radio's *The Diane Rehm Show.* His appearances on national television and radio include a major role in the

HBO film *Letting Go: A Hospice Journey,* and interviews on *Final Blessings* (NBC), *Nightline* (ABC), *Before I Die: Medical Care and Personal Choices* (PBS), *All Things Considered* (NPR), *Dateline* (NBC), *60 Minutes* (CBS), and *Summit for a Cure* (MSNBC).

There are two mottos that motivate Dr. Byock's work with the dying: "Nobody should have to die in pain," and "Nobody should have to die alone." But there is a third motto that clearly motivates Dr. Byock's work, and which is a theme running throughout his best-selling book, *Dying Well* (1997). Having sat by the bedside of hundreds of dying patients, including that of his own father, having comforted their families and counseled their healthcare practitioners, Dr. Byock has come to the conclusion that, for many, the most important steps we take in life, spiritually and psychologically, very often come when we are at the very end of it. "I have learned from my patients and their families," he writes, "a surprising truth about dying: this stage of life holds remarkable possibilities." His work with the dying has convinced Dr. Byock that in the final moments of life lay tremendous opportunities to gain wisdom and insight, to repair broken relationships, to heal the heart and soul, and sometimes to discover what life is supposed to be all about in the first place.

You will read here of one such story, taken from *Dying Well,* and which featured prominently in HBO's film on dying, *Letting Go.* In this story Dr. Byock describes a patient named Michael, a young boy who at the age of three succumbed to a fatal "mysterious" disease that resembled polio. As the story very poignantly shows, death is not only a great tragedy, it is also a great teacher of life's most difficult-to-learn truths.

Michael began showing the first signs of misfortune at age three. His head was abnormally small, he was having seizures, and he was not developing normal toddler skills. His CT brain scan, which was not quite normal, pointed to a degenerative and potentially progressive central nervous system disease. Suspecting a congenital, genetic condition, Dr. Hardy sent Michael to see Mary Anne Guggenheim. Her initial diagnosis was the poignantly named Fragile X syndrome, and she detailed for Mike, the boy's father, what he could expect to see in his son. Yet from the beginning, Michael did not follow any predictable patterns. Despite the forecast, he slowly learned to walk, speak a few words, and use the toilet. But at around age five he stopped growing, and within two years had regressed into infancy, unable to feed himself or move around without help. For the rest of his life he would be a cheerful, babbling, bedridden baby with the mental age of a ten-month-old.

A single parent, Mike Merseal was raising Michael and his older sister, Krystle, by himself. Their mother had led a troubled life, and she and Mike had separated when the kids were four and five years old, so Mike provided both the mothering and the fathering. Parenting came naturally to him. He instinctively knew when to discipline and when to listen, when to expect childishness and when to demand maturity. Michael and Krystle looked like siblings. Both had dark red hair, freckles across their noses, and fair, pink complexions. Michael's frequent smile radiated from two large buck teeth. Krystle's face usually bore the expression of a sunny nine-year-old, but at other times she exhibited the solemnity and wisdom of a grandmother.

The Merseals lived in a yellow frame house on the north side of Missoula with a dog named Ginger and a large black-and-white cat named Pooh that Krystle adored. Her attic bedroom was plastered with posters of cats and kittens. Before little Michael had become bedridden, Mike and the kids loved to pile into his pickup and drive to Seeley Lake for picnics and fishing. When Michael's seizures, which often involved incontinence followed by long "post-ictal" periods of being dazed and confused, with episodes of gagging, kept them close to home, the family still enjoyed times together. Mike taught Krystle how to cook their favorite desert, Buffalo Chip cookies, made with chocolate chips, marshmallows, and oatmeal. Together Mike and Krystle liked to read Dr. Seuss to Michael and sing to him. Michael loved music, and the household was never quiet. From rock-and-roll oldies to contemporary country tunes, the radio or record player was always going. During the day, a nurse paid for through a state fund cared for Michael while Mike worked as a custodian at the University of Montana. When Mike and Krystle got home in the late afternoon, she helped her dad prepare the liquid supplement for Michael's tube feedings and played with her brother. She rattled his toys, and he gurgled and reflexively grinned, giggled, and chewed on anything within reach.

I met the Merseals when Michael was eight and his health was rapidly deteriorating. He had just been hospitalized because of persistent vomiting, and the doctors at St. Patrick's had recommended surgically inserting a tracheostomy tube into his neck to prevent choking. When Mike refused to approve the surgery,

declaring that his son had already been through too many procedures, the family was referred to hospice. Mike had long known that his son's illness was terminal, and possessed equal measures of fatalism and practicality When he heard from Dr. Guggenheim that Michael had only months to live, he grimly accepted this turn of fate and concentrated on ensuring his son's comfort and contentment, no matter how short-lived they might be.

When hospice became involved, Michael's seizures were occurring back to back, and his vomiting and choking were becoming almost hourly events. His son's suffering tormented Mike. Even moistening Michael's lips and mouth provoked a reflexive gag, and tears welled up in his eyes before he stiffened dramatically and finally went limp. Although little Michael could not speak to express his pain, Mike read the signs in his son's frantic eyes during his seizures and choking and in his listless body afterward. After he was discharged from the hospital, Michael was put on a number of medications to control his seizures, and his father cut back on his tube feedings and fluids in order to diminish the horrible gagging. But neither measure worked. Dr. Hardy had kept in touch with Dr. Guggenheim by phone, and now, in the final phase of his patient's illness, he asked me to help.

When I called to set up an appointment, Mike said that he had been expecting my call and asked me to the house to talk about further reducing or stopping tube feedings and fluids. It was early afternoon; I sat with the family—Mike, his sister, Kathy, and their father, Ted—

around the kitchen table. Krystle was in school. James Taylor was singing on the radio. The kitchen was tucked into an alcove off the living room, where Michael slept on the couch. As we talked, we could hear his rattling breaths. At one point, we had to interrupt our discussion to suction phlegm from Michael's windpipe. I noticed that Mike performed the task adeptly.

Ted Merseal apparently was a recent addition to the household. Before Michael's hospitalization, Mike and his father had not spoken for ten years. When Michael was hospitalized, Kathy had telephoned their father and told him what was happening to his grandson. He had come to the hospital within an hour. Since Michael had been discharged, Ted had shown up at the house daily. Although he looked like a working farmer, always dressed in denim overalls, flannel shirt, and a cap with a feed company logo, he was mostly retired, and he readily volunteered to run errands or sit with Michael. He usually stayed in the kitchen and made sure there was always hot, fresh coffee. Ted and Mike mostly spoke to each other in clipped though not unfriendly tones. They exchanged practical words about things like meals, the day's shopping list, or a new problem with one of the cars. Whatever had caused their estrangement had been buried and replaced by Ted's support of the hard decisions Mike was having to make, and Mike's appreciation of that support and his father's presence.

Mike and Kathy bore little resemblance to one another. Mike was short and stocky, with straight blond hair long enough for a ponytail, and although Kathy was also broad in the shoulders, she was taller, with short, coffee-brown hair. Nevertheless, they interacted like twins, sharing unspoken thoughts and emotions. They often mirrored each other in their reactions to situations or people. Michael's illness had brought them even closer, if that was possible. Kathy had moved in after Michael's first hospitalization, and she and Mike juggled their jobs and caring for Michael in a carefully choreographed duet.

As our visit began, we chatted about who had visited Michael, breaking the ice by gossiping about a new pizza place in town before the conversation shifted to Michael's condition. As we got down to business, the mood was glum. Michael's seizures were not abating despite a barrage of anticonvulsant medications, and his choking was worse despite the reduction of tube feedings. Mike was sleeping only a few hours each night. often getting up to check on Michael's breathing. The worst time was the early morning when he came into the living room. If Michael was feeling well, he was awake and chirpy, but in the past few weeks, Mike had always found him silent and listless.

In the middle of the table, Mike had assembled all of his son's medications. He ticked off the names without mispronouncing a syllable: Reglan, Tegretol, Felbamate, Depakote, plus a multivitamin. "It seems to me that the medications are making him throw up, not the other way around," Mike said. "He had twelve seizures yesterday, and they're getting worse, putting him out longer and longer."

"How much Jevity are you giving him?" I asked about the liquid nutrient he was getting through his tube.

"Only a can a day, and about four hundred cc's of electrolyte solution," Mike responded. As he mashed one cigarette he lit another, and cradled his coffee cup.

"Does propping him up help at all?"

"Not really," he answered, and waited.

"It is hard to say what Michael is able to sense or experience." I began. "Certainly, his seizures trigger a physiological response. His body stiffens, and there are tears in his eyes. But beyond that . . . " My voice trailed off. Everyone was gazing into a coffee mug, heads bowed. "As you know, cutting back further, or stopping his tube feedings and fluids, is an option. I want you to know what all the possibilities are, Mike, and I will tell you everything I know. The decision will remain yours. You're driving the bus here." We had a lot to discuss, but I paused before continuing.

"Clearly, Michael will die of some complication from his neurological deterioration. It may be an infection or the result of a prolonged seizure that causes hypoxia, that is, robs the oxygen from his brain. Cutting back on calories and fluid may be an option worth considering."

"You mean starve him to death?" Kathy whispered, her eyes wide.

I explained that the reality did not match the gruesome image the word *starvation* brings to mind. Kathy, like most people, harbored understandable misconceptions about this way of dying. People imagine that malnutrition and dehydration are painful, horrible ways of dying. But with an advanced illness like cancer,

heart, or lung disease, kidney failure, or AIDS, the reality does not match the awful image. Over the years I have seen that malnourishment and dehydration do not increase a terminally ill person's suffering, and can actually contribute to a comfortable passage from life.

"Kathy, I would never suggest that we refuse Michael his baby bottle or food if he could take it, but now even his bottle causes him to gag uncontrollably. The tube feedings are also causing him to choke, and we've tried all the things that should be making it better. It's unlikely that Michael will feel much discomfort or suffer if you decide to cut back on his feedings further. Hunger disappears after a day or two of withholding calories, and dehydration in someone terminally ill is usually experienced as a dry mouth and throat, which we can easily relieve with tiny sips or a spray of fluid. Although there's no way of knowing exactly what Michael is feeling, my experience with other patients has been that this is a comfortable way to die. Often people even experience mild euphoria, probably because of the change in their chemistry from not taking in calories."

For years hospice people have avoided this subject, fearing that it might be misinterpreted as encouraging suicide. But it is not suicide to refuse an operation when one can no longer swallow, nor is it suicide to decline food when hunger is a distant memory and death is one's immediate future. The social climate is rapidly changing, and one good effect of the assisted suicide movement has been to make discussion of suicidal feelings and not eating more common. The family of a person who can no longer eat normally or communicate his desires often struggles with decisions about life prolonging procedures such as surgery to place a tube for formula feeding. In deciding that a loved one will not be allowed to die of malnourishment, a family is making a tacit decision to let the person die of something else. Thus, the declaration by the daughter of an eighty-seven-year-old comatose patient, "I would never let Mom die of starvation," is a decision that Mom must, therefore, succumb to infection or stroke or seizure or blood clot or gastrointestinal hemorrhage. Each complication that is treated merely shifts the physiology of the person's dying, it does not halt it. A patient who is artificially fed and hydrated may live longer but is more likely to die with episodes of acute pain or breathlessness or, as in Michael's case, from a seizure. For Mike, the issue was not about how, precisely, his son would die but the quality of his life in the final days—that is, how much physical distress he would feel.

"You have done a magnificent job taking care of Michael," I told Mike. "You've given him more love and attention in his few years than most people get in their whole life. And I recognize how tough it must be, trying to take care of him and at the same time making sure Krystle does not feel neglected. But somehow, you've managed. I know of no institution or medical people who could have done it as well as you have. You have earned my lasting respect. Whatever you decide, you should feel confident that you have done everything for this little guy. I don't think there are any wrong decisions to be made here."

Mike's eyes watered. "He's not holding down any of his food. I can tell it's really hurting him when he throws up," he said. As if on cue, Ted rose from the table to check on Michael's breathing while Mike briefly diverted himself by pulling a Mountain Dew from the refrigerator.

"You don't have to decide anything this moment," I said. "This is wrenching stuff, so take as much time as you need. None of us, in the months to come, and especially after Michael has died, wants to look back and wonder whether we did the right thing. Think about it. We don't need to make any changes today. One thing I would like to do right away, Mike, is to begin to back off on his usual seizure medications and start him on a low dose of Versed around the clock."

I explained that Versed was a fast-acting, powerful medication like Valium that would have to be given by subcutaneous or intravenous infusion but would very likely control Michael's seizures. This was another big topic we needed to talk about today, and I was glad that Andi had discussed it with him when they were preparing for Michael's discharge from the hospital. She had introduced Mike to Versed and the other drugs included in the hospice "crisis pack." The medications and syringes, and the idea that he would eventually learn to use them, had intimidated him. "Am I supposed to use these needles?" he had asked her, his mouth open and brow arched. The person she had described then was different from the resolute man sitting across from me now.

"The Versed will give him relief from the seizures. But he'll probably be pretty sedated. We'll start at a fairly low dose and adjust it to keep him from convulsing. You need to know, however, that if a large dose is required, there's always a chance that it could suppress his breathing and he will die. It's not likely, but there's a chance," I said.

"I understand. Andi and I talked about this for a long time. Whatever it takes, we've got to stop his seizures. I'd like a day or two to think about the tube feedings and fluids. Maybe tonight we can put him on Gatorade and water. You know; gradually cut back to see how he does," Mike said. "I've just got a feeling that he might snap out of this. I don't know why, just a feeling."

Mike would not be human or a father if he did not hold a kernel of hope. I knew he was looking for middle ground between this sliver of wishful thinking and the desire to end his son's suffering. And, as happened time and again with this family, little Michael showed the way.

Before I left the Merseals that first day, I told Mike that I would talk with Dr. Hardy and get in touch with Dr. Guggenheim as well for any new thoughts she might have on controlling the seizures, and any other suggestions. In truth, I did not expect to hear anything new, but I wanted to give Mike as much time as he needed to decide which way to go next. As important as Michael's medical care was, my treatments as a doctor—and those of the other hospice people— had become secondary to the family's emotional needs. In this respect, hospice care differs noticeably from the modern medical approach to dying. Typically, as a hospice patient nears death, the medical

details become almost automatic and attention focuses on the personal nature of this final transition, what the patient and family are going through emotionally and spiritually. In the more established system, even as people die, medical procedures remain the first priority.

With hospice they move to the background as the personal comes to the fore.

Andi gave me daily reports about the effects of the Versed; it was slowing the tempo of the seizures. Michael slept most of the time but occasionally shifted to groggy wakefulness. Finally, the gagging stopped. Mike spoke about the various treatment issues with Kathy and Ted, and debated the pros and cons aloud with himself and with the hospice chaplain, Tom King, who had become a trusted friend. A couple of days after our talk, he asked Andi to lower Michael's fluid intake to three cans of Jevity and five ounces of water a day. Three days later, they cut it to one-and-a-half cans, and after another three days Mike decided to stop the nutritional supplement completely.

Less than a week after the decision was made, I was finishing dinner at the Hob Nob Cafe in the old Union Hall downtown when I received a page from the Merseal home. Joy, the hospice nurse on call, needed to speak with me. "Michael's making these strange noises," she reported. "I don't know what I'm listening to. I think you should come over."

"Is he in distress?"

"I don't think so," Joy said.

"Has he been seizing?"

"Mike says Michael hasn't had a seizure in three days."

"I'll be over in a few minutes."

Every light in the Merseal home was on. The family, along with Toy, a friend of Kathy's, were clustered around Michael's couch. He slept here for two reasons, one practical and one symbolic. The couch offered more space for the stuffed animals, pillows, and dog that crowded it, and the living room gave everybody easy access to the medical tubes and machines Michael needed. Symbolically, this was the center of the home and the family, and it had become Michael's place. Installed in the living room, beneath a blue quilt on the wall pinned with pictures of Barney and a rocking horse, he was the first thing people saw when they visited. Here, everyone who entered was reminded that this boy was the polestar of the family.

Mike greeted me at the door; for a few moments I stood there, watching Michael and his sister. Krystle, pigtailed and in her pajamas, was snuggling beside her little brother and making silly noises, mimicking his own. She whistled and popped and screeched to him, and Michael watched, his eyes wide open. I was stunned, he was *watching* her.

Mike gave me a quizzical look, and Joy shook her head in mystification. I knelt beside Michael and tested his eyes. Sure enough, they were tracking, something he hadn't done in months. My mind raced as I listened to his chest and heart. Finally, it struck me; I stood up and declared, "I think he's cooing!"

Krystle was shaking a rattle for Michael; his eyes got wider, and he kept reaching out to grab it. "He wants to chew!" she said excitedly.

I had never seen anything like this before. This little boy was supposed to be in a coma and dying. He had not had any nourishment to speak of for days, only a few ounces of water a day, and was now on no antiseizure medications other than the Versed, which was supposed to sedate him. But "supposed to's" aside, here he was, awake and ready to play.

"He hasn't had a seizure since the day before yesterday," Mike volunteered.

"My best guess is that until we started the Versed the seizures had been coming so frequently that he's been in that post-ictal, sort-of-irritable, 'gorked' state almost continuously for weeks. It was like a hibernation. And now that he seems to have stopped seizing, he's woken up." I shook my head with amazement and grinned at Mike. "The good news is that I think, for the moment at least, your son's doing great! The bad news is, I also think he's rested, and you're going to be up for awhile!" Mike gave me a lopsided smile.

The improvement was dramatic. With Michael temporarily resurrected, we all changed gears. He was offered his baby bottle and drank without any choking or gagging. We steadily increased his fluids and formula. Mike now discovered that his son, like a growing infant who has outgrown the bottle, was hungry for solid food. The family resumed its picnics, now in the backyard, with Michael wearing a brightly colored baseball cap in his wheelchair and Krystle climbing a tree or chasing Pooh. Michael was very thin and his father was anxious for him to regain his strength. He spoon-fed him macaroni salad, ham, cereal, marshmallows—virtually anything in the pantry. The day his son punched him, he was delighted. "He had finished eating, and I asked him how he was doing, and he doubled up his fist and hit me in the mouth! He didn't mean it, but I've never seen him do that before. I grabbed some toilet paper for my bloody mouth, and started laughing, because he was getting his strength back," Mike recalls.

The Merseal household came alive with visitors, people who were eager to see Michael when they heard about his astonishing comeback. Mike was having to juggle all the people who wanted to sit with and care for his son. A nurse's aide who had been assigned to another patient asked if she could come by on weekends. Michael's teenage cousin brought tapes of his favorite music. Preschool teachers from years past visited with coloring books and toys. Even Krystle's friends hung around after school just for the chance to giggle and play with her brother. Soon after Mike rose every morning, someone would appear at the door to see Michael, and the traffic continued through the day and into the evening. Michael's night-owl hours kept the lights on, coffee brewing, and company coming until well after midnight.

Mike felt more than one reason to welcome all the visitors. Michael loved the company—the noise, the voices, the activity—and frequently squealed with delight. A lively house also enabled Mike to avoid stewing about his son. "If there wasn't anybody in the house, I would sit there and think about Michael and what was going to happen. Anybody could walk through my door and I'd be happy to see them. Anybody except Michael and Krystle's mother," he said.

Through July, August, and into September, Michael flourished. He was doing so well that Mike resumed working at the university, from which he had taken unpaid leave months before. I marveled at Michael every time I visited. Except for his size, he was like a happy six-month-old child. He defied medical axioms. Although an MRI showed deterioration of cerebral tissue, with the current dose of Versed, his brain looked relatively calm on an EEG. I told Mike that his son might be on a long-term plateau.

As we both knew, this was not entirely good news. The uncertainty of Michael's present condition and the certainty of his demise in the uncharted future pushed Mike and Krystle into an emotional roller coaster. Mike had no illusions about his son's prognosis. He read a copy of a letter Dr. Guggenheim had written about Michael to his pediatrician and myself so many times that he memorized phrases; especially the last paragraph: "I am sure that we all appreciate how complex this is for Michael's father and other family members when we had anticipated that Michael was in the last few weeks of life. Now, we have to reassess and recognize that part of his terminal state was apparently caused by the anti-epileptic medications and at this point, I cannot accurately judge his actual life expectancy."

Mike reiterated his plan not to do anything dramatic if Michael suddenly became ill again, relinquishing any wistful ideas of a complete reversal and lasting good health. Nevertheless, every time he saw Michael laugh or grab a toy, he hoped it was forever.

Krystle's roller coaster traveled higher peaks and deeper lows. Some days she was inseparable from her little brother. She would curl up beside him on the couch and whisper into his ear or prop him up, and with her arm guiding his, fill in a coloring book, repeatedly removing the crayon from his mouth and chattering sweetly to him. Occasionally he drooled on her, and she nonchalantly wiped it off. Yet on other days she declared that she did not want to play with him or she ignored him. Out of self-protection, part of Krystle was withdrawing from her dying brother.

For me, Michael's fluctuations in health were a repeated lesson in humility and the potential arrogance of supposed knowledge. I could not make any assumptions about how this little boy would fare from day to day, or even week to week. Instead of imposing on the situation what I already knew about his medical condition and prognosis, I had to admit to the myriad unknowns and stay open to the next lesson. I felt like a surfer catching huge waves and trying to stay upright in a rolling sea. With each successive wave, I wondered what Michael would teach me next.

Michael remained stable through the fall, and we began to wonder if we should transfer his care from hospice to the less intensive services of home health. All of us on Michael's hospice team agonized over the thought of withdrawing from this family we had grown to love. But the plateau did not last beyond Thanksgiving. Michael's seizures gradually returned, stealing a couple days of sentient life each time. After the initial shock of a seizure, he became irritable and lethargic

and vomited frequently. His fluttering eyelids would signal a coming seizure, and his father would hold his son and rub his head as his body stiffened and shook like a marionette with a cruel master. "Hang in there, Tiger," he soothed. "We'll get through this one, we've been through worse. Hang in there."

While the electrical storms in Michael's brain grew worse, the love around him grew stronger. People who had known him through the Medicaid office or his preschool formed a constant stream of visitors. Virtual strangers to Mike would drop by the house, introduce themselves and their connection to Michael, and ask if they could sit with him for a few hours. As I witnessed this parade of pilgrims, I marveled at how Michael's dying belied medical wisdom. His chart and medical history—the description of a boy with a hopeless illness whose life was a litany of misery and debilitation—looked like only tragedy. Yet when I removed the medical filters from my eyes, I was struck by how powerfully his life was affecting his family and friends and by the loving relationships he inspired.

Around the middle of December, Mike realized that his son was slipping away for the last time. The light in his eyes dulled. Mike told his son to hang on and make it through Christmas for his sister's sake. Mike took Krystle out of school a week early and they decorated the house with colored lights, red ribbons, and pine boughs.

I stopped by the house to check Michael and take his vital signs. Mike paced and chain-smoked as I sat on the edge of the couch.

"Are you getting out at all?" I asked.

"Not much. It makes me nervous to go anywhere." He lit another Newport and looked straight at me. "In the last twenty-four hours, he's had three of the hard seizures and at least twenty of the fluttering ones, Ira. They *have* to stop, he can't take it anymore. I can't watch it anymore. They're getting worse and longer."

Krystle was puttering around the kitchen as we spoke, and I watched her scoop out a mound of chocolate ice cream for lunch. She fiddled with the radio and found a station playing Christmas carols.

"I understand, Mike. We can increase the Versed infusion further and give a bolus injection each time you see a sequence of the milder seizures that tell us he is beginning to kindle. That way, maybe we can stop the grand mal seizures from happening." I smoothed Michael's brow and saw that someone had pinned a sticker that read "Don't Ever Give Up" on the quilt over the couch.

"You understand that full sedation may be necessary to control the seizures." This step meant crossing another major threshold and giving him intravenous barbiturates, something we have very rarely had to do. But I did not have to tell Mike this. By now, he was achingly familiar with the signs of suffering and the potential consequences of treatment.

"Yup, I know. But they have to stop, even if he's in a coma," he insisted. "The look in his eyes last night, the pain and stuff. He can't take it anymore, even if it again means stopping the feedings and fluid. They're not making him feel any better, and they're just prolonging the agony." I nodded as he traversed this sad, familiar ground. I said that for the moment we would adjust the Versed dose and start liquid Phenobarbital through his peg tube. The front door opened and Ted and Andi came in, having driven up simultaneously. Andi was starting her shift, and Ted carried a bag of groceries. Ted gave a soft hello; Andi sat down beside me. She took Michael's hand, noting his pulse and skin tone.

"You saw we're up to two milligrams an hour?" she asked me, referring to the Versed.

"Yeah. Mike and I are talking about holding off on the tube feedings and cutting back on the fluid."

No one said anything for a few minutes. Krystle came over to the couch and sat on the end. Ginger hopped up beside her. She held a music box that played "When You Wish upon a Star."

Ted was in the kitchen, and I smelled coffee. The house seemed enveloped in a blanket of calm. I packed my medical bag and prepared to leave. I reassured Mike that we were doing everything humanly possible to make his son comfortable. Once again, I said I thought he was acting carefully and out of love in reducing Michael's tube feedings. But I had a further concern.

"Mike, even though I feel you are doing the right thing, and I think I would make the same choices if Michael were my son, I want to present this case to the ethics committee at St. Pat's. Because Michael is a child, and because his treatment plan goes beyond ordinary measures, I want to make absolutely certain we leave no stone unturned. I want to do this in the light of day, so to speak. If someone criticizes your decision, or our care, after Michael passes away, it will be important to all of us to be able to say we asked everyone we could think of for help and made these decisions in the open. OK with you?"

Mike's response was immediate and unequivocal. "Sure, I've got nothing to hide."

As a doctor treating a terminally ill child, I felt it was important that our actions be known and understood within the medical community. Michael's story was receiving some public attention. The *Missoulian* was planning to run a front-page account about him, and a film crew from Maysles Films, a production company for Home Box Office, was capturing his story for a documentary about hospice. The spotlight on a child who was dying and whose family and doctor have decided to cut back on nutrition made all of us sensitive to appearances.

I had already discussed my decision to solicit input from the ethics committee with the hospice team. No one had any doubts about the rightness of Mike's decision, and I took some heat for my insistence that the ethics committee discuss the case. A few members of the team feared that the committee's questions would intrude on this family and might result in a second-guessing of their decision. I held firm. Three or six months after Michael died, I did not want anyone, his family or us, accused of killing him. Any inconvenience or intrusion on the Merseals now would pale in comparison to the sort of inquiry and fuss they might be vulnerable to later. I felt it was

imperative to anticipate, prepare for, and prevent such a possibility. Without violating the bounds of medical confidentiality, we had to make people understand the situation. It was paramount that, if anyone in the medical community—or the community at large—investigated, they understand that we were not euthanizing this little boy but remaining focused on his comfort and the support of his family. At times in hospice care the line between ensuring comfort and hastening death becomes fine; in Michael's case, I felt it was best to walk that line in bright light.

In my letter to the chairman of the ethics committee, I explained: "This case is not controversial in the usual sense. There is no conflict with the family. Indeed, relationships with the family are warm and supportive. However, all involved realize the poignancy of the situation. While this decision seems within the ethical and legal authority of this patient's father to refuse unwanted medical intervention, we are aware that the situation might appear to an outside observer as constituting euthanasia."

I was braced for a lengthy and arduous session with the committee. Instead the meeting lasted just over an hour. The two doctors, the nurse, the social worker, the nonmedical businessperson, the hospital administrator, and the community pastor who comprise the committee had all read my letter and a summary of the medical aspects of the case. They asked pertinent questions and probed to find out whether all available options had been explored. They did not question the family's motive or decision but marveled over the exceptional care of Michael. At the conclusion of the meeting, the committee asked me to communicate to Michael's family and the hospice team its understanding, continued interest, and support.

Less than a week later, the *Missoulian's* front-page story, "Michael's Gift: Dying Child Leaves Family Stronger Still," described what was happening in the Merseal household. It quoted Andi: "Michael has taught a lot of people, hospice workers included, not what dying is but what living means. This is not a sad house. This is a remarkable place." The story had unexpected consequences. Michael's mother, Leslie, read it, called Mike, and asked to see her son.

Four years earlier, Leslie had left behind an angry husband, a frightened daughter, and an uncomprehending son. Even after years of peace without her, Mike's anger still burned, and Krystle was still terrified that she might be forced to live with her mother. Krystle happened to answer the phone when Leslie called, and in a few short minutes, Krystle was terribly upset. Mike refused to let Leslie come to the house.

Michael lived through Christmas, still very much a part of the family, though he was sedated most of the time. Santa Claus gave him a big brown stuffed bear and a Lion King T-shirt, and gave Krystle a new pair of skates, a cookbook for kids, and a stuffed kitten. On Christmas afternoon, a day gray and drizzling outside but lit inside with candles and colored lights, Michael opened his eyes for the last time. Mike was immediately by his side with a cool washcloth for his sweaty brow. His eyes briefly tracked, picking up a Snoopy doll Mike wagged for him.

When Andi and Tom King came by later that afternoon, Mike and Krystle were baking Christmas cookies. But Mike was clearly on edge.

"This is scaring me real bad," he said, after describing Michael's condition. "I don't think he'll last another week. I can't let him go on anymore, he's gone through too much. I've got to let him go. I've been thinking about it for days. This is making me nervous, it's got my whole body shaking. I can't sleep."

Two days later Mike left a note on Leslie's windshield saying that she could visit her son the following evening. When he told Krystle that her mother was coming over, the little girl insisted on going to her grandfather's house. Leslie appeared around eight o'clock—petite, with long brown hair, delicate, fine features, and a doll-like beauty. Mike let her in with a cold hello and retreated into the kitchen area. He had asked Andi, Tom, and Kathy to be there. Mike and his sister stood in the kitchen, leaning against the sink, and mostly avoided looking at Leslie as she sat beside her sedated son and rubbed his back.

"Michael's in a sleep-like state," Andi explained. "He was having terrible seizures, and this was the only way to make him comfortable. But I always act as if it's possible he knows I'm here and can hear me," she suggested. "We keep his mouth moist, so he won't be thirsty." She showed Leslie a sponge swab. "He's also getting a little fluid through the tube."

Crying as she spoke, Leslie remarked on how much Michael had grown and pulled back the blanket to caress his legs and feet. Although Michael had been bedridden for months, his many caregivers had made sure that he had no sores or raw spots. The only physical sign of his failing health was a bluish tinge at the ends of his limbs and other extremities. Leslie noticed that the tips of his ears looked blue, and Andi explained that it was due to lack of oxygen. With tears silently running down her cheeks, Leslie studied Michael's hand, which looked warm, kissed it, and began to wail.

"I wanted to read him a story," she said helplessly. Tom King knelt beside the couch and wordlessly held Leslie's hand. "It'll be OK, I believe that with all my heart," Andi said, and left to get fresh syringes from her car. The house was crammed with people, but the loudest sound was the gurgling of Michael's breathing. When Andi returned, Mike stepped forward to help her. Adept with tubes and needles, he helped her give Michael his nine-o'clock dose of liquid Phenobarbital through the tube. Leslie watched as Mike then gently slipped a soft plastic suction tube into Michael's mouth and throat to clear the collected saliva. As Mike suctioned him, he intoned, "It's OK, Tiger. You'll be OK, Tiger."

When Mike finished, Leslie marveled, as if she had not known what her ex-husband was capable of.

Over the next two hours Mike, Andi, Leslie, and Tom hovered over Michael, tending to his every twitch, his every irregular breath. Concerned about a seizure breaking through the sedation, Andi checked and rechecked the subcutaneous Versed infusion line. Mike changed the Foley catheter bag, even though it contained barely a cup of urine. Together, they cleared his mouth and throat. Throughout it all, Michael's mother grew visibly hollow-eyed and pale.

When they could do no more, Andi said to Mike, "He's not suffering. He's in a different place." "Do you think he's going?" Mike asked. "Yes," Andi replied softly. "I'm not sure tonight, but it feels like it."

The need for suctioning became more frequent, and Mike worked the tube while Andi held Michael's head from behind at a slight tilt. Frightened by the long plastic tube that disappeared into her son's nose, Leslie stood back and watched. But as time went on, she edged closer and closer.

Mike, Andi, and Leslie hovered over the comatose boy. His hands and face were turning grayish blue. Andi softly murmured, "It's all right, sweet boy." Mike sat on the edge of the couch close to his son's head and held his hand. On the other side, Leslie leaned close to her son's face, almost lying down beside him. The room jangled with discordant sounds: light rock on the radio, Michael's talking bear reciting a story, and the slurping and rattling of the suctioning tube.

Through his tears, Mike urged, "Let go, Michael. You're beautiful." Leslie was beyond words: she wrapped her arm around Michael and wailed. The two hospice workers moved closer and enveloped the grieving parents in their arms.

Sensing that Michael's heart had finally stopped, Andi consoled them. "He did more than fight the good fight," she said. Bereft, yet composed, Mike agreed. "Yeah, he needed to rest."

I was not there when Michael died, but I had been visiting almost daily. As Michael was dying, the Merseal household felt like a sacred place, almost a temple, where people selflessly poured their love into a little boy. The family dynamics— Mike's enormous growth as a father, Krystle's uncanny ability to be both child and mature sibling, Ted's and Kathy's coalescing into a tight unit—evolved by the day and changed what some might have considered a dysfunctional, disparate family into a committed whole. This family grew immensely in the face of this seemingly senseless tragedy. Even as a vital part of it was being amputated, long-festering wounds and previously severed relationships were healed, and the family assumed a new and stronger identity. Clearly, this was neither a painless nor perfect process. People and families all have their flaws; certainly the Merseals were no exception. Mike never reconciled with or forgave his ex-wife for leaving. Nevertheless, for the sake of his son, he put aside his burning resentment of her. When Krystle returned home after Michael had died and Leslie had gone, her first thought was that her mother had taken her brother. She was relieved to learn that he had peacefully died. Although Krystle could not forgive or forget that her mother had left them, she recognized this special time in her family's life and suppressed her nine-year-old emotions. Leslie, too, transcended ancient emotions, at least for a few hours. Despite being surrounded by rejection, she did not flee or back away. It was too important to stay with her son.

Many people believe that the dying of someone who is unconscious has little value and that it stresses family members and caregivers far beyond the usual sadness it brings. What is the point, they wonder, of allowing an unconscious, terminally ill patient to linger? The patient is mentally gone, and the family is suffering from emotional and financial demands. Isn't this the kind of situation that cries out for euthanasia? Michael's story certainly attests to the value such a dying can hold for a family. As Mike cared for his comatose son on Christmas Eve, I remember someone saying to him, "You must wish it was over." He replied, "Oh, no, I still have hope, I still have my family." Mike would not have wanted Michael's death to have come any sooner than it was destined to. Up until his final breath, Michael united and fortified the family.

Questions

1. Which person in Michael's story did you most identify with, and why?
2. According to Dr. Byock, what are the differences between hospice care and "the modern medical approach to dying"?
3. What were the advantages of Michael's dying at home as opposed to a hospital?

6 Mitch Albom, *Tuesdays with Morrie*

Maybe it was a grandparent, or a teacher, or a colleague. Someone older, patient and wise, who understood you when you were young and searching, helped you see the world as a more profound place, gave you sound advice to help you make your way through it. For Mitch Albom, that person was Morrie Schwartz, his former college professor and mentor.

When Mitch saw Professor Schwartz being interviewed by Ted Koppel on *Nightline,* he knew he had to make contact. Schwartz was dying of ALS, "Lou Gehrig's disease," and did not have much time left. Albom called up his old professor and made an appointment to see him the next Tuesday. Tuesdays had always been the day the two would meet at college. It was the day Professor Schwartz held office hours, and the day he usually taught his classes. "We are Tuesday people," Schwartz liked to say. Mitch flew from his home in Detroit to be with the ailing Schwartz in Boston. This one-time visit turned into a string of fourteen visits that became the basis of Albom's best-selling book, *Tuesdays with Morrie.* Their rekindled relationship turned into one final "class": lessons in "how to live."

Mitch Albom is a sports columnist for the *Detroit Free Press,* and has been voted America's number one sports columnist ten times by the Associated Press Sports Editors. He hosts a daily radio show in Detroit, is the author of two previous bestsellers, *Bo* and *Fab Five,* and has published four collections of his columns.

The following selection from *Tuesdays with Morrie* is taken from the last chapter, "The Fourteenth Tuesday: We Say Goodbye." After visiting Morrie on thirteen previous occasions, and enjoying both lighthearted and deeply moving conversation, Mitch arrives to find Morrie bedridden and near death. With frank openness Mitch narrates the emotion he felt upon seeing his great friend in this state. What is especially important to note is the way Mitch responds when he sees this drastic change in Morrie's condition.

It was cold and damp as I walked up the steps to Morrie's house. I took in little details, things I hadn't noticed for all the times I'd visited. The cut of the hill. The stone façade of the house. The pachysandra plants, the low shrubs. I walked slowly, taking my time, stepping on dead wet leaves that flattened beneath my feet.

Charlotte had called the day before to tell me Morrie "was not doing well." This was her way of saying the final days had arrived. Morrie had canceled all of his appointments and had been sleeping much of the time, which was unlike him. He never cared for sleeping, not when there were people he could talk with.

"He wants you to come visit," Charlotte said, "but Mitch . . . "

Yes?

"He's very weak."

The porch steps. The glass in the front door. I absorbed these things in a slow, observant manner, as if seeing them for the first time. I felt the tape recorder in the bag on my shoulder, and I unzipped it to make sure I had tapes. I don't know why. I always had tapes.

Connie answered the bell. Normally buoyant, she had a drawn look on her face. Her hello was softly spoken.

"How's he doing?" I said.

"Not so good." She bit her lower lip. "I don't like to think about it. He's such a sweet man, you know?"

I knew.

"This is such a shame."

Charlotte came down the hall and hugged me. She said that Morrie was still sleeping, even though it was 10 a.m. We went into the kitchen. I helped her straighten up, noticing all the bottles of pills, lined up on the table, a small army of brown plastic soldiers with white caps. My old professor was taking morphine now to ease his breathing.

I put the food I had brought with me into the refrigerator—soup, vegetable cakes, tuna salad. I apologized to Charlotte for bringing it. Morrie hadn't chewed food like this in months, we both knew that, but it had become a small tradition. Sometimes, when you're losing someone, you hang on to whatever tradition you can.

I waited in the living room, where Morrie and Ted Koppel had done their first interview. I read the newspaper that was lying on the table. Two Minnesota children had shot each other playing with their fathers' guns. A baby had been found buried in a garbage can in an alley in Los Angeles.

I put down the paper and stared into the empty fireplace. I tapped my shoe lightly on the hardwood floor. Eventually, I heard a door open and close, then Charlotte's footsteps coming toward me.

"All right," she said softly. "He's ready for you."

I rose and turned toward our familiar spot, then saw a strange woman sitting at the end of the hall in a folding chair, her eyes on a book, her legs crossed. This was a hospice nurse, part of the twenty-four watch.

Morrie's study was empty. I was confused. Then I turned back hesitantly to the bedroom, and there he was, lying in bed, under the sheet. I had seen him like this only one other time—when he was getting massaged—and the echo of his aphorism "When you're in bed, you're dead" began anew inside my head.

I entered, pushing a smile onto my face. He wore a yellow pajama-like top, and a blanket covered him from the chest down. The lump of his form was so withered that I almost thought there was something missing. He was as small as a child.

Morrie's mouth was open, and his skin was pale and tight against his cheekbones. When his eyes rolled toward me, he tried to speak, but I heard only a soft grunt.

There he is, I said, mustering all the excitement I could find in my empty till.

He exhaled, shut his eyes, then smiled, the very effort seeming to tire him.

"My . . . dear friend . . . " he finally said.

I am your friend, I said.

"I'm not . . . so good today . . . "

Tomorrow will be better.

He pushed out another breath and forced a nod. He was struggling with something beneath the sheets, and I realized he was trying to move his hands toward the opening.

"Hold . . . " he said.

I pulled the covers down and grasped his fingers. They disappeared inside my own. I leaned in close, a few inches from his face. It was the first time I had seen him unshaven, the small white whiskers looking so out of place, as if someone had shaken salt neatly across his cheeks and chin. How could there be new life in his beard when it was draining everywhere else?

Morrie, I said softly.

"Coach," he corrected.

Coach, I said. I felt a shiver. He spoke in short bursts, inhaling air, exhaling words. His voice was thin and raspy. He smelled of ointment.

"You . . . are a good soul."

A good soul.

"Touched me . . ." he whispered. He moved my hands to his heart. "Here."

It felt as if I had a pit in my throat.

Coach?

"Ahh?"

I don't know how to say good-bye.

He patted my hand weakly, keeping it on his chest.

"This . . . is how we say . . . good-bye . . ."

He breathed softly, in and out, I could feel his ribcage rise and fall. Then he looked right at me.

"Love . . . you," he rasped.

I love you too, Coach.

"Know you do . . . know . . . something else . . ."

What else do you know?

"You . . . always have . . ."

His eyes got small, and then he cried, his face contorting like a baby who hasn't figured how his tear ducts work. I held him close for several minutes. I rubbed his loose skin. I stroked his hair. I put a palm against his face and felt the bones close to the flesh and the tiny wet tears, as if squeezed from a dropper.

When his breathing approached normal again, I cleared my throat and said I knew he was tired, so I would be back next Tuesday, and I expected him to be a little more alert, thank you. He snorted lightly, as close as he could come to a laugh. It was a sad sound just the same.

I picked up the unopened bag with the tape recorder. Why had I even brought this? I knew we would never use it. I leaned in and kissed him closely, my face against his, whiskers on whiskers, skin on skin, holding it there, longer than normal, in case it gave him even a split second of pleasure.

Okay, then? I said, pulling away.

I blinked back the tears, and he smacked his lips together and raised his eyebrows at the sight of my face. I like to think it was a fleeting moment of satisfaction for my dear old professor: he had finally made me cry.

"Okay then," he whispered.

Questions

1. List all the ways in which Mitch responds to Morrie's change of condition. What does he do, say, not do, not say?

2. Of the several ways Mitch responds to Morrie's near-death state, which do you think is the most helpful to Morrie, and why?

3. Describe a time when you were with someone who was in a helpless, sorrowful state such as the one Morrie was in. How did you respond? What did you do or say that was helpful? What might you change about your response if you could be there again?

Small Group Exercises

1. In your small group discuss an experience you have had with someone you knew who was dying, or suffering from serious illness. Apply Kübler-Ross's "five stages" theory to this person. Try to identify what stage or stages the person was in at that time.

2. In your small group, watch the film *Letting Go: A Hospice Journey* (HBO Films, 1996). The film depicts the dying process of three individuals and their families. Identify the different stages of dying you think the individuals and their families are in. Note how these stages change over time as the patients come closer to death. Present your findings to the class, showing clips from the film to illustrate Kübler-Ross's theory.

3. In your small group, write out a short play around the theme of "being with someone who is dying." Use all the members of your group as characters. Include doctors, nurses, chaplains, and family members in the drama. Rehearse the play and then present it to the class.

Practical Learning Component

1. Arrange to make hospital visitations with the chaplain of your local hospital. Ask to be able to visit patients in the cancer (oncology) ward and ICU (Intensive Care Unit) if possible. Simply observe the chaplain at work. After the visitations, spend time with the chaplain discussing how the visits went. Ask questions about this kind of work: what are the difficulties? what are the rewards? etc.

2. Arrange to visit a nursing home that has a hospice unit attached to it. Spend some time with the elderly there who are in hospice care. Pay attention to your own emotions as you visit with these folks in their last days of life.

3. Volunteer some of your time with your local chapter of hospice nurses as they go on their daily rounds. Offer to share a talent you have with the dying patients (singing, playing an instrument, reading poetry, etc.). Perhaps you can offer a foot massage, to play a game of cards, or simply to be there with the patient.

Chapter 5

Suicide

There is but one truly serious philosophical problem,
and that is suicide. Judging whether life is or is not worth
living amounts to answering the fundamental question
of philosophy.

—Albert Camus

Suicide literally means self-killing, the intentional taking of one's own life. Nearly 30,000 people in the United States die by suicide and over half a million people attempt suicide, each year.[25] It is the country's eleventh leading cause of death, and the third leading cause of death among young people. The most frequently used method of suicide is a firearm, which accounts for 62 percent of all suicides. More women than men attempt suicide, but men succeed more often than women. Contrary to popular conception, suicides are not more frequent during holidays. They are highest during the summer months, and are least likely to happen in the month of December. Suicide per capita rates tend to be higher among whites than among blacks, among the young and elderly than the middle-aged, and among homosexuals than heterosexuals. White male college students possess the highest suicide risk of any social demographic.

Although posing a severe psychobiological problem—how can a species hardwired for survival kill itself?—suicidal behavior has been observed among all cultures with varying degrees of acceptance. The Scythians, for example, a nomadic tribe in ancient Persia, welcomed the voluntary immolation of the elderly and infirm as a way of maintaining the mobility of the clan. In ancient Eskimo culture, the aged used to place themselves on blocks of ice and float off into the horizon, equipped with all they needed for life in the next world. In this way they could avoid becoming a burden on the younger members of the tribe. In ancient Greece, supplies of hemlock were kept by local magistrates for the purpose of suicide. All one had to do was to offer proof of the hopelessness of one's life and one would be given the remedy. Accepted forms of such despair included inconsolable grief and terminal illness.

In some Eastern cultures, there are ritualistic forms of suicide deemed acceptable in certain social settings. In India, for example, *suttee* is still occasionally practiced in more rural areas as an appropriate form of grieving. Though outlawed in 1829 by British law, the act of a wife throwing herself on her husband's funeral pyre was viewed as an act of extreme devotion and faithfulness. Failure to do so was looked upon with great social disapproval.

Seppuku, the Japanese formal term for ritual suicide (*Hara-kiri* is the common term), was an integral aspect of feudal Japan (1192–1868). To the samurai warrior, seppuku or "ritual disembowelment" in the face of enemy capture or a failure to obey orders was thought of as a demonstration of one's courage, loyalty, and honor. Although suicide is deplored in Japan today, it does not have the same sinful overtones that are common in the west. Japanese are occasionally known to commit suicide for failed businesses, involvement in love triangles, or even failing school examinations. In such cases death is preferred to dishonor.

In our own culture, suicide is looked upon as an unquestionable taboo. Indeed, it was only in recent decades that a failed attempt at suicide ceased to be prosecuted. This prohibition may be largely attributed to the Judeo-Christian structure of Western culture, within which humans are understood to be the only aspect of creation made in God's "image and likeness." As such they are endowed with the highest value. The destruction of human life in any other way than through natural means is seen, therefore, as the worst of crimes. Moreover, suicide is understood in Christian theology as the ultimate act of despair, and as such it expresses a complete loss of the faith that is the sufficient means of salvation.

THE CAUSES AND PREVENTION OF SUICIDE

Suicide is often characterized as an emotional or even irrational response to a single, traumatic event or set of life circumstances. However, unlike these popular conceptions suicide is a much more involved phenomenon. The factors that contribute to any particular suicide are diverse and complex. Normally, depression, substance abuse, or a history of family violence or abuse are among the contributing factors, but sometimes the reasons someone commits suicide are more subtle and harder to detect. The effort to understand suicide must therefore incorporate many approaches, including psychological, sociological, and neurobiological methods of study.

There are many resources devoted to educating the public on issues related to suicide. One such resource is the group known as SAVE (Suicide Awareness Voices of Education), a consortium of mental health professionals out of Minneapolis committed to teaching others about suicide and suicide prevention. They are especially knowledgeable about the connection between suicide and depression. SAVE makes note of several "myths" surrounding the suicidal person, including:[26]

"People who talk about suicide won't really do it."
Not True. Almost everyone who commits or attempts suicide has given some clue or warning. Do not ignore suicide threats. Statements like "you'll be sorry when I'm dead," "I can't see any way out"—no matter how casually or jokingly said—may indicate serious suicidal feelings.

"Anyone who tries to kill him/herself must be crazy."
Not True. Most suicidal people are not psychotic or insane. They must be upset, grief-stricken, depressed, or despairing, but extreme distress and emotional pain are not necessarily signs of mental illness.

"If a person is determined to kill him/herself, nothing is going to stop him/her."
Not True. Even the most severely depressed person has mixed feelings about death, wavering until the very last moment between wanting to live and wanting to die. Most suicidal people do not want death; they want the pain to stop. The impulse to end it all, however overpowering, does not last forever.

"People who commit suicide are people who were unwilling to seek help."
Not True. Studies of suicide victims have shown that more than half had sought medical help within six months before their deaths.

"Talking about suicide may give someone the idea."
Not True. You don't give a suicidal person morbid ideas by talking about suicide. The opposite is true—bringing up the subject of suicide and discussing it openly is one of the most helpful things you can do.

Death and Dying Facts

Suicide statistics from the Center for Disease Control (CDC), Washington, DC

- *Suicide took the lives of 29,350 Americans in 2000.*
- *In 2000, there were 1.7 times as many suicides as homicides.*
- *In 1999, white males accounted for 72% of all suicides. Together, white males and white females accounted for over 90% of all suicides.*
- *From 1979–1992, suicide rates for Native Americans were 1.5 times the national rates. Males aged 15–24 accounted for 64% of all suicides by Native Americans.*
- *Suicide rates are generally higher in the western states and lower in the eastern and midwestern states.*
- *57% of suicides in 2000 were committed with a firearm.*
- *Suicide rates are highest among Americans aged 65 years and older.*
- *Men accounted for 84% of suicides among persons aged 65 years and older in 2000.*
- *Suicide rates among the elderly are highest for those who are divorced or widowed.*
- *In 1999, more teenagers and young adults died from suicide than from cancer, heart disease, AIDS, birth defects, stroke, and chronic lung disease combined.*
- *The risk for suicide among young people is greatest among young white males; however, from 1980 through 1995, suicide rates increased most rapidly among young black males.*

So what are the warning signs to look out for if you suspect someone is suicidal? Since 90 percent of all suicides are related to the suffering of depression in some way, then signs of severe depression in someone who may have other risk factors should be taken seriously. Signs of depression can include: changes in sleeping patterns, changes in appetite and/or body weight, unusual irritability, withdrawal from normal social activities, inability to make common decisions, unusual forgetfulness, and anxiety disorders. Other signs to watch out for in a potentially suicidal person are:

- verbal clues such as "I can't go on," "Nothing matters anymore," "I want to die"
- an inordinate obsession with death and suicide
- reckless, daredevil behavior
- getting one's affairs in order, giving away prized possessions
- loss of interest in hobbies, favorite sport, school, work
- dramatic changes in appearance (weight, clothes, mannerisms)
- abuse of alcohol and/or drugs
- self-mutilation, self-abuse
- changes in, or struggles with, sexual desires

- spending more and more time alone, rejecting social invitations
- excessive crying, often for no apparent reason
- not coping well after a major loss or setback

Background conditions that act to increase the risk of suicidal thoughts and behavior can include:

- family history of suicide or violence
- sexual or physical abuse
- death of a close friend or family member
- divorce or separation, ending a relationship
- failing academic performance, impending exams, exam results
- job loss, problems at work
- impending legal action
- impending arrest or prison sentence
- recent imprisonment or upcoming release

Suicide prevention strategies usually begin with open confrontation of the suicidal person, as talking about suicide with a suicidal person is one of the best ways of getting the person to change his or her mind about committing it. Suicide prevention professionals recommend addressing the specifics of the act: get the person to admit a date and time of the planned suicide, to specify the method to be used, to indicate whether he or she has access to the required materials (for example, a gun or poison), etc. This helps the caregiver know just how serious the suicidal person is, and how much time might be left in which to try to dissuade the person from attempting the suicide. It also forces the suicidal person to make the act real; to move beyond the stage of daydreaming about it. While this may seem to encourage suicide, in fact it often has the opposite effect. Most people come to realize that it is one thing to talk about suicide as a way of coping with emotional pain, but it is quite a more serious and disagreeable thing to actually take the steps necessary to carrying it out.

The larger part of suicide prevention strategies, however, deal with treating the underlying causes that led the person to this point of despair in the first place. In some instances this involves treating acute mental illness with antipsychotic or antidepressant agents, and/or psychotherapy. In other cases, drug rehab may be called for. But with most suicidal people, these forms of therapy are not welcomed and therefore are not a practical means of prevention. In such cases the best the caregiver can do is to bring a sympathetic, nonjudgmental, listening presence to the person in despair. Lecturing on the moral or religious problems associated with suicide is normally not helpful with someone considering suicide; in fact, it may push the person closer to attempting. One of the struggles suicidal people often have is feeling disconnected from others or feeling unlike others, and a judgmental attitude will only reinforce these feelings. Rather, the best approach is one of calm acceptance; you are taking his or her pleas for help seriously, and you care enough to want to help.

Other steps in suicide prevention involve active intervention. The caregiver is advised to remove from the person's environment any instrument that might be used to commit suicide: guns, pills, knives, razor blades, etc. Professional help should also be sought immediately. The suicidal person may request sworn secrecy as he or she shares feelings of hopelessness and plans for suicide, but it is in his or her best interests if this secrecy is broken, and others are involved.

TYPES OF SUICIDE

One of the issues that arises in the discussion of suicide is defining the concept. Clearly someone in deep psychological distress who puts a loaded gun to his head and pulls the trigger has committed a suicide. But does a man commit suicide who throws himself into an icy river to save a drowning child? When an activist stands in front of a heavily armored tank in protest, is she "suicidal"? If a religious devotee chooses to be burned at the stake rather than reject his beliefs, is he willfully ending his own life? Just what makes suicide a suicide?

For a self-willed death to be considered a genuine suicide, three conditions must be met: the person must be sane, in despair, and must consider death a form of relief from that despair. Clearly the examples of the hero, activist, and saint cited above satisfy none of these conditions. These are examples of what we might call "altruistic suicide." Though not a suicide in the strong sense, an altruistic suicide occurs when someone willingly accepts an otherwise avoidable death in order to bring benefit to others or to uphold a conviction or belief. Examples of altruistic suicide abound on the battlefield, in religious history, and during natural disasters.

A genuine suicide, rather, is an act freely and consciously chosen by those in great psychological and/or physical distress, who understand death to be the only thing that will bring immediate and lasting relief to that distress. The suicide's suffering might come in the form of a terminal illness, a grieved loss or separation, or a profound public humiliation. But whatever its form, the pain is perceived as so great, and so intractable, that death is the only solution.

This form of suicide might be called "reasonable suicide." The sufferer comes to the conclusion that death is the only solution to his or her problems because the dictates of logic demand that it be so. The argument for such a conclusion might run as follows:

- Premise 1: My life is intolerably painful.
- Premise 2: Death puts an end to life.
- Conclusion: Death puts an end to my intolerable pain.

Clearly the tautology of premise 2 cannot be questioned. But premise 1 presents a subjective assessment that requires justification. It may well be reasonable that a person at the end of a long and happy life, now faced with a painful, terminal illness, can choose to hasten death without violating his or her sense of integrity. But the notion of intolerability may be subjectively manipulated by the sufferer in less than rational ways. For example, someone with extreme low self-esteem may find an experience of failure "intolerably painful," when in fact there are many ways of treating failure so that its negative emotional effects are lessened, or even turned into positive effects. Or someone may feel suicidal because life has lost its meaning and as such is "intolerable," when what is needed is not death but a restructuring of life's values and commitments.

This latter group may be engaging in a form of "unreasonable suicide." Suicides that stem from chronic, deep depression can fall into this category. The depression itself, as a disease that affects human judgment, can induce in the sufferer the sensation of hopelessness; that no change in life's circumstances, no therapy or medication, will ever alleviate the pain and suffering of life. While most forms of depression do not impair logical reasoning to the extent that one is tempted to put one's own life in danger, more extreme forms of depression can have this effect. Such suicides are termed "unreasonable" because the depression clouds the person's judgment to such a degree that suicide seems to be to him or her the only option available. Other examples of unreasonable suicide are suicides committed by people suffering from hallucinatory psychosis of some kind, or from severe bipolar disorder.

Finally there is what Edwin Schneidman calls "subintentional suicide." A subintentional suicide is one in which "the person plays some partial, covert, subliminal, or unconscious role in hastening his own demise."[27] Examples of subintentional suicide may include excessive drinking which leads to terminal liver damage, drug overdose, excessive drug abuse which hastens death, chain-smoking, and "daredevil" behavior. While these behaviors are not always compatible with the intention to commit suicide, they do suggest the presence of a "death wish" of some kind.

The readings that follow move beyond the topics just discussed to address the question of the legitimacy of suicide. If life is experienced with such intense suffering that we feel it is no longer worth living, do we then have a right to put an end to that suffering through suicide? If we do have that right, at what point does the quality of life become so poor that we may legitimately exercise it? And if we do not have that right, what are we to do with people whose bodies are not yet ready to die, but for reasons of illness or injury are suffering terribly? In the following passages you will hear from several thinkers on these and other related questions.

1 Tom Beauchamp, *The Problem of Defining Suicide*

Defining the term "suicide" and other terms associated with suicidal behavior is important for a number of reasons:

1. Deaths from suicide raise different legal and moral issues than do deaths from other causes;
2. The identification of statistical trends in suicide and related phenomena is only possible if these events are clearly and consistently defined over time and across national and cultural boundaries;
3. Evaluation, intervention, and prevention strategies depend on clear definitions of suicidal phenomena and a consistent application of these definitions by those who classify deaths and other outcomes.[28]

In the following selection, Professor Tom Beauchamp argues that the term "suicide" is not as straightforward as we might suppose. If we find someone dead at the base of a tall building, for example, it would be reasonable to assume that the death was a result of suicide. But if we later learn that the man had been coerced into jumping by murderous threats against his family, we might want to rethink that label. Moreover, there are certain acts people engage in—like hang-gliding, chain-smoking, and overeating—that may appear to some to be "suicidal." But clearly we cannot classify such acts as suicidal, even if they result in death, as long as the intent to kill oneself is not present.

What Beauchamp outlines, therefore, is a more restricted definition of suicide, one that takes into account the intentionality or willful desire of the victim to die, the noncoerced or active nature of the act, and the "nonfatal" (i.e., nonterminal) condition of the victim. This is to say that, according to Beauchamp, a death can rightfully be called a suicide only when the otherwise healthy victim has, without any outside pressure, willfully arranged the circumstances that brought about his or her death, and has assumed that death would result of those circumstances. Beauchamp also deals with the question of whether a soldier who throws himself on a grenade to save his comrades has committed suicide (Beauchamp claims he has not), or whether a monk who kills himself to protest an inhumane war has committed suicide (Beauchamp claims he has). In the end, Beauchamp is forced to admit that "suicide is an ill-ordered concept."

A death is commonly considered a suicide if it is an intentionally caused self-destruction. However, problems are presented by refusals of treatment with the intent to die, sacrificial deaths, and the like. Many problems about whether a death is a suicide result from incomplete evidence about a person's intentions and the role of those intentions in a circumstance in which the person died. We, therefore, should be prepared to encounter borderline cases of suicide and to find that it is an untidy concept.

Standard Definitions of Suicide

Three general types of definition of suicide have been popular. The first, which might be called the *intentional-death definition*, is straightforward: Suicide occurs if and only if there is an intentional termination of one's life. Case law and several contemporary moral philosophers have used this definition. The second definition, by contrast, does not require a specific intent to terminate life. It has been used by courts in a few isolated legal cases, but its main influence has come from sociologist Emile Durkheim: "The term suicide is applied to all cases of death resulting directly or indirectly from a positive or negative act of the victim himself, which he knows will produce this result." This *foreknowledge definition*—like the first definition—requires foreknowledge of death, but not an intention to produce death. The third definition is still broader and has fittingly been called *the omnibus definition*: "Suicide occurs when an individual engages in a life-style that he knows might kill him (other than living another day)—and it does [kill him]."

The primary problem with both the foreknowledge and the omnibus definitions is that they are too broad, allowing actions to be classified as suicides that should not be so classified. The third is far too broad: Those who frequently engage in waterfall rafting, hang gliding, police bomb-squad work, mountain diving (into oceans), and space explorations of an adventuresome sort—and who die as a result of these activities—are suicides under this definition. Smokers, drug addicts, excessively fast drivers, and those who voluntarily serve in a dangerous division of the armed services and die as a result would similarly be suicides. Moreover, the definition fails to preserve the distinction between accidental death and suicide in cases in which high risks are commonly taken—for example, the risks taken by terrorists in hijacking airplanes, martyrs and ascetics who inflict intense privations on themselves and die, and military commanders who lead life-endangering charges into battle. Accordingly, the omnibus definition seems to require too much of a change in our ordinary notion of suicide, and for insufficient reasons.

Durkheim's foreknowledge definition is also too broad, as can be illustrated by the problem of the soldier who throws himself on a grenade in a sacrificial attempt to save his friends. He knows the act will bring about his death, so under the foreknowledge definition he is a suicide. Even the soldier who jumps from a trench in a hail of gunfire at his lieutenant's command knowing that he will die is a suicide under this definition. Similarly, a woman who resists a man's attempted rape with the knowledge that his threat to kill her will be carried out if she refuses is a suicide on Durkheim's definition, an absurd outcome.

Both the foreknowledge and the omnibus definitions suffer from a common defect: They overlook the difference between a suicide and what is sometimes loosely called suicidal conduct.

A problem with the intentional death and the foreknowledge definitions is that they omit all mention of the precise nature of the motivation, intention, or knowledge involved in a suicide. I agree that suicide must be an *intentional* self-killing, but more needs to be said both about what can or must cause the action and precisely what can or must be intended. Consider a captured soldier who, given the choice by an enemy of being executed or of executing himself, chooses self-execution. Because coercion to death underlies this self-killing, I am reluctant to classify the act as a suicide. The reason we exclude death by coercion from the category of suicide is that a coerced person does not act autonomously. Rather, the will of another deprives the person of autonomy. The act is intended, but not freely intended.

Should Cases of Refusal of Treatment Be Excluded?

Physicians and nurses have long worried that when they stop treatment and a patient dies, they will be accused of killing the patient. There has been a parallel concern that patients who withdraw from or forego treatment are killing themselves and that health professionals are assisting in the suicide. When death occurs by the patient's withdrawing from or withholding treatment, these acts *can* be suicides, because *any* means productive of death can be arranged to the end of killing oneself. This is so even if death is inevitable or the cause of death is natural. Pulling the plug on one's respirator is not relevantly different from plunging a knife into one's heart, if the conditions and the reason for putting an end to life are relevantly similar. Suicidal intent may occur in any circumstance of refusal of treatment.

Three features of such situations need to be distinguished:

1. whether *death is intended* by the agent;
2. whether an *active cause* of death is arranged by the agent;

3. whether a *nonfatal condition* is present (no terminal disease or mortal injury exists).

The closer we are to an unmistakable action that involves an *intentionally self-caused death* using an active means where there is a *nonfatal* condition, the more inclined we are to classify the act as a suicide; but the more these conditions are peeled away, the less inclined we are to classify the acts as suicides. For example, if a nonmortally wounded soldier in pain turns his rifle on himself and intentionally brings about his death, the act is a suicide. But what are we to say about the terminally ill patient who is ambivalent about whether he wishes to die, and refuses yet another blood transfusion knowing that death will ensue?

A passively allowed, natural death is typically excluded from the notion of suicide, but not all such naturally caused deaths can be eliminated from consideration as suicides, because of the agent's intention and causal role. The person might be using a passive means (for example, failing to take requisite drugs) as a socially acceptable and convenient way of ending it all. People who so intend to end their lives cannot be excluded as suicides merely because they select a passive means to this end. Given this mixture of elements, the following is an attractive hypothesis: An act is *not* a suicide if the person who dies suffers from a terminal disease or from a mortal injury that, by refusal of treatment, he or she allows to cause death. If the person intends to die and in refusing treatment arranges this outcome when the condition is treatable, the behavior does amount to suicide.

The precise causal role the agent plays in these cases is important, because it determines whether decisions made by the person who died were the relevant cause of death or whether some other cause was responsible. Suicide requires self-inflicted death, whereas in *pure* treatment-refusal cases death is disease inflicted or injury inflicted. The reason why in some refusal of treatment cases we categorize the death as suicide is that injury or disease is not the real cause, but rather a kind of manufactured cause used as a way to perform suicide. If, for example, a man is seriously burned but could by conventional treatment be restored to health, and if he refuses treatment because he prefers dying to living with such disfigurement, then this is a suicide despite its connection to refusal of treatment. We accept pre-existing conditions such as disease and injury to be the relevant cause of death only if they are *not treatable* or *not controllable* so as to allow the person to go on living.

Clearly intention, not merely causation, plays a major role in our judgment. The more a person lacks a specific intention to cause death, and has only an intention such as relieving suffering, ending agony, or trying to live without dependence on a machine, the less are we inclined to classify the action as suicide. But the more the specific intent to cause death rises to the surface, the more we move in the direction of suicide. Thus far, then, the notion of suicide seems to require the conditions earlier mentioned (intended death and noncoercion), and *in addition* some form of

causal arranging that exceeds mere refusal of treatment.

Should Cases of Self-Sacrifice Be Excluded?

There remains the problem of whether altruistically motivated self-caused death should be excluded as suicide and, if so, which altruistic acts are excluded. Perhaps intentional self-sacrifice is excluded as suicide because the action has, from the suicide's point of view, plausible claim to justification for *other-regarding*, not *self-regarding*, reasons. We may not regard these acts as *actually* justified, but we can frame them as justified from the point of view of the agent. However, we need to be cautious with this claim, because a person with sacrificial intent may also have suicidal intent.

People who act from self-sacrificial motives are suicides if they intentionally arrange the life-threatening conditions that cause their deaths *for the purpose of bringing about death* (whether this purpose be primary or not). Because the monk who kills himself in protesting a war arranges the conditions, precisely for this purpose, he is a suicide, whereas because the soldier falling on the grenade does not hurl his body over the grenade for this purpose (of ending it all), he is *not* a suicide.

A good test case for my analysis is the classic case of Captain Oates, who walked into the Antarctic snow to die because he was suffering from an illness that hindered the progress of a party attempting to make its way out of a severe blizzard. According to the contemporary English philosopher R. F. Holland, Oates was not a suicide because: "in Oates's case I can say, 'No [he didn't kill himself]; the blizzard killed him.' Had Oates taken out a revolver and shot himself I should have agreed he was a suicide." In contrast, I believe that Oates's heroic sacrifice is plausibly a suicide because of the active steps that he took to bring about his death. Although the fierce climatic conditions proximately caused his death, he knowingly and willingly brought about the relevant life-threatening condition causing his death with the intention that he die.

A Final Definition of Suicide

I can now formulate a definition of suicide:

> An act or omission is a suicide if a person intentionally brings about his or her death, unless the death (a) is coerced or (b) is caused by conditions that are not specifically arranged by the agent for the purpose of bringing about the death.

Under this definition, a person must believe the act will result in self-caused death, and the death must occur in accordance with the agent's plan to produce his or her death. It is not suicide if disease or injury has not been arranged to be the cause, or if the person does not believe death will be caused by the action, or if death occurs in a way other than in accordance with the final plan selected by the agent.

My definition has several advantages over competing definitions. First, the definition is consistent with a long legal (and

I think ordinary-language) tradition of determining when persons are or are not suicides by reference to their intentions. Second, the definition does not prejudge the morality of suicide. Unlike categories such as self-murder, this definition is morally neutral, and does not contain as a part of its *meaning* whether suicide is to be morally commended or condemned. Third, the definition takes account of our reluctance to categorize certain forms of coercion and treatment refusal as suicides.

Whatever the advantages of my definition, Manny Velasquez has objected to it, and I need to confront his objections. He writes as follows: "Beauchamp's view that death resulting from coercion is not suicide . . . seems mistaken. A person who is coerced into self-destruction by the threat of blackmail will be said to have committed suicide." This claim may misunderstand blackmail, likely misunderstands coercion, and certainly misunderstands my definition. *Blackmail* occurs only by extortion of money through a threat, not extortion of life, so Velasquez may be working with a faulty counterexample. Nonetheless, suppose there was an attempted blackmail, by, say, a threat of loss of reputation, and the person threatened *chose* self-caused death rather than the payment of money demanded (or after a revelation of corrupt activities). In this circumstance, the act is not a case of coercion to self-caused death and is a suicide on my definition.

Perhaps Velasquez is thinking of a circumstance in which one person coerces another person to suicide by threatening blackmail if he does not commit suicide. If the threat is credible, and such that the threatened person cannot reasonably resist the threat, which is required for coercion, then we do have a bona fide situation involving coercion to self-caused death, and the death is not a suicide. This case seems to me no different than the following: If a man threatens me with unbearable and prolonged torture that will eventuate in my dying unless I take a painless drug that will kill me, I am no more a suicide if I take the pill than if he forces the pill down my throat or if I do nothing and he tortures me to death. Similarly, the woman who kills herself under the credible threat of death to her children unless she kills herself does not commit suicide, in my view, any more than Socrates did. She does not freely aim at death; rather, under menace she takes the only course she has to save her children. In all these cases the person is deprived of autonomy because of the coercion. Velasquez's analysis would force us to the unacceptable conclusion that coerced acts are not merely intentional but also autonomous. Since Velasquez agrees with me that Socrates did not commit suicide, there seems to be an incoherence in his analysis unless he too accepts this conclusion.

It is, however, difficult to capture precisely which intention is required for suicide, and what the right excluding conditions are. Suicide is an ill-ordered concept, and the linguistic intuitions of indigenous users of the language are inadequate to correct it. As we have seen, there are clear cases of suicide, clear cases of what is not suicide, and many cases where native speakers of the language find it difficult to reach a clear judgment. My definition does not eliminate all problems of imprecise boundaries. All one can ask from such an analysis is that most users of the language will find the definition congenial to the mainstream of their linguistic intuitions.

Questions

1. In your own words, describe the three parameters Beauchamp uses to define the concept of "suicide."

2. According to Beauchamp, would a man who throws himself overboard from a lifeboat to allow those remaining in it to survive be committing suicide? Why or why not?

3. What, in your opinion, are the reasons for so carefully defining the concept of suicide?

---

2 Joel Feinberg, *Whose Life Is It Anyway?*

Dr. Joel Feinberg, professor emeritus of philosophy at the University of Arizona, is recognized as a leading political and social theorist. He has published widely on moral issues such as capital punishment, the treatment of the mentally ill, civil disobedience, and environmental ethics. Before joining the University of Arizona, he served on the faculties of Brown, Princeton, and Rockefeller Universities. He was awarded a Fulbright Scholarship in 1987 to work on the issue of suicide in Japan. He was chairman of the National Board of Officers in the American Philosophical Association for three years in the mid-1980s.

In his widely reviewed 1986 book, *Harm to Self,* Professor Feinberg staunchly argues that individuals have full rights over what they do to their bodies. They may ruin their health with drugs, suffer from neglect, or rid themselves of life through suicide, but in the end, these actions are all within their rights as individuals so long as no harm is done to anyone else in the process.

Professor Feinberg argues that personal autonomy over what one does with one's life is intimately connected with the notions of personal integrity, independence, and self-reliance. Drawing a political analogy, Feinberg views individuals as sovereign nations whose "territories" ought not to be invaded. In the following selection from the book, Feinberg presents four antipaternalistic arguments, i.e., arguments that support the human right to self-autonomy. Feinberg uses these arguments to show that intervention to prevent a rational suicide is a denial of independence and a wrongful invasion of one's private rights to control one's own life and destiny. In Feinberg's analysis, respect for autonomy always takes precedence over protecting a person's welfare.

It stands to reason that occasionally a person who has been convicted of serious crimes and sentenced to incarceration for a large part or all of his natural life, who is loathed and mistreated by his guards, and distrusted and abused by his fellow prisoners, might genuinely prefer to die, and would kill himself if only he could find the means to do so cleanly. Can we be certain that a formal death request from such a person must have been coerced, ill-informed, or the product of impairment or distraction? Surely not; but prisons are highly coercive institutions, seething with barely contained violence, and founded on mutual distrust. Penal authorities always have an incentive to get rid of trouble-makers if they can. The suspicion of manipulation or intimidation would always be present, no matter how authentic the request might seem, and furthermore, once euthanasia of prisoners was approved in principle, the incentive for foul play would be all the greater. It is quite understandable why self-destruction in prisons should be prohibited absolutely.

The more likely place to look then for verifiably voluntary death requests from persons who are *not* in severe pain and *not* suffering from terminal illnesses is in the hospitals that sustain quadriplegics and others suffering from permanent and near totally disabling physical "handicaps." The best example for our purposes is a fictitious but highly believable one. On March 12, 1972, Granada TV in Great Britain produced an hour-long drama by Brian Clark called *Whose Life Is It Anyway?* The television play was taped, replayed, and widely distributed. It was adapted for the stage and produced in London in 1978 and in New York a year later. In 1982 it was made into a motion picture and widely seen. The story is about Ken Harrison, a young man of great wit and charm who is a sculptor who loves his work, a creative and sensual man in his late twenties. His spine has been ruptured in an automobile accident, and in the first scene he learns from Dr. Emerson that his paralysis from the neck down is incurable, and that he must remain hospitalized for the rest of his life. He has suspected that fearful fact for most of the six months that have elapsed since the accident. He has deliberated calmly and continuously over that period, and decided finally that he prefers to die now rather than live out his remaining four or five decades in a hospital. Since he is physically incapable of killing himself, and active euthanasia is forbidden by law, the only way he can satisfy his desire is to be released from the hospital and sent home where, without his sustaining treatments, he is sure to die within a week.

Dr. Emerson, speaking for the hospital, will not permit it. It is his duty as a doctor, he says, to preserve life. Besides, Mr. Harrison is suffering from depression and is therefore "incapable of making a rational decision about life and death." Mr. Harrison, unimpressed by this argument, consults his solicitor who then petitions a court on his behalf for a writ of *habeas corpus*, alleging that his client has been deprived of liberty without proper cause. The writ is issued; the hospital accepts the challenge of showing that the detention is proper; and a judicial hearing is hastily arranged to be held in the petitioner's hospital room with a presiding judge, Mr. Harrison and his counsel, a "friendly" outside psychiatrist, Dr. Emerson, *his* counsel, and the hospital staff psychiatrist all in attendance.

The hearing is brief, the testimony terse but trenchant, the relevant philosophical arguments on both sides given their due. Dr. Emerson testifies about Harrison's physical injuries and the projected course of treatment. "It is common in these cases," he adds, "that depression and the tendency to make wrong decisions goes on for months, even years." But under cross-examination he admits that there are no objective tests or measurements that can be used to distinguish between a medical syndrome and a "sane,

even justified, depression," and that he must rely simply on his "thirty years of experience as a physician dealing with both types." Dr. Barr, the consulting psychiatrist selected by Harrison's lawyer, testifies in rebuttal. He does not dispute that Harrison is depressed but judges that his attitude is not simply an expression of clinical depression; rather ". . . he is reacting in a perfectly rational way to a very bad situation." He too concedes that since the patient's physical condition masks the usual symptoms of clinical depression, there is no objective way of telling which sort of depression he has, save "by experience," and "by discovering when I talk to him that he has a remarkably incisive mind and is perfectly capable of understanding his position and of deciding what to do about it." Then comes the question with the dramatically surprising but philosophically stimulating answer: "One last thing, Doctor, do you think Mr. Harrison has made the right decision?" The psychiatrist answers without hesitation: "No, I thought he made the wrong decision."

Harrison himself is not called upon to testify, but he agrees to a brief interrogation by the judge who then concludes that he is satisfied that "Mr. Harrison is a brave and cool man who is in complete control of his mental faculties, and I shall therefore make an order for him to be set free" (p. 144). Harrison's only remaining life prospect now is "to get a room some place" and begin the gradual and inevitably messy dying process. One would think that by this point, when he has won every other victory, a painless lethal injection would be a humane favor, a decent thing to do, but of course that is impossible under the prevailing law. . . . Instead, Dr. Emerson offers the most that his conscience and the criminal law will permit, a room in the hospital with cessation of treatment and even feeding stopped if the patient wishes—a kind of supervised passive euthanasia. "You'll be unconscious in three days, dead in six at most" (p. 146). Dr. Emerson wants to be as kind as he can, but he also wants witnesses at hand in case the patient undergoes a last minute change of mind. And so the story ends with mutual respect between the antagonists, and British decency all around, but no ground given in the moral and philosophical debate.

This fictional tale serves as a much better test for the soft paternalist's position and its attendant theory of personal autonomy than do the more common cases of aged patients with painful terminal diseases, because it isolates the factor of voluntary choice and focuses our attention on it. . . . Its moral (if one can be attributed to it) is that respect for personal autonomy alone justifies our noninterference with a competent person's primarily self-regarding choice of death, quite independently of further humanitarian considerations. Mr. Harrison is not a terminal patient. He can expect to live on for another forty years or more if he stays in a hospital. (He becomes "terminal" only after the judge's release order). No rule is applied which limits the recognition of voluntariness to choices of death by persons whose whole reason is the desire to escape pain and who will die soon in any case. Whatever Mr. Harrison's reasons are, they are good enough, provided only they are *his* reasons. The soft paternalist,

if he can be convinced that the choice is voluntary enough by reasonable tests, is firmly committed to a policy of noninterference with its implementation, for the life at stake is Mr. Harrison's life not ours. The person in sovereign control over it is precisely he.

In his final exchange with the judge, Harrison cites as the chief reason for his choice (and of course in his view the ground of its reasonableness or correctness) his desire for *dignity.* He is eloquent about the indignity of being forced to live in total dependence on others for even the basic primitive functions. In response to the judge, he then concedes that "many people with appalling physical handicaps have overcome them and lived essentially creative, dignified lives" (p. 142), but the point, he insists, is that "the dignity begins with their choice." It would be an indignity to force the others to die against their will, but an equal indignity to force him to remain alive, as a kind of "medical achievement," against his will. Human dignity is not possible without the acknowledgement of personal sovereignty. . . .

Mr. Harrison's reply (as he puts it later in the play) to the physician's diagnosis of "acute depression" is to concede the point, and then add "Is that surprising? I am almost totally paralyzed. I'd be insane if I weren't depressed" (p. 138). Some depression then is *understandable,* even proper, rational, and justifiable, a state of mind any normal person would experience if he were to suffer certain losses. "Depression" is also the name of a clinical syndrome marked by "affective disorders," involving "an accentuation in the intensity or duration of otherwise normal emotions." Psychologists have not agreed on any simple criterion for distinguishing accentuated affective states that are "clinical" from those that are less extreme or less debilitating conditions, but they often speak of a plurality of symptoms, at least some of which are present in clinical depression, in addition to the depressed or "disphoric" mood (sadness, gloominess) that is common to both the clinical and nonclinical species. . . .

Mistaken inferences from depression to some specific incompetence are often profoundly unfair to the depressed person. Characteristically they deprive him, a priori as it were, of any opportunity to make a case for himself. Argumentatively, he is trapped in a destructive dilemma that defeats him from the start, leaving him no conceivable ground on which to stand. Mr. Harrison, at one point in the play (p. 97), complains that one of the justifications for refusing his request to die is a version of Catch-22. The term "Catch-22" comes from Joseph Heller's 1961 anti-military novel of that name, in which it is used characteristically for a certain kind of military rule that places a petitioning soldier in an inescapable dilemma, in effect barring approval of his petition a priori in language that falsely suggest that there are conditions under which the request could be granted, when in fact those "conditions" are contradictory. . . .

Actually, there are as many as four Catch-22 arguments in *Whose Life Is It Anyway?* that beg the question against Mr. Harrison and make it *a priori* impossible for him to prove the voluntariness of his request. Consider Catch-22, number 1. This version focuses on suicide, a passive version of which is essentially that

for which Harrison requests permission. Dr. Emerson and the friendly psychiatrist agree that the crucial question is whether or not Harrison's acknowledged clinical depression is the sort that impairs judgment. Dr. Emerson finds the answer self-evident. "You haven't understood," he says to Dr. Travers with ill-concealed impatience. "He's *suicidal.* He's determined to kill himself." The assumption apparently is that if a depressed person requests to die that *proves* that his depression impairs judgment, and his request therefore is insufficiently voluntary to be granted. This argument suggests that only persons who are happy are capable of voluntarily choosing suicide, and of course they are precisely the ones who won't apply. Thus if you are unhappy you *cannot* voluntarily choose suicide, and if you are happy you *will not* commit suicide. The conclusion: no suicide. Yet the context of discussion presupposes that the issue is initially an open question to be settled by discussion and evidence. Catch-22 rules out all evidence *a priori.* The assumption that no choice of suicide can be voluntary is the very question at issue in the case at hand, not one presumed to be settled in advance.

The second Catch-22 argument follows closely on the first, and is also concerned with the voluntariness of death requests. Another party takes up the argument against Dr. Emerson, one of his subordinate physicians, Dr. Scott, who reminds him that "It's *his* [Harrison's] life." Emerson replies "But my responsibility." "Only if he is incapable of making his own decision," rejoins Dr. Scott. "But he isn't capable," insists Emerson––"I refuse to believe that a man with a mind as quick as his, a man with enormous mental resources, would calmly choose suicide." Scott replies: "But he has done just that." "And therefore," interjects Emerson, "I say he is unbalanced" (pp. 91–92). Again the case is begged against the petitioner. His request cannot possibly be voluntary, not because it fails to satisfy independent formal tests of voluntariness, but entirely because of what it is a request *for*. . . .

Catch-22 number 3 is a closely related corollary of the preceding. The hospital staff psychiatrist, Dr. Travers, warns Harrison: "But your obvious intelligence weakens your case. I'm not saying that you would find life easy, but you do have resources that an unintelligent person doesn't have." This is the observation that prompts Harrison's remark about Catch-22: "If you're clever and sane enough to put up an invincible case for suicide, it demonstrates that you ought not to die" (p. 97). The characterization of this requirement as "Catch-22" is perfectly apt. The authorities meet to hear the petitioner's case. They invite him to present his arguments for their granting his request. It is understood that if his arguments are weak, they will turn him down. Better then that the arguments should be cogent, except for Catch-22, which declares that if the arguments are convincing then the request cannot be granted, for in that case the petitioner's obvious intellectual resources undermine the case for his death. However he argues, he cannot win. Why then have the hearing at all?

The final Catch-22 argument is put forward half-heartedly by the sympathetic Dr. Scott, when she senses Harrison's excitement at the approach of his life-or-death judicial hearing, and his zest for the debate. "I think you are enjoying all this," she says. "I suppose I am in a way," he replies, "for the first time in six months I feel like a human being again" (p. 108). This exchange underlines the paradox: Harrison is never so alive as when he is staging and winning his fight for death. But to make too much of the point is once again to put the petitioner in the position of Catch-22. If he enjoys getting what he wants (permission to die), then he is not depressed and has less reason to die, but if he is not pleased at his victory then he must not really have wanted to die after all, and that casts doubt on the authenticity of his prior desire. . . .

Before leaving *Whose Life Is It Anyway?*, we should pay some heed to Dr. Barr's surprising admission that Harrison's decision to die, while carefully reasoned and voluntary, is nevertheless in his opinion the wrong decision. He might very well have put the point by saying that the decision is unreasonable (not one Dr. Barr would have made in the circumstances) but not irrational, and hence not involuntary. Why should a person be permitted to implement a "wrong" or "unreasonable" decision to die? The only answer possible is simply that it is *his* decision and *his* life, and that the choice falls within the domain of his morally inviolate personal sovereignty. But why does Dr. Barr think that the decision was the wrong one to make? In the play, the question is left for our conjecture, but we may surmise that Dr. Barr's reason is his anticipation that in the course of time, if only Harrison would wait more patiently, his mind would change, and he would be happy that he had not chosen death earlier. Harrison himself admits that possibility in an earlier discussion with the sympathetic Dr. Scott (pp. 68–69):

H: I grant you, I may become lethargic and quiescent. Happy when a nurse comes to put in a new catheter, or give me an enema, or to turn me over. These could become the high spots of my day. I might even learn to do wonderful things like turn the pages of a book with some miracle of modern science, or to type letters with flicking my eyelids. And you would look at me and say: "Wasn't it worth waiting?" and I would say: "Yes," and be proud of my achievements. Really proud. I grant you all that, but it doesn't alter the validity of my present position.

S: But if you became happy?

H: But I don't want to become happy by becoming the computer section of a complex machine. And morally you must accept my decision.

Exactly so. . . . In order to become reconciled at a later date to his condition (a sculptor without the use of his hands; a sensualist without the use of his genitalia; a living tribute to the ingenuity of modern technology), he will have to become a very different person with very different values, and the person he is now, applying the values that he has now, prefers not to become the repugnant future person. The future self does not yet exist; the sovereign chooser is the clearheaded and determined present self. Whatever the hypothetical future self would say, it is only the actual present self who has the right to decide. The choice is squarely within the temporal boundaries of his sovereign domain.

Questions

1. Describe Mr. Harrison's predicament in the play, *Whose Life Is It Anyway?*, and his reasons for wanting to die. Do you agree or disagree with his arguments, and why?

2. Put into your own words what is at issue in the four "Catch-22" arguments Feinberg uses to support his antipaternalist position of self-autonomy.

3. Do you agree with Feinberg's position on personal autonomy? Why or why not?

---

3 Arthur Schopenhauer, *On Suicide*

Arthur Schopenhauer was born in Danzig, Germany, in 1788, where his family owned a large trading business. It was expected that the young Schopenhauer would inherit the family business after his university studies, and accordingly he trained as an apprentice in one of the family's offices. But after his father committed suicide, Schopenhauer quit the business and entered Göttingen University to study science. The following year, he took up philosophy. In 1811, he went to Berlin for doctoral studies, and after their completion he began work on his *magnum opus, The World as Will and Idea.* Schopenhauer had hoped this work would bring him international fame as a philosopher, but throughout his lifetime it went largely unread.

Living mostly on inherited money, Schopenhauer took up part-time university lectureships following graduation, but was overshadowed by the great German philosopher of his day, Hegel. Most of his time, therefore, was devoted to reading, writing, mastering languages (he was fluent in seven!), traveling, and entertaining friends. The fame which Schopenhauer so earnestly sought was finally granted him upon the publication of his *Parerga and Paralipomena,* a collection of essays, dialogues, and aphorisms from which the following selection is taken.

Schopenhauer is considered one of the great masters of "spiritual philosophy," that form of philosophical thinking that combines the great teachings of Western philosophers with the insights and wisdom of Eastern religious writers. In the passage you are about to read, the philosopher argues that suicide is not necessarily a crime. He calls it a "mistake," and certainly a grave one, for it goes against the most solid moral principle known to humanity: the will to live. But Schopenhauer suggests that the religious and civil authorities are wrong to brand it a sin or crime. He also readily admits that if killing oneself were not so painful, many more might try it, for life as it is ordinarily lived is often unbearable to the point of wanting death more than anything else.

As far as I can see, it is only the monotheistic, that is to say Jewish, religions whose members regard self-destruction as a crime. This is all the more striking in that neither in the Old nor in the New Testament is there to be found any prohibition or even definite disapproval of it; so that religious teachers have to base their proscription of suicide on philosophical grounds of their own invention, which are however so poor that what their arguments lack in strength they have to try to make up for by the strength of the terms in which they express their abhorrence; that is to say, they resort to abuse. Thus we hear that suicide is the most cowardly of acts, that only a madman would commit it, and similar insipidities; or the senseless assertion that suicide is "wrong," though it is obvious there is nothing in the world a man has a more incontestable *right* to than his own life and person. Let us for once allow moral feelings to decide this question, and compare the impression made on us by the news that an acquaintance of ours has committed a *crime,* for instance a murder, an act of cruelty, a betrayal, a theft, with that produced by the news that he has voluntarily ended his life. While the former will evoke a lively indignation, anger, the demand for punishment or revenge, the latter will excite pity and sorrow, which are more likely to be accompanied by admiration for his courage than by moral disapproval. Who has not had acquaintances, friends, relatives who have departed this world voluntarily?—and is one supposed to think of them with repugnance, as if they were criminals? In my opinion it ought rather to be demanded of the clergy that they tell us by what authority they go to their pulpits or their desks and preach as a crime an action which many people we honour and love have performed and deny an honourable burial to those who have departed this world voluntarily—since they cannot point to a single biblical authority, nor produce a single sound philosophical argument; it being made clear that what one wants are *reasons* and not empty phrases or abuse. If the criminal law proscribes suicide this is no valid reason for the Church to do so, and is moreover a decidedly ludicrous proceeding, for what punishment can deter him who is looking for death? If one punishes attempted suicide, it is the ineptitude of the attempt one punishes.

The only cogent moral argument against suicide is that it is opposed to the achievement of the highest moral goal, inasmuch as it substitutes for a true redemption from this world of misery a merely apparent one. But it is a very long way from a mistake of this kind to a crime, which is what the Christian clergy want to call it.

Christianity carries in its innermost heart the truth that suffering (the Cross) is the true aim of life: that is why it repudiates suicide, which is opposed to this aim, while antiquity from a lower viewpoint approved of and indeed honoured it. This argument against suicide is however an ascetic one, and is therefore valid only from a far higher ethical standpoint than any which European moral philosophers have ever assumed. If we descend from this very high standpoint there no longer remains any tenable moral reason for damning suicide. It therefore seems that the extraordinary zeal in opposing it displayed by the clergy of monotheistic religions—a zeal which is not supported by the Bible or by any cogent reasons—must have some hidden reason behind it: may this not be that the voluntary surrender of life is an ill compliment to him who said that all things were very good? If so, it is another instance of the obligatory optimism of these religions, which denounces self-destruction so as not to be denounced by it.

Questions

1. Schopenhauer suggests that we think of a person who "voluntarily" ends his life with "admiration for his courage." Do you agree or disagree, and why?

2. According to Schopenhauer, why does Christianity consider suicide a sin? Do you agree with his assessment? Why or why not?

3. Schopenhauer suggests that there are fundamental moral differences between the killing of another and the killing of oneself. Do you agree? Why or why not?

---

4 St. Thomas Aquinas, *Whether It Is Lawful to Kill Oneself*

St. Thomas Aquinas (1225–1274) is considered by many scholars to be the most important Christian philosopher. Born near Naples, Italy, he became a Dominican monk and devoted his life to prayer, scholarship, and teaching. His great work, the multivolume *Summa Theologica,* was in his day considered a radically new way of expressing the Christian faith. Aquinas had revived the ancient philosophy of Aristotle, and used it to defend and explain traditional theological concepts. Shortly before his death, and before his great work could be completed, Aquinas is reported to have had a vision of Christ while serving Mass. "In the light of that vision," said Aquinas, "all my scholarly work is like straw!" He never wrote another word after that, and died the next year on his way to a conference where the Pope had planned to make him a cardinal. Thomas Aquinas was canonized in 1323, and proclaimed a doctor of the Church in 1567.

In the following selection from the *Summa Theologica*, St. Thomas discusses the morality of suicide in light of teachings found in Aristotle's *Nicomachean Ethics*. Aquinas makes the claim that suicide—literally a "self-murder"—is at once a sin against the self, a sin against society, and ultimately a sin against God. It is therefore altogether "unlawful." He also offers a possible exception to the rule that suicide is a sin: it may, in fact, not be a sin if it is done under the "secret" injunction of "the Holy Ghost," a teaching that can have serious ethical consequences in an our age of suicide bombings and terrorist attacks.

Aquinas begins his argument in the fashion that was common in his day: the objections to his own position are stated, as if he were playing his own devil's advocate. He then states his view on the matter, citing relevant sources for support: an earlier saint, Augustine; "the Philosopher," Aristotle; and a passage from the Bible. He concludes by replying to each of the objections he had earlier set up against his position.

Objection 1. It would seem lawful for a man to kill himself. For murder is a sin insofar as it is contrary to justice. But no man can do an injustice to himself, as is proved in *Ethic.* v.11. Therefore no man sins by killing himself.

Objection 2. Further, it is lawful, for one who exercises public authority, to kill evil-doers. Now he who exercises public authority is sometimes an evildoer. Therefore he may lawfully kill himself.

Objection 3. Further, it is lawful for a man to suffer spontaneously a lesser danger that he may avoid a greater: thus it is lawful for a man to cut off a decayed limb even from himself, that he may save his whole body. Now sometimes a man, by killing himself, avoids a greater evil, for example an unhappy life, or the shame of sin. Therefore a man may kill himself.

Objection 4. Further, Samson killed himself, as related to Judges xvi., and yet he is numbered among the saints (Heb. xi). Therefore it is lawful for a man to kill himself.

Objection 5. Further, it is related (2 Mach. xiv: 42) that a certain Razias killed himself, *choosing to die nobly rather than to fall into the hands of the wicked, and to suffer abuses unbecoming his noble birth.* Now nothing that is done nobly and

bravely is unlawful. Therefore suicide is not unlawful.

On the contrary, Augustine says (*De Civ. Dei* i.20): *Hence it follows that the words "Thou shalt not kill" refer to the killing of a man;—not another man; therefore, not even thyself. For he who kills himself kills nothing else than a man.*

I answer that, It is altogether unlawful to kill oneself, for three reasons. First, because everything naturally loves itself, the result being that everything naturally keeps itself in being, and resists corruptions so far as it can. Wherefore suicide is contrary to the inclination of nature, and to charity whereby every man should love himself. Hence suicide is always a mortal sin, as being contrary to the natural law and to charity. Secondly, because every part, as such, belongs to the whole. Now every man is part of the community, and so, as such, he belongs to the community. Hence by killing himself he injures the community, as the Philosopher declares (*Ethic.* v.11).

Thirdly, because life is God's gift to man, and is subject to His power, Who kills and makes to live. Hence whoever takes his own life, sins against God, even as he who kills another's slave, sins against that slave's master, and as he who usurps to himself judgment of a matter not entrusted to him. For it belongs to God alone to pronounce sentence of death and life, according to Deut. xxxii. 39, *I will kill and I will make to live.*

Reply Obj. 1. Murder is a sin, not only because it is contrary to justice, but also because it is opposed to charity which a man should have towards himself: in this respect suicide is a sin in relation to oneself. In relation to the community and to God, it is sinful, by reason also of its opposition to justice.

Reply Obj. 2. One who exercises public authority may lawfully put to death an evil doer, since he can pass judgment on him. But no man is judge of himself. Wherefore it is not lawful for one who exercises public authority to put himself to death for any sin whatever: although he may lawfully commit himself to the judgment of others.

Reply Obj. 3. Man is made master of himself through his free-will: wherefore he can lawfully dispose of himself as to those matters which pertain to this life which is ruled by man's free-will. But the passage from this life to another and happier one is subject not to man's free-will but to the power of God. Hence it is not lawful for man to take his own life that he may pass to a happier life, nor that he may escape any unhappiness whatsoever of the present life, because the ultimate and most fearsome evil of this life is death, as the Philosopher states (*Ethic.* iii.6). Therefore to bring death upon oneself in order to escape the other afflictions of this life, is to adopt a greater evil in order to avoid a lesser. In like manner it is unlawful to take one's own life on account of one's having committed a sin, both because by so doing one does oneself a

very great injury, by depriving oneself of the time needful for repentance, and because it is not lawful to slay an evildoer except by the sentence of the public authority. Again it is unlawful for a woman to kill herself lest she be violated, because she ought not to commit on herself the very great sin of suicide, to avoid the lesser sin of another. For she commits no sin in being violated by force, provided she does not consent, since *without consent of the mind there is no stain on the body,* as the Blessed Lucy declared. Now it is evident that fornication and adultery are less grievous sins than taking a man's, especially one's own, life: since the latter is most grievous, because one injures oneself, to whom one owes the greatest love. Moreover it is most dangerous since no time is left wherein to expiate it by repentance. Again it is not lawful for anyone to take his own life for fear he should consent to sin, because *evil must not be done that good may come* (Rom. iii.8) or that evil may be avoided. Especially if the evil be of small account and an uncertain event, for it is uncertain whether one will at some future time consent to a sin, since God is able to deliver man from sin under any temptation whatever.

Reply Obj. 4. As Augustine says (*De Civ. Dei* i.21), *not even Samson is to be excused that he crushed himself together with his enemies under the ruins of the house, except the Holy Ghost, Who had wrought many wonders through him, had secretly commanded him to do this.* He assigns the same reason in the case of certain holy women, who at the time of persecution took their own lives, and who are commemorated by the Church.

Reply Obj. 5. It belongs to fortitude that a man does not shrink from being slain by another, for the sake of the good of virtue, and that he may avoid sin. But that a man takes his own life in order to avoid penal evils has indeed an appearance of fortitude (for which reason some, among whom was Razias, have killed themselves thinking to act from fortitude), yet it is not true fortitude, but rather a weakness of soul unable to bear penal evils, as the Philosopher (*Ethic.* iii.7) and Augustine (*De Civ. Dei* i. 22, 23) declare.

Questions

1. What is the one exception St. Thomas mentions to the rule that suicide is always unlawful? Discuss the ethical implications of this exception.

2. Detail what, for St. Thomas, makes suicide a sin against God. Offer a critical evaluation of this teaching. Is his teaching persuasive? Why or why not?

3. What arguments does St. Thomas make that might convince an atheist that suicide is wrong? Why might they be convincing?

Small Group Exercises

1. In your small group, discuss experiences you have had with someone you knew who was thinking about or actually attempted suicide. Describe what possible signs there were that this person was considering suicide, and any intervention strategy you may have used. Talk through how things might have gone better (or worse).

2. In your small group, watch the film *Sylvia* together. The film portrays the true life story of Sylvia Plath, an American writer married to poet Ted Hughes. In 1963, having become a mother of two children and attained some degree of success for her poetry, Plath committed suicide. Discuss the role depression played in Plath's suicide.

3. Prepare a debate in your small group on the claim: "Suicide is not murder." Draw up arguments for both sides of the debate and present the debate to the class.

Practical Learning Component

1. Arrange to volunteer some time on a suicide "hotline" in your local community. Usually you will receive some training in suicide prevention and general counseling techniques.

2. Interview the school psychologist at your college on the subject of suicide and suicide prevention. Ask him or her to go over strategies one can use when a friend or roommate is thought to be suicidal. Gather written materials he or she may have on suicide prevention and distribute them in class.

3. Contact a local chapter of the suicide survivors' network of support groups. You will find an up-to-date list on the website of the American Association of Suicidology. Attend one of the meetings and share what you learned with the rest of the class.

Chapter 6

⎯⤝⎯

The Rights of the Dying

The difficulty, my friends, is not in avoiding death, but in
avoiding unrighteousness; for that runs faster than death.
—Socrates

Any discussion of death and dying would be incomplete without mention of the ethical issues that attend the dying of human beings. The list of such issues comes straight from today's headlines: abortion, capital punishment, living wills, the soaring costs of end-of-life care, organ harvesting, etc. But the one ethical debate that involves nearly everyone at some point in their lives is this: If I am dying a slow and painful death, or if a loved one is dying such a death, is it not ethical to hasten the dying process in some way? Should not physicians, who are called upon to be administers of comfort and relief, offer their terminal patients effective means of escaping the horrors of prolonged dying?

These and similar questions raise the issue of euthanasia (Greek; literally, "a good/happy death," from *eu-*, "good, well" and *thanatos,* "death"). Euthanasia is often translated into English as "mercy killing." It was accepted by the ancient Greeks and Romans but remains criminalized in its active form in nearly all developed nations. Two types of patients are involved in euthanasia. The first is a patient in a "persistent vegetative state" (PVS). Such a patient has no higher brain functions and is only kept alive by various means of artificial life support. The second is a patient with a terminal illness or injury who is experiencing, or is expected to experience, discomfort, psychological suffering, and loss of dignity. Such a patient may or may not be on life support.

Those who debate the issue distinguish between two types of euthanasia: active euthanasia—an act of commission, which involves hastening death, usually by means

193

of lethal injection; and passive euthanasia—an act of omission, in which a person is allowed to die by taking no action to maintain life. Passive euthanasia can involve the withholding or withdrawing of water, food, drugs, medical or surgical procedures, resuscitation like CPR, and other means of life support such as a respirator or heart-lung machine. The patient is then left to die from the underlying disease. Euthanasia is understood to be "voluntary" when the patient makes the decision and performs the act, "nonvoluntary" when the decision and act are made by another person for an unconscious patient, and "involuntary" when the decision and act are made contrary to the patient's wishes.

THE HIPPOCRATIC OATH

Tangential to the debate on euthanasia is the question as to whether physicians, who still swear to uphold some version of the Hippocratic Oath, have the obligation to facilitate that right in any way. The Hippocratic Oath is one of the oldest binding documents in history. Written in ancient Greece by the founding father of Western medicine, Hippocrates, its principles are held sacred by doctors to this day: treat the sick to the best of one's ability, preserve patient privacy, teach the secrets of medicine to the next generation, and so on. "The Oath of Hippocrates," holds the American Medical Association's *Code of Medical Ethics* (1996 edition), "has remained in Western civilization as an expression of ideal conduct for the physician." Today, most graduating medical school students swear to some form of the oath, usually a modernized version. Indeed, oath-taking in recent decades has risen to near uniformity, with just 24 percent of U.S. medical schools administering the oath in 1928 to nearly 100 percent today.

Here is how the oath read in Hippocrates' day[29]:

> I swear by Apollo Physician and Asclepius and Hygieia and Panaceia and all the gods and goddesses, making them my witnesses, that I will fulfill according to my ability and judgment this oath and this covenant:
>
> To hold him who has taught me this art as equal to my parents and to live my life in partnership with him, and if he is in need of money to give him a share of mine, and to regard his offspring as equal to my brothers in male lineage and to teach them this art—if they desire to learn it—without fee and covenant; to give a share of precepts and oral instruction and all the other learning to my sons and to the sons of him who has instructed me and to pupils who have signed the covenant and have taken an oath according to the medical law, but no one else.
>
> I will apply dietetic measures for the benefit of the sick according to my ability and judgment; I will keep them from harm and injustice.

I will neither give a deadly drug to anybody who asked for it, nor will I make a suggestion to this effect. Similarly I will not give to a woman an abortive remedy. In purity and holiness I will guard my life and my art.

I will not use the knife, not even on sufferers from stone, but will withdraw in favor of such men as are engaged in this work.

Whatever houses I may visit, I will come for the benefit of the sick, remaining free of all intentional injustice, of all mischief and in particular of sexual relations with both female and male persons, be they free or slaves.

What I may see or hear in the course of the treatment or even outside of the treatment in regard to the life of men, which on no account one must spread abroad, I will keep to myself, holding such things shameful to be spoken about.

If I fulfill this oath and do not violate it, may it be granted to me to enjoy life and art, being honored with fame among all men for all time to come; if I transgress it and swear falsely, may the opposite of all this be my lot.

The language in the oath about swearing to the gods and "not using the knife" no longer apply in today's world of secular, highly technical medicine, but there now exist numerous modernizations of the original wording. The most popular of these was written by Louis Lasagna, professor of medicine at Tufts University, in 1964. It continues to be used by a majority of medical schools around the country. This newer version of the classic oath, sworn to by thousands of future doctors on their medical school graduation day, reads as follows:

I swear to fulfill, to the best of my ability and judgment, this covenant:

I will respect the hard-won scientific gains of those physicians in whose steps I walk, and gladly share such knowledge as is mine with those who are to follow.

I will apply, for the benefit of the sick, all measures which are required, avoiding those twin traps of overtreatment and therapeutic nihilism.

I will remember that there is art to medicine as well as science, and that warmth, sympathy, and understanding may outweigh the surgeon's knife or the chemist's drug.

I will not be ashamed to say "I know not," nor will I fail to call in my colleagues when the skills of another are needed for a patient's recovery.

I will respect the privacy of my patients, for their problems are not disclosed to me that the world may know. Most especially must I tread with care in matters of life and death. If it is given me to save a life, all thanks. But it may also be within my power to take a life; this awesome responsibility must be faced with great humbleness and awareness of my own frailty. Above all, I must not play at God.

I will remember that I do not treat a fever chart, a cancerous growth, but a sick human being, whose illness may affect the person's family and economic stability. My responsibility includes these related problems, if I am to care adequately for the sick.

I will prevent disease whenever I can, for prevention is preferable to cure.

I will remember that I remain a member of society, with special obligations to all my fellow human beings, those sound of mind and body as well as the infirm.

If I do not violate this oath, may I enjoy life and art, respected while I live and remembered with affection thereafter. May I always act so as to preserve the finest traditions of my calling and may I long experience the joy of healing those who seek my help.

A growing number of physicians have come to feel that the Hippocratic Oath is inadequate to address the realities of a medical world that has witnessed huge scientific, economic, political, and social changes; a world of legalized abortion, extreme medical costs, high malpractice premiums, and diseases unheard of in Hippocrates' time. Some doctors have begun asking pointed questions regarding the oath's relevance. In an environment of increasing medical specialization, for example, should physicians of such different forms of practice swear to a single oath? With governments and healthcare organizations demanding patient information as never before, how can a doctor maintain a patient's privacy? Are physicians morally obligated to treat patients who suffer from such lethal new diseases as AIDS, SARS, or the Ebola virus?

Perhaps more pointedly, some doctors argue that with the advance of medical technology, and with the public expectation that medical personnel will use that technology to "keep the patient alive as long as possible," the original oath's prohibiting the doctor from giving "a deadly drug to anybody who asked for it" may not always be in the patient's best interests. Increasingly, doctors are faced with a "Catch-22" type of dilemma: either use aggressive measures to prolong the person's life, but at the expense of physical comfort and loss of personal autonomy; or hasten the dying process in order to maintain dignity and avoid further discomfort, but at the expense of the ethical obligation placed on physicians to "do no harm" to their patients.

LEGISLATIVE ISSUES

At issue in this dilemma is the normally low *quality of life* experienced by a terminal patient when on life-support equipment. Immobile, drifting in and out of a morphine haze, with a feeding tube running up the nose and down the esophagus, a breathing apparatus forcing air into the lungs, a pacemaker keeping the heart pumping, a kidney dialysis machine filtering the blood, and a host of intravenous shunts dripping fluids into various veins, one can hardly say a patient on life-support equipment has much quality of life.

Though subjectively determined, quality of life as it refers to terminal illness is a complex of observable components:

- The ability to care for oneself (feeding, simple hygiene, using the toilet, etc.)
- Clarity of thinking and reasoning
- Freedom from pain and discomfort

- Freedom of mobility
- Interaction with friends and family
- Meaningful ways to pass the time

When these components are compromised by the complications of illness or injury, the question arises, "Is life really worth living?" Most people faced with a state of dependence, physical discomfort, and inconvenience nevertheless find other means of enjoying life. They find solace in simple interactions with people, in spiritual disciplines, and in simply being in the presence of others. But some, used to a life of activity and freedom, find the confines of the illness or injury too burdensome to bear. For such people, active euthanasia becomes a "live possibility."

The issue of the "right to die" was placed at the forefront of the American social agenda when, in 1975, a twenty-one-year-old woman named Karen Ann Quinlan was admitted to a New Jersey hospital after consuming a large amount of alcohol and barbiturates. Quinlan lapsed into a "persistent vegetative state" from which she was not expected to recover. She was put on a feeding tube and an artificial respirator. Severe brain damage caused her body to curl up into a rigid fetal position. Her beleaguered parents asked to have the respirator removed so that their daughter could die a natural death. When the medical personnel in charge of Quinlan's care refused, the case ended up in the New Jersey Superior Court. The court decided in favor of the medical staff, but this decision was soon overturned by the State Supreme Court. The respirator was removed, and Quinlan was moved to a nursing care facility.

In an ironic twist to this story, Quinlan remained alive, breathing on her own, for ten more years. She eventually died of pneumonia. Following her death, a book about her story was published, and was later made into a TV movie, drawing the issue of the "right to die" into the public spotlight. Quinlan became the "poster child" for those who upheld "dying with dignity" in the face of terminal illness or permanent coma as a constitutional right.

As of this writing, Oregon is the only state in the U.S. which allows physicians to hasten the death of a terminal patient by means of lethal medication. Currently, twenty-six states have criminalized active euthanasia, while the remainder have chosen simply to abide by the federal legislative prohibition. Among the European Union, only the Netherlands has passed a "Death with Dignity Act."

Oregon's Death with Dignity Act requires that the Oregon Health Services (OHS) monitor compliance with the law, collect information about the patients and physicians who exercise the right, and publish an annual statistical report. The Act was first passed by Oregon voters in November 1994 by a margin of 51 to 49 percent. Immediate implementation of the Act was delayed by a legal injunction. After a petition was denied by the United States Supreme Court, the Ninth Circuit Court of Appeals lifted the injunction in October of 1997, and physician-assisted suicide then became a legal option for terminally ill patients in the state.

Death and Dying Fact

Oregon's Death with Dignity Act

In 1994 and again in 1997, Oregonians voted in favor of the legal provision of the means for active euthanasia, granted certain requirements are met. The requirements of the Oregon Death with Dignity Act are as follows:

- *The request must be voluntary*
- *No doctor is forced to comply*
- *The patient must be an adult who is terminally ill and mentally competent*
- *The request must be an enduring one; a 15-day waiting period is required*
- *An examination by a mental health professional may be required*
- *The request must be made orally and in writing and witnessed*
- *All alternatives will be explained to the patient*
- *The patient receives a prescription for a lethal dose of medication which must be self-administered*
- *The patient must be allowed to change his or her mind at any time*

To date, similar bills have been introduced in 26 state legislatures.

The Death with Dignity Act allows terminally ill Oregon residents to obtain and use prescriptions for self-administered, lethal medications. The Act states that ending one's life in accordance with the law does not constitute suicide. Oregon's Death with Dignity Act legalizes physician-assisted suicide, but specifically prohibits active euthanasia, where a physician or other person directly administers a medication to end another's life. The act of suicide must in all cases be self-facilitated, self-intended, and self-administered for all legal requirements to be met.

ARGUMENTS FOR AND AGAINST

Opponents of active euthanasia often group their arguments against it into five general types

• The *religious argument* relies on a belief in an all-powerful, divine creator who, as the first cause of human life, is solely responsible for ending such life. It is often said by those who use this argument that physicians are "playing God" when they prescribe lethal medication for their terminal patients. Although the Roman Catholic church has no official position on the matter, its representatives often use this argument to lobby politicians in states about to vote on death with dignity acts.

• The *doctor as enemy argument* would remind the medical community of its Hippocratic obligations to uphold the value of life, and to fight against anything that would compromise that value. This argument suggests that there is a danger in legalizing active euthanasia inasmuch as it turns the doctor into a potential enemy of life, one who can just as easily kill as heal. The doctor as enemy argument is also used to call into question the motives of hospital administrators, in whose best interests it may be to euthanize terminal patients rather than have to cover their medical costs long after insurance limits have been met.

• The *hospice argument,* as the name implies, is used to remind us that in the final days of a terminal patient's life, many wonderful things can happen to that person and to his or her loved ones. Assuming the patient is awake and competent, there is the opportunity to put closure on relationships, make restitution for past wrongs, and seek spiritual growth. It is the primary aim of hospice, in fact, to facilitate this kind of relational closure through the use of proper pain medication, counseling, and spiritual guidance. If the patient were euthanized, so the argument runs, there is the risk of missing out on these important aspects of life.

• The *unexpected cure argument* states that with the exponential rate at which medical research advances in this country, it seems reasonable to allow a dying or persistently vegetative patient every possible chance to be the recipient of the latest wonder drug. This argument highlights the many diseases that in former times were an automatic death sentence, but which now are either preventable or treatable. Another version of this argument holds that as much time as possible ought to be given a patient so that God can perform a miraculous cure.

• Finally, there is the *slippery slope or thin edge of the wedge argument.* Opponents of physician-assisted suicide reason that there is a fine line between allowing terminally ill patients to kill themselves, and allowing nonterminal but suffering patients to kill themselves. If we allow terminally ill patients to commit supervised suicide now, what is to stop us later from allowing those who suffer, but whose lives are sustainable, from doing the same? And once we legalize euthanasia for such people, what will hold us back at an even later date from affording nonterminal but mentally ill patients the same right? One case in support of this argument appears to be the situation in Holland which, after legalizing euthanasia for the terminally ill, went on to legalize it for the severely mentally retarded. Supporters of this argument also sometimes mention what the Nazis did to imprisoned Jews during the Holocaust: many who were physically disabled were used in medical experiments which resulted in their deaths. Slippery slope proponents argue that we must put in place any and all legislative safeguards that will prevent anything like this from ever happening again.

Those who support the legalization of active euthanasia counter such arguments with their own set of standards:

• In response to the *religious argument,* some right-to-die advocates argue that a) there may not be a God (sometimes called the *atheist argument*), and if not then there is no higher possessor of responsibility for the preservation of life than us humans; or b) even if there is a God, the State has no right passing legislation on such a basis due to the constitutional separation of religious from civil authority; or c) there is a God, but one who is by nature full of compassion and who therefore abhors human suffering (sometimes called the *theological argument*). Such a God would presumably support the hastening of death if it would cease needless suffering in a terminal patient.

• In response to the *doctor as enemy argument,* right-to-die advocates suggest that, on the contrary, a physician who has the means at his or her disposal to put a permanent end to futile suffering should well be viewed as a "friend," not an enemy. The *doctor as friend argument* suggests putting the focus not on the physician, but on the ever more sophisticated medical technology as the real enemy. When it is used to keep a dying body alive beyond its natural abilities, say the users of this argument, technology is rightly viewed as an evil thing.

• In response to the *hospice argument,* there is the *dying with dignity argument.* The latter argues that the final days of a person's life should not be marked by pain, physical and mental helplessness, immobility, and complete reliance on others for even simple tasks like feeding oneself, bathing, and going to the bathroom. Moreover, it is understood as psychological damaging for all involved for a patient to be seen in such a condition by loved ones, especially when there are small children involved. This argument suggests that to force a person to live in such a state of indignity constitutes a form of torture.

• The *economic argument* points to the spiralling costs of end-of-life care. It was recently estimated that up to 12 percent of the total U.S. budget for health care, and 30 percent of the Medicare budget, are spent on people aged 65 and older in their last year of life. Studies show that as much as 40 percent of these costs could be saved by decriminalizing active euthanasia. This translates into a savings in the tens of billions of dollars which, as proponents of this argument suggest, could be used to further research on preventable diseases and health for the needy young.[30]

• While there is no direct counterargument to the *slippery slope argument,* except to talk about putting regulations in place to prevent such a misuse of privilege, right-to-die advocates use the right to autonomy (self-rule) argument to uphold the values of individual liberty and agency. It is argued that our bodies are uniquely our own, not the property of the state nor the product of a deity's power. We are each free to decide for ourselves when and how we are to die. It is within our rights, therefore, to kill ourselves in any set of circumstances, and especially so when faced with the threat of a painful death through terminal disease or injury.

Most religious traditions familiar to the West take a stand on the issue of active euthanasia. Jewish teachings, for example, hold that God both created and owns the rights to a person's body. While individuals are to be caretakers of their bodies, no human has a right to do intentional harm to his or her own body, let alone anyone else's. It is also taught in Judaism that human life is of infinite value, because it was created by God and owned by God; and that this value is independent of its quality. In other words, even if the quality of a person's life is very low, the value of that life remains infinitely high. Orthodox and Conservative Jews ordinarily apply these teachings to any situation in which active euthanasia might be desired, ruling out that possibility as morally unacceptable. Indeed there are direct statements in the *Mishnah* and the *Talmud* that equate hastening death with murder.[31] The twelfth-century Jewish philosopher Maimonides, regarded by Jews as an authoritative voice on ethical issues, wrote:

> One who is in a dying condition is regarded as a living person in all respects . . . He who touches him is guilty of shedding blood. To what may he be compared? To a flickering flame, which is extinguished as soon as one touches it. Whoever closes the eyes of the dying while the soul is about to depart is shedding blood. One should wait a while; perhaps he is only in a swoon.[32]

With its ethical and theological roots firmly planted in Jewish soil, Christianity shares a similar emphasis on the created nature of human life and God's ultimate ownership of that life. But Christians differ from Jews in placing ultimate value in God alone; while human life is sacred, its value is not innate. Rather, the value of human life is derived from the ultimate value of God's act of creation and is therefore relative to that act. Moreover, Christians view the nature of God to be revealed definitively in the person of Jesus. While Christianity holds human suffering to be redemptive when ordered rightly, they see in Jesus someone whose compassion led him to alleviate suffering through healing. Thus there is in Christianity a potential for openness to viewing euthanasia in a more positive light. But in general the religion prohibits any form of self-harm or hastening of death on grounds of God's ownership over human life.

While Islam has no definitive statement on active euthanasia—there is no formal hierarchy in the religion from which such a statement might issue—there are clear prohibitions placed on suicide in the *Qu'ran,* Islam's holy book. Moreover, the *Islamic Code of Medical Ethics,* a guide to physicians and researchers seeking to apply *Shari'ah* or Islamic Law to their medical practices, states that while passive means may legitimately be used to allow a terminal patient to perish naturally, "the doctor shall not take positive measures to terminate the patient's life."[33]

Eastern religions bring a different set of religious values to the question of the ethical legitimacy of active euthanasia. On the one hand, both Hinduism and Buddhism teach that this present life is not the only life we will lead. Following death we will incarnate again in another body, just as our current body is an incarnation subsequent to lives we have lived in the past. With this teaching of reincarnation comes the doctrine of *karma,* the inviolable law of the consequences of our actions. Eastern religions teach that if we suffer in this life, it is because we gathered to ourselves bad karma through evil deeds done in a previous lifetime. If we therefore cut our suffering short by committing suicide, we run the risk of interfering with the process of working off that bad debt. At the same time, both religions teach compassion for all suffering creatures. Gandhi himself wrote, "Should my child be attacked with rabies and there was no helpful remedy to relieve his agony, I should consider it my duty to take his life."[34] It has been said that such complementary values might well support a set of questions useful in determining when assisted suicide is ethically plausible. Is the suffering tolerable enough for the individual to mindfully pursue spiritual disciplines? Then the law of karma should take precedence and suicide should be postponed. Is the suffering to such an extent that mindfulness is no longer possible? Then the law of compassion should take precedence and suicide should be an option.

In the following section you will first read two articles which stand on opposite sides of the euthanasia debate. The first, written by a practicing physician, argues in favor of decriminalizing active euthanasia, while the second, written by a professor of medical ethics, argues against such a change. This section concludes with a discussion of the related issue of the spiraling costs of end-of-life care.

---

1 Timothy Quill, *Death and Dignity: A Case of Individualized Decision Making*

Dr. Timothy Quill, an oncologist from the state of New York and a leading figure in the fight to decriminalize active euthanasia, describes in the following essay one of his patients, a forty-five-year-old leukemia sufferer whom he had been treating for several years. The patient, Diane, was given a 25 percent chance of survival if she agreed to submit to a very painful and physically devastating routine of chemotherapy, radiation, and bone-marrow transplant. Married with a college-age son, Diane considered her chances too slim to suffer the torment, and so opted to refuse treatment. But she also wanted, when the time was right, to end her life before the disease had a chance to destroy her body completely. And she wanted Dr. Quill to help her. Quill describes himself as a long-time advocate of active, informed patient control of medical treatment, of a patient's right to refuse such treatment, and to die with as much dignity as possible. So Quill agreed, prescribing for Diane a lethal dose of barbiturates along with the instructions on how to take them for the desired effect. The laws of New York consider this to be an act of civil disobedience, for physician-assisted suicide is illegal there.

At the time of this writing, physician-assisted suicide is illegal in all states but Oregon, and in all European countries but Holland. It is legal to "pull the plug" on life support, or to withhold nutrition and hydration from terminal patients, if they or their legal powers of attorney wish it. But the more active forms of euthanasia, like prescribing a lethal dose of sleeping pills, are strictly prohibited. It is a live debate presently whether there is any real moral difference between the two kinds of euthanasia, passive and active. But it is clear that, since approximately 75 percent of Americans favor making active euthanasia a legal option, and several other states beyond Oregon are getting ready to take the issue to the polls, the argument will be with us very prominently over the next decade or two.

Diane was feeling tired and had a rash. A common scenario, though there was something subliminally worrisome that prompted me to check her blood count. Her hematocrit was 22, and the white-cell count was 4.3 with some metamyelocytes and unusual white cells. I wanted it to be viral, trying to deny what was staring me in the face. Perhaps in a repeated count it would disappear. I called Diane and told her it might be more serious than I had initially thought—that the test needed to be repeated and that if she felt worse, we might have to move quickly. When she pressed for the possibilities, I reluctantly opened the door to leukemia. Hearing the word seemed to make it exist. "Oh, shit!" she said. "Don't tell me that." Oh, shit! I thought, I wish I didn't have to.

Diane was no ordinary person (although no one I have ever come to know has been really ordinary). She was raised in an alcoholic family and had felt alone for much of her life. She had vaginal cancer as a young woman. Through much of her adult life, she had struggled with depression and her own alcoholism. I had come to know, respect, and admire her over the previous eight years as she confronted these problems and gradually overcame them. She was an incredibly clear, at times brutally honest, thinker and communicator. As she took

control of her life, she developed a strong sense of independence and confidence. In the previous 3½ years, her hard work had paid off. She was completely abstinent from alcohol, she had established much deeper connections with her husband, college-age son, and several friends, and her business and her artistic work were blossoming. She felt she was really living fully for the first time.

Not surprisingly, the repeated blood count was abnormal, and detailed examination of the peripheral-blood smear showed myelocytes. I advised her to come into the hospital, explaining that we needed to do a bone marrow biopsy and make some decisions relatively rapidly. She came to the hospital knowing what we would find. She was terrified, angry, and sad. Although we knew the odds, we both clung to the thread of possibility that it might be something else.

The bone marrow confirmed the worst: acute myelomonocytic leukemia. In the face of this tragedy, we looked for signs of hope. This is an area of medicine in which technological intervention has been successful, with cures 25 percent of the time—long-term cures. As I probed the costs of these cures, I heard about induction chemotherapy (three weeks in the hospital, prolonged neutropenia, probable infectious complications, and hair loss;

75 percent of patients respond, 25 percent do not). For the survivors, this is followed by consolidation chemotherapy (with similar side effects; another 25 percent die, for a net survival of 50 percent). Those still alive, to have a reasonable chance of long-term survival, then need bone marrow transplantation (hospitalization for two months and whole-body irradiation, with complete killing of the bone marrow, infectious complications, and the possibility for graft-versus-host disease—with a survival of approximately 50 percent, or 25 percent of the original group). Though hematologists may argue over the exact percentages, they don't argue about the outcome of no treatment—certain death in days, weeks, or at most a few months.

Believing that delay was dangerous, our oncologist broke the news to Diane and began making plans to insert a Hickman catheter and begin induction chemotherapy that afternoon. When I saw her shortly thereafter, she was enraged at his presumption that she would want treatment, and devastated by the finality of the diagnosis. All she wanted to do was go home and be with her family. She had no further questions about treatment and in fact had decided that she wanted none. Together we lamented her tragedy and the unfairness of life. Before she left, I felt the need to be sure that she and her husband understood that there was some risk in delay, that the problem was not going to go away, and that we needed to keep considering the options over the next several days. We agreed to meet in two days.

She returned in two days with her husband and son. They had talked extensively about the problem and the options. She remained very clear about her wish not to undergo chemotherapy and to live whatever time she had left outside the hospital. As we explored her thinking further, it became clear that she was convinced she would die during the period of treatment and would suffer unspeakably in the process (from hospitalization, from lack of control over her body, from the side effects of chemotherapy, and from pain and anguish). Although I could offer support and my best effort to minimize her suffering if she chose treatment, there was no way I could say any of this would not occur. In fact, the last four patients with acute leukemia at our hospital had died very painful deaths in the hospital during various stages of treatment (a fact I did not share with her). Her family wished she would choose treatment but sadly accepted her decision. She articulated very clearly that it was she who would be experiencing all the side effects of treatment and that odds of 25 percent were not good enough for her to undergo so toxic a course of therapy, given her expectations of chemotherapy and hospitalization and the absence of a closely matched bone marrow donor. I had her repeat her understanding of the treatment, the odds, and what to expect if there were no treatment. I clarified a few misunderstandings, but she had a remarkable grasp of the options and implications.

I have been a longtime advocate of active, informed patient choice of treatment or nontreatment, and of a patient's right to die with as much control and dignity as possible. Yet there was something about her giving up a 25 percent chance of long-term survival in favor of almost certain death that disturbed me. I had seen Diane fight and use her considerable inner resources to overcome alcoholism and depression, and I half expected her to change her mind over the next week. Since the window of time in which effective treatment can be initiated is rather narrow, we met several times that week. We obtained a second hematology consultation and talked at length about the meaning and implications of treatment and nontreatment. She talked to a psychologist she had seen in the past. I gradually understood the decision from her perspective and became convinced that it was the right decision for her. We arranged for home hospice care (although at that time Diane felt reasonably well, was active, and looked healthy), left the door open for her to change her mind, and tried to anticipate how to keep her comfortable in the time she had left.

Just as I was adjusting to her decision, she opened up another area that would stretch me profoundly. It was extraordinarily important to Diane to maintain control of herself and her own dignity during the time remaining to her. When this was no longer possible, she clearly wanted to die. As a former director of a hospice program, I know how to use pain medicines to keep patients comfortable and lessen suffering. I explained the philosophy of comfort care, which I strongly believe in. Although Diane understood and appreciated this, she had known of people lingering in what was called relative comfort, and she wanted no part of it. When the time came, she wanted to take her life in the least painful way possible.

Knowing of her desire for independence and her decision to stay in control, I thought this request made perfect sense. I acknowledged and explored this wish but also thought that it was out of the realm of currently accepted medical practice and that it was more than I could offer or promise. In our discussion, it became clear that preoccupation with her fear of a lingering death would interfere with Diane's getting the most out of the time she had left until she found a safe way to ensure her death. I feared the effects of a violent death on her family, the consequences of an ineffective suicide that would leave her lingering in precisely the state she dreaded so much, and the possibility that a family member would be forced to assist her, with all the legal and personal repercussions that would follow. She discussed this at length with her family. They believed that they should respect her choice. With this in mind, I told Diane that information was available from the Hemlock Society that might be helpful to her.

A week later she phoned me with a request for barbiturates for sleep. Since I knew that this was an essential ingredient in a Hemlock Society suicide, I asked her to come to the office to talk things over. She was more than willing to protect me by participating in a superficial conversation about her insomnia, but it was important to me to know how she planned to use the drugs and to be sure that she was not in despair or overwhelmed in a way that might color her judgment. In our discussion, it was apparent that she was having trouble sleeping, but it was also evident that the security of having enough barbiturates available to commit suicide when and if the time came would leave her secure enough to live fully and concentrate on the present. It was clear that she was not despondent and that in fact she was making deep, personal connections with her family and close friends. I made sure that she knew how to use the barbiturates for sleep, and also that she knew the amount needed to commit suicide. We agreed to meet regularly, and she promised to meet with me before taking her life, to ensure that all other avenues had been exhausted. I wrote the prescription with an uneasy feeling about the boundaries I was exploring—spiritual, legal, professional, and personal. Yet I also felt strongly that I was setting her free to get the most out of the time she had left, and to maintain dignity and control on her own terms until her death.

The next several months were very intense and important for Diane. Her son stayed home from college, and they were able to be with one another and say much that had not been said earlier. Her husband did his work at home so that he and Diane could spend more time together. She spent time with her closest friends. I had her come into the hospital for a conference with our residents, at which she illustrated in a most profound and personal way the importance of informed decision making, the right to refuse treatment, and the extraordinarily personal effects of illness and interaction with the medical system. There were emotional and physical hardships as well. She had periods of intense sadness and anger. Several times she became very weak, but she received transfusions as an outpatient and responded with marked improvement of symptoms. She had two serious infections that responded surprisingly well to empirical courses of oral antibiotics. After three tumultuous months, there were two weeks of relative calm and well-being, and fantasies of a miracle began to surface.

Unfortunately, we had no miracle. Bone pain, weakness, fatigue, and fevers began to dominate her life. Although the hospice workers, family members, and I tried our best to minimize the suffering and promote comfort, it was clear that the end was approaching. Diane's immediate future held what she feared the most—increasing discomfort, dependence, and hard choices between pain and sedation. She called up her closest friends and asked them to come over to say goodbye, telling them that she would be leaving soon. As we had agreed, she let me know as well. When we met, it was clear that she knew what she was doing, that she was sad and frightened to be leaving, but that she would be even more terrified to stay and suffer. In our tearful goodbye, she promised a reunion in the future at her favorite spot on the edge of Lake Geneva, with dragons swimming in the sunset.

Two days later her husband called to say that Diane had died. She had said her final goodbyes to her husband and son, that morning, and asked them to leave her alone for an hour. After an hour, which must have seemed like an eternity, they found her on the couch, lying very still and covered by her favorite shawl. There was no sign of struggle. She seemed to be at peace. They called me for advice about how to proceed. When I arrived at their house, Diane indeed seemed peaceful. Her husband and son were quiet. We talked about what a remarkable person she had been. They seemed to have no doubts about the course she had chosen or about their cooperation, although the unfairness of her illness and the finality of her death were overwhelming to us all.

I called the medical examiner to inform him that a hospice patient had died. When asked about the cause of death, I said, "acute leukemia." He said that was fine and that we should call a funeral director. Although acute leukemia was the truth, it was not the whole story. Yet any mention of suicide would have given rise to a police investigation and probably brought the arrival of an ambulance crew for resuscitation. Diane would have become a "coroner's case," and the decision to perform an autopsy would have been made at the discretion of the medical examiner. The family or I could have been subject to criminal prosecution, and I to professional review, for our roles in support of Diane's choices. Although I truly believe that the family and I gave her the best care possible, allowing her to define her limits and directions as much as possible, I am not sure the law, society, or the medical profession would agree. So I said "acute leukemia" to protect all of us, to protect Diane from an invasion into her past and her body, and to continue to shield society from the knowledge of the degree of suffering that people often undergo in the process of dying. Suffering can be lessened to some extent, but in no way eliminated, or made benign, by the careful intervention of a competent,

caring physician, given current social constraints.

Diane taught me about the range of help I can provide if I know people well and if I allow them to say what they really want. She taught me about life, death, and honesty and about taking charge and facing tragedy squarely when it strikes. She taught me that I can take small risks for people that I really know and care about. Although I did not assist in her suicide directly, I helped indirectly to make it possible, successful, and relatively painless. Although I know we have measures to help control pain and lessen suffering, to think that people do not suffer in the process of dying is an illusion. Prolonged dying can occasionally be peaceful, but more often the role of the physician and family is limited to lessening but not eliminating severe suffering.

I wonder how many families and physicians secretly help patients over the edge into death in the face of such severe suffering. I wonder how many severely ill or dying patients secretly take their lives, dying alone in despair. I wonder whether the image of Diane's final aloneness will persist in the minds of her family, or if they will remember more the intense meaningful months they had together before she died. I wonder whether Diane struggled in that last hour, and whether the Hemlock Society's way of death by suicide is the most benign. I wonder why Diane, who gave so much to so many of us, had to be alone for the last hour of her life. I wonder whether I will see Diane again, on the shore of Lake Geneva at sunset, with dragons swimming on the horizon.

Questions

1. Describe and evaluate the grounds on which Dr. Quill made the decision to assist Diane in her desire to commit suicide.

2. Describe the ways in which Diane chose to spend her final days.

3. If you were in Diane's place, would you have made the same decision? Why or why not?

---

2 Edmund Pellegrino, *Distortion of the Healing Relationship*

Edmund Pellegrino, M.D., is a professor emeritus of medicine and medical ethics at the Center for Clinical Medical Ethics at Georgetown University Medical Center. He was the John Carroll Professor of Medicine and Medical Ethics and the former director of the Kennedy Institute of Ethics, the Center for the Advanced Study of Ethics at Georgetown University, and the Center for Clinical Bioethics. Dr. Pellegrino is the author of over 550 published items in medical science, philosophy, and ethics and a member of numerous editorial boards. He is the recipient of forty-seven honorary degrees and awards, including the Benjamin Rush Award from the American Medical Association, the Abraham Flexner Award of the Association of American Medical Colleges, and the Beecher Award for Life Achievement in Bioethics from The Hastings Center.

Dr. Pellegrino argues against Dr. Quill, and thus against the decriminalization of physician-assisted suicide. It is his position that the physician-patient relationship is one built primarily upon trust: the patient trusts that the physician will, to the best of his or her ability, provide medical care and helpful treatment options. This relationship is structured by the concepts of cure, prevention, and palliation of pain and disability. To introduce "killing" into that mix is, in Pellegrino's view, to distort the true nature of the physician's calling. He goes on to argue that giving physicians the right to kill their patients, or even the right to aid them in killing themselves, will eventually lead to a great deal of distrust of the physician's role, and even to abuse by the physician of the autonomous right of the patient to life itself. Here Pellegrino combines two traditional arguments that are set forth against active euthanasia: the "doctor as enemy argument," which states that when doctors are given the right to kill their patients, they can easily be seen as the enemy of patients rather than as their friends; and the "slippery slope argument," which suggests that once active euthanasia is legalized for terminally ill patients, it will soon be used on other such "social undesirables" as the mentally disabled and criminals.

Distortions of Beneficence

The strongest arguments in favor of euthanasia and assisted suicide are based in appeals to two basic principles of contemporary medical ethics—beneficence and respect for autonomy. Protagonists of intentional death argue when the patient is suffering intolerably, is ready to meet death, and able to give consent, that it is compassionate, merciful, and beneficent to kill the patient or assist him or her in killing oneself. Not to do so would be to act maleficently, to violate the dignity and autonomy of the suffering person, and to inflict harm on another human—in effect, to abandon a person in a time of greatest need: Since the doctor has the requisite knowledge to make death easy and painless, it is not only cruel but immoral not to accede to the patient's request. Some would carry the argument: further into the realm of justice. They would make euthanasia a moral obligation. Not to "assist" an incompetent patient is to act discriminatorily, for it deprives the comatose, the retarded, and infants the "benefit" of an early death. When the patient's intention cannot be expressed, the obligation, in justice, is to provide involuntary or nonvoluntary access to the same benefit of death accessible to the competent patient. The Dutch Pediatric Society is already moving in this direction in the case of badly handicapped infants.

It will not do to argue that one is not intending to kill but only to relieve suffering. This is a misuse of the principle of double effect. In this regard, it is interesting that the Remmelink Report shows that only 10 of the 187 cases of patients studied who asked for active euthanasia in Holland did so for relief of pain alone, while 46% mentioned pain in combination with loss of dignity, unworthy dying, dependence, or surfeit with life.

At this juncture, those who see euthanasia as beneficent may reply that, in fact, physicians do not manage pain optimally, that they are not educated to do so, and that they ignore contemporary methods of analgesia. It is concluded that we cannot realistically expect or trust physicians to control pain and this justifies killing the patient out of compassion. In this way, we make the victim of medical ineptitude a victim twice over. In fact, legitimating euthanasia in any form would relieve physicians of the time, effort, and care

required to control *both* pain and suffering. The moral mandate is not to extinguish the life of the patient because doctors are inept at pain control but to better educate physicians in modern methods of analgesia.

A familiar argument used in many contexts today is that what is illegal or morally forbidden but desired by many should be "regularized" to keep it within respectable bounds. Examples of this kind of thinking include legalization of drug use, prostitution, commercialization of organ procurement, and so on. This argument misses the fact that the more decorous and regulated injection of a lethal dose of morphine or potassium chloride to bring about death in a hospital or one's own bedroom by one's family practitioner is not morally different from Kevorkian's crude methodology. The intention is the same—to kill or to help the patient kill oneself. Efficiency in the killing does not eradicate the unethical nature of the act.

Arguments based on euthanasia as a way to preserve the patient's dignity in dying are grounded in a misconception about dignity. Patients do not lose their dignity as humans simply because they are suffering, in pain, perhaps disfigured by illness, incontinent, or comatose. A patient's dignity resides in his humanity. It cannot be lost, even through the ravages of disease. When proponents of euthanasia speak of loss of dignity, they are speaking more for their own reactions to seeing, living with, or treating terminally ill patients. When patients speak of their fear of a loss of "dignity," for the most part, they are speaking of the way they appear to, or are regarded by, others—by physicians, nurses, other patients, and even their families. This type of "dignity" is the fabrication of the observer, not a quality of the person observed.

For the patient, this is not death with "dignity"; it is more like death as a remedy for the shame they feel, or are made to feel. Shame is a potent cause of suffering. It is far more human to treat that cause by treating the patient with true dignity. Acceding to the patient's request to die is not helping to restore his dignity. It is a confirmation of the loss of worth he has suffered in the eyes of those who behold him as an object of pity.

Distortion of Autonomy

Protagonists of euthanasia and assisted suicide argue that assisting the patient to die is a beneficent act since it respects the principle of autonomy. On this view, those who refuse to comply with the autonomous request of a competent patient are in violation of respect for persons. Such absolutization of autonomy has two serious moral limitations that make any form of euthanasia or assisted suicide a maleficent rather than a beneficent act. For one thing, the mere assertion of a request cannot, of itself, bind another person within, or outside the physician-patient relationship. When a demand becomes a command, it can violate another person's autonomy. Even more problematic is whether a person desperate enough to ask to be killed or assisted in killing herself can act autonomously. In the end, the person

who opts for euthanasia uses her autonomy to give up her autonomy. She chooses to eradicate the basis on which autonomy is possible—consciousness and rationality.

At the other extreme, when death is imminent, the empirical questions of autonomy are equally problematic. The person who is fatally ill is a person, often in pain, anxious, and rejected by those who are healthy, afflicted with a sense of guilt and unworthiness, perceiving himself as a social, economic, and emotional burden to others. Can a person in this state satisfy the criteria for autonomous choice? How well could these patients safeguard their autonomy if euthanasia were legalized? Chronically ill and dying patients are extremely sensitive to even the most subtle suggestions of unworthiness by their medical attendants, family, and friends. Any sign—verbal or nonverbal—that reinforces guilt or shame will be picked up as a subtle suggestion to take the "noble" way out.

The degree to which pain, guilt, and unworthiness may compromise autonomy is evident in the fact that when these are removed or ameliorated, patients do not ask to be killed. Even if euthanasia were legalized, a first obligation under both principles of beneficence and autonomy would be to diagnose, ameliorate, or remove those causes of the patient's despondency and suffering that lead to a request for euthanasia in the first place.

Distortion of Trust

Trust plays an inescapable role in whatever model of physician-patient relationship one chooses. The patient trusts the physician to do what is in the patient's best interests as it is indicated by the diagnosis, prognosis, and therapeutic possibilities. When patients know that euthanasia is a legitimate choice and that some physicians may see killing as healing, they know they are vulnerable to violations of trust.

A much more common danger at present is the possibility that the physician's values and acceptance of euthanasia may unconsciously shape how vigorously she treats the patient or presents the possibility of assisted suicide. How is the patient to know, when his doctor is persuading or even subtly coercing him to choose death? The doctor's motives may be unconsciously to advance her own beliefs that euthanasia is a social good to relieve herself of the frustrating difficulties of caring for the patient, of her distress with the quality of life the patient is forced to lead, or promote her desire to conserve society's resources, etc. How will a patient ever be sure of the true motive for his doctor's recommendation? When is the doctor depreciating the value of available methods of pain relief or comprehensive palliative care because he believes the really "good" death is a planned death?

The power of physicians to shape their patient's choices is well-known to every experienced clinician. Physicians can get a patient to agree to almost any decision they want by the way they present the alternatives. All judgments may be influenced by the physician's attitude on euthanasia or her emotional and physical frustrations in treating a difficult patient. How realistic is patient autonomy in such circumstances? How effective can the criteria proposed to prevent abuses of legalized euthanasia really be?

Assisted Suicide: Is There a Moral Difference between Quill and Kevorkian?

What I have attempted to show is the way in which intentional killing, if accepted into the body of medical ethics, would distort the ethics and purposes of the healing relationship in at least three of its dimensions—beneficence, protection of autonomy, and fidelity to trust. One may justifiably ask: Is the ethical situation different if the physician intends only to advise the patient on how to attain the goal of a "good" death by assisting the patient to kill oneself? Is not the causal and intentional relationship of the physician to the death of the patient essentially different?

I do not believe a convincing case can be made for a moral difference between the two. This is a classical instance of a distinction without a difference in kind. The intentional end sought in either case is the death of the patient: in active euthanasia, the physician is the immediate cause; in assisted suicide, the physician is the necessary cooperating cause, a moral accomplice without whom the patient could not kill oneself. In assisted suicide, the doctor fully shares the patient's intention to end his or her life. The doctor provides the lethal medication, advises on the proper dose, on how it should be taken to be most effective, and on what to do if the dose is regurgitated. The physician's cooperation is necessary if the act is to be carried out at all.

The physician shares equal responsibility with the patient just as she or he would in active euthanasia.

This moral complicity is obvious in the cases reported by Dr. Timothy Quill and Dr. Jack Kevorkian. In both cases, the physician provided the means fully knowing the patient would use them and encouraging the patient to do so when they felt the time was right. Kevorkian's "death machine" was operated by the patient but designed and provided by Kevorkian. Quill's patient took the sedatives he prescribed. To be sure, Quill's account of his assistance in the death of a young woman with leukemia elicits more sympathy because of the length and intensity of his professional relationship with her. Kevorkian's cases, in contrast, are remarkable for the brevity of the relationships, the absence of any serious attempt to provide palliative medical or psychiatric assistance, and the brusqueness with which the decisions are made and carried out. Kevorkian is the technician of death; Quill, its artist.

Quill's *modus operandi* is gentler and more deliberate, but this does not change the nature of the action in any essential way. Indeed, in some ways, Quill's approach is more dangerous to patient beneficence and autonomy because it compromises the patient more subtly and is conducted under the intention of "treatment." But when does the intention to treat become synonymous with the intent to assist in, or actively accelerate, death? Kevorkian's patients at least approach him with the intention already in their minds to commit suicide and to gain access to his machine. He is, after all, a pathologist, and his patients do not start out thinking he might be able to treat their illnesses. Quill's patients presumably come to him as a physician primarily, not as a minister of death. This may well change now that Quill has attained so much notoriety through his public zeal for assisted suicide.

Questions

1. Pellegrino states that, "A patient's dignity . . . cannot be lost, even through the ravages of disease." Do you agree with this? Why or why not?
2. Explain how, according to Pellegrino, the motives of the doctor toward the patient might be changed were active euthanasia to be decriminalized.
3. How does Pellegrino answer his own question, "Is there a moral difference between Quill and Kevorkian?"

---

3 Hans Küng, *The Theological Controversy of Physician-Assisted Suicide*

Dr. Hans Küng is a scholar of theology and philosophy and a prolific writer. Born in Switzerland in 1928, he studied philosophy and theology at the Gregorian University (Rome), the Sorbonne, and the Institut Catholique de Paris. He was ordained into the Roman Catholic priesthood in 1954. In 1960 he was appointed to a teaching position in the Catholic Faculty of Theology at Tübingen University in Germany where he remained until his retirement from a full professorship in 1996. From 1962 to 1965 he served as official theological consultant (peritus) to the Second Vatican Council appointed by Pope John XXIII. Dr. Küng holds numerous awards and honorary degrees from several universities.

A persistent critic of papal authority, which he claims is man-made (and thus reversible) rather than instituted by God, Küng became the first major Roman Catholic theologian to reject the nineteenth-century doctrine of papal infallibility. Following several failed attempts by Vatican authorities to extricate from Küng a confession of error, in December of 1979 Küng was stripped of his right to teach as a Catholic theologian. Küng continued to teach at Tübingen University, however, once he was tenured there as professor of ecumenical theology, a position he held until his retirement. He also established and served as director of the Institute for Ecumenical Research at Tübingen.

Dr. Küng is co-editor of several journals and has written many books, including *Justification; The Catholic Church: A Short History; On Being a Christian; Does God Exist?; Theology for the Third Millenium; Christianity and the World Religions; Judaism; Christianity: Essence, History, and Future; Global Responsibility; A Global Ethic for Global Politics and Economics;* and *Tracing the Way: Spiritual Dimensions of the World Religions.* He was the drafter of *Towards a Global Ethic: An Initial Declaration* of the Parliament of the World's Religions in 1993, and of the proposal of the InterAction Council for a Universal Declaration of Human Responsibilities in 1997. Most recently Dr. Küng was asked by Kofi Annan, Secretary General of the United Nations, to draft a statement for the U.N. regarding the need for a global standard of ethical behavior in the wake of war in the Middle East. Küng obliged, publishing *A Global Ethic: Development and Goals* in 2003.

The following reading comes from Küng's 1985 book, *Eternal Life: Life After Death as a Medical, Philosophical, and Theological Problem.* In this passage, Küng raises the issue of suicide, particularly physician-assisted suicide, as a problem of human responsibility rather than divine commandment.

The theological controversy is centered on the question of whether man has the right to dispose of his life even up to his death. It should be noted that for us the question arises here, not in regard to the healthy person, but to someone who is seriously ill and even doomed to die (moribund). That is to say, I am not talking here about the person who is suffering—and often only for a time—simply from weariness of life, of a young person—for instance—whose first love affair falls to pieces and who now despairs of life. No, we are talking about at the end of life, inescapably approaching his death, caused by an incurable disease. Can he dispose of his life?

Yes, say the advocates of active assisted dying: man has this right in virtue of his autonomous power of disposal over himself, and the liberal constitutional state together with its courts has to enable him to use this right; but the churches must not try to impose their own moral and religious views on ideological minorities.

No, say not only most theologians, but also most jurists and doctors. They point out that the person himself may not dispose of his life; that the doctor is there to heal, not to kill. Moreover, it is striking that more healthy and young than old and sick people are calling for permission for mercy killing. It is completely different in the concrete situation of hopeless sickness; a wish of this kind, as a result of medical experiences, is only rarely expressed. It is precisely in the interests of a properly understood freedom of the human person—say the jurists—that the constitutional state cannot permit killing on demand. And some theologians add that human life is based on God's consent to man, that it is God's creation and gift and therefore outside human control.

The situation in regard to the arguments is extremely complicated and full of objective difficulties. But are the theological arguments in particular—and it is to these that I must mainly devote my attention—completely convincing for the suffering, doomed sick person or the senile person? Human life is God's "gift," certainly. But is it not also—according to the Creator's mandate—also man's *responsibility*? Man must hold out to his "appointed" end. But what is the end appointed? A "premature withdrawal" of life is human refusal of the divine consent. But what is the meaning of "premature" when we are speaking of a life that has been destroyed physically or psychologically?

In this respect we must not attempt to construct false counterarguments. No advocate of a more active assisted death thinks that the person becomes "non-human" or "no longer human" as a result of incurable sickness, senility or definitive unconsciousness. On the contrary, precisely because man is and remains human, he has a right to live a life worthy of a human being and to die with human dignity, a right that may *possibly* be denied him if he is continually dependent on surgical apparatus and medicaments: that is,

when all that is possible is to go on merely vegetating, to sustain a merely vegetative existence. In this light none of the three partial objectives of assisted dying—prolongation of life, diminishing suffering and preservation of freedom—may be made absolute, but must all be brought into harmony with each other.

Countless people were unable to understand those American doctors who preserved artificially for months the life, that could not have been saved anyway, of the unconscious Karen Ann Quinlan, even against the wishes of her parents. On the other hand, countless people did understand that Dutch woman doctor who let her semiparalyzed, depressive seventy-eight-year-old mother pass away as a result of an overdose of morphine. Some described it as "killing," others called it "compassion," "mercy," "helpful love." If we look more closely, the gray areas in the process of distinguishing between active and passive assisted dying increase in size. Is the breaking off of a life-preserving medical aid—for instance, the disconnection of a heart-lung machine—an active or a passive aid to dying? From the standpoint of the effect (oncoming death), the termination of active treatment (normal dose of morphine and stoppage of artificial feeding) can be precisely the same thing as active treatment (overdose of morphine). What can be clearly distinguished conceptually often cannot be kept apart in the concrete; here the boundaries between all these ideas of aids—between active and passive, natural and artificial, life-preserving and life-terminating—are obviously fluid. And it is typical of the uncertain situation that the competent Dutch court condemned that doctor, as the (existing) law required, but was content at the same time with a symbolic prison sentence of ten days, which the doctor did not have to serve.

Are these exceptional cases? Do we perhaps identify ourselves too emotionally with someone in a tragic situation and thus sacrifice sacred principles? That would be an oversimplified view. Might it not also here be a question of the rapid change in the sense of values and norms, which must be taken into account in the enormous influence of the rapidly growing scientific-medical establishment on our feeling for life? Control over the processes of life is increasingly possible and placed under human responsibility. We have already experienced such a rapid change in the sense of values and norms in regard to the *beginning* of human life. At one time many moral theologians interpreted and rejected active, "artificial" birth control as a denial of God's sovereignty over life, until they had to admit that the beginning also of human life had been placed by God under man's responsibility (not at his arbitrary choice). Is it conceivable that the end too of human life has been placed more than hitherto under the responsibility (not at the whim) of man by the same God, who does not want us to shift off onto him a responsibility that we ourselves can and should bear?

With these observations on a highly controversial question, I do not want to support any definitive, irreformable doctrine, but to put forward for reflection what seem to me to be a few justifiable questions which might lead to a more relaxed discussion. Otherwise it seems to me that there is a great danger of the formation of rigid fronts similar to those adopted in the debate on abortion . . . The question of assisted dying must be removed from the theological taboo zone, in which it remained for a long time. But it is completely clear what disastrous consequences any deviation from the principle of the inviolability of human life can have, even though those on the other side are not to be regarded simply as supporters of the Nazi compulsory euthanasia, which of course no one really wants now. Just as there is no life that is "unfit to live," neither is there any life "worth living" under all circumstances, as if a life that is only capable of purely biological functions were the supreme good.

What I am advocating then is permission not for mercy killing but for a reflection on human responsibility even for the dying and for a little less fear and nervousness about decisions in this respect, both on the side of the patient and on the side of the doctor. I am advocating man's responsibility, particularly from a specifically theological viewpoint, which attempts to take seriously belief not merely in a temporal, but also in an eternal life. For:

If man does not die pointlessly into nothingness, but into an absolutely last, absolutely first reality, if then his dying is not merely absurd departure and decline, but incoming and homecoming, then what follows can be justified:

• The doctor need never regard the process of dying or even the death of a patient (even when recorded) as a personal defeat, which he has to cover up as far as possible from himself and others. Certainly he should do everything possible to cure the person, but not everything to postpone death artificially and technically for hours, days or even years often in the midst of intolerable torment.

• A therapy remains meaningful only as long as it leads, not merely to a continual vegetation, but to the rehabilitation—that is, to the restoration—of vital bodily functions that have lapsed and thus to the restoration of the whole human person. Even an operation or intensive therapy may never be an end in itself, but must always be a means to the end of a new life of human dignity. The distinction then must constantly be made between what is technically feasible and what is medically meaningful.

• The patient himself has the right to refuse treatment intended to prolong life; he is not to be brought back under all circumstances even out of his agony. The dying person is not to be pushed off into isolation (into a side room), but should remain as far as possible integrated within the hospital, so that he is not denied contact with other human beings—the most important aid to dying—particularly in the final moments of fear.

• The task in regard to the dying person then should not be restricted to medical treatment alone, but—as required by the particular situation—should also include the human devotion of doctors, nurses, pastors, relatives and friends.

Questions

1. Name two questions at the heart of the assisted suicide debate that Dr. Küng raises. Answer these questions from your personal perspective on the issue.
2. Küng shifts the theological focus of the euthanasia issue from divine command to human responsibility. What is your opinion of this shift?
3. How does Küng use the notion of "eternal life" to strengthen his argument? Do you agree or disagree with him, and why?

---

4 Dan Brock, *When Is Patient Care Not Costworthy?*

Suppose you were an elderly person dying of a terminal illness, and your doctor gave you anywhere from one week to one month to live. Now suppose that your doctor goes on to tell you that through an expensive series of procedures you could be nearly guaranteed another three months of life. What would you do? Would you choose to prolong your life at the cost of tens of thousands of dollars, some of which your insurance may pick up, but the rest of which would have to be paid by your family, or failing that, by the hospital? Or would you forgo the expensive treatment and simply let nature take its course? This is the issue Professor Dan Brock takes up in the following essay.

Dan Brock is the Charles C. Tillinghast Jr. University Professor of Philosophy and Biomedical Ethics, and director of the Center for Biomedical Ethics at Brown University. His research has focused on the issue of euthanasia, and particularly on the prioritization and distribution of healthcare resources. He has written extensively on the subject since 1989. His research into the increasing costs of end-of-life care of the elderly at the expense of medical research has led him to take a stand in favor of legalizing active euthanasia.

Relevant questions that are addressed in the debate around the rationing of healthcare dollars, especially in cases of so-called "futile care"—i.e., care which very likely will not benefit the patient in any therapeutic way—include the following:

- Who is to decide whether certain medical procedures are or are not futile?
- If a patient desires futile care, does he or she have a right to it?
- What rights do HMOs and hospital administrators have in rationing health care?
- Ought taxpayers to pick up the bill when insurance companies refuse to pay for end-of-life care?
- Should spending caps be placed on end-of-life costs for the terminal and elderly in order to allocate more funds to medical research and care for the young?

Dan Brock does not address all of these questions in his essay. But he does argue that the physicians themselves are not the ones who should be making any of these decisions. Their role as healthcare providers, as the promoters of life, might be compromised, Brock reasons, if they also had to decide who does and does not get admitted into the intensive-care unit.

The following dialogue occurred during Grand Rounds: . . .

Gertrude Handel, a sixty-year-old woman, has had cancer of the pancreas for six months. The cancer has metastasized despite her participation in an experimental chemotherapy program. Currently, 95 percent of her liver is cancerous, she has metastases in her lungs, and her peritoneal cavity is filled with malignant ascites [cancerous fluid]. The patient has become anuric [her kidneys have stopped functioning], and she is encephalopathic [has suffered severe brain damage] due to kidney and liver failure.

The family has been told that she is dying and that there is nothing further that medical science can do for her. They have been advised that the present aim should be to keep the patient free from pain and as comfortable as possible. However, the family refuses to accept this and insists on placing the patient in the Intensive Care Unit to receive all available aggressive treatment. . . .

Intensive care would prolong the patient's life for a few days at most. The patient has no chance of recovering from the brain damage. Further, this is a particularly unresponsive form of cancer. Studies indicate that those who have it, even those who have participated in experimental protocols, invariably die. . . . The beds in the ICU are all occupied. . . . there is [no] other patient who could be safely discharged to make room for the patient.

[The family says] that the patient has told them on several occasions that she would want everything possible done to keep her alive if she should ever become terminally ill. . . . Dr. Bernstein said, "The patient has catastrophic health care insurance, and the effect of the costs of her care would not be felt by the family. It seemed the wrong time to bring up costs with them, as they were very upset, and the costs do not directly affect them. . . . Although the expenses incurred by additional treatment won't financially devastate the patient and her family, they *do* affect the costs of medical care to others who are in the patient's insurance pool. This has been overlooked by patients and physicians and is one reason why the costs of medical care have been rising so rapidly. Another reason is that we don't stop to consider whether some of the medical care we are providing is worth its high cost—or whether it is wasteful or useless. Some expensive medical treatments should be carried out . . . because they can restore patients to a meaningful life. But in this case, further treatments cannot do that. They would be futile, and it seems wrong to ask others to pay for them.". . .

Dr. Lean replied, "I believe that [another physician] is way off base if he thinks that doctors should consider the costs of care that they provide to patients. It is essential to the ethic of medicine that physicians ignore costs. Once we begin to talk about whether money should be spent on some patients and not others, we get into a devilish kind of reasoning that ends in allowing elderly people to die because their care is too expensive and that dumps poor people out of ERs because they have no insurance coverage. No one has a right to put a price on a patient's life. I know that I could never consider how much money each procedure costs when making a treatment decision for my patients. It would be contrary to everything that I stand for as a doctor. . . . I must admit that I, too, am bothered by the idea of giving the patient treatment that will only keep her alive for a few more days at great expense. I just want someone else, not me, to decide when treatment is too costly to provide. We shouldn't make these kinds of decisions at the bedside. We need some kind of policy that we know is ethical for

determining when treatment is just not worth its costs.". . .

Should Mrs. Handel be denied admission to the ICU because her care would not be costworthy? If so, should her family be apprised of this?

Commentary by Dan W. Brock

The central issue raised by this case is what role, if any, physicians should play in rationing health care when benefits seem not worth its costs. More specifically, should Mrs. Handel's physicians make decisions "at the bedside" about whether particular health care for her is worth its cost? It is easy to sympathize with Dr. Bernstein's concern about the social bill for expensive care such as that which Mrs. Handel's family seeks for her, since it appears to be both wasteful and inappropriate. At the same time, it is also easy to sympathize with Dr. Lean's concern that if physicians ever begin to decide whether care for their patients is worth its cost, they will inevitably be carried down a slippery slope toward clearly wrongful denials of care to the old or poor. Any plausible response for limiting use of noncostworthy care must be sensitive to both these concerns.

It is sometimes said that for so important a good as health care, cost should never be a consideration in whether a particular patient receives it. I believe it is easy to see that this cannot be correct. There is wide agreement that it is ethically permissible for a competent patient to decide to forgo any life-sustaining care that he or she judges to be unduly burdensome. One of the burdens of care is the financial cost that it imposes on the patient or others about whom the patient cares. Patient resources used for health care will not be available for other uses. Thus, a patient might freely choose not to undergo some forms of even life-sustaining treatment in order, for example, to preserve an inheritance for his family. Few would find such a choice based on consideration of financial costs ethically objectionable.

When a patient is incompetent to make treatment choices for him or herself, a surrogate, commonly a family member who knows the patient best, must decide for the patient. The widely accepted substituted judgment principle requires that surrogates attempt to decide as the patient would have decided in the circumstances if he or she had capacity. If there is clear and compelling evidence that the patient would not have wanted a particular treatment, in part because of its expense, respecting the patient's self-determination strongly supports the decision of the patient's surrogate against the costly care. Thus, there is nothing intrinsically unethical in either patients or their surrogates sometimes deciding to forgo treatment because of its cost.

The specific issue this case raises, however, is whether Mrs. Handel's physicians should take it upon themselves to deny care to her that she and her surrogates want solely on grounds that its benefits do not warrant its costs. I believe there are several important reasons why they should not. First, Mrs. Handel has obtained catastrophic health care insurance presumably in order to be able to pay the costs of care in circumstances like

these. While this does not obligate her physicians to offer whatever care her surrogates might demand for her, it probably does obligate them not to deny her care on grounds of its cost. Her insurance, in effect, creates both an entitlement and a legitimate expectation that any medically appropriate care covered by her policy will be paid for by the insurance. While the insurance payments for her care will come from the pooled funds largely of others; all members of a private insurance pool join together to pool their funds precisely in order to fund members' entitlements to reimbursement for catastrophic health care costs. Even if the insurance comes from a government program funded by general tax revenues, that program would have the same democratic legitimacy as would other government spending programs, and the entitlements the program establishes should be honored, not surreptitiously undermined, by Mrs. Handel's physicians.

Institutions such as the government, employers, and health insurers all have an interest in holding down their bill for health care. They should not expect or pressure physicians, however, to deny care to patients in circumstances like Mrs. Handel's in which patients have an entitlement to be reimbursed for the financial costs of care. That would be to put the physicians in an ethically unacceptable position. It is ethically acceptable for physicians to help patients or their surrogates weigh the true costs of care against its benefits when the patients or surrogates wish to do so. I believe it is also ethically acceptable for the incentive structures of reimbursement systems to encourage patients or surrogates to weigh the true costs of care against its benefits more than is now common, so long as that does not result in denying patients an adequate level of care. The main reason this is so notoriously difficult to do is that health care insurance, the means of reimbursement for most health care in our country today, reduces or eliminates both out-of-pocket costs to the patient for care utilized, and in turn, the patient's economic incentive to consider or even learn the true costs of care. Yet the unpredictability and great variability in the amount and cost of health care that an individual may need provide powerful reasons to have insurance for health care costs.

A second important reason why Mrs. Handel's physicians should not take it upon themselves to decide whether her care is too costly to the other members of her insurance pool is that they lack any social, moral, or legal authorization to do so. If there is to be a serious public debate in this country about limiting utilization of noncostworthy care, particularly if that is life-sustaining care, then we are now only in the early stages of that debate. Any authorization for physicians to act as health care rationers with their individual patients should come as a result of such a debate, and not merely from pressures from third party payors to reduce their health care outlays. These pressures would be likely to fall most heavily on the vulnerable and powerless and would perhaps end up realizing Dr. Lean's worst fears.

When cost containment measures are openly adopted in financially closed health care systems like HMO's, then both physicians and patients can have reasonable assurance that cost savings will be passed on in the form of lower rates, improved quality of care, or new available forms of care to members who have forgone care to produce the savings. In such settings, it is possible for patients and physicians to cooperate together with the shared goal of providing good quality health care while limiting health care costs. When physicians instead only reduce "society's" overall health care cost by denying care that may benefit or be wanted by their patients, their justification cannot be that the savings are returned to those denied the care for them to spend in alternative ways.

A third serious concern about physicians assuming the role of health care rationers with their individual patients is whether denials of noncostworthy care would be equitably or fairly applied to different patients. If physicians are left to determine without further guidance what care is costworthy for individual patients at the bedside, then almost certainly the effects of these attempts to control health care costs will not be equitable. This is because physicians, in the absence of clear standards of costworthy care, would inevitably reach differing conclusions about what care is costworthy and would also be susceptible to allowing ethically irrelevant factors, such as the social worth of the patient, subtly to influence their judgments. The relatively vulnerable and powerless could be expected to suffer a disproportionate share of the effects of such rationing.

A fourth major concern about physicians becoming "bedside rationers" is that this will create new conflicts of interest between patients and their physicians and so be likely to undermine the trust necessary for well-functioning physician/patient relationships. If physicians come to think of themselves as responsible for ensuring that society's resources are prudently spent, patients' trust that the treatment recommendations and decisions of their physicians are guided first and foremost by concern for their patients' well-being will quite justifiably erode. I think that this concern lies behind Dr. Lean's view that physicians should remain unconstrained advocates for their patients and that "someone else . . . should decide when treatment is too costly to provide."

These various worries about physicians becoming bedside rationers do not imply that economic considerations should never play any role in decisions concerning life-sustaining treatment. Instead, they support an ethical case: (1) that decisions about standards and/or procedures for identifying care that will not be provided to patients because it is not costworthy be arrived at through public processes that allow substantial input to those who will be affected; (2) that health care institutions limiting access to noncostworthy care inform current and potential patients of those limitations; (3) that procedures be put in place to monitor the application of limitations on provision of noncostworthy care to insure that it is done equitably and without denying patients access at least to an adequate level of health care.

The appropriate decision-making bodies for defining limitations on noncost-worthy care will vary depending on the context. For example, in an HMO these issues might be addressed by a committee within the HMO with substantial patient member representation. For government insurance programs, open debate at relevant points in the political process such as legislatures, public hearings, and so forth, would be appropriate. In other cases, participant input may be fostered by employers and health insurers that provide their employees and insurees with a greater range of alternative insurance plans that attempt to define and limit reimbursement for noncostworthy care to varying extents. There is no single institutional mechanism or group of persons that should address and make decisions about what care is costworthy. Nor is there any single correct definition of costworthy care, or any ethical necessity for societal uniformity in the definitions arrived at.

These several reasons for Mrs. Handel's physicians not to deny her the aggressive care she seems to have wanted because it is too costly do not mean she must go to the ICU.

Questions

1. Do you agree with Dr. Lean that physicians should not consider the costs of the health care when they are treating a patient? Why or why not?
2. Summarize in your own words the four major concerns Brock has with physicians needing to make decisions about the rationing of health care.
3. Do you agree with Dr. Brock that there should be "limitations on noncostworthy care"? Why or why not?

5 John Harris, *The Value of Life*

Many writers working in medical ethics have recently argued that, for the sake of society as a whole, healthcare costs ought to be contained for those in the final weeks of life, and for whom aggressive medical treatment would be futile. They argue primarily for economic reasons, and for reasons of the fair distribution of limited resources. When medical resources are spent on terminal patients—here, resources mean everything from X rays and MRIs to the time doctors and nurses spend with each patient—those resources cannot be spent on other patients for whom they might be more effective. Moreover, when medical insurance companies have to spend money on futile care, they are forced to pass on those costs to their healthier clients in the form of increased premiums, a form of taxation which has ripple effects in the larger global economy.

But John Harris in the following essay argues that these opinions are "ageist." Dr. Harris is the Sir David Alliance Professor of Bioethics and Research Director for Social Ethics and Policy at the University of Manchester in England. He is the author of the definitive textbook used in bioethics courses around the world.

Dr. Harris considers it an injustice not to do all that is possible to prolong life, regardless of the cost. He presents an argument that is sometimes called the "fair innings" argument, and then offers his opposition to it. The fair innings argument is based on the view that a given span of years—seventy years, say—constitutes a reasonable, complete life, and that anyone who has lived that long has had a fair shake at life and should therefore not demand that any extraordinary, and expensive, measures be done to them simply to prolong their life a few months more. Harris rejects this argument, holding that it has limited application in the selection of patients for medical treatment.

Suppose that only one place is available on a renal dialysis programme or that only one bed is vacant in a vital transplantation unit or that resuscitation could be given in the time and with the resources available to only one patient. Suppose further that of the two patients requiring any of these resources, one is a 70-year-old widower, friendless and living alone, and the other a 40-year-old mother of three young children with a husband and a career. . . .

The Moral Significance of Age

Many, perhaps most, people feel that, in cases like the one with which we began, there is some moral reason to save the 40-year-old mother rather than the 70-year-old widower. A smaller, but perhaps growing, group of people would see this as a sort of "ageist" prejudice which, in a number of important areas of resource allocation and care, involves giving the old a much worse deal than the younger members of society. This is an exceptionally difficult issue to resolve. A number of the ways of thinking about the issue of the moral relevance of age yield opposed conclusions or seem to tug in opposite directions.

I want first to look at an argument which denies that we should prefer the young mother in our opening example. It is an anti-ageist argument so that is what I will call it, but it is not perhaps the usual sort of argument used to defend the rights of the old.

The Anti-Ageist Argument

All of us who wish to go on living have something that each of us values equally although for each it is different in character, for some a much richer prize than for others, and we none of us know its true extent. This thing is of course "the rest of our lives." So long as we do not know the date of our deaths then for each of us the "rest of our lives" is of indefinite duration. Whether we are 17 or 70, in perfect health or suffering from a terminal disease we each have the rest of our lives to lead. So long as we each fervently wish to live out the rest of our lives, however long that turns out to be, then if we do not deserve to die, we each suffer the same injustice if our wishes are deliberately frustrated and we are cut off prematurely. Indeed there may well be a double injustice in deciding that those whose life expectation is short should not benefit from rescue or resuscitation. Suppose I am told today that I have terminal cancer with only approximately six months or so to live, but I want to live until I die, or at least until I decide that life is no longer worth living. Suppose I then am involved in an accident and because my condition is known to my potential rescuers and there are not enough resources to treat all who could immediately be saved I am marked among those who will not be helped. I am then the victim of a double tragedy and a double injustice. I am stricken first by cancer and the knowledge that I have only a short time to live and I'm then stricken again when I'm told that because of my first tragedy a second and more immediate one is to be visited upon me. Because I have once been unlucky I'm now no longer worth saving.

The point is a simple but powerful one. However short or long my life will be, so long as I want to go on living it then I suffer a terrible injustice when that life is prematurely cut short. Imagine a group of people all of an age, say a class of students all in their mid-20s. If fire trapped all in the lecture theatre and only twenty could be rescued in time should the rescuers shout "youngest first!"? Suppose they had time to debate the question or had been debating it "academically" before the first? It would surely seem invidious to deny some what all value so dearly merely because of an accident of birth? It might be argued that age here provides no criterion precisely because although the lifespans of such a group might be expected to vary widely, there would be no way of knowing who was most likely to live longest. But suppose a reliable astrologer could make very realistic estimates or, what amounts to the same thing, suppose the age range of the students to be much greater, say 17 to 55. Does not the invidiousness of selecting by birth-date remain? Should a 17-year-old be saved before a 29-year-old or she before the 45-year-old and should the 55-year-old clearly be the last to be saved or the first to be sacrificed?

Our normal intuitions would share this sense of the invidiousness of choosing between our imaginary students by reason of their respective ages, but would start to want to make age relevant at some extremes, say if there were a 2-day-old baby and a 90-year-old grandmother. We will be returning to discuss a possible basis for this intuition in a moment. However, it is important to be clear that the anti-ageist argument denies the relevance of age or life expectancy as a criterion absolutely. It argues that even if I know for certain that I have only a little space to live, that space, however short, may be very precious to me. Precious, precisely because it is all the time I have left, and just as precious to me on that account as all the time you have left is precious to you, however much those two timespans differ in length. So that where we both want, equally strongly, to go on living, then we each suffer the same injustice when our lives are cut short or are cut further short.

It might seem that someone who would insist on living out the last few months of his life when by "going quietly" someone else might have the chance to live for a much longer time would be a very selfish person. But this would be true only if the anti-ageist argument is false. It will be true only if it is not plausible to claim that living out the rest of one's life could be equally valuable to the individual whose life it is irrespective of the amount of unelapsed time that is left. And this is of course precisely the usual situation when individuals do not normally have anything but the haziest of ideas as to how long it is that they might have left.

I think the anti-ageist argument has much plausibility. It locates the wrongness of ending an individual's life in the evil of thwarting that person's desire to go on living and argues that it is profoundly unjust to frustrate that desire merely because some of those who have exactly the same desire, held no more strongly, also have a longer life expectancy than the others. However, there are a number of arguments that pull in the opposite direction and these we must now consider.

The Fair Innings Argument

One problem with the anti-ageist argument is our feeling that there is something unfair about a person who has lived a long and happy life hanging on grimly at the end, while someone who has not been so fortunate suffers a related double misfortune, of losing out in a lottery in which his life happened to be in the balance with that of the grim octogenarian. It might be argued that we could accept the part of the anti-ageist argument which focuses on the equal value of unelapsed time, if this could be tempered in some way. How can it be just that someone who has already had more than her fair share of life and its delights should be preferred or even given an equal chance of continued survival with the young person who has not been so favoured? One strategy that seems to take account of our feeling that there is something wrong with taking steps to prolong the lives of the very old at the expense of those much younger is the fair innings argument.

The fair innings argument takes the view that there is some span of years that we consider a reasonable life, a fair innings. Let's say that a fair share of life is the traditional three score and ten, seventy years. Anyone who does not reach 70 suffers, on this view, the injustice of being cut off in their prime. They have missed out on a reasonable share of life; they have been short-changed. Those, however, who do make 70 suffer no such injustice, they have not lost out but rather must consider any additional years a sort of bonus beyond that which could reasonably be hoped for. The fair innings argument requires that everyone be given an equal chance to have a fair innings, to reach the appropriate threshold but, having reached it, they have received their entitlement. The rest of their life is the sort of bonus which may be cancelled when this is necessary to help others reach the threshold.

The attraction of the fair innings argument is that it preserves and incorporates many of the features that made the anti-ageist argument plausible, but allows us to preserve our feeling that the old who have had a good run for their money should not be endlessly propped up at the expense of those who have not had the same chance. We can preserve the conclusion of the anti-ageist argument, that so long as life is equally valued by the person whose life it is, it should be given an equal chance of preservation, and we can go on taking this view until the people in question have reached a fair innings.

There is, however, an important difficulty with the fair innings argument. It is that the very arguments which support the setting of the threshold at an age which might plausibly be considered to be a reasonable lifespan, equally support the setting of the threshold at any age at all, so long as an argument from fairness can be used to support so doing. Suppose that there is only one place available on the dialysis programme and two patients are in competition for it. One is 30, and the other 40 years of age. The fair innings argument requires that neither be preferred on the grounds of age since both are below the threshold and are entitled to an equal chance of reaching it. If there is no other reason to choose between them we should do something like toss a coin. However, the 30-year-old can argue that the considerations which support the fair innings argument require that she be given the place. After all, what's fair about the fair innings argument is precisely that each individual should have an equal chance of enjoying the benefits of a reasonable lifespan. The younger patient can argue that from where she's standing, the age of 40 looks much more reasonable a span than that of 30, and that she should be given the chance to benefit from those ten extra years.

This argument generalised becomes a reason for always preferring to save younger rather than older people, whatever the age difference, and makes the original anti-ageist argument begin to look again the more attractive line to take. For the younger person can always argue that the older has had a fairer innings, and should now give way. It is difficult to stop whatever span is taken to be a fair innings collapsing towards zero under pressure from those younger candidates who see their innings as less fair than that of those with a larger share.

But perhaps this objection to the fair innings argument is mistaken? If seventy years is a fair innings it does not follow that the nearer a span life approaches seventy years, the fairer an innings it is. This may be revealed by considering a different sort of threshold. Suppose that most people can run a mile in seven minutes, and that two people are given the opportunity to show that they can run a mile in that time. They both expect to be given seven minutes. However, if one is in fact given only three minutes and the other only four, it's not true that the latter is given a fairer running time: for people with average abilities four minutes is no more realistic a time in which to run a mile than is three. Four minutes is neither a fair threshold in itself, nor a fairer one than three minutes would be.

Nor does the argument that establishes seven minutes as an appropriate threshold lend itself to variation downwards. For that argument just is that seven is the number of minutes that an average adult takes to run a mile. Why then is it different for lifespans? If three score and ten is the number of years available to most people for getting what life has to offer, and is also the number of years people can reasonably expect to have, then it is a misfortune to be allowed anything less however much less one is allowed, if nothing less than the full span normally suffices forgetting what can be got out of life. It's true that the 40-year-old gets more time than the 30-year-old, but the frame of reference is not time only, but time normally required for a full life.

This objection has some force, but its failure to be a good analogy reveals that two sorts of considerations go to make an innings fair. For while living a full or complete life, just in the sense of experiencing all the ages of man, is one mark of a fair innings, there is also value in living through as many ages as possible. Just as completing the mile is one value, it is not the only one. Runners in the race of life also value ground covered, and generally judge success in terms of distance run.

What the fair innings argument needs to do is to capture and express in a workable form the truth that while it is always a *misfortune* to die when one wants to go

on living, it is not a *tragedy* to die in old age; but it is on the other hand, both a tragedy and a misfortune to be cut off prematurely. Of course ideas like "old age" and "premature death" are inescapably vague, and may vary from society to society, and over time as techniques for postponing death improve. We must also remember that while it may be invidious to choose between a 30- and a 40-year-old on the grounds that one has had a fairer innings than the other, it may not be invidious to choose between the 30- and the 65-year-old on those grounds.

If we remember, too, that it will remain wrong to end the life of someone who wants to live or to fail to save them, and that the fair innings argument will only operate as a principle of selection where we are forced to choose between lives, then something workable might well be salvaged.

While "old age" is irredeemably vague, we can tell the old from the young, and even the old from the middle-aged. So that without attempting precise formulation, a reasonable form of the fair innings argument might hold; and might hold that people who had achieved old age or who were closely approaching it would not have their lives further prolonged when this could only be achieved at the cost of the lives of those who were not nearing old age. These categories could be left vague, the idea being that it would be morally defensible to prefer to save the lives of those who "still had their lives before them" rather than those who had "already lived full lives." The criterion to be employed in each case would simply be what reasonable people would say about whether someone had had a fair innings. Where reasonable people would be in no doubt that a particular individual was nearing old age and that the person's life could only be further prolonged at the expense of the life of someone that no reasonable person would classify as nearing old age, then the fair innings argument would apply, and it would be justifiable to save the younger candidate. . . .

Fair Innings or No Ageism?

We have then two principles which can in hard cases pull in opposite directions. What should we do in the sorts of hard cases we have been considering? First, we should be clear that while the very old and those with terminal conditions are alike, in that they both have a short life expectancy, they may well differ with respect to whether or not they have had a fair innings. I do not believe that this issue is at all clear cut but I am inclined to believe that where two individuals both equally wish to go on living for as long as possible our duty to respect this wish is paramount. It is, as I have suggested, the most important part of what is involved in valuing the lives of others. Each person's desire to stay alive should be regarded as of the same importance and as deserving the same respect as that of anyone else, irrespective of the quality of their life or its expected duration.

This would hold good in all cases in which we have to choose between lives, except one. And that is where one individual has had a fair innings and the other not. In this case, while both equally wish to have their lives further prolonged one, but not the other, has had a fair innings. In this case, although there is nothing to choose between the two candidates from the point of view of their respective will to live and both would suffer the injustice of having their life cut short when it might continue, only one would suffer the further injustice of being deprived of a fair innings—a benefit that the other has received.

Questions

1. Put into your own words the "anti-ageist" argument that Dr. Harris proposes.
2. Put into your own words the "fair innings" argument that Dr. Harris outlines.
3. Which side of the dilemma do you support, the anti-ageist argument or the fair innings argument, and why?

Small Group Exercises

1. Prepare a debate in your small group on the claim, "Active euthanasia should be legalized." Draw up arguments for both sides of the debate and present the debate to the class.

2. In your small group, discuss the merits of withholding medical treatment from a patient who in all likelihood, due to the severity of his or her condition, will not be able to benefit from it. In whose best interests would this act be? If this option became mandatory in hospitals today, would it change your opinion of medical care in this country? If you were in this situation as the patient, would you demand to be treated? Why or why not?

3. Discuss ways in which a state like Oregon might take its decriminalization of active euthanasia "to the next level" by decriminalizing active euthanasia for other, nonterminal sufferers. If such legislation were proposed, would you support it? Why or why not? If you support it, where would you draw the final line as to who could legitimately be a recipient of the "right to die"?

Practical Learning Component

1. Visit a local chapter of End-of-Life Choices (formerly the Hemlock Society), the world's most active support network for the legalization of active euthanasia. Interview chapter members as to their views on the subject. Ask about personal experiences that may have led to their commitment to this organization.

2. Contact members of your local chapter of the National Right to Life organization, or attend one of their sponsored events. Interview chapter members as to their views on the subject. Ask about personal experiences that may have led to their commitment to this organization.

3. Interview several doctors who frequently work with dying patients (oncologists, cardiac specialists, brain surgeons, etc.). Ask pointed questions about their views on the subject of active euthanasia. If they are opposed to legalizing it, find out the reasons why. If they are in favor of legalizing it, ask whether they fear this might affect the way the public views their profession. If possible, try to interview doctors of both genders, and of various ages.

Chapter 7

Near-Death Experiences

Man's task is . . . to become conscious of the contents that
press upward from the unconscious. As far as we can discern,
the sole purpose of human existence is to kindle a light in the
darkness of mere being.

— CARL JUNG

Late one night in southern California, under the influence of drugs and alcohol, a woman was driving too fast on a slick mountain road. She hit a patch of ice and careened off the pavement, slamming her car into a road sign. The impact caused her unrestrained body to fly through the windshield, over 20 feet of grassy earth, and to crash headfirst into a second road sign. She lay in a bleeding, crumpled heap at the bottom of the sign for three hours before rescue crews arrived, applied first aid, and rushed her to the hospital. She remained in a coma for two weeks, her body fighting for life.

When she awoke from the coma, she displayed no brain or other neurological damage. In a fully conscious state she related a story of what took place as her body flew the short space between windshield and road sign. In midair, fully aware of her plight, she felt separated from her body, as if she were watching herself fly through the air on a movie screen. Then she saw a tunnel open above her. Brilliant colors and warm, inviting music emanated from the tunnel, and she willingly ventured in. As she traveled down the tunnel, she lost all sensation of pain and fear and felt immersed in a feeling of blissful anticipation. At the end of the tunnel she found herself in the presence of a bright light and other spiritual beings. She recognized and had a brief conversation with her sister who had died just a few months before. The light seemed to coax out of her the lengthy, detailed story of her life. In response she was given full understanding of her struggles, and loving encouragement to improve herself. She then heard the words, "It is not your time to die," after which she found herself sailing quickly down the tunnel and back into her pain-wracked body.

Since this experience the woman entered rehab, graduated from a local university with a degree in business, married happily, and is now raising two sons while managing a successful insurance firm. She claims to have no fear of death, that her life is more meaningful, and that she feels a vital connection to God. The woman had what recent literature is calling a "near-death experience" (NDE) and it changed her life, as it has for the nearly twelve million Americans who have had similar sorts of experiences.

ELEMENTS OF THE NDE

History records that near-death experiences and the beliefs they engender have been part of human consciousness from its beginning. The Tibetan *Book of the Dead,* the Egyptian *Book of the Dead,* the pre-Socratic philosophers, Plato, the New Testament's *Book of the Apocalypse,* the early Church Fathers—all relate stories that speak of a life beyond death as told by those who "died" and came back to life again. A recent study of medieval Christianity demonstrates that NDEs were a vital part of the Church's teaching ministry. And NDEs find their place in the founding histories of Islam, Methodism, and Mormonism; and in the annals of the Revolutionary and Civil Wars.

The academic and scientific study of NDEs, however, is a relatively recent phenomenon. One of the primary causes behind the current fascination with NDEs is the work of Dr. Raymond Moody, a psychiatrist and former professor of philosophy from the University of Virginia. At the publication of his 1975 book, *Life After Life,* Dr. Moody single-handedly made NDEs a household phrase. The book went on to sell more than five million copies after being translated into thirty-six different languages. Moody wrote three more books, all detailing the nature, causes, and effects of near-death experiences.

For *Life After Life,* Moody interviewed 150 patients at the University of Virginia Medical Center who were referred to him after having close brushes with death. As one patient after another told Moody of seemingly impossible experiences that occurred right at the time of their clinical "death," Moody began to piece together a common pattern to their stories. Despite a great deal of variety, these experiences "near death" contained recurring elements that led Moody to conclude that there must be some empirical reality behind them. While Moody was careful in his writing to refrain from making any absolute rendering of these NDEs as genuine spiritual experiences, he nevertheless found himself profoundly moved by his research. At the end of *Life After Life,* Moody writes,

> I am left, not with conclusions or evidence or proofs, but with something much less definite—feelings, questions, analogies, puzzling facts to be explained. In fact, it might be more appropriate to ask, not what conclusions I have drawn on the basis of my study, but rather how the study has affected me personally. In response I can only say: There is something very persuasive about seeing a person describe his experience which cannot easily be conveyed in writing. Their near-death experiences were very

real events to these people, and through my association with them the experiences have become real events to me.[35]

Moody notes that all NDEs begin with some kind of trauma to the body. Most often this occurs on the operating table as, for example, a simple operation goes badly, or an overdose of anesthesia is delivered. Sometimes NDEs are triggered by life-threatening accidents—a car crash, accidental drowning, electrocution, etc. Usually this trauma forces the person into "clinical" or "cardiopulmonary" death, where the heart and lungs stop functioning for a period of time. Occasionally, however, NDEs are precipitated by non-dying events. They can be caused by an impending accident that hasn't occurred yet, such as when a mountain climber falls and has an NDE on the way down before hitting the ground. And history records experiences that sound much like NDEs occurring to persons during prolonged periods of fasting, prayer, and meditation.

What then follows, says Moody, is the experience of one or more of the following NDE "elements" or "traits."[36]

• *experiencing deep peace and a complete cessation of pain:* An element common to nearly all NDEs is the feeling of bliss, peace, and painlessness that begins at the moment of clinical death; this feeling contrasts sharply with the pain and anxiety associated with the precipitating trauma.

• *hearing noises:* They hear noises that are similar to common earthly sounds, some of which are pleasant (beautiful music, soft humming, wind chimes), while others (buzzing, rushing wind, banging, roaring, whistling) are more irritating.

• *out-of-body experience:* Most NDEs are marked by an experience in which the person finds himself floating above his dead body, looking down on it, and able to hover and maneuver bodiless in the air.

• *traveling down an enclosure:* Near-death survivors describe being dragged down a dark or dimly lit tunnel or some other form of enclosed space (a well, funnel, sewer pipe, or valley).

• *meeting others:* NDErs sometimes report seeing dead relatives or friends who appear to help them make the transition from life to death. Sometimes religious figures like Jesus and Mary are met; in other experiences angelic beings are met, or something like a guardian angel appears.

• *meeting a being of light:* The most important element of the experience, NDErs often describe meeting, and sometimes merging with, a being of brilliant light who is experienced as personal, loving, understanding, caring, and nonjudgmental, and is often associated with God, Christ, or an angel. The light emanating from this being is often described as being brighter and more brilliant than any earthly light; music is sometimes associated with the light.

• *a life review:* NDErs describe an experience of total recall of every aspect of their lives as it flashed before them in vibrant color and depth. Everything they have ever said and done is reviewed, usually in the presence of the being of light; understanding is sometimes given as to why certain mistakes were made, and wisdom for how to live life better upon return to the body.

• *a border or limit:* If the NDE is experienced as a kind of journey, it usually reaches a point beyond which the person is not able to travel; if that point is breached, it is understood that there is no way of returning; that it is the point of genuine death. Sometimes a variant of the following words are heard, "It is not your time to die."

• *receiving special knowledge:* Although rare, some NDErs claim that at some point during their near-death journey they learned the "secrets of the universe," the "meaning of it all"; they are given answers to all the great questions that have perplexed humankind for centuries.

• *returning to the body:* NDEs usually end with a decision to return to the body—perhaps in response to a sense of "unfinished business"—a return venture down the tunnel, and the painful re-entry into the traumatized body.

• *sense of ineffability:* Those who survive such a close brush with death often claim that what they experienced of the afterlife is so unlike our lives on earth that it is impossible to put it into words.

• *lasting changes in attitude, belief, and behavior:* Most NDErs experience profound change in their perspective and life orientation. While most do not become more religious in a conventional sense, they do adopt a more philosophical attitude toward life, feel less anxiety and greater peace, lose all fear of death, and sometimes take up a new direction in life.

Moody's listing of the most common elements of the NDE has for years fueled a stereotype of the NDE that it is a straightforward, sequential journey from pain to bliss by means of a tunnel, meeting God and having a life review. However, further research has revealed a much more complex picture. One of those putting that picture together is Moody's former colleague from the University of Virginia, and now a professor of psychology at the University of Connecticut, Dr. Kenneth Ring. Although accepting of the NDE as a genuine phenomenon of consciousness, Dr. Ring nonetheless remains skeptical of the reductionism implied by Moody's work.

Dr. Ring lists three issues of concern raised by Moody's work on the general pattern of the NDE. The first of these is that not all those who have an NDE experience all the elements. Assuming the NDE to be a genuine spiritual experience of an objective reality, one would expect that every NDE would more or less look the same: that all NDErs would travel down the same type of tunnel, that all would have a life review (most do not), that all would meet a loving being of light, etc. The fact is that NDEs vary wildly from person to person. While most are positive, not all are. While meeting the being of light and having a life review are powerfully significant to those who experience them, less than a third of all NDEs have both. Tunnels vary in kind, dimension, and quality, and some people do not have any kind of "enclosure" experience. Some are warmly greeted by angels, friends, and family while others go through the experience alone. Again, if the NDE opens a window on a space-time dimension other than the one we normally inhabit, we would expect a degree of agreement among those privileged to get a glimpse of it.

Dr. Ring suggests that the discrepancy among the elements observed in NDEs may be due to differences in the amount of time the experiencer is clinically dead. The longer the person is in cardiopulmonary death, Ring reasons, the more elements that are experienced. But this theory was discounted by research performed by cardiologist Maurice Rawlings.[37] Dr. Rawlings recorded the amount of time patients undergoing open-heart surgery were clinically dead (such "death" is often a routine part of the surgery) and correlated that with the number of elements they experienced in the NDEs they related. Rawlings found no significant correlation between the time of cardiopulmonary death and the number of elements experienced.

A second problem associated with Moody's description of the NDE is that recent cross-cultural studies reveal that the tone and visual references of NDEs vary from culture to culture as well as person to person. The ground-breaking work of Allan Kellehear, published in his 1996 book, *Experiences Near Death,* demonstrates that some of the fundamental archetypes of the Western NDE simple do not appear in the NDEs of other cultures, or they appear under different forms. Tunnels become gates or doors, for example, in the NDEs of people from India and China. The life review, so important to the Western NDE experience, are very rare in the NDEs of the aboriginal peoples of Australia, New Zealand, and North America. Most notably, while those living in countries influenced by the Judeo-Christian tradition tend to see and converse with Jesus (there are notable differences, it should be said, between Catholic and Protestant NDEs), those living in Islamic countries tend to see Mohammed, those in Buddhist lands tend to see the Buddha, and those in India tend to see Krishna or one of the Hindu gods. Even the architecture of the NDE differs from culture to culture: an NDEr in Europe will enter into a building that resembles the Vatican while an NDEr in Saudi Arabia enters into a building that looks like the al-Haram, the "Great Mosque," in Mecca. NDErs in New Delhi speak of grand, gilded temples, while NDErs in London speak of English gardens and tables laid out for afternoon tea!

Naturally all this begs the question: Are NDEs merely the neurological construction of a dying brain, and as such merely hallucinatory social constructs derived from a lifetime's experiences, values, and beliefs? Would this then explain why they appear to be so different across cultures? For if they are not merely that, if they are objectively real in the strong, spiritualist sense—meaning they are indeed out of body experiences that transfer the disembodied soul to another space-time dimension—then one would be forced to conclude that this dimension is itself partitioned according to religious (or nonreligious) culture, language, ethnicity, and so on; which is to say, that there are different heavenly realms for all the different sociocultural units that make up our diverse human world. And for many, neither answer is fully satisfactory.

Finally, a third problem with the NDE as described by Moody is that it leaves us with the impression that everyone who experiences clinical death also experiences an NDE, and this is simply not true. To be fair, Moody does mention once at the beginning of *Life After Life* that he has "talked with a few people who were pronounced dead, resuscitated, and came back reporting none of these common elements."[38] But his anecdotal research methodology, which only treats those who have had an NDE, fails to render the full picture. Studies conducted by several researchers conclude that less than half of those who experience clinical "death" also experience an NDE; in some studies the number of experiences was as few as 25 percent.[39] Most people whose heart stops beating and whose lungs stop breathing for a period of time, and who are resuscitated, experience nothing but empty blackness while they are unconscious. This again leaves us wondering: if this is a genuine spiritual experience, why do some experience nothing at the moment of death while some go on to have a profound, life-changing experience?

One simple answer that has been given to this question is that NDEs are a gift from God offered to a select few who have either merited the experience because of their faith and good deeds, or who needed it in order to fulfill their calling in life. There is no scientific way to refute this answer, of course. But it is interesting to note that while prior religious faith appears to have direct impact on the elemental details of an NDE, it has no correlation to whether or not one has an NDE. In fact, research performed in 1980 by Kenneth Ring, and in 1982 by Michael Sabom, shows that atheists and agnostics are twice as likely than theists to have an NDE.[40]

Death and Dying Fact

A Brief History of Interest in NDEs[41]

In 1892, Albert von St. Gallen Heim published a collection of accounts by mountain climbers who had fallen in the Alps and soldiers wounded in war who reported experiencing life after death.

In 1943, Dr. George Ritchie suffered mortal injuries during World War II. As his body was being wheeled to the morgue an orderly saw his hand move. After his revival his life was completely transformed. He later published the experiences he underwent while clinically dead.

In 1965, philosophy student Raymond Moody heard George Ritchie tell his story and became fascinated by it. In 1975, after becoming a medical doctor, Moody published an account of 150 stories he gathered. The book, *Life After Life,* was the first bestseller on the phenomenon of near-death experiences.

In 1981, after five years of research, Dr. Kenneth Ring was able to verify the research of Dr. Raymond Moody and published his findings in "Life After Life." Dr. Kenneth Ring's scientific study established the near-death experience as a genuine subject of mainline academic research.

(Continued)

(Continued)

In 1982, Dr. Ring's work was furthered by a study of NDEs in children performed by Dr. Melvin Morse.

In 1982, the Gallup polling organization discovered that eight million adult Americans have had near-death experiences. This is about one person in twenty.

In 1993, Dr. Susan Blackmore published research suggesting the NDE is nothing more than a mental state produced by the dying brain.

In 1997, the *U.S. News & World Report* survey found that over fifteen million adult Americans have claimed to have had an NDE.

With conflicting evidence mounting against the NDE as a true glimpse of life after death, several theories have arisen in recent years to explain the NDE in purely psychological or biological terms. Generally, the psychological theories fall into three basic types:

- that the NDE is a defensive emotional reaction to the shock and stress of death, and as such involves a *depersonalization* or *detachment* from one's body and situation;
- that the NDE is a form of *fantasy* or *wish-fulfillment* in the face of the horrors of death, which then creates the positive hallucinations and memories of one's experiences;
- that the NDE is an experience that taps into certain *mythological archetypes* that have been "wired" into our brains through evolution as a way of keeping us calm during death and thus increasing our chances of survival.

The biological explanations for the NDE tend to be more complex inasmuch as they involve detailed discussion of brain anatomy and hormonal chemistry. These explanations usually include one or more of the following theories:

- *metabolic disturbances:* the NDE is the product of certain dramatic imbalances in the body's systems which occur during death—such as toxins leaked into the blood from a dying liver; high fever; lack of oxygen, etc.
- *drug overload:* the NDE is the product of too much anesthesia during surgery which creates the hallucinations and out-of-body experiences common to NDEs
- *endorphins:* the morphinelike substance in our brain produced during trauma and physical exertion—which creates the so-called "runner's high"—is produced in excessive amounts during the trauma of dying, inducing the sensations of deep peace and joy
- *limbic lobe seizure:* the area in the brain that controls both mood and memory seizes up during the dying process, much as it does in an epileptic during a seizure, and thus creates both the NDE hallucinations and a life review

- *visual cortex hyperactivity:* the area in the brain responsible for processing visual stimuli overreacts during death, creating a sensation of a bright light at the center of the visual field surrounded by darkness. As the brain is dying, this bright light becomes more intense, leading to the sensation of traveling down a tunnel toward the light[42]

When taken together, psychological and biological explanations for the NDE can move us toward a coherent working hypothesis for why there is often such a powerful, life-changing experience as the human body approaches death. They reveal the immense complexities of human consciousness, and the need for further research into the phenomena associated with the brain. On their own, however, such materialistic theories fall short on several counts.

First, comparisons of near-death visionary experiences with the sort of hallucinations caused by metabolic disturbances, brain seizures, and drug overdoses highlight dramatic, qualitative differences between the two types of dissociations while the former are described as "real," "three-dimensional," and "clear," the latter are usually described as "dreamlike" and "flat." While the former are almost universally associated with feelings of bliss and joy and are interpreted as spiritually meaningful, the latter are often described as filled with pain and discomfort, and as being spiritually meaningless. The former often cause the experiencers to change their lives for the better, while the latter rarely do.

Moreover, some who have NDEs go on to make claims of having sensory experiences that could not have been perceived through normal means during clinical death. For example, some who have an NDE go on to recall conversations that took place between the doctors and nurses who were working to revive them. Some can recall precise measurements on the life-support machines attached to their bodies, or the exact time the heart monitor went to flatline. A rare few even remember overhearing conversations that took place in adjoining rooms, or even further away from the site of the trauma. While some of this recollection can be attributed to normal sensory perception that can occur even while unconscious or anesthetized, some of it clearly cannot.

A recent study of NDEs experienced by the blind offers further evidence that the NDE may be more than merely a psychological or biological response to a dying brain.[43] Among those born blind, the study reveals, there is a kind of sight that is experienced during an NDE. When tested after an NDE, the blind were able to describe familiar objects with accuracy. Even some of those who had lost their sight at birth were able to recognize the unique physical features of their doctors and nurses following their brush with death.

Lastly, there are some NDErs who approach death and recover, and then go on to report that while they were dying they were met by previously deceased relatives or friends. While visions of this kind, like other aspects of the NDE, may represent a defensive attempt to reduce fear, there are cases of this type that defy such explanation. For example, there are instances in which a near-death experiencer reports meeting a deceased family member or friend whose death could not have been known in any other way. In one Dutch study, there is recorded a case of a young boy who lost his family in a tragic car accident. He was brought to the hospital unconscious and remained in a coma for days. He could not have known about his loss by any normal means. Upon recovery, however, as he was informed that his parents and younger sister were dead, he responded that he knew already; he had been told of the news by his parents and sister during an NDE.[44]

The problem with such evidence in support of a more "paranormal" explanation of the NDE is that it is anecdotal in form, and often reported long after the near-death event itself. It may be collected by researchers anxious to disprove reductionist theories, or zealous to promote a particular religious agenda. In most cases, the evidence has not been, or cannot be, corroborated in any rigorous way.

Nevertheless, NDEs represent a genuine, powerful, life-changing experience for those who have them. Whatever is going on in the body at the time of the experience, subjectively speaking the NDE is of such high quality that all other human experiences seem to pale by comparison. While they are not able to provide definitive "proof" that there is life after death, they do open up that possibility for many who would otherwise be disinclined to accept the idea. Perhaps the best method of approaching NDEs is to walk a middle path. As Carol Zaleski has written, "We need to find a middle path between the extremes of dismissing near-death experience as 'nothing but' and embracing it as 'proof.'"[45]

In the readings that follow, you will be introduced to some of the leading figures in the ongoing research into this fascinating phenomenon. You will hear from Raymond Moody himself, the "founding father" of near-death research. Allan Kellehear will introduce you to some of his studies of near-death experiences across cultures. Carol Zaleski and Susan Blackmore will discuss the science lying behind the NDE, the first from the perspective of someone who is critical of merely reductionistic accounts, and the second of someone who is critical of merely spiritualist accounts. And in a final group of readings, you will learn of some of the life lessons that NDEs can impart to the rest of us.

---

1 Raymond Moody, *The Light Beyond*

Raymond Moody is to the near-death experience what Elisabeth Kübler-Ross is to the death and dying movement—namely, the primary popularizer of what is an ancient, but now widely considered, phenomenon. Dr. Moody has a Ph.D. in philosophy from the University of Virginia, where he also served as a medical resident after receiving his M.D. degree. In 1975, Moody published a collection of stories he had been gathering during his years as a resident and young intern in Virginia. He had come in contact with over 150 patients who, according to their own testimonies, had been clinically dead, but were brought back to life again by medical means.

Near-death experiences have been a part of Western literature since the time of Plato. But at no time have they been more popular, and more talked about, than in our own. This is in part due to the increase in medical technology and its ability to bring people back from the brink of death. As a result, more and more people are experiencing bouts with death and living to tell the tale. But it is also due to the immense popularity of Moody's first book, *Life After Life*. Moody himself is quick to say that the NDE does not prove scientifically that there is life after death (after all, the experiencers themselves are brought back to life again, so by definition, they have not really died at all). But he does admit that the NDE may be a kind of passageway to another form of reality that lies beyond the one to which we are normally accustomed.

The following passage is taken from Dr. Moody's follow-up study to *Life After Life*, published in 1988 under the title *The Light Beyond*. In this reading taken from the introductory section of the book, you will learn in great detail the many different ways people who have an NDE experience its various elements.

What happens when people die? That is probably mankind's most often asked and perplexing question. Do we simply cease to live, with nothing but our mortal remains to mark our time on earth? Are we resurrected later by a Supreme Being only if we have good marks in the Book of Life? Do we come back as animals, as the Hindus believe, or perhaps as different people generations later?

We are no closer to answering the basic question of the afterlife now than we were thousands of years ago when it was first pondered by ancient man. But there are many ordinary people who have been to the brink of death and reported miraculous glimpses of a world beyond, a world that glows with love and understanding that can be reached only by an exciting trip through a tunnel or passageway.

This world is attended by deceased relatives bathed in glorious light and ruled by a Supreme Being who guides the new arrival through a review of his life before sending him back to live longer on earth.

Upon return, the persons who "died" are never the same. They embrace life to its fullest and express the belief that love and knowledge are the most important of all things because they are the only things you can take with you.

For want of a better phrase to describe these incidents, we can say these people have had near-death experiences (NDEs).

I coined this phrase several years ago in my first book, *Life After Life*. Other people have called it other things, including "other world journeys," "flight of the alone to the Alone," "breaking of the plane," "near-death visions." But the traits of these episodes—no matter what they are called—all point to a similar experience. NDEers experience some or all of the following events: a sense of being dead, peace and painlessness even during a "painful" experience, bodily separation, entering a dark region or tunnel, rising rapidly into the heavens, meeting deceased friends and relatives who are bathed in light, encountering a Supreme Being, reviewing one's life, and feeling reluctance to return to the world of the living.

I isolated these traits over two decades ago in personal research that started by coincidence when I was a twenty-year-old philosophy student at the University of Virginia.

I was sitting with a dozen or so students in a seminar room listening to Professor John Marshall discuss the philosophical issues related to death. Marshall mentioned that he knew a psychiatrist in town—Dr. George Ritchie—who had been pronounced dead of double pneumonia and then successfully resuscitated. While he was "dead," Ritchie had the remarkable experience of passing through a tunnel and seeing beings of light.

This experience, my professor remarked, had profoundly affected this physician, who was convinced that he had been allowed to peek into the afterlife.

Frankly, at that point in my life, the prospect that we might survive spiritually after physical death had never occurred to me. I had always assumed that death was an obliteration of one's physical body as well as one's consciousness. Naturally I was intrigued that a respected physician would be confident enough to publicly admit having a glimpse of the afterlife.

A few months later I heard the psychiatrist himself describe his experience to a group of students. He told us of viewing from a distance his own apparently dead body as it lay on a hospital bed, of entering into a brilliant light that emanated love, and of seeing every event of his life reviewed in a three-dimensional panorama.

I filed Ritchie's story away in my memory and went on with my studies, finishing my Ph.D. in philosophy in 1969. It was when I began teaching at the university that I ran into another near-death experience.

One of my students had almost died the year before, and I asked him what the experience was like. I was overwhelmed to find that he'd had an episode almost exactly like the one I had heard from Ritchie over four years before.

I began to find other students who knew of other NDEs. By the time I entered medical school in 1972, I had no fewer than eight NDE case studies from reliable, sincere people.

In medical school I found more cases and soon had enough case studies to compile *Life After Life,* which became an international best-seller. There was clearly a thirst for knowledge about what happens to us in the hereafter.

The book posed many questions it couldn't answer and raised the ire of skeptics who found the case studies of a few hundred people to be worthless in the realm of "real" scientific study. Many doctors claimed that they had never heard of near-death experiences despite having resuscitated hundreds of people. Others claimed it was simply a form of mental illness, like schizophrenia. Some said these NDEs only happened to extremely religious people, while others felt it was a form of demon possession. These experiences never happen to children, some doctors said, because they haven't been "culturally polluted" like adults. Too few people have NDEs for them to be significant, others said.

Some people were interested in researching the subject of NDEs further, myself included. The work we have done over the last decade has shed a tremendous amount of light on this subject. We have been able to address most of the questions put forth by those who feel that the near-death experience is little more than a mental illness or the brain playing tricks on itself. Frankly, it has been good to have the skeptics around, because it has made us look at this phenomenon much harder than we probably would have otherwise. Much of what we researchers have found is included in this book.

Who, How Many, and Why

One thing I would like to discuss in this chapter is the great number of NDEs that actually happen. When I started looking into this phenomenon, I thought there were very few people who actually experienced it. I had no figures and there were certainly none referred to in medical literature, but if I had to guess I would say that one in eight people who were resuscitated or had a similar brush with mortality had at least one of the traits of an NDE.

When I began lecturing and asking large groups of people if they had ever had an NDE themselves or knew anyone who had, my perception of the frequency of this phenomenon changed dramatically. At lectures I would ask the audience, "How many of you have had a near-death experience or know of someone who has?" About one person in thirty raised his hand in reply.

Pollster George Gallup, Jr., found that eight million adults in the United States have had an NDE. That equals one person in twenty.

He was further able to analyze the content of these NDEs by polling for their elements. Here is what he found:

Element	Percent
Out of body	26
Accurate visual perception	23
Audible sounds or voices	17
Feelings of peace, painlessness	32
Light phenomena	14
Life review	32
Being in another world	32
Encountering other beings	23
Tunnel experience	9
Precognition	6

Such a poll clearly showed the NDEs are much more common in society than any of the NDE researchers ever thought.

The NDE Traits

As I mentioned earlier, I was able to derive a set of nine traits that define the near-death experience. I did this by questioning hundreds of people and examining their unique episodes for those common elements.

In *Life After Life* I said that I had never met anyone who had experienced all of these traits while undergoing an NDE. But since writing that book, I have interviewed more than a thousand NDEers and have found several who had "full-blown" episodes that exhibited all nine NDE traits.

Still, it's important to note that not all people who undergo a near-death experience have all of the following symptoms. Some might have one or two, others five or six. It is the presence of one or more of these traits that defines the NDE.

A Sense of Being Dead

Many people don't realize that the near-death experience they are having has anything to do with death. They will find themselves floating above their body, looking at it from a distance, and suddenly feel fear and/or confusion. They will wonder, "How is it that I can be up here, looking at myself down there?" It doesn't make any sense to them and they become very confused.

At this point, they may not actually recognize the physical body they are looking at as being their own.

One person told me that while he was out of his body, he passed through an army hospital ward and was amazed at how many young men there were who were about his age and shape who looked like him. He was actually looking at these different bodies, wondering which one was his.

Another person who was in a horrible accident in which he lost two of his limbs remembered lingering over his body on the operating table and feeling sorry for the maimed person on it. Then he realized it was him!

NDEers often feel fear at this point, which then gives way to perfect understanding of what is going on. They can understand what the doctors and nurses are trying to convey to each other (even though they frequently have no formal medical training), but when they try to talk to them or other people present, no one is able to see or hear them.

At this point, they may try to attract the attention of the people present by touching them. But when they do, their hands go right through the person's arm as though nothing was there.

This was described to me by a woman I personally resuscitated. I saw her have a cardiac arrest and immediately started chest massage. She told me later that while I was working on restarting her heart, she was going up above her body and looking down. She was standing behind me, trying to tell me to stop, that she was fine where she was. When I didn't hear her, she tried to grab my arm to keep me from inserting a needle in her arm for injecting intravenous fluid. Her hand passed right through my arm. But when she did that, she later claimed that she felt something that was the consistency of "very rarified gelatin" that seemed to have an electric current running through it.

I have heard similar descriptions from other patients.

After trying to communicate with others, NDEers frequently have an increased sense of self-identity. One NDEer described this stage as being "a time when you are not the wife of your husband, you are not the parent of your children, you are not the child of your parents. You are totally and completely you." Another woman said she felt like she was going through "a cutting of ribbons," like the freedom given to a balloon when its strings are cut.

It is at this point that fear turns to bliss, as well as understanding.

Peace and Painlessness

While the patient is in his or her body, there can frequently be intense pain. But when the "ribbons are cut," there is a very real sense of peace and painlessness.

I have talked to cardiac arrest patients who say that the intense pain of their heart attack turns from agony to an almost intense pleasure. Some researchers have theorized that the brain, when it experiences such intense pain, releases a self-made chemical that stops the pain. I discuss this theory [elsewhere] but I will say here that no one has ever done experiments to prove or disprove it. But even if it is true, it doesn't explain the other symptoms of this phenomenon.

Out-of-Body Experience

Frequently about the time that the doctor says, "We've lost him (or her)," the patient undergoes a complete change of perspective. He feels himself rising up and viewing his own body below.

Most people say they are not just some spot of consciousness when this happens. They still seem to be in some kind of body even though they are out of their physical bodies. They say the spiritual body has shape and form unlike our physical bodies. It has arms and a shape although most are at a loss to describe what it looks like. Some people describe it as a cloud of colors, or an energy field.

One NDEer I spoke to several years ago said he studied his hands while he was in this state and saw them to be composed of light with tiny structures in them. He could see the delicate whorls of his fingerprints and tubes of light up his arms.

The Tunnel Experience

The tunnel experience generally happens after bodily separation. I didn't notice until I wrote *Life After Life* that it isn't until people undergo the "cutting of the ribbons" and the out-of-body experience that they truly realize that their experience has something to do with death.

At this point, a portal or tunnel opens to them and they are propelled into darkness. They start going through this dark space and at the end they come into the brilliant light that we'll deal with next.

Some people go up stairways instead of through a tunnel. One woman said she was with her son as he was dying of lung cancer. One of the last things he said was that he saw a beautiful spiral staircase going upward. He put his mother's mind at peace when he told her that he thought he was going up those stairs.

Some people have described going through beautiful, ornate doors, which seems very symbolic of a passage into another realm.

Some people hear a *whoosh* as they go into the tunnel. Or they hear an electric vibrating sensation or a humming.

The tunnel experience is not something I discovered. There is a fifteenth-century painting by Hieronymus Bosch called "The Ascent into the Empyrean" that virtually describes this experience. In the foreground are people who are dying. Surrounding them are spiritual beings who are trying to direct their attention upward. They pass through a dark tunnel and come out into a light. As they go into this light, they kneel reverently.

In one of the most amazing tunnel experiences I've ever heard the tunnel was described as being almost infinite in length and width and filled with light.

The descriptions are many, but the sense of what is happening remains the same: the person is going through a passageway toward an intense light.

People of Light

Once through the tunnel, the person usually meets beings of light. These beings aren't composed of ordinary light. They glow with a beautiful and intense luminescence that seems to permeate everything and fill the person with love. In fact, one person who went through this experience said, "I could describe this as 'light' or 'love' and it would mean the same thing." Some say it's almost like being drenched by a rainstorm of light.

They also describe this light as being much brighter than anything we experience on earth. But still, despite its brilliant intensity, it doesn't hurt the eyes. Instead, it's warm, vibrant, and alive.

In this situation, NDEers frequently meet up with friends and relatives who have died. Often, they speak of these people as being in the same indescribable bodies as theirs.

Besides bright light and luminescent friends and relatives, some people have described beautiful pastoral scenes. One woman I know spoke of a meadow that was surrounded by plants, each with its own inner light.

Occasionally, people see beautiful cities of light that defy description in their grandeur.

In this state, communication doesn't take place in words as we know them, but in telepathic, nonverbal ways that result in immediate understanding.

The Being of Light

After meeting several beings in light, the NDEer usually meets a supreme Being of Light. People with a Christian background often describe Him as God or Jesus. Those with other religious backgrounds may call him Buddha or Allah. But some have said that it's neither God nor Jesus, but someone very holy nonetheless.

Whoever he is, the Being radiates total love and understanding. So much so, that most people want to be with it forever.

But they can't. At this point they are told, usually by the Being of Light, that they have to return to their earthly body. But first it's his job to take them on a life review.

The Life Review

When the life review occurs, there are no more physical surroundings. In their place is a full color, three-dimensional, panoramic review of every single thing the NDEers have done in their lives.

This usually takes place in a third-person perspective and doesn't occur in time as we know it. The closest description I've heard of it is that the person's whole life is there at once.

In this situation, you not only see every action that you have ever done, but you also perceive immediately the effects of every single one of your actions upon the people in your life.

So for instance, if I see myself doing an unloving act, then immediately I am in the consciousness of the person I did that act to, so that I feel their sadness, hurt, and regret.

On the other hand, if I do a loving act to someone, then I am immediately in their place and I can feel the kind and happy feelings.

Through all of this, the Being is with those people, asking them what good they have done with their lives. He helps them through this review and helps them put all the events of their life in perspective.

All of the people who go through this come away believing that the most important thing in their life is love.

For most of them, the second most important thing in life is knowledge. As they see life scenes in which they are learning things, the Being points out that one of the things they can take with them at death is knowledge. The other is love.

When people come back they have a thirst for knowledge. Frequently, NDEers become avid readers, even if they weren't very fond of books before, or they enroll in school to study a different field than the one they are in.

Rising Rapidly into the Heavens

I should point out that not all NDEers have a tunnel experience. Some report a "floating experience," in which they rise rapidly into the heavens, seeing the universe from a perspective reserved for satellites and astronauts.

The psychotherapist C. G. Jung had an experience like this in 1944 when he had a heart attack. He said that he felt himself rise rapidly to a point far above the earth.

One child I talked to said that he felt himself rise far above the earth, passing through the stars and finding himself up with the angels. Another NDEer described himself as zooming up and seeing the planets all around him and the earth below, like a blue marble.

Reluctance to Return

For many people, the NDE is such a pleasant event that they don't want to return. As a result, they are frequently very angry at their doctors for bringing them back.

Two physician friends of mine first discovered NDEs for themselves when patients they saved became hostile.

One of them was resuscitating another physician who had just had a cardiac arrest. When the stricken man revived, he said angrily: "Carl, don't you ever do that to me again."

Carl was bewildered as to why this anger should arise. But later the revived physician took him aside and apologized for his behavior and explained his experience. "I was mad because you brought me back to death instead of life."

Another physician friend of mine discovered the NDE phenomenon when he resuscitated a man who then yelled at him for taking him out of "that beautiful and bright place."

NDEers frequently act this way. But it is a short-lived feeling. If you talk to them a week or so later, they are happy to have returned. Although they miss the blissful state, they are glad to have the chance to go on living.

Interestingly, many NDEers feel they are given a choice to return or stay. It may be the Being of Light who offers this choice to them, or a relative who has died.

All of the persons I have talked to would stay if they had only themselves to think of. But they usually say they want to go back because they have children left to raise or because their spouses or parents might miss them.

One woman in Los Angeles has faced this question from the Being of Light twice in her life. Once in the late fifties when she was in a coma following an automobile accident, the Being told her it was time to die and go to heaven.

She argued with him, complaining that she was too young to die. But the Being wouldn't budge until she said, "But I'm young, I haven't danced enough yet."

At that point the Being gave out a hearty laugh and allowed her to live.

About thirty years later, she had a cardiac arrest while undergoing minor surgery. Again she passed through the tunnel and found herself with the Being, and again he told her it was her time to die.

This time she argued that she had children to raise and couldn't leave them at this point in their lives.

"Okay," said the Being. "But this is the last time. The next time you have to stay."

Different Time and Space

In addition to these nine traits, people who have undergone NDEs say that time is greatly compressed and nothing like the time we keep with our watches. NDEers have described it as "being in eternity." One woman, when asked how long her experience lasted, told me, "You could say it lasted one second or that it lasted ten thousand years and it wouldn't make any difference how you put it."

The boundaries imposed by space in our everyday lives are often broken in NDEs. During the experience, if NDEers want to go somewhere, they can often just think themselves there. People say that while they were out of their body but watching the doctors work on them in the operating room, they could simply wish their way into the waiting room to see their relatives.

Such experiences are perhaps the best answer to people who think NDEs are the brain playing tricks on itself. After all, on the surface it is entirely possible that the brain, while in great distress, could try to calm itself by creating tunnel experiences and Beings of Light to put the person to rest. But NDEers who can tell you what was going on in other rooms while having their episodes are truly having out-of-body experiences.

I have several examples of people who had out-of-body experiences during their resuscitations and were able to leave the operating room to observe relatives in other parts of the hospital.

One woman who left her body went into the waiting room and saw that her daughter was wearing mismatched plaids. What had happened was that the maid had brought the child to the hospital and in her haste had just grabbed the first two things off the laundry pile.

Later, when she told her family about her experience and the fact that she had seen the girl in these mismatched clothes, they knew that she must have been in that waiting room with them.

Another woman had an out-of-body experience and left the room where her body was being resuscitated. From across the hospital lobby, she watched her brother-in-law as some business associate approached him and asked what he was doing in the hospital.

"Well, I was going out of town on a business trip," said the brother-in-law. "But it looks like June is going to kick the bucket, so I better stay around and be a pallbearer."

A few days later when she was recovering, the brother-in-law came to visit. She told him that she was in the room as he spoke to his friend, and erased any doubt by saying, "Next time I die, you go off on your business trip because I'll be just fine." He turned so pale that she thought he was about to have a near-death experience himself.

Another of these experiences happened to an elderly woman I was resuscitating. I was giving her closed heart massage on an emergency room examining table and the nurse assisting me ran into another room to get a vial of medication that we needed.

It was a glass-necked vial that you're supposed to hold in a paper towel while breaking off the top so you don't cut yourself. When the nurse returned, the neck was broken so I could use the medicine right away.

When the old woman came to, she looked very sweetly at the nurse and said, "Honey, I saw what you did in that room, and you're going to cut yourself doing that." The nurse was shocked. She admitted that in her haste to open the medicine, she had broken the glass neck with her bare fingers.

The woman told us that while we were resuscitating her, she had followed the nurse back to the room to watch what she was doing.

In the absence of firm scientific proof, people frequently ask me what I believe:

Are NDEs evidence of life after life? My answer is "Yes."

There are several things about NDEs that make me feel so strongly. One of these is the verifiable out-of-body experiences that I mentioned [above]. What greater proof is needed that persons survive the death of their physical bodies than many examples of individuals leaving their bodies and witnessing attempts to save it?

Although these out-of-body experiences might be the most solid scientific reason to believe in life hereafter, the most impressive thing about NDEs to me is the enormous changes in personality that they bring about in people. That NDEs totally transform the people to whom they happen shows their reality and power.

After twenty-two years of looking at the near-death experience, I think there isn't enough scientific proof to show conclusively that there is life after death. But that means scientific proof.

Matters of the heart are different. They are open to judgments that don't require a strictly scientific view of the world. But with researchers like myself, they do call for educated analysis.

Based on such examination, I am convinced that NDEers do get a glimpse of the beyond, a brief passage into a whole other reality.

The psychotherapist C. G. Jung summed up my feeling on life after life in a letter he wrote in 1944. This letter is especially significant since Jung himself had an NDE during a heart attack just a few months before he wrote it:

What happens after death is so unspeakably glorious that our imaginations and our feelings do not suffice to form even an approximate conception of it. . . .

Sooner or later, the dead all become what we also are. But in this reality, we know little or nothing about that mode of being. And what shall we still know of this earth after death? The dissolution of our timebound form in eternity brings no loss of meaning. Rather, does the little finger know itself a member of the hand.

Questions

1. Why is it that, according to Moody, some people who have an NDE do not think the experience has anything to do with death?

2. Of the NDE traits that Moody describes in the reading, which one would have the most impact on you (emotionally, spiritually, intellectually, etc.), and why?

3. After reading the stories Moody narrates of NDEs, is there any change in your perception of death? If so, explain this change. If not, why not?

---

2 Allan Kellehear, *Non-Western Near-Death Experiences*

Allan Kellehear was born and educated in Sydney, Australia, where he received a Ph.D. in sociology from the University of New South Wales. He is currently a senior lecturer in sociology at La Trobe University in Melbourne, Australia, and is the author of numerous books on the subject of death and dying, including the one from which this essay is taken, *Experiences Near Death: Beyond Medicine and Religion*.

Professor Kellehear's work on near-death experiences is among the most original of all published NDE research. The fact that Oxford University Press chose to publish it speaks well to the thoroughness and rigor with which Kellehear approaches the subject. Among the many books published about NDEs every year, Kellehear's is the first, and perhaps only, book-length consideration of the NDE from a cross-cultural perspective. Kellehear explores what the NDE is like in countries outside the United States and Europe, and discovers not only many similarities, but also many startling differences. In this passage, you will read of some of his multicultural findings.

China

Contemporary accounts of Chinese NDE in the academic literature are fragmentary and piecemeal. What we know about Chinese NDE comes to us primarily through the historical work of Carl Becker and the more recent empirical work by Zhi-ying and Jian-Xun. Becker reviewed three traditional biographical accounts of well-known Chinese monks who were important to the founding of pure land Buddhism. Each monk experienced a serious illness that resulted in either an NDE or a deathbed vision while still reasonably conscious. In each of these accounts, no tunnel experience is reported, although one person proceeded "through a void." Neither the OBE experience nor the life review was mentioned in these accounts. Encountering other beings, usually religious figures, and observing supernatural environs, usually interpreted as the paradisical "pure land," are consistent throughout the three narratives. In a later work, Becker provided a secondary analysis of the works of Ogasawara and Lai. Ogasawara documents about 20 accounts of deathbed visions, and Lai documents up to 100. Becker argues that the analysis of deathbed visions reveals features of the NDE that are strikingly parallel, an observation made earlier by the parapsychologists Osis and Haraldsson. Once again, though, there is no report of a tunnel sensation. However, emerging from a "dark tubular calyx" is reported. There is no report of an OBE, but life review is suggested by one person who saw all his "sinful deeds." Once again, supernatural environs and beings of light are witnessed.

Physicians Feng Zhi-ying and Liu Jianxun conducted a recent study of Chinese NDE. They interviewed eighty-one survivors of the Tangshan earthquake of 1976 and found that thirty-two of them reported NDEs. Their survey suggested that most of the Western NDE phenomenology was also present in their sample. OBE, the tunnel sensation, a sensation of peace, life reviews, meeting deceased beings, and sighting of an unearthly realm of existence were all reported in their study. Unfortunately, they did not include descriptive cases that we can analyze for content; thus, observations about their data cannot be scrutinized further. For example, although Zhi-ying and Jian-xun assert that "a tunnel-like dark region" was reported by their respondents, this is, in fact, a response to a prior descriptive category offered to them. Thus, we are unsure whether the tunnel sensation is a volunteered descriptor for this part of their experience.

Finally, a recent survey some colleagues and I conducted in China indicates that the Chinese experience and/or understanding of the NDE may not be very different from the Anglo-European one. Similar to Zhi-ying and Jian-xun, we presented a typical Anglo-European vignette of an NDE to a sample of 197 Chinese in Beijing. Twenty-six of these respondents claimed to have had an experience similar to the one described in that survey. Overall it seems that, from the historical and survey evidence available, the Chinese NDE may be very similar to the Anglo-European NDE.

India

The first major report of NDEs from India came to us from the work of Osis and Haraldsson, who interviewed 704 Indian medical personnel about their experiences with the dying. In this sample there were sixty-four reports of NDEs. The remaining reports concerned near-death visions. More recently and directly, Pasricha and Stevenson reported sixteen cases of NDE from India. In the majority of cases (ten) the respondents were actually interviewed by the authors, while in most of the others a "firsthand informant" was interviewed. In later studies, by Pasricha, another twenty-nine cases of Indian NDE were uncovered In a total of forty-five cases, then, Pasricha, and Pasricha with Stevenson, found no evidence of a tunnel sensation. There was one case report of an OBE. A life review was regularly reported, but this took the form of a reading by others of the record of the percipient's life. The panoramic review commonly mentioned by Anglo-Europeans is not reported in this Indian sample. The reading of a person's record is a traditional Hindu belief that, according to the authors, is apparently widely held or known to the people of India. Finally, observing religious figures and deceased beings is part of these Indian NDE reports. These beings are observed in a supernatural world whose features resemble the traditional view of the "other realm."

The Indian NDE accounts collected by Pasricha and Stevenson do not seem to exhibit tunnel and OBE features. However, Osis and Haraldsson, in their interviews with Indian health personnel, found several reports of OBE in Indian patients near death. Blackmore claims to have found cases of tunnel sensation in Indian NDE in her survey of eight respondents. However, on closer inspection, all three of those who supposedly reported tunnel sensation actually reported a sensation of darkness. One respondent agreed that her experience of darkness was "tunnel like" only after accepting this suggestion from Blackmore. This raises two important methodological problems. First, the acceptance of one descriptor does not mean that the description offered is entirely satisfactory. Another, less geometric descriptor, such as an experience of twilight or night darkness, may also be accepted, even preferred, if this is offered as a choice. Second, because Blackmore recruited her respondents through an advertisement in an English newspaper in India (rather than a Hindi newspaper), her respondents were not typical of people from India. We are therefore unable to

draw any conclusion on this subject from Blackmore's study.

Life review and observing a transcendent world in Indian NDEs have parallels with Anglo-European accounts. However, the figures observed in this world, deceased acquaintances aside for the moment, are those suggested by traditional Indian or Chinese mythology. Nevertheless, as Pasricha and Stevenson warn, social variations in another realm, if it exists, should be expected, just as they exist in our own world. The appearance of familiar cultural images may be psychological, but it may also be sociological and empirical. In other words, either projection may account for the visions or the visions may actually be observations of another empirical world that resembles the world of its "expatriate" inhabitants.

Guam

School psychologist Green reported four cases of NDE among the Chammorro of Guam. Two of these cases involved direct interviews conducted by Green. The other two cases were collected by a local man who was interested in the subject of NDEs.

Like the NDEs gathered in India and China, the Chammorro cases report visits to a paradisical place of gardenlike appearance. Here the NDEr is met by deceased beings, some of whom are relatives. Unlike the Indian and Chinese cases, however, OBEs are reported; the respondents recount flying "through the clouds" and making invisible visits to living relatives in America. There is no mention of life review of any sort in these accounts or of any tunnel experience. Indeed, the transition from the ill and unconscious state to the OBE appearance is unexplained. Respondents suddenly find themselves flying through the sky or walking on a road. The emphasis of the narrative is on the social experiences while unconscious, that is, of meeting deceased relatives or experiencing a flying visit to living ones.

Western New Britain

Counts reported three cases of NDE among the Kaliai as part of her 1981 anthropological fieldwork. "Andrew," the subject of the case cited at length in the previous chapter, was one of the three interviewees. Once again, other realms are visited and deceased relations and friends are met. The afterlife environment, as in previous accounts, has a strong physical and social resemblance to the usual world of the percipient. So far these two features of the NDE, encountering other worlds and deceased beings, is a steady, recurring feature of NDEs. As we shall see in other non-Western cases, this trend will continue.

There are two points to note about these particular Melanesian cases. The first is the single report of a life review, the second is the absence of an OBE or tunnel experience. However, the picture is somewhat more complex than these first impressions may suggest. Although one person reported a life review, this respondent stated that he also witnessed a review of someone else's life also—a sorcerer. This review was narrated by the NDEr as a visit to a place where sorcerers are placed "on trial." Each person stands on a series of

magnetic "manhole covers." If these hold the person fast, so that others must assist him in freeing himself, then he is called to account. If his explanation is unsatisfactory or unforthcoming, a series of punishing events occurs, ending with burning by fire. This is an unusual account, for as Counts notes, "there was no precontact notion of judgment of the dead for their sins."

However, Counts notes that the western New Britain area has been "missionized" by Catholicism since 1949. Many of the Kaliai are at least nominally Catholic, although traditional and Christian ideas often exist side by side. This may account for the life review in this case. This is not the first case of mixed cultural imagery in an NDE. Pasricha and Stevenson report an American follower of Sai Baba (an Indian holy man) who almost died in a hotel. His NDE featured the Indian life review of having his life record read by others.

Although no OBE was reported in the Kaliai NDE reports, one case is reported by Counts that may be a vivid dream, hypnagogic imagery, or an OBE. Its nature is difficult to discern in that account because no dead or sleeping body is observed, nor is a new body identified. An ability to see unusual sights and travel vast distances is connected with characteristics of the spirit world. The question of OBE among the Kaliai, then, must be left open. There is a possibility that interpretations of similar experiences by Westerners may favor an OBE explanation, while those of the Kaliai may not.

Finally, in no case was a tunnel experience identified. All informants report the early part of their NDE as walking on a road. However, in one case the NDE began in darkness, which gave way to a walk in a field of flowers. Only after this part of the experience did the walk continue onto a road.

Native America

Schorer reports two cases of NDE from native North Americans. These accounts were identified from H. R. Schoolcraft's nineteenth-century work *Travels in the Central Portion of the Mississippi Valley.* In these accounts, OBE and encountering other realms and deceased beings are reported. The other realm, as in all previous cases, is similar to the former world of the percipient.

Absent from these two accounts are any reference to a tunnel experience or a life review. Similar to the accounts from Guam and western New Britain, percipients emphasize their journey. The narrative is a series of tales about what happened to them after they discovered that they were dead. This pattern is repeated in the only account to appear from South America. Gomez-Jeria reports a single NDE account from the Mapuche people in Chile. In this account, an old man named Fermin was considered by his family and friends to be dead for two days. When he finally woke, he reported visiting another realm.

> He said that all his dead acquaintances, his own parents, his children, his wife, and other children that he did not know were all in there. There was also a German gentleman reading and writing

in big books. When the German saw him, he asked what he wanted.

"I am following my son," said the old man.

"What is his name?" asked the German gentleman

"Francisco Leufuhue."

He called the guard and ordered him to inform Francisco.

After passing through a series of noisy gates, Fermin is reunited with his son, who tells him that it is not his father's time.

> When the time comes, I myself shall go to the side of the house to look for you. Then you will come. Now, go away.

Note again, in this account, the absence of tunnel sensation or life review. The NDE reported here contains a visit to other worlds and the meeting of deceased beings. Jeria asserts that the presence of the German gentleman is an indication that culture "contributes in part to shaping the content of mental experiences." This may be true for certain structural elements, such as, for example, *the presence or absence of review phenomena,* but we must be cautious *in explaining even the smallest detail of NDEs in cultural terms lest our cultural analysis fall prey to reductionist tendencies.* Clearly, NDErs meet an assortment of social beings, and their prior experiences shape their *interpretation* of the identity, function, and meaning of these beings. Only if we have strong evidence that these NDE accounts are purely subjective, like dreams, can we link even small details of the NDE content to culture and biography. We do not, at this stage, have that type of evidence.

Aboriginal Australia

An isolated account of an NDE among Australian aborigines has appeared in several ethnographies during this century. It is, by all accounts, an unusual story in aboriginal terms because it is not a mythical account that can be interpreted as part of the aboriginal "dream time." On the contrary, the most interesting feature of this story, of which there are several versions, is that it is an historically real account of a human being who visits the "land of the dead."

Lloyd Warner retells a version of the account as "Barnumbi—and the Island of the Dead" in *A Black Civilisation*. More recently, the Berndts (1989) have reported the same story told to them as "Yawalngura dies twice?" According to the Berndts, the story is now quite old and part of a long oral tradition.

The account is a long one, so I will only summarize the main elements. Yawalngura was out gathering turtle eggs with his two wives. He ate some of the eggs, after which he lay down and "died." Later, his wives returned from their own search and found him dead. They returned his body to the main camp and with others built a mortuary platform for him. After this, Yawalngura revived and told others that he became curious about the land of the dead. He decided to build a canoe so that he could travel there to visit. This he did and set off on a journey lasting for several days and nights.

Finally, he arrived at an island where he met traditional spirits (e.g., the Turtle Man Spirit) and deceased beings who recognized that he was alive and had to return. These spirits then danced for Yawalngura and gave him gifts, such as a Morning Star emblem and yams for his return journey.

> Yawalngura took those things which were given to him. All the spirit people danced at that special spring (well), and they told Yawalngura that he had to return: "You have to return, you're not dead properly, you've still got bones. You can come back to us when you die properly."

Yawalngura returned and told others of his fantastic epic journey. "Two or three days afterwards," however, Yawalngura died again, "only this time he did so properly."

In this account, deceased beings and a land of the dead are visited. Again, both the people and the place have traditional mythical qualities. However, no tunnel experience and no life review are mentioned. Although the OBE is regarded as common in aboriginal Australia, especially during sleep and dreaming, no OBE is mentioned in this NDE account. These are also features of the final non-Western account from New Zealand.

Maori New Zealand

In an autobiographical exploration of New Zealand white culture and its encounter with the native Maori culture, King recounts a Maori NDE. Nga was a Maori woman who encountered her first white person when she was "a girl just over school age." A favorite story of Nga's was apparently one about the occasion when she believed she had died.

I became seriously ill for the only time in my life. I became so ill that my spirit actually passed out of my body. My family believed I was dead because my breathing stopped. They took me to the marae, laid out my body and began to call people for the tangi. Meanwhile, in my spirit, I had hovered over my head then left the room and travelled northwards, towards the Tail of the Fish. I passed over the Waikato River, across the Manukau, over Ngati Whatua, Ngapuhi, Te Rarawe and Te Aupouri until at last I came to Te Rerenga Wairua, the leaping off place of spirits.

At this sacred place she performed the ablutions expected of the departed. Ascending to a ledge, she gazed down at the entrance to the underworld. After performing a dance, she prepared to descend into the subterranean passage leading to the realm of the spirits. At this point, she was stopped by a voice who told her that that her time had not come and that she must return until called again. She then returned to her body and awoke to see her anxious living relatives.

In this Maori account, no mention of a tunnel is made; instead, Nga flies to the land of the dead after her OBE (e.g., "I had hovered over my head then left the room"). However, the story of Nga

takes us to the entrance of a subterranean underworld, and this, had she traveled to it, may have constituted a tunnel experience. This subterranean passage is a common feature of some Pacific cultures and may mean, for the purpose of this review, that a tunnel experience cannot be excluded. If the experience had lasted longer, perhaps Nga would have descended to that underworld place through the traditional dark passage. So the absence of a tunnel sensation must be seen as a conditional matter that may relate idiosyncratically to this single account. Nevertheless, another characteristic, such as the life review, is unequivocally missing in this account.

Summary of Non-Western NDE Features

Table 7.1 summarizes the preceding review of the non-Western NDE. It identifies features that seem cross-cultural, those that appear to be culture-specific, and those in which the question of universality remains ambiguous. In every case discussed, deceased or supernatural beings are encountered.

These are often met in another realm, variously described as the "land of the dead," the "island of the dead," the "pure land," and so on. Consistently, the other realm is a social world not dissimilar to the one the percipient is from. The major difference is that this world is often much more pleasant socially and physically. Clearly, the consistency of these reports from highly diverse cultures suggests that at least these two features of the NDE are indeed cross-cultural.

TABLE 7.1 SUMMARY OF NON-WESTERN NDE FEATURES

Culture	Source	Cases	Tunnel	OBE	Life review	Other beings	Other world
China	Becker (1981, 1984); Zhi-ying and Jian-xun (1992)	100–180	/2	/	/	/	/
India	Osis and Haraldsson (1977); Pasricha (1992, 1993); Pasricha and Stevenson (1986)	64 29 16	X	/	/	/	/
Western New Britain	Counts (1983)	3	X1	X1	/2	/	/
Guam	Green (1984)	4	X	/	X	/	/
Native America	Schorer (1985–86); Gomez-Jeria (1993)	3	X	/	X	/	/
Australian Aborigine	Berndt (1989)	1	X1	X	X	/	/
N. Z. Maori	King (1985)	1	X1	/	X	/	/

Key: X, none reported; /, reported; X1, conditional negative; /2 conditional positive.

This distinction is less clear in the findings about the OBE. Some cultures, such as the New Zealand Maori, native American, and Chammorro, clearly experience some kind of OBE with their NDE. However, the Chinese do not report this feature. Finally, the Australian aborigines do not report an OBE, but OBEs are known in this culture. In fact, OBEs are known in the vast majority of cultures, but these may not necessarily occur, or occur consistently, in NDEs in these cultures. The apparent randomness of the finding concerning OBEs makes conclusions about them in relation to the NDE ambiguous. On the basis of the present data, we are unable to judge whether these are cross-cultural or culture-specific features. However, clearer patterns emerge when the life reviews and tunnel experiences are examined in the different non-Western cases.

Life review is a definite feature of the Chinese and Indian NDE accounts. In at least one Chinese account one's "sinful deeds" are observed, and in several Indian accounts one's life record is read from a book. A life review is also noted in connection with a Melanesian account, but this is a conditional finding. The life review described in the Melanesian account contrasts sharply with traditional—that is, precontact—notions of death and judgment. This particular feature and case may be better explained as a function of Western influence. Because many of the Kaliai are under Catholic influence, this may have altered either the experience or the narrative. This possibility gains some support from the observation that judgment is not part of the precontact Melanesian beliefs about death.

Life review is absent from all other accounts from Guam, Native America, aboriginal Australia, and Maori New Zealand. In other words, except for one ambiguous case in Melanesia, all accounts from hunter-gatherer, primitive cultivator, and herdsman cultures do not exhibit the feature of life review. Accounts from India and China, however, definitely do exhibit this feature.

Finally, the tunnel experience does not seem to be a feature of most non-Western NDE accounts. The cases from Native America, Guam, and India give no indication of a tunnel experience or sensation. There is, however, some suggestion that a tunnel experience may occur to those NDErs if their experience is prolonged.

This attaches conditions to any conclusion about this finding in the New Zealand case, as already noted, because the Maori NDEr traveled via a subterranean entrance to the land of the dead. Had she traveled to that place, she might have experienced a dark tunnel-like experience, and this would have occurred after her OBE—as it does in some Western accounts. In the Australian aboriginal account, much may have been lost in its development into an oral tradition. For example, the visit to the land of the dead occurred after the percipient revived rather than during the time he was unconscious and "dead." It is difficult to speculate about what message or meaning is intended in this interesting turn to the story. Perhaps, having been dead, that person inherited special privileges/powers as a result of the experience that allowed him to travel while "alive" to the land of the dead. Perhaps the account has simply been altered via its oral transmission through the normal passage of time and embellishment. In any case, the trip to the land of the dead reports a journey of successive "nights," which indicates the importance in the account of light and darkness. This theme is also important in other aspects of the account, particularly when a struggle takes place over a "star."

In the western New Britain account, most of the NDErs describe how they suddenly appeared on a road, but one account does note that the individual emerged from darkness into a field of flowers. However, he did not describe this darkness as a tunnel. And in China, there exists at least one report of emerging from a similar darkness described as a dark void or "dark, tubular calyx." This calyx, of course, is the throatlike part of a flower and complements the lotus imagery of much pure land Buddhist narrative. In any case, Zhi-ying and Jian-xun report several accounts of tunnel sensation in their study of Chinese NDEs.

Overall, then, the present review has revealed that the major crosscultural features of the NDE appear to include encountering other beings and other realms on the brink of death. Life review and the tunnel experience seem to be culture-specific features. Life review seems to be a feature of Western, Chinese, and Indian NDE accounts. Cases collected from hunter-gatherer, primitive cultivator, and herdsmen societies do not exhibit this feature. The tunnel experience is not described in most non-Western accounts, though an experience of darkness of sorts is often reported. The present review has revealed no major pattern in reports about the OBE in non-Western NDE accounts, and therefore this finding must be viewed as inconclusive. I now turn to a discussion of these findings, focusing on the following question: How are we to account for these differences in the pattern of non-Western NDEs, comparing them with each other and with Western accounts?

Discussion

The universality of NDEs/visions, in which individuals purport to see new worlds and beings beyond death's door, is not a particularly new or interesting finding. In relation to this recurring feature of death or NDEs, there has been a long tradition of medical social science literature, as well as similar concerns in the humanities and in religious thought generally. The conclusion is either that these visions represent observations of another empirical reality or that these are simply hallucinations. As delusions or visions of a dying organism, the sight of deceased relatives in a world beyond death may reflect archetypal forms, as outlined by the famous psychoanalyst Carl Jung. They may represent a major cultural source of myths, but these myths may reflect neuronal activities and patterns, thus representing something of a cerebral map or blueprint. Others have argued that perhaps the belief in and desire for the afterlife represents a strong unconscious need to deny the annihilating reality of death. I will not attempt to arbitrate on an issue such as this, a task that is clearly beyond the scope of this book. Suffice to say that the universality of human experiences such as these has created and will continue to generate fierce, complex debate. Culture-specific findings are somewhat more modest in their demand for explanation, and I now turn my attention to these.

Blackmore and Troscianko asks two questions about the tunnel feature so often reported in the Western NDE: First, why is the tunnel so often a regular feature of the NDE? Second, why do other symbols not appear, for example, gates or doors? The present review has not found tunnel experiences in any of the non-Western case material. However, there were several mentions of darkness described as a void, a calyx, or simply darkness. This suggests that tunnel experiences are not cross-cultural but that a period of darkness may be. This darkness is then subject to culture-specific interpretations: a tunnel for Westerners, subterranean caverns for Melanesians, and so on. NDErs who do not report darkness may not view this aspect of the experience as an important part of their account or narrative. Because an account of an event is a social exchange based on mutual expectations about what is or is not important information, recall may sometimes be selective and shaped to the perceived requirements of the listener. This may be an important methodological point for a review such as this because the sample of cases is too small to allow us to gauge if darkness is important or unimportant in all regional accounts. On the other hand, unless appropriate images can be selected that may convey traditional meanings about darkness, no image at all may be chosen to explain the experience. The first question that Blackmore and Troscianko asked must now be reformulated as follows: Why is the frequently reported sensation of traveling through darkness by Western NDErs so often described as a tunnel experience? In other words, why do many Western NDErs choose the term *tunnel* to denote their experience of darkness?

The term *tunnel* has two major meanings in the English-speaking world, and both of them are relevant to the NDE. In a literal vein, tunnels are shafts or structures similar to the inside of a chimney. They may resemble subterranean passages or they may denote tubes, pipes, or simply deep openings that channel partway into other structures. Drab argues that tunnels have specific properties that make them enclosed spaces whose length is greater than their diameter. This definition emphasizes the technical but in doing so omits the metaphorical, representational, and symbolic. This would not be important except that, in social communication terms, dimensions such as these must be viewed as equally influential in a person's choice of words. This is even more true when one considers that the NDE is often described as ineffable, that is, beyond words. Excluding the symbolic meaning involves excluding the figurative meaning, and the figurative meaning may be the most critical.

As a figurative term, *tunnel* may also denote a period of prolonged suffering or difficulty, as embodied in such expressions as "light at the end of the tunnel." Tunnels are often viewed as experiences of darkness that lead to other experiences. This representational view is well grounded in common experiences of the Western workaday world. It may begin in childhood, as for example, with stories such as *Alice in Wonderland,* reading of Alice's long fall down a dark rabbit hole that signals the start of a journey into a wondrous and confusing world. Or it may begin with accounts of Santa Claus, who is expected to appear at the bottom of the family's chimney every December. From a child's kaleidoscope to the adult's experiences of gazing through telescopes, microscopes, and binoculars, Western people have grown accustomed to seeing strange new worlds through the dimness of tunnels. Through dark tunnels, and in the light that appears at the end of them, people leave the ordinary momentarily to experience the strange and unfamiliar.

Furthermore, tunnels are common images for the idea of transition, of traversing from one side to another. Drab objects to this notion of transition, arguing that often the tunnel in NDEs does not lead anywhere. However, this ignores the social fact that people may believe or expect the tunnel to lead them somewhere. Social experiences can rarely be understood in terms of concrete events separated from their interpretations, and these interpretive processes are constructed from attitudes, beliefs, expectations, and/or assumptions. If percipients are moving along in a shaft or space of darkness, some may choose a term that commonly denotes that experience. The tunnel is a symbol that, in Western industrial societies, is readily associated with that kind of experience. This brings us to Blackmore and Troscianko's second question: Why a tunnel and not other symbols such as a gate, door, or bridges?

However, gates, doors, bridges, and many other symbols do appear as images in the NDE, as Blackmore and Troscianko readily admit, but frequently alongside or after experiences of the tunnel. They rarely seem to substitute for the tunnel, and this should be no mystery. The major and most obvious reason why gates or doors seldom substitute for tunnels is that NDErs are attempting to describe some

kind of movement through darkness. It is the tunnel, therefore, rather than gates or doors, that best captures this experience. This is a further problem with a technical definition of tunnels that relies on shape as its primary characteristic. Shape reflects architecture rather than experience, but it is experience that is being described by NDErs. Because the experience is difficult to communicate, the descriptions will always be rich in interpretations that lean more toward metaphor than toward measurement.

The life review is the second feature of the Western NDE that seems to be limited in other cultures. Indian and Chinese NDEs seem to exhibit features of the life review, but NDEs in Australia, the Pacific, and Native North America do not. This might be explained by the scarcity of cases from these areas. A larger sample from these areas might turn up NDEs with life reviews. There is, however, much in the medical and anthropological literature to suggest that this will not be the case.

Butler argues that life review is always something of an identity search. He uses the mirror as an example of an identity search metaphor that recurs in Western literature. In the Narcissus myth, the story of Snow White, stories from the Arabian nights, and also in the preoccupation of adolescents and the aged, the mirror reveals the face, the life, and the person. The mirror and the life review

serves the self and its continuity; it entertains us; it shames us; it pains us. Memory can tell us our origins; it can be explanatory and it can deceive.

This sense of self as interior, as inwardly responsible, driven and reflective from within, is a social construction of identity recently born in the development of what Bellah calls *historic religions.* In historic religions, such as Buddhism, Christianity, Islam, and Hinduism, two worlds exist: the material and the divine. The self and the material world are devalued. Human nature is flawed and in need of rehabilitation and redemption, while the material world is mere illusion. The responsibility for rehabilitation lies in the action of the self.

In primitives and archaic religions such as those of Native Americans, Australian aborigines, and many Pacific cultures, the distinction between self and the world is less explicit. "Mind" as a store for social experience is not paramount, for experience is also drawn from the animistic world of animals, vegetation, rocks, landforms, and climate. The mythological and actual worlds are not sharply separate but heavily overlapping. Individuals are no more responsible than the world. Anxiety, guilt, and responsibility are in-the-world properties or characteristics, not located purely within the private orbit of an individual's makeup.

Roheim observed that the psychology of the Australian aborigines, for example, was based on much less internalizing of social sanctions. They have a very good opinion of themselves, are easygoing, and fear the social consequences of transgression much more than private guilt, remorse, or anxiety. Laws are obeyed because they fear being caught.

Roheim discusses what happened when Christian missionaries began their proselytizing practices among the Aranda aborigines. In their religious wisdom and magnanimity of those days, white missionaries promptly observed that the Arunda were all basically sinful and wicked and needed forgiveness before God. In response to this rather novel view of themselves, the Arunda retorted with understandable indignation. "Arunda inkaraka mara," they declared; the Arunda are all good. These were hardly a people who would seek a life review in evaluative terms or be impressed by a biographical review of their individual deeds.

So, although Indian and Chinese cultures may appear quite different from Anglo-European ones, in terms of social custom and language they are broadly similar in terms of religious development. Historic religion, whether Hinduism or Christianity, emphasizes the cultivation and development of the moral self vis-à-vis the divine world and its demands. Historic religions actively appeal to the notion of individual conscience. And conscience places great importance on past thought and action in the process of self-evaluation. As Weber has reminded us, when belief in spirits is transformed into belief in god, "transgression against the will of god is an ethical sin which burdens the conscience, quite apart from its direct results." Since these religions link death with conscience, and conscience with identity after death, it is little wonder that some kind of life review takes place in near-death circumstances among people from these cultures. In a different world view altogether, members of aboriginal and Pacific cultures may not review their past personal lives in search of sense of identity. As mentioned earlier, the store of social experience is contained not within the self, but rather in the animistic and communal life of the physical and social world. There is probably little private use or function for a life review in individuals from this type of society.

Questions

1. Describe the similarities and differences between Chinese and Indian NDEs, on the one hand, and those found in Europe and America on the other hand. What do you think might be responsible for some of the differences?

2. Describe the unique features of NDEs in hunter-gatherer, primitive cultivator, and herdsmen societies. How are these NDEs different from those found in other types of cultures?

3. If NDEs are real and culture-specific, as Kellehear's research suggests, what then might this say about what awaits us beyond death?

---

3 Carol Zaleski, *NDEs as Symbolic Narratives*

Carol Zaleski, Ph.D., teaches religious studies at Smith College in Massachusetts. Her scholarly treatment of the NDE in her award-winning 1987 book, *Otherworldly Journeys,* has been well received as a balanced yet sympathetic account. It has been translated into French, German, and Japanese, and has revolutionized the way scholars think about NDEs. Dr. Zaleski's work challenges the view of most academics who generally dismiss the NDE as a modern, unsophisticated fabrication of the "New Age" movement. On the contrary, Dr. Zaleski demonstrates that NDEs are vital to understanding both the history of the Christian church and the inner workings of the religious imagination.

Dr. Zaleski's work in *Otherworldly Journeys* was the first to narrate the role of cultural experience in shaping the spiritual visions associated with NDEs. She compares the contemporary NDE account to similar accounts in early Christian writings. She finds many parallels, as well as vital differences. One of the main differences she finds among the two genres is that in medieval accounts, stories of heaven and hell were often used by NDErs to try to persuade their listeners that death is something to be feared, and that conversion to the Christian faith is therefore essential for eternal salvation. But in contemporary accounts, where hell is seldom experienced and heaven is open to all, an evangelistic tone is rarely used. Instead, the NDE is more often used to promote the view that all people ultimately will be saved, and that death is nothing to be feared.

In the following essay, Dr. Zaleski offers a convenient summary of the current theological opinion of NDEs. After discussing objections to a literal interpretation of the NDE—objections which come both from conservative Christians (that NDEs are a "Satanic trick") and materialistic scientists (that they are merely "hallucinations stored in the brain")—she argues that the most appropriate rendering of NDEs is to view them as symbolic narratives, as "works of the religious imagination, whose function is to communicate meaning through symbolic forms rather than to copy external facts."[46]

Experiential Claims

One conclusion to which the present study leads is that the West has seen no steady progress from literal to literary use of the otherworld journey motif. The line between fiction and confession is necessarily blurry, but contemporary near-death reports—like their medieval predecessors—at least claim to represent actual experience. In this final chapter we will consider whether it is possible to take this claim seriously without being naïve.

Some might feel inclined to disregard the question, as do the social and literary historians who concern themselves only with the cultural transmission of otherworld journey imagery. For if we take visionary accounts at face value, as a factual description of what happens after death, we run the risk of enclosing ourselves in a shrunken utopia, cut off from the scientific and historical awareness that is our culture's special gift. Theologians, as much as other intellectuals, might wish to ignore experiential claims in order to avoid having to weigh testimony that either conflicts with accepted religious and scientific principles or brings the mysteries of life, death, and the hereafter embarrassingly close. It is safer to treat the otherworld journey solely as a metaphor or literary motif that illustrates a psychological or moral truth. In this way, we render it harmless; we attenuate the visionary virus until it is so weak that it produces immunity instead of contagion.

This approach fails to account, however, for what makes the other world such a powerful symbol. We have seen that the otherworld journey motif remains potent only as long as it retains at least a hint of correspondence to a sensed, dreamed, or imagined reality. An image like the review of deeds continues to have some vitality because we imagine ourselves undergoing such an experience, we visualize this experience as taking place in another world, and we sense that the image has further possibilities as yet unexplored. By contrast, an expression like "The road to hell is paved with good intentions," which we recognize as exclusively metaphorical, seems trite. It has become a dead circuit, no longer connected to real or imagined experience. The experiential dimension must therefore be considered if we are to understand the whole range of otherworld journey imagery—from its vestiges in our ordinary discourse to the more overt forms found in near-death literature.

It is, moreover, unfair to the individuals who report near-death experience to discount their claims in advance. The current controversy surrounding the rights and needs of the dying—and the fact that many people are turning to books like *Life After Life* for guidance or consolation—puts us under an obligation to assess near-death literature in an informed and sympathetic way.

It is a good sign, then, that some religious thinkers have taken an interest in interpreting near-death literature. Before I make suggestions of my own, it will be useful to consider the main currents of theological opinion on the subject.

When *Life After Life* appeared, it provoked widely varying reactions (Moody, 1975). In *Reflections of Life After Life,* Moody remarks that there were some among the clergy who accused him of selling "cheap grace," while others thanked him for producing a book that was such an asset to their pastoral work with the dying and bereaved (Moody, 1977). This pattern of response continues as public awareness of near-death experience grows. The loudest reaction against *Life After Life* and its successors comes from the conservative Christians who see these books as a Satanic trick, designed to lull us into a false sense of security about the future life, to lure us into occult practices such as astral projection, to beguile us into accepting the advances of demons disguised as departed spirits, and to sell us a secular (but fundamentally diabolic) bill of goods about salvation without Christ. At the same time, as we noted above, there has been a proliferation of "born again" versions of near-death experience—complete with recollections of hell which, according to Maurice Rawlings, are "repressed" by the Life After Lifers (Rawling, 1978).

On the other side, Moody reports that Christian clergy often tell him that *Life After Life* has strengthened their faith in the traditional Church teachings which it is their office to represent. It gave one minister the confidence to affirm at a funeral that the woman he eulogized had gone to join her deceased husband with Christ: "I wasn't speaking figuratively or symbolically; I meant it. This gave them comfort. . . ." (Moody, 1997, 54). Near-death testimonials play a similar role in the pages of *Guideposts, Soul Searcher, Spiritual Frontiers*, and other magazines of Christian or Christian/spiritualist inspiration.

Among professional Christian theologians, the idea that near-death testimony might make a case for life after death has received critical attention both favorable and dissenting. A few mavericks—notably John Hick and Paul Badham—suggest that clinical and parapsychological evidence might provide just the empirical elixir we need to invigorate our culture's withered eschatological imagination. Nonetheless, neither of these theologians relies on empirical arguments alone. In *Death and Eternal Life*, Hick combines the evidence from mediumship and parapsychology with scientific, philosophical, and moral grounds for conceiving the future life on an evolutionary mode. Badham's view is that near-death experiences and other psychic phenomena, although they provide no guarantee of immortality, can at least disarm naturalisitic objections and make room for a faith founded on the experience of relationship to God (Badham, 1980, 1982).

In general, however, academic circles have not seen much theological debate over the implications of near-death research. The predominant trend has been to ignore or repudiate efforts to find evidence for existence after death. One reason for this is that many Christian thinkers believe that the idea of personal survival has been rendered obsolete by recent scientific, philosophical, and linguistic discoveries. Beyond this standard and widespread skepticism, however, several generations of liberal and neo-orthodox theologians have warned against preoccupation with the hereafter. It is a narcissistic distraction from the ethical and social mission of the church, they argue, and it is moreover both childish and arrogant to expect more from rational or empirical proofs than from biblical promises. A Lutheran pastor writes, "If life after death could be empirically verified 'beyond a shadow of a doubt,' then there would seem to be little need for faith."

For some religious critics, the most serious flaw in near-death literature is its portrait of death as a pleasant, gentle transition. Converging streams of Freudian, existentialist, and neo-orthodox thought, along with modern biblical scholarship, have produced a strong sentiment among theologian that it is essential to the Christian message to affirm the reality and sting of death. Ever since Oscar Cullmann drew (perhaps overdrew) the distinction between the resurrection faith of Christianity and the Greek philosophical idea of natural immortality, this contrast has been a recurrent theme, even a rallying cry, of theological writing. Stephen Vicchio speaks for many when he complains that "the empty tomb for Kübler-Ross and Moody is superfluous if not redundant. There is no need for Easter if we are immortal."

Those who pit Cullmann against Kübler-Ross and her ilk are heirs to a long tradition of Christian polemic against the opponent—pagan or straw man—who would ground our hopes in knowledge rather than faith, in nature rather than sacred history, in the soul's intrinsic purity rather than God's willingness to cleanse it. Pragmatically speaking, however, the real issue in these debates is whether the alternative views make a difference in religious life; do they breed complacency or catalyze conversion? The answer to this question cannot be decided solely on biblical, doctrinal, or philosophical grounds. A great deal depends on social climate and personal temperament; as I shall suggest below, the history of religion tells us that similar eschatological conceptions may serve, under different circumstances, either to awaken efforts to merit an afterlife or to make such efforts redundant by feeding people pie-in-the-sky consolations.

In the current atmosphere of skepticism and cultural fragmentation, fears and doubts about survival of death can be just as morally and spiritually paralyzing as a monolithic faith in its certainty. Those who testify to the transforming effect of near-death experience often say that their conviction that death is not the end gave them the freedom and energy to change their way of life. On the other hand, when the quest for immortality is isolated from other religious concerns, as in psychical research, it can become something tawdry, egoistic, and this-worldly. So, too, medieval Christian vision literature runs the gamut from profound to mechanical understanding of penance, purgatory, and conversion. Perhaps the doctrine itself is not at fault, but only its abuse; the present danger is not that people will become convinced of immortality, but that the whole subject will be trivialized by a narrow focus on the case for or against survival.

Clearly, a new approach is needed; to make near-death testimony an arena for restaging old philosophical or theological battles will not suffice. It appears to be impossible, in any case, to determine objectively whether near-death reports are accurate or inaccurate depictions of the future life. It might therefore be more fruitful for theologians to consider near-death visions as works of the religious imagination, whose function is to communicate meaning through symbolic forms rather than to copy external facts. This is the aspect of near-death literature that I have attempted to highlight.

Double Vision

The purpose of comparing medieval and modern vision narratives has been to benefit from the stereoscopic effect, the depth perception, which the juxtaposition of two separate perspectives can provide. It will be helpful, then, to review the results of this comparison before proceeding to generalize about the religious implications of otherworld journey narration.

In broad terms, the similarities we found were as follows; both medieval and modern narratives depict the death and revival of individuals whose experience is held up as an example of what we can expect in our own final moments. The manner of death—departure of the spirit from the body—is described in frankly dualistic terms, the separated spirit looking down upon its former dwelling place with indifference or contempt.

After leaving the body, the visionary finds himself in a liminal condition hovering just overhead and watching the scene of crisis in a mood of detachment. The beginning of the otherworld journey proper is signaled by the advent of a guide and by motifs of visionary topography and travel such as paths, valleys, and tunnels. The guide, who is the narrator's alter ego, escorts the visionary from place to place, pushing the story forward and interpreting the inner significance of otherworld scenes; he thus calls attention to the symbolic character of the other world, and to the need for spiritual instruction in this life and the next.

In the pivotal episode of both medieval and modern journeys, the visionary confronts himself by means of various graphic representations. He meets his thoughts, words, and deeds; learns the weight of his soul; or reviews his life in a book, play or movie—and in such fashion brings judgment upon himself.

Although medieval hell and purgatory scenes find scarcely any counterparts in the near-death testimony collected by Moody and his colleagues, motifs of paradise topography are much the same in both periods: shining edifices, gardens, meadows, heavenly cities, and so forth. In addition, the ultimate experience of contemplative vision, though treated only rarely and briefly by medieval otherworld journey narratives, is consistently described as a comprehensive vision of the whole, in which cognitive and affective power fuse. It is a moment when the dramatic action of the otherworld journey seems to be suspended and unmediated awareness floods in; but an instant later the play resumes, a message is formulated, and the visionary feels compelled, against his desires, to return to life.

Upon revival, the visionary is physically and spiritually changed. Reticent and overwhelmed at first, he is eventually persuaded to communicate his discoveries and share his mission with others. Once an ordinary *vir quidam,* average guy, or "just a housewife," the visionary takes on a prophetic role, teaching by word and by the example of a transformed life.

We also saw that in both periods the otherworld journey narrative evolves through the visionary's conversation with others, and that the narrator shapes the account to conform to the conventions of the genre in which it will appear, whether sermon, allegory, chronicle, Christian polemic, contemporary best-seller, tabloid testimonial, statistical study, or television talk show. In all these different formats, the vision story retains its didactic aim: the other world is described not to satisfy theoretical curiosity, but to serve as a goad toward transformation.

There is bound to be disagreement over whether these recurrent motifs—guides, paths, barriers, encounters with deeds, and so forth—constitute a universal lexicon or whether they provide only the syntactic structure of the otherworld vision. Many of the areas of similarity appear to be formal rather than material; for when we fill in the picture, supplying the emotional content and the culturally specific features that make up a concrete vision, we discover significant divergences.

Thus, despite the structural resemblance between descriptions of the soul's exit from the body, we find that medieval visions exemplify the two deaths theme, while modern visions portray only the comforting prospect of a good death. So, too, although the guide is essential in both periods as a narrative expedient, didactic instrument, guardian of the threshold, and psychopomp, his character and relation to the visionary are understood quite differently. In medieval visions, the guide stands for hierarchical and feudal authority; in modern visions, he represents benevolent parental acceptance. His role appears to be determined by presuppositions about social and family structure, judicial process, education, and pastoral or psychological cure of souls.

The most glaring difference is the prominence in medieval accounts of obstacles and tests, purificatory torments, and outright doom. Aside from continuing the hellfire traditions of early Christian apocalyptic, medieval narratives serve as vehicles for the consolidation of Catholic teachings on purgatory and penance. In modern accounts, on the other hand, a sense of inevitable progress softens the rigors of final reckoning; the review of deeds is transformed from an ordeal into an education experience; and the only serious obstacle is the barrier marking the point of no return. These narratives are shaped throughout by optimistic, democratic, "healthy-minded" principles that transparently reflect a contemporary ideology and mood.

The contrast to medieval accounts is sharpened when we set near-death narratives against the background of nineteenth- and twentieth-century spiritualism and its intellectual offshoot, the psychical research movement. The spiritualist other world, like that of near-death literature, is a social utopia, mirroring the progressive causes with which many spiritualist and psychical researchers have been connected; prison, insane asylum, and school reform; abolition; feminism; socialism; Christian perfectionism; and other high-minded liberal concerns have been validated by mediumistic and clairvoyant descriptions of the ideal conditions of the spirit world.

Although ours is a less fertile period for generating utopian schemes, near-death literature expresses and provides other-world validation for similar progressivist ideas. It is no wonder, then, that it provokes the ire of conservative religious thinkers, whose objections to current near-death studies echo earlier reactions against spiritualism.

In its otherworld cosmology, as well, near-death literature is as close to spiritualism as it is distant from medieval visions. Medieval vision narratives, as we saw, are the outcome of a long history of development and suppression of cosmological schemes for the soul's journey to God; they retain vestiges, sometimes sublimated or confused, of older conceptions of the planetary spheres as places of interrogation and punishment. Naturally, this idiom is completely foreign to modern accounts; near-death literature reflects instead a short history of attempts to reconcile the spirit world with the world of Faraday, Maxwell, Darwin, and Einstein. Though less inclined than spiritualism to localize the other world in the outer atmosphere, modern narratives make similar use of scientific vocabulary—energy, magnetism, vibrations, dimensions, evolution—now supplemented by terms drawn from relativity theory, quantum mechanics, and holography to update the imaginative cosmology.

In focusing on the reports of those who return from death, however, modern accounts are closer to their medieval counterparts than to spiritualist literature. The return-from-death story, unlike mediumistic accounts of the afterlife, conforms to the pattern of a conversion narrative.

Rather than mapping the spirit world in great detail, the return-from-death story emphasizes the visionary's special task, the message he is charged to bring back to humanity, and the transformation of his way of life.

On the other hand, medieval and modern narratives differ considerably in their understanding of the nature of the visionary's message, commission, and conversion. Moral rehabilitation is too vague a goal for medieval visions; they are concerned, as we have seen, to promote particular penitential and monastic institutions. Modern narratives, however, advocate the renunciation of worries and fears and conversion to a life of love, learning, and service; this is an individualistic, anti-institutional, humanistic ideal, of which churches, hospices, and other service organizations may be the incidental beneficiaries. Considered closely, then, the differences between medieval and modern accounts of return-from-death conversion are as impressive as the similarities.

These comparative observations force us to conclude that the visionaries of our own age are no more free of cultural influence than those of less pluralistic eras. We have seen that the otherworld journey story—which comprises every level of the experience to which we have access, as well as every layer of narrative reconstruction—is through and through a work of the socially conditioned religious imagination; it is formed in conversation with society, even if it takes place in the solitude of the deathbed and in the private chamber of inner experience.

Once we recognize this, we can no longer insist that *Life After Life*, Gregory's

Dialogues, or any other work of visionary eschatology paints a true picture of what occurs at the extreme border of life. If we wish to avoid the self-defeating extremes of shallow relativism and naïve affirmation, then our only recourse is to focus on the imaginative and symbolic character of otherworld visions.

The remainder of this chapter will consider whether this approach can yield a fuller understanding of near-death literature and of visionary and religious testimony in general. I should explain at the outset, however, that I am not attempting to provide a systematic theory of near-death visions. Such a theory would require the collaborative efforts of many different interpreters. Perhaps the solution to the puzzle of near-death experience will always remain in the distance, drawing us along by receding as we approach it. What I offer here is not a conclusion designed to close the book on the subject, but a set of suggestions and thought experiments intended to point out promising directions for further inquiry.

Although this discussion is preliminary and open-ended, it is guided by certain assumptions about the symbolic character of religious discourse; in case these assumptions are not by now apparent, I will make them explicit.

In speaking of *symbolism,* I have in mind a definition that the reader may not share but may be willing to grant for the purpose of discussion. According to most dictionaries, a symbol is an image or object that represents something beyond itself. To this minimal definition I would add— following the view expressed in various ways by Samuel Taylor Coleridge, Paul Tillich, Ernst Cassirer, Suzanne Langer, and Paul Ricoeur, among others—that a symbol participates in the reality that it represents. It does not copy or fully contain that reality, but it does communicate some of its power. Unlike a metaphor, it cannot adequately be translated into conceptual terms.

By *religious imagination,* I understand the capacity to create or to appreciate religious symbols. In this book, we have caught a glimpse of some of the features of the religious symbols. We have seen that it works not only with universal patterns—such as death and birth—but also with culturally specific and idiosyncratic material, and that it can fuse the universal and the particular into a seamless narrative whole.

Connected to this understanding of symbol and religious imagination is an assumption about the nature of religious discourse and of theology. *Theology,* as I understand it, is a discipline of critical reflection on religious experience and religious language. As such, no matter how objective of systematic it becomes, it cannot escape the fundamental limitations that apply to religious discourse in general.

To put it bluntly, I do not believe that any of our notions of God, the soul, or the other world are likely to be true in the ordinary sense of the word. One reason for this is human weakness: we are too thick-headed, twisted, or frightened to see clearly. Another reason, which perhaps brings less discredit, is that we have no mode of expression that combines the virtues of analytic and symbolic thought: our concepts are too abstract and one-dimensional while our images and symbols are too concrete; we sense that both modes of understanding are necessary, yet they seem incompatible. For this and other reasons that have been adduced by countless philosophers and religious thinkers, there is no sensory, imaginative, or intellectual form capable of fully expressing the transcendent. We can intuit and be forever changed by a higher reality, but we cannot apprehend or describe it in the direct and unequivocal manner with which we seem to know the objects of ordinary experience. Such understanding as we do receive of the transcendent comes to us through symbols, and it is through symbols that we communicate this understand to one another.

Thus, although theology involves analytic thought, its fundamental material is symbol. Its task is to assess the health of our symbols, for when one judges a symbol, one cannot say whether it is true or false, but only whether it is vital or weak. When a contemporary theologian announces, for example, that God is dead or that God is only Father but also Mother, he or she is not describing the facts per se, but is evaluating the potency of our culture's images for God—their capacity to evoke a sense of relationship to the transcendent.

To say that theology is a diagnostic discipline is also to say that its method is pragmatic. In evaluating religious ideas and images, theology deals with ranges of experience that cannot be verified—which even overflow our normal categories of thought. One need not abandon the idea

that there is an ultimate truth in order to recognize that for now, at least, pragmatic criteria must be used. If we have no direct sensory or conceptual access to the reality for which we aim, then we must judge those images and ideas valid that serve a remedial function, healing the intellect and the will. In this sense, all theology is pastoral theology, for its proper task in not to describe the truth but to promote and assist the quest for truth.

I suggest, therefore, that a pragmatic method and a sensitivity to symbol must go hand in hand if we wish to give a fair hearing to the claims of near-death literature. If we fully recognize the symbolic nature of near-death testimony (and accept the limits that imposes on us), then in the end we will be able to accord it a value and a validity that would not otherwise be possible; this in turn will yield further insight into the visionary, imaginative, and therapeutic aspects of religious thought in general.

Questions

1. Name some of the reasons why modern theologians and Christian thinkers seek to dismiss NDE accounts.

2. What did Dr. Zaleski learn when she compared medieval with modern accounts of the NDE? What are some of the similarities and differences between the two?

3. What does Dr. Zaleski mean when she says that "the otherworld journey story . . . is through and through a work of the socially constructed religious imagination"? What conclusions does she draw from this?

4 Susan Blackmore, *Near-Death Experiences: In or Out of the Body?*

Susan Blackmore, Ph.D., is currently a freelance writer and part-time lecturer in psychology at the University of the West of England in Bristol. She has written several books about the near-death experience, including her most recent, *Dying to Live: Science and the Near-Death Experience,* from which the following essay is taken. Though initially interested in the NDE after having one of her own, Dr. Blackmore eventually came to adopt a more scientific, materialist stance. She narrated this journey from naïve belief to critical skepticism in the 1986 book, *The Adventures of a Parapsychologist,* which established her reputation as a leading thinker among NDE debunkers. She remains critical of any attempt to describe the NDE in anything other than scientific terms.

Though Dr. Blackmore is not the first researcher to offer a reductionist interpretation of the NDE, her account is unique in its complexity. From her scientific background, Blackmore is able to relate various elements of the NDE, especially the tunnel experience and the seeing of a being of light, to the way the visual cortex of the brain is structured. She also can account for the life review by means of her psychological understanding of the memory centers of the brain, and for the feeling of warmth and love in the presence of love by means of her training in body chemistry: it is endorphins, she says, the body's natural opiates that kick in during periods of physical stress, that make us feel peaceful at the point of death. Finally, she incorporates insights from her training in Zen Buddhism to assert that the NDE, although powerfully comforting in the face of life's greatest struggle, is merely an illusory hallucination, an imaginary projection of the imaginary self we believe ourselves to be. NDE survivors return with this insight, reasons Dr. Blackmore, and so this explains why they tend to be less attached to the material world, and to selfish desires.

What is it like to die? Although most of us fear death to a greater or lesser extent, there are now more and more people who have "come back" from states close to death and have told stories of usually very pleasant and even joyful experiences at death's door.

For many experiencers, their adventures seem unquestionably to provide evidence for life after death, and the profound effects the experience can have on them is just added confirmation. By contrast, for many scientists these experiences are just hallucinations produced by the dying brain and of no more interest than an especially vivid dream.

So which is right? Are near-death experiences (NDEs) the prelude to our life after death or the very last experience we have before oblivion? I shall argue that neither is quite right: NDEs provide no evidence for life after death, and we can best understand them by looking at neurochemistry, physiology, and psychology, but they are much more interesting than any dream. They seem completely real and can transform people's lives. Any satisfactory theory has to understand that too—and that leads us to questions about minds, selves, and the nature of consciousness.

Deathbed Experiences

Toward the end of the last century the physical sciences and the new theory of evolution were making great progress. But many people felt that science was forcing out the traditional ideas of the spirit and soul. Spiritualism began to flourish, and people flocked to mediums to get in contact with their dead friends and relatives "on the other side." Spiritualists claimed, and indeed still claim, to have found proof of survival.

In 1882, the Society for Psychical Research was founded, and serious research on the phenomena began; but convincing evidence for survival is still lacking over one hundred years later (Blackmore, 1988). In 1926, a psychical researcher and Fellow of the Royal Society, Sir William Barrett (1926), published a little book on deathbed visions. The dying apparently saw other worlds before they died and even saw and spoke to the dead. There were cases of music heard at the time of death and reports of attendants actually seeing the spirit leave the body.

With modern medical techniques, deathbed visions like these have become far less common. In those days people died at home with little or no medication and surrounded by their family and friends. Today most people die in the hospital and all too often alone. Paradoxically it is also improved medicine that has led to an increase in quite a different kind of report—that of the near-death experience.

Close Brushes with Death

Resuscitation from ever more serious heart failure has provided accounts of extraordinary experiences (although this is not the only cause of NDEs). These remained largely ignored until about fifteen years ago, when Raymond Moody (1975), an American physician, published his best-selling *Life After Life*. He had talked with many people who had "come back from death," and he put together an account of a typical NDE. In his idealized experience a person hears himself pronounced dead. Then comes a loud buzzing or ringing noise and a long, dark tunnel. He can see his own body from a distance and watch what is happening. Soon he meets others and a "being of light" who shows him a playback of events from his life and helps him to evaluate it. At some point he gets to a barrier and knows that he has to go back. Even though he feels joy, love, and peace there, he returns to his body and life. Later he tries to tell others; but they don't understand, and he soon gives up. Nevertheless the experience deeply affects him, especially his views about life and death.

Many scientists reacted with disbelief. They assumed Moody was at least exaggerating, but he claimed that no one had noticed the experiences before because the patients were too frightened to talk about them. The matter was soon settled by further research. One cardiologist had talked to more than 2,000 people over a period of nearly twenty years and claimed that more than half reported Moody-type experiences (Schoonmaker, 1979). In 1982, a Gallup poll found that about one in seven adult Americans had been close to death and about one in twenty had had an NDE. It appeared that Moody, at least in outline, was right. In my own research I have come across numerous reports like this one, sent to me by a woman from Cyprus:

> An emergency gastrectomy was performed. On the fourth day following that operation I went into shock and became unconscious for several hours. . . . Although thought to be unconscious, I remembered, for years afterwards, the entire, detailed conversation that passed between the surgeon and anaesthetist present. . . . I was lying above my own body, totally free of pain, and looking down at my own self with compassion for the agony I could see on the face; I was floating peacefully. Then . . . I was going elsewhere, floating towards a dark but not frightening, curtain-like area. . . . Then I felt total peace. . . . Suddenly it all changed—I was slammed back into my body again, very much aware of the agony again.

Within a few years some of the basic questions were being answered. Kenneth Ring (1980), at the University of Connecticut, surveyed 102 people who had come close to death and found almost fifty percent had had what he called a "core experience." He broke this into five stages: peace, body separation, entering the darkness (which is like the tunnel), seeing the light, and entering the light. He found that the later stages were reached by fewer people, which seems to imply that there is an ordered set of experiences waiting to unfold.

One interesting question is whether NDEs are culture specific. What little research there is suggests that in other cultures NDEs have basically the same structure, although religious background seems to influence the way it is interpreted. A few NDEs have even been recorded in children. It is interesting to note that nowadays children are more likely to see living friends than those who have died, presumably because their playmates only rarely die of diseases like scarlet fever or smallpox (Morse et al., 1986).

Perhaps more important is whether you have to be nearly dead to have an NDE. The answer is clearly no (e.g., Morse et al., 1989). Many very similar experiences are recorded of people who have taken certain drugs, were extremely tired, or, occasionally, were just carrying on their ordinary activities.

I must emphasize that these experiences seem completely real—even more real (whatever that may mean) than everyday life. The tunnel experience is not like just imagining going along a tunnel. The view from out of the body seems completely realistic, not like a dream, but as though you really are up there and looking down. Few people experience such profound emotion and insight again during their lifetimes. They do not say, "I've been hallucinating," "I imagined I went to heaven," or "Can I tell you about my lovely dream?" They are more likely to say, "I have been out of my body" or "I saw Grandma in heaven."

Since not everyone who comes close to death has an NDE, it is interesting to ask what sort of people are more likely to have them. Certainly you don't need to be mentally unstable. NDEers do not differ from others in terms of their psychological health or background. Moreover, the NDE does seem to produce profound and positive personality changes (Ring, 1984). After this extraordinary experience people claim that they are no longer so motivated by greed and material achievement but are more concerned about other people and their needs. Any theory of the NDE needs to account for this effect.

Explanations of the NDE

Astral Projection and the Next World

Could we have another body that is the vehicle of consciousness and leaves the physical body at death to go on to another world? This, essentially, is the doctrine of astral projection. In various forms it is very popular and appears in a great deal of New Age and occult literature.

One reason may be that out-of-body experiences (OBEs) are quite common, quite apart from their role in NDEs. Surveys have shown that anywhere from eight percent (in Iceland) to as much as fifty percent (in special groups, such as marijuana users) had OBEs at some time during their lives. In my own survey of residents of Bristol I found twelve percent. Typically these people had been resting or lying down and suddenly felt they had left their bodies, usually for no more than a minute or two (Blackmore, 1984).

A survey of more than fifty different cultures showed that almost all of them believe in a spirit or soul that could leave the body (Sheils, 1978). So both the OBE and the belief in body are common, but what does this mean? Is it just that we cannot bring ourselves to believe that we are nothing more than a mortal body and that death is the end? Or is there really another body?

You might think that such a theory has no place in science and ought to be ignored. I disagree. The only ideas that science can do nothing with are the purely metaphysical ones—ideas that have no measurable consequences and no testable predictions. But if a theory makes predictions, however bizarre, then it can be tested.

The theory of astral projection is, at least in some forms, testable. In the earliest experiments mediums claimed they were able to project their astral bodies to distant rooms and see what was happening. They claimed not to taste bitter aloes on their real tongues, but immediately screwed up their faces in disgust when the substance was placed on their (invisible) astral tongues. Unfortunately these experiments were not properly controlled (Blackmore, 1982).

In other experiments, dying people were weighed to try to detect the astral body as it left. Early this century a weight of about one ounce was claimed, but as the apparatus became more sensitive the weight dropped, implying that it was not a real effect. More recent experiments have used sophisticated detectors of ultraviolet and infrared, magnetic flux or field strength, temperature, or weight to try to capture the astral body of someone having an out-of-body experience. They have even used animals and human "detectors," but no one has yet succeeded in detecting anything reliably (Morris et al., 1978).

If something really leaves the body in OBEs, then you might expect it to be able to see at a distance, in other words to have extrasensory perception (ESP). There have been several experiments with concealed targets. One success was Tart's subject, who lay on a bed with a five-digit number on a shelf above it (Tart, 1968). During the night she had an OBE and correctly reported the number, but critics argued that she could have climbed out of the bed to look. Apart from this one, the experiments tend, like so many in parapsychology, to provide equivocal results and no clear signs of any ESP.

So, this theory has been tested but seems to have failed its tests. If there really were astral bodies, I would have expected us to have found something out about them by now—other than how hard it is to track them down!

In addition there are major theoretical objections to the idea of astral bodies. If you imagine that the person has gone to another world, perhaps along some "real" tunnel, then you have to ask what relationship there is between this world and the other one. If the other world is an extension of the physical, then it ought to be observable and measurable. The astral body, astral world, and tunnel ought to be detectable in some way, and we ought to be able to say where exactly the tunnel is going. The fact that we can't leads many people to say the astral world is "on another plane," at a "higher level of vibration," and the like. But unless you can specify just what these mean, the ideas are completely empty even though

they may sound appealing. Of course we can never prove that astral bodies don't exist, but my guess is that they probably don't and that this theory is not a useful way to understand OBEs.

Birth and the NDE

Another popular theory makes dying analogous with being born: that the out-of-body experience is literally just that—reliving the moment when you emerged from your mother's body. The tunnel is the birth canal and the white light is the light of the world into which you were born. Even the being of light can be "explained" as an attendant at the birth.

This theory was proposed by Stanislav Grof and Joan Halifax (1977) and popularized by the astronomer Carl Sagan (1979), but it is pitifully inadequate to explain the NDE. For a start the newborn infant would not see anything like a tunnel as it was being born. The birth canal is stretched and compressed and the baby usually forced through it with the top of its head, not with its eyes (which are closed anyway) pointing forward. Also it does not have the mental skills to recognize the people around, and these capacities change so much during growing up that adults cannot reconstruct what it was like to be an infant.

"Hypnotic regression to past lives" is another popular claim. In fact much research shows that people who have been hypnotically regressed give the appearance of acting like a baby or a child, but it is no more than acting. For example, they don't make drawings like a real five-year-old would do, but like an adult imagines children do. Their vocabulary is too large and in general they overestimate the abilities of children at any given age. There is no evidence (even if the idea made sense) of their "really" going back in time.

Of course the most important question is whether this theory could be tested, and to some extent it can. For example, it predicts that people born by Caesarean section should not have the same tunnel experiences and OBEs. I conducted a survey of people born normally and those born by Caesarean (190 and 36 people, respectively). Almost exactly equal percentages of both groups had had tunnel experiences (36 percent) and OBEs (29 percent). I have not compared the type of birth of people coming close to death, but this would provide further evidence (Blackmore, 1982b).

In response to these findings some people have argued that it is not one's own birth that is relived, but the idea of birth in general. However, this just reduces the theory to complete vacuousness.

Just Hallucinations

Perhaps we should give up and conclude that all the experiences are "just imagination" or "nothing but hallucinations." However, this is the weakest theory of all. The experiences must, in some sense, be hallucinations, but this is not, on its own, any explanation. We have to ask why are they these kinds of hallucinations? Why tunnels?

Some say the tunnel is a symbolic representation of the gateway to another world. But then why always a tunnel and not, say, a gate, doorway, or even the great River Styx? Why the light at the end of the tunnel? And why always above the body, not below it? I have no objection to the theory that the experiences are hallucinations. I only object to the idea you can explain them by saying, "They are just hallucinations." This explains nothing. A viable theory would answer these questions without dismissing the experiences. That, even if only in tentative form, is what I shall try to provide.

The Physiology of the Tunnel

Tunnels do not only occur near death. They are also experienced in epilepsy and migraine, when falling asleep, meditating, or just relaxing, with pressure on both eyeballs, and with certain drugs, such as LSD, psilocybin, and mescaline. I have experienced them many times myself. It is as though the whole world becomes a rushing, roaring tunnel and you are flying along it toward a bright light at the end. No doubt many readers have also been there, for surveys show that about a third of people have—like this terrified man of 28 who had just had the anesthetic for circumcision:

> I seemed to be hauled at "lightning speed" in a direct line tunnel into outer space; (not a floating sensation . . .) but like a rocket at a terrific speed. I appeared to have left my body.

In the 1930s, Heinrich Kluver, the University of Chicago, noted four form constants in hallucinations: the tunnel, the spiral, the lattice or grating, and the cobweb. Their origin probably lies in the structure of the visual cortex, the part of the brain that processes visual information. Imagine that the outside world is mapped onto the back of the eye (on the retina), and then again in the cortex. The mathematics of this mapping (at least to a reasonable approximation) is well known.

Jack Cowan, a neurobiologist at the University of Chicago, has used the mapping to account for the tunnel (Cowan, 1982). Brain activity is normally kept stable by some cells inhibiting others. Disinhibition (the reduction of this inhibitory activity) produces too much activity in the brain. This can occur near death (because of lack of oxygen) or with drugs like LSD, which interfere with inhibition. Cowan uses an analogy with fluid mechanics to argue that disinhibition will induce stripes of activity that move across the cortex. Using the mapping it can easily be shown that stripes in the cortex would appear like concentric rings or spirals in the visual world. In other words, if you have stripes in the cortex you will seem to see a tunnel-like pattern of spirals or rings.

This theory is important in showing how the structure of the brain could produce the same hallucination for everyone. However, I was dubious about the idea of these moving stripes, and also Cowan's theory doesn't readily explain the bright light at the center. So Tom Troscianko and I, at the University of Bristol, tried to develop a simpler theory (Blackmore and Troscianko, 1989). The most obvious thing about the representation in the cortex is that there are lots of cells representing the center of the visual field but very few for the edges. This means that you can see small things very clearly in the center, but if they are out at the edges you cannot. We took just this simple fact

as a starting point and used a computer to simulate what would happen when you have gradually increasing electrical noise in the visual cortex.

The computer program starts with thinly spread dots of light, mapped in the same way as the cortex, with more toward the middle and very few at the edges. Gradually the number of dots increases, mimicking the increasing noise. Now the center begins to look like a white blob and the outer edges gradually get more and more dots. And so it expands until eventually the whole screen is filled with light. The appearance is just like a dark speckly tunnel with a white light at the end, and the light grows bigger and bigger (or nearer and nearer) until it fills the whole screen.

If it seems odd that such a simple picture can give the impression that you are moving, consider two points. First, it is known that random movements in the periphery of the visual field are more likely to he interpreted by the brain as outward than inward movements (Georgeson and Harris, 1978). Second, the brain infers our own movement to a great extent from what we see. Therefore, presented with an apparently growing patch of flickering white light your brain will easily interpret it as yourself moving forward into a tunnel.

The theory also makes a prediction about NDEs in the blind. If they are blind because of problems in the eye but have a normal cortex, then they too should see tunnels. But if their blindness stems from a faulty or damaged cortex, they should not. These predictions have yet to be tested.

According to this kind of theory there is, of course, no real tunnel. Nevertheless there is a real physical cause of the tunnel experience. It is noise in the visual cortex. This way we can explain the origin of the tunnel without just dismissing the experiences and without needing to invent other bodies or other worlds.

Out-of-Body Experiences

Like tunnels, OBEs are not confined to near death. They too can occur when just relaxing and falling asleep, with meditation, and in epilepsy and migraine. They can also, at least by a few people, be induced at will. I have been interested in OBEs since I had a long and dramatic experience myself (Blackmore, 1982a).

It is important to remember that these experiences seem quite real. People don't describe them as dreams or fantasies, but as events that actually happened. This is, I presume, why they seek explanations in terms of other bodies or other worlds.

However, we have seen how poorly the astral projection and birth theories cope with OBEs. What we need is a theory that involves no unmeasurable entities or untestable other worlds but explains why the experiences happen and why they seem so real.

I would start by asking why anything seems real. You might think this is obvious—after all, the things we see out there are real, aren't they? Well no, in a sense they aren't. As perceiving creatures all we know is what our senses tell us. And our senses tell us what is "out there" by constructing models of the world with ourselves in it. The whole of the world "out there" and our own bodies are really constructions of our minds. Yet we are sure, all the time, that this construction—if you like, this "model of reality"—is "real" while the other fleeting thoughts we have are unreal. We call the rest of them daydreams, imagination, fantasies, and so on. Our brains have no trouble distinguishing "reality" from "imagination." But this distinction is not given. It is one the brain has to make for itself by deciding which of its own models represents the world "out there." I suggest it does this by comparing all the models it has at any time and choosing the stable one as "reality."

This will normally work very well. The model created by the senses is the best and most stable the system has. It is obviously "reality," while that image I have of the bar I'm going to go to later is unstable and brief. The choice is easy. By comparison, when you are almost asleep, very frightened, or nearly dying, the model from the senses will be confused and unstable. If you are under terrible stress or suffering oxygen deprivation, then the choice won't be so easy. All the models will be unstable.

So what will happen now? Possibly the tunnel being created by noise in the visual cortex will be the most stable model and so, according to my supposition, this will seem real. Fantasies and imagery might become more stable than the sensory model, and so seem real. The system will have lost input control.

What then should a sensible biological system do to get back to normal? I would suggest that it could try to ask itself—as it were—"Where am I? What is happening?" Even a person under severe stress will have some memory left. They might recall the accident, or know that they were in hospital for an operation, or remember the pain of the heart attack. So they will try to reconstruct, from what little they can remember, what is happening.

Now we know something very interesting about memory models. Often they are constructed in a bird's-eye view. That is, the events or scenes are seen as though from above. If you find this strange, try to remember the last time you went to a pub or the last time you walked along the seashore. Where are "you" looking from in this recalled scene? If you are looking from above you will see what I mean.

So my explanation of the OBE becomes clear. A memory model in bird's eye view has taken over from the sensory model. It seems perfectly real because it is the best model the system has got at the time. Indeed, it seems real for just the same reason anything ever seems real.

This theory of the OBE leads to many testable predictions, for example, that people who habitually use bird's-eye views should be more likely to have OBEs. Both Harvey Irwin (1986), an Australian psychologist, and myself (Blackmore 1987) have found that people who dream as though they were spectators have more OBEs, although there seems to be no difference for the waking use of different viewpoints. I have also found that people who can more easily switch viewpoints in their imagination are also more likely to report OBEs.

Of course this theory says that the OBE world is only a memory model. It should only match the real world when the person has already known about something or can deduce it from available information. This presents a big challenge for research on near death. Some researchers claim that people near death can actually see things that they couldn't possibly have known about. For example, the American cardiologist Michael Sabom (1982) claims that patients reported the exact behavior of needles and monitoring apparatus when they had their eyes closed and appeared to be unconscious. Further, he compared these descriptions with those of people imagining they were being resuscitated and found that the real patients gave far more accurate and detailed descriptions.

There are problems with this comparison. Most important, the people really being resuscitated could probably feel some of the manipulations being done on them and hear what was going on. Hearing is the last sense to be lost and, as you will realize if you ever listen to radio plays or news, you can imagine a very clear visual image when you can only hear something. So the dying person could build up a fairly accurate picture this way. Of course hearing doesn't allow you to see the behavior of needles, and so if Sabom is right, I am wrong. We can only await further research to find out.

The Life Review

The experience of seeing excerpts from your life flash before you is not really as mysterious as it first seems. It has long been known that stimulation of cells in the temporal lobe of the brain can produce instant experiences that seem like the reliving of memories. Also, temporal lobe epilepsy can produce similar experiences, and such seizures can involve other limbic structures in the brain, such as the amygdala and hippocampus, which are also associated with memory.

Imagine that the noise in the dying brain stimulates cells like this. The memories will be aroused and, according to my hypothesis, if they are the most stable model the system has at that time they will seem real. For the dying person they may well be more stable than the confused and noisy sensory model.

The link between temporal-lobe epilepsy and the NDE has formed the basis of a thorough neurobiological model of the NDE (Saavedra-Aguilar and Gomez-Jeria, 1989). They suggest that the brain stress consequent on the near-death episode leads to the release of neuropeptides and neurotransmitters (in particular the endogenous endorphins). These then stimulate the limbic system and other connected areas. In addition, the effect of the endorphins could account for the blissful and other positive emotional states so often associated with the NDE.

Morse provided evidence that some children deprived of oxygen and treated with opiates did not have NDE-like hallucinations, and he and his colleagues (Morse et al., 1986) have developed a theory based on the role of the neurotransmitter serotonin, rather than the endorphins. Research on the neurochemistry of the NDE is just beginning and should provide us with much more detailed understanding of the life review.

Of course there is more to the life review than just memories. The person feels as though she or he is judging these life events, being shown their significance and meaning. But this too, I suggest, is not so very strange. When the normal world of the senses is gone and memories seem real, our perspective on our life changes. We can no longer be so attached to our plans, hopes, ambitions, and fears, which fade away and become unimportant, while the past comes to life again. We can only accept it as it is, and there is no one to judge it but ourselves. This is, I think, why so many NDEers say they faced their past life with acceptance and equanimity.

Other Worlds

Now we come to what might seem the most extraordinary parts of the NDE; the worlds beyond the tunnel and OBE. But I think you can now see that they are not so extraordinary at all. In this state the outside world is no longer real, and inner worlds are. Whatever we can imagine clearly enough will seem real. And what will we imagine when we know we are dying? I am sure for many people it is the world they expect or hope to see. Their minds may turn to people they have known who have died before them or to the world they hope to enter next. Like the other images we have been considering, these will seem perfectly real.

Finally, there are those aspects of the NDE that are ineffable—they cannot be put into words. I suspect that this is because some people take yet another step, a step into nonbeing. I shall try to explain this by asking another question. What is consciousness? If you say it is a thing, another body, a substance, you will only get into the kinds of difficulty we got into with OBEs. I prefer to say that consciousness is just what it is like being a mental model. In other words, all the mental models in any person's mind are all conscious, but only one is a model of "me." This is the one that I think of as myself and to which I relate everything else. It gives a core to my life. It allows me to think that I am a person, something that lives on all the time. It allows me to ignore the fact that "I" change from moment to moment and even disappear every night in sleep.

Now when the brain comes close to death, this model of self may simply fall apart. Now there is no self. It is a strange and dramatic experience. For there is no longer an experiencer—yet there is experience.

This state is obviously hard to describe, for the "you" who is trying to describe it cannot imagine not being. Yet this profound experience leaves its mark. The self never seems quite the same again.

The After Effects

I think we can now see why an essentially physiological event can change people's lives so profoundly. The experience has jolted their usual (and erroneous) view of the relationship between themselves and the world. We all too easily assume that we are some kind of persistent entity inhabiting a perishable body. But, as the Buddha taught, we have to see through that illusion. The world is only a construction of an information-processing system, and the self is too. I believe that the NDE gives people a glimpse into the nature of their own minds that is hard to get any other way. Drugs can produce it temporarily, mystical experiences can do it for rare people, and long years of practice in meditation or mindfulness can do it. But the NDE can out of the blue strike anyone and show them what they never knew before, that their body is only that—a lump of flesh—that they are not so very important after all. And that is a very freeing and enlightening experience.

And Afterwards?

If my analysis of the NDE is correct, we can extrapolate to the next stage. Lack of oxygen first produces increased activity through disinhibition, but eventually it all stops. Since it is this activity that produces the mental models that give rise to consciousness, then all this will cease. There will be no more experience, no more self, and so that, as far as my constructed self is concerned, is the end.

So, are NDEs in or out of the body?

I should say neither, for neither experiences nor selves have any location. It is finally death that dissolves the illusion that we are a solid self inside a body.

Questions

1. Put into your own words and evaluate both the "astral projection" and "reliving birth" theories of the NDE.

2. How does Dr. Blackmore explain the "tunnel" experience in physiological terms? Does this sound plausible to you? Why or why not?

3. Knowing what you now know about the NDE, do you agree with Blackmore's reductionist account that the NDE is merely the product of a dying brain? Why or why not?

5 P. M. H. Atwater, L. H. D. *What Is Not Being Said About the Near-Death Experience*

P. M. H. Atwater, Ph.D., lives in Virginia and travels the country as a freelance speaker on the subject of near-death experiences. She is herself a survivor of three NDEs. She had her first during a miscarriage that caused a massive amount of internal hemorrhaging. According to her own testimony, Dr. Atwater traveled out of her body, met Christ and several deceased family members, had a complete life review, and witnessed a cyclonelike funnel of souls, along with an explosive energy center in the cyclone that brought her to God.

Following her recovery from the miscarriage, Dr. Atwater published her story in the book *Coming Back to Life: The After-Effects of the Near-Death Experience* (1988). She then went on to research the NDE phenomenon by interviewing scores of other experiencers. As she did so, she discovered something that none of the other researchers had ever mentioned: that not all NDEs are positive experiences. In contrast to the joyous, peaceful experiences that Raymond Moody mentions in his best-selling *Life After Life,* Dr. Atwater described the experiences of several of her interviewees in which a dark sense of doom dominated, and in which lifeless, threatening beings were encountered. In these more "hellish" visions, the experiencers recount feeling a sense of danger, of cold emptiness and evil. Dr. Atwater also discovered that the NDE, even if joyous, does not always make the experiencer a saint; that some simply return to their former lives without much change. "Surviving [death] does not make you enlightened or super-human," she writes. Or sometimes, when the experiencer returns with new spiritual insights and gifts, turns away from materialism and toward spirituality, and feels a profound love for all people, he or she can confuse family and friends who experience the sudden changes as threatening. This can lead to things like depression, divorce, and the severing of friendships. But generally, Dr. Atwater considers the near-death experience meaningful as a kind of "wake-up call" from God.

The near-death experience represents an incredible unknown, resisting thus far many attempts to clinically define its scope or the "need" that drives it. We do know a lot about the phenomenon. After thirty years of study and the efforts of well over a hundred researchers, we have a better grasp today of the phenomenon's dynamics and aftereffects. Still, we have hardly scratched the surface of what can be learned about this incredible mystery. *We do not know as much as we think.*

I say this because I am not just a researcher. I have had three near-death experiences (Atwater 1988, 1994, 2004). My research is informed by powerful personal experiences of the subject in question. Although my initial motive for doing this work was to save my sanity, I have always been guided by revelations made to me while on "the other side" of death, revelations that gave me a purpose: clarifying and giving perspective to soul awakenings. The Russian proverb "Trust, but verify" has set my course as I have interviewed nearly 4,000 near-death experiencers of all ages, from many countries, 2,000 of them in depth, plus numerous "significant others."

My own three near-death experiences were precipitated by my 1977 miscarriage and extreme hemorrhaging. Months later I suffered three relapses, one of which was adrenal failure. As a result, I had to relearn how to crawl, stand, walk, climb stairs, run, tell the difference between left and right, see and hear properly, and rebuild my belief systems. I was never hospitalized, seeing doctors only after the fact, but it is both my opinion and that of the specialist who diagnosed my problems that I had indeed died. Each time I met death, I had a visionary experience, and each was different, although one seemed somehow to lead into the next.

Elisabeth Kübler-Ross first helped me understand that I am a near-death survivor when we met at O'Hare Airport in 1978. Although her description of the phenomenon's universal pattern was helpful, I was left with more questions than answers. I launched my own research project shortly afterward, employing the skills of investigative observation and analysis that were taught to me when a child by my police officer father. I was rigorous in cross-checking my work and in forcing myself to be objective, even if that meant acknowledging what I did not want to face.

This effort convinced me that the near-death phenomenon is more complex and many-faceted than is commonly believed. Far from describing some heavenly travelogue or providing "proof" of an afterlife, the phenomenon actually challenges us to reconsider our very *aliveness* and the existence of *spirit*.

Because I kept the individual's near-death scenario in context with their previous and present life, I was able to find multiple connections, correlations, and parallels that led me to conclude that the experience could be "needed" by those who had it. It seems that a near-death experience quite probably is one of nature's more accelerated growth events, a powerful and complex dynamic that can foster major

psychological and physiological changes in both adults and children. Viewing the near-death phenomenon in this manner, I have identified four distinctive types of experience with a general psychological profile for each category (Atwater, 1994).

The Four Types of Near-Death Experiences

1. **Initial Experience (sometimes referred to as the "non-experience")**

   Involves elements such as a loving nothingness, the living dark, a friendly voice, a brief out-of-body experience, or a manifestation of some type. Usually experienced by those who seem to need the least amount of evidence for proof of survival, or who need the least amount of shakeup in their lives at that point in time. Often this becomes a "seed" experience or an introduction to other ways of perceiving and recognizing reality.

   Incident rate: 76% with child
   experiencers
   20% with adult
   experiencers

2. **Unpleasant and/or Hell-Like Experience (inner cleansing and self-confrontation)**

   Encounter with a threatening void or stark limbo or hellish purgatory, or scenes of a startling and unexpected indifference, even "hauntings" from one's own past. Usually experienced by those who seem to have deeply suppressed or repressed guilts, fears, and angers and/or those who expect some kind of punishment or discomfort after death.

Incident rate: 3% with child
            experiencers
            15% with adult
            experiencers

3. **Pleasant and/or Heaven-Like Experience (reassurance and self-validation)**
Heaven-like scenarios of loving family reunions with those who have died previously, reassuring religious figures or light beings, validation that life counts, affirmative and inspiring dialogue. Usually experienced by those who most need to know how loved they are and how important life is and how every effort has a purpose in the overall scheme of things.
Incident rate: 19% with child
            experiencers
            47% with adult
            experiencers

4. **Transcendent Experience (expansive revelations, alternate realities)**
Exposure to otherworldly dimensions and scenes beyond the individual's frame of reference; sometimes includes revelations of greater truths. Seldom personal in content. Usually experienced by those who are ready for a "mind-stretching" challenge and/or individuals who are more apt to utilize (to whatever degree) the truths that are revealed to them.
Incident rate: 2% with child
            experiencers
            18% with adult
            experiencers

I have found that all four types can occur during the same near-death experience, can exist in varying combinations, or can spread out across a series of episodes. What may seem as negative or positive concerning any of these four types is very relative. *The value and meaning of an NDE depend on each individual involved and his or her response to what happened.*

1. The Initial Experience

One group of people had very brief experiences with one or two elements. Hardly more than "snatches" of anything otherworldly, these seemingly inconsequential events can have an impact on an individual every bit as powerful as a full-blown near-death scenario. Uncomplicated or simple out-of-body episodes account for about half of them.

What happened to the novelist Ernest Hemingway is an example of this type. During World War I, Hemingway was wounded by shrapnel while fighting in Italy. He made this cryptic statement in a letter he wrote from his hospital bed: "Dying is a very simple thing. I've looked at death and really I know." Years later, Hemingway confided to a friend the details that had occurred on that fateful night in 1918:

> A big Austrian trench mortar bomb, of the type that used to be called ash cans, exploded in the darkness. I died then. I felt my soul or something coming right out of my body, like you'd pull a silk handkerchief out of a pocket by one corner. It flew around and then came back and went in again and I wasn't dead anymore. (Josephs, Hoffman, 108)

Hemingway remained deeply affected by this out-of-body initial near-death experience throughout his life, and was never again as "hard-boiled" as he once had been. *A Farewell to Arms* contains a passage where the character Frederic Henry undergoes the same confrontation with death that Hemingway did:

> I ate the end of my piece of cheese and took a swallow of wine. Through the other noise I heard a cough, then came the chuh-chuh-chuh-chuh—then there was a flash, as when a blast-furnace door is swung open, and a roar that started white and went red and on and on in a rushing wind. I tried to breathe but my breath would not come and I felt myself rush bodily out of myself and out and out and out and all the time bodily in the wind. I went out swiftly, all of myself, and I knew I was dead and that it had all been a mistake to think you just died. Then I floated, and instead of going on I felt myself slide back. I breathed and I was back. (Hemingway, 54)

Those who have this type of near-death episode respond as if they had been suddenly "stimulated." They appear more alert, curious and open, exhibiting expanded sensory abilities. This is a "seed" event, an experience that grows over time, inspiring the survivor to think more creatively and abstractly. And, like most seed events, it can lead to lifestyle and personality changes. It seems that shorter lengths of exposure to other-worldly realities are quite enough for this stage in survivors' development. Young children often undergo this type of episode.

2. Unpleasant or Hellish Experience

This kind of fearful terror was experienced by Jeanne Eppley of Columbus, Ohio. She told me that, during the birth of her first child, she was frightened when:

> Everything was bright yellow. There was a tiny black dot in the center of all the yellow. Somehow I knew that the dot was me. The dot began to divide. First there was two, then four, then eight. After there had been enough division, the dots formed into a pinwheel and began to spin. As the pinwheel spun, the dots began to rejoin in the same manner as they had divided. I knew that when they were all one again, I would be dead, so I began to fight. The next thing I remember is the doctor trying to awaken me and keep me on the delivery table, because I was getting up.

Eppley expressed disappointment that her case did not match all the wonderful stories that other near-death survivors tell. A fellow experiencer suggested that maybe the reason for this was her refusal to "let go" and surrender to the experience. The battle she had waged so fiercely may have blocked any further development of an uplifting scenario. Other researchers have suggested that "surrender" may indeed be the factor that determines not only depth of experience, but who might possibly have an NDE to begin with.

Yet, if you explore Eppley's life before and after, a startling pattern emerges. This painful experience evoked some needed strength. It foreshadowed two disappointing marriages, the birth of three more children, verbal and physical abuse, an attempt on her life, plus the ordeal of raising her family without support. The battle fear generated in her near-death episode was *the first time* she had ever stood up for herself. By her own admission, the strength she gained from that fight enabled her to call upon deep reservoirs of power that she never knew she had. Thus, winning one battle gave her the courage to win many others. She has since remarried, and is now a radiantly happy woman. What was originally fearsome turned out to be a godsend.

Would Eppley have benefited as much as she did had her scenario been sweetly angelic? In Eppley's case developing psychological muscle was more advantageous than becoming spiritually pious. She needed to get tougher and what happened helped her to do so. I have observed this curious characteristic with all the people I have interviewed: The phenomenon tends to provide experiencers with an opportunity to rectify behavior flaws or heal an emptiness; in some way the NDE inspires them to loosen up, open up, and grow.

With unpleasant cases, seldom has anyone I have met said anything about fiery hot or burning sensations where they went. Rather, most comment on how cold it was, or clammy or shivery or "hard" or empty. The light was dull, sometimes gray or "heavy" as if overcast or foggy. Invariably an attack of some kind or a shunning would occur, resulting in pain or surges of anxiety. The experiencer would have to defend him or herself or fight for survival. Common are themes of good and evil, devils and angels, great storms, sucking vortexes and a frightening void.

Also common with the frightening type are reports of hauntings after the individual revives and resumes life's routines. These hauntings are perceived as physically solid and real. I have heard numerous stories of "evil ones" who suddenly appear in broad daylight to chase the experiencer and do battle over his or her soul, then disappear. Manifestations such as these are depicted in the 1990 movie "Flatliners."

One out of seven in my research had unpleasant or hellish experiences, yet truly demonic scenarios were in the minority. Three puzzles emerged for me concerning this finding:

- *Elements* (Contrary Evaluations)— The same thing that one person would describe as "horrific," another would term "wondrous."
- *Scenarios* (Coping)—Whether or not an individual could cope with the experience stemmed more from their evaluation of "heavenly" or "hellish" than the actual content.
- *Experiencers* (Age)—Older children and adults reported the most unpleasant or hellish episodes; little ones seldom did.

When I focused on these puzzles I noticed a glaring contrast in language among those I spoke with, even though many described *similar images in similar settings*. This chart compares these descriptive contrasts:

Comparison of Heavenly and Hellish Experiences

Heavenly Cases	Hellish Cases
Friendly beings	Lifeless or threatening apparitions
Beautiful, lovely environments	Barren or ugly expanses
Conversations and dialogue	Threats, screams, silence
Total acceptance and an overwhelming sensation of love	Danger and possible violence or torture
A feeling of warmth and a sense of heaven	A feeling of temperature extremes, usually cold, and a sense of hell

These conundrums took on new meaning once I recognized a common denominator present in *every* episode of this type that I investigated: distressing near-death experiences seem to outpicture a process of inner purification, a fantastic housecleaning that operates on levels more powerful than personal or religious beliefs. Along this same line I noticed that those experiencers willing to confront "the shadow self," that aspect of their own nature either repressed or denied, were the ones who reported miraculous healings more often than did the others.

3. Pleasant or Heavenly Experience

Since these constitute the largest number of cases, it is no wonder that the basic story-line has become virtually mythologized as the classic NDE. But, just as there is more to the hellish version than meets the eye, more can also be found in tales of heaven.

For example, in 1932 Arthur Yensen, a university graduate and staunch materialist turned syndicated cartoonist, decided to take some time off to research his weekly cartoon strip, *Adventurous Willie Wispo*. Since his main character was a hobo, Yensen became one for a while, blending with the Depression's sixteen million unemployed. He bummed rides from Chicago into Minnesota, where he was picked up by a young man driving a convertible. Going too fast for road conditions, the car hit oiled gravel and flipped into a series of violent somersaults. Both men were catapulted through the cloth top before the car smashed into a ditch. The driver escaped unharmed, but Yensen was injured and nearly died:

Gradually the earth scene faded away, and through it loomed a bright, new, beautiful world—beautiful beyond imagination! For half a minute I could see both worlds at once. Finally, when the earth was all gone, I stood in a glory that could only be heaven.

In the background were two beautiful, round-topped mountains, similar to Fujiyama in Japan. The tops were snow-capped, and the slopes were adorned with foliage of indescribable beauty. The mountains appeared to be about fifteen miles away, yet I could see individual flowers growing on their slopes. I estimated my vision to be about one hundred times better than on earth.

To the left was a shimmering lake containing a different kind of water—clear, golden, radiant, and alluring. It seemed to be alive. The whole landscape was carpeted with grass so vivid, clear and green that it defies description. To the right was a grove of large, luxuriant trees, composed of the same clear material that seemed to make up everything. (Yensen)

Yensen's rapturous visit was lengthy and involved many insights and teachings given to him by a heavenly being. His case rivals any of modern vintage. To say he was transformed and transfigured after his experience would be an understatement, yet his life is a study in contradiction. Forcefed religion as a youngster, he turned against church and challenged his parents at every turn, including the way they ate. His defiance of convention was compounded by his near-death event. Suddenly "knowing" more than before, he switched from atheism to mysticism and became a political activist, educator, organic gardener and nutrition expert. He married, helped raise three sons, and later was named one of Idaho's "Most Distinguished Citizens."

Even though he healed and helped thousands of people during his long life, Yensen died still questioning his worth and whether he had accomplished his mission in life. He suffered a deep loneliness and often claimed that it was his near-death experience that kept him going.

I have observed that once those who have a heavenly scenario experience and encounter what they recognize as true love, they feel tremendous pressure to pass it on. This may not be because they have become a fountain of that love—for many sense, as did Yensen, a gross inadequacy in themselves and are never quite able to accept the validity of "worthiness"—but

because they now know they are connected to and in communion with a Greater Reality. They have faced the awesome visage of RESPONSIBILITY and returned with a sense of mission.

Both pain and joy can be as instructive. Heavenly visions may leave some pain, and hellish experiences may stimulate some joy. I have consistently found this in my research. I no longer consider one type of near-death scenario to be more important than another. Rather, I now view all four categories as ways that evolving consciousness uses to stimulate progress.

4. The Transcendent Experience

Usually lengthy, complex and seldom personal, these cases are so otherworldly that they defy ordinary understanding. Scenarios can range from riding a light ray throughout the universe, or viewing creation as it happened, or witnessing the beginning and end of history, to attending classes in some "heavenly" university. Invariably the people who have them are inspired to take action when they return, to make a difference in the world. Although hearing remarkable claims by near-death survivors that they were privy to all knowledge during their experience is typical, coming back with that knowledge rarely occurs.

History gives us an example that shows how society can be affected by an individual who has had a transcendent episode. In 1837 a Chinese peasant farmer's son Hung Hsiu-ch'uan failed for the third time to pass the official state examination. He fell into a prolonged delirium, his body wasting away as he lay near death for forty days. He revived after having a miraculous vision that portrayed him and an "elder brother" searching out and slaying legions of evil demons in accordance with divine will. Six years later Hsiu-ch'uan came across a Christian missionary pamphlet. He used what he read in the pamphlet to "substantiate" his conviction that his vision was real and that he, as the younger brother of Jesus Christ and God's Divine Representative, was ready and willing to overthrow the forces of evil, which he saw as the Manchus and Confucianism. With the help of converts to his cause, he established the God Worshippers Society, a puritanical and absolutist group that quickly swelled to the ranks of a revolutionary army. Hsiu-ch'uan joined forces with the Taiping Rebellion of 1850 to help lead a massive, bloody civil uprising which lasted fourteen years and cost the lives of twenty million people (Chien 10, 36; Curwen, 11; Hamberg; Lee).

Near-death survivors such as Hsiu-ch'uan (who changed his name to T'ien Wang, the Heavenly King) may be transformed by their unusual near-death experiences and become zealous in their desire to "wake up" the so-called "deluded." They may be convinced that only REAL TRUTH has been revealed to them, and thus it is their sacred duty to "save" the populace. In the case of Hsiu-ch'uan, his near-death experience led to wholesale carnage and helped to forge a "Heavenly Dynasty" that ripped asunder the very fabric of China.

Transcendent cases are powerful in both content and consequences, yet they are a risky business because they can affect experiencers' lives plus the lives of countless others. This enigma repeats itself each time an individual is changed so utterly by the near-death phenomenon. Clearly, seeing "heaven" does not make one holy, nor does it make anyone "chosen" or "savior." *No single case* is more profound, complete, or better than any other. In truth, the real strength of near-death stories comes from *the combined message of the many*, a chorus that speaks with a voice of thunder about the reality of God, Soul and Oneness.

Only 21 percent of those I had sessions with denied the existence of aftereffects, even though their families often disagreed, claiming they did indeed exhibit the pattern of aftereffects. Of these experiences, most reported having had only the initial type. The rest reported significant, life-changing differences afterward, 19 percent claimed radical psychological and spiritual turnarounds, almost as if they had become another person.

Any notion that, as a compensatory gift, some people are privileged to survive death, see heaven, and return dedicated to selfless service for all humankind, I call the "myth of Amazing Grace." That's because there are both positive and negative aspects to the aftereffects. Passing through death's door seems merely to be step one. Integrating the experience is the real adventure. Making what was learned real and workable in everyday life is difficult. No "set of instructions" covers how to do this. Thus lengthy bouts with depression are typical.

Psychological Aftereffects

I have observed that it seems to take a minimum of seven years for most experiencers to integrate the aftereffects (2001). Although these cannot be faked, an individual can delay the onset of them or deny their existence. Seven major elements comprise the universal pattern.

1. Unconditional love—Experiencers perceive themselves as equally and fully loving of each and all, openly generous, excited about the potential and wonder of each person they see. Confused family members tend to regard this sudden switch in behavior as oddly threatening, as if their loved one had become aloof, unresponsive, even uncaring or unloving.

2. Lack of boundaries—Familiar codes of conduct can lose relevance or disappear altogether as unlimited avenues of interest and inquiry take priority. This new frame of reference can infuse experiencers with such an accepting nature that they can and do display childlike naiveté. With the fading of previous norms and standards, basic cautions and discernments can also fade.

3. Timelessness—Most experiencers begin to "flow" with the natural shift of time, rejecting clocks and schedules as they exhibit a heightened awareness of the present moment and the importance of "now." They are easily distracted and can appear "spacey" until they readjust to the demands of daily routines.

4. Psychic insights—Extrasensory perception and various types of psychic phenomena become normal and ordinary in the lives of experiencers. A person's religious beliefs do not prevent this expansion of faculties or enlargements of perceptual range. This can frighten the unprepared and be misconstrued as "the devil's work," whereas it is actually more akin to "gifts of the spirit."

5. Reality switches—Hard-driving achievers and materialists can transform into easy-going philosophers. But, by the same token, those previously more relaxed or uncommitted can become energetic "movers and shakers," determined to make a difference in the world. Such switches seem to depend more on what is "needed" to round out the individual's growth than on any uniform result.

6. The soul as self—Most come to recognize themselves as an immortal soul currently resident within material form so lessons can be learned while sojourning in the earthplane. They know they are not their body; it is a "jacket" they wear. The majority develop an interest in reincarnation, and some accept it as valid.

7. Modes of communication—what was once foreign becomes familiar, what was once familiar becomes foreign. Rationality of any kind tends to lose its logic as experiencers begin to think more abstractly and in grandiose terms. New ways of using language, even whole new vocabularies, emerge.

Within some households, relatives are so impressed by what they witness with their loved one that they too change, making the near-death experience a shared event. In other families, though, the response is so negative that alienation, separation, or divorce results. The situation with children, who undergo the same aftereffects as adults, can be doubly challenging, since they lack the ability to speak up for themselves, negotiate, or seek alternatives. Pattern specifies (based on 3,000 adults, 277 children).

Psychological Aftereffects of near-death states:

Most Common (between 80 to 99%)—loss of the fear of death; become more spiritual/less religious; more generous and charitable; handle stress easier; philosophical;

more open and accepting of the new and different; disregard for time and schedules; regard things as new even when they're not (boredom levels decrease); form expansive concepts of love while at the same time challenged to initiate and maintain satisfying relationships; become psychic/intuitive; know things (closer connection to Deity/God, prayerful); deal with bouts of depression; less competitive.

Quite common (50 to 79%)—displays of psychic phenomena; vivid dreams and visions; "inner child" issues exaggerate; convinced of life purpose/mission; rejection of previous limitations/norms; episodes of future knowing common; more detached and objective (dissociation); "merge" easily (absorption); hunger for knowledge; difficulty communicating and with language; can go through deep periods of depression and feelings of alienation from others; synchronicity commonplace; more or less sexual; less desire for possessions and money; service oriented; healing ability; attract animals (good with plants); aware of invisible energy fields/auras; preference for open doors and open windows/shades; drawn to crystals; laugh more; adults younger afterward/children more mature (wiser) afterward.

Physiological Aftereffects

More than the psyche is affected by the near-death phenomenon. A person's body and its patterns undergo change too. Mundane chores can take on surrealistic dimensions. I have found a number of typical physiological aftereffects, including: altered energy levels, hypersensitivity to light and sound, unusual sensitivity to chemicals (especially pharmaceuticals),

reduced stress, lowered blood pressure, and even electrical sensitivity. This last effect makes a person's energy field affect electrical and electronic devices; many can no longer wear watches because they break, or microphones "fight" them. Pattern specifies (based on 3,000 adults, 277 children).

Psychological Aftereffects of near-death states:

Most common (between 80 to 95%)—more sensitive to light, especially sunlight, and to sound (tastes in music change); look younger/act younger/more playful; substantial change in energy levels (can have energy surges); changes in thought processing (switch from sequential/selective thinking to clustered/abstracting, with an acceptance of ambiguity); insatiable curiosity; lower blood pressure; brighter skin and eyes; reversal of brain hemisphere dominance commonplace; heal quicker.

Quite common (50 to 79%)—reversal of body clock, electrical sensitivity, heightened intelligence, metabolic changes (doesn't take that long to process food, bowel movements can increase); assimilate substances into bloodstream quicker (takes less for full effect); loss of pharmaceutical tolerance (many turn to alternative/complimentary healing measures—holistic); heightened response to taste/touch/texture/smell/pressure; more creative and inventive; synesthesia (multiple sensing); increased allergies; preference for more vegetables, less meat with adults/more meat less vegetables with children; latent talents surface; display indications of changes in brain structure and function (changes in nervous and digestive systems, skin sensitivity).

External Verification

Every near-death incident I studied that had elements in it unknowable to the experiencer that could be checked, was checked, and every one of those details was verified. For example, in one of my cases, a four-year-old boy drowned in his parents' backyard swimming pool. Emergency crews were called. After fifteen minutes, the boy revived. Incredibly, but typical of most near-death incidents, there was no brain damage. Immediately, he spoke of meeting his little brother on "the other side," a little brother about two years old, yet able to converse. Since the youngster was an only child, his parents rightfully assumed that he was hallucinating—until the story spilled out.

Mommy made a "mistake" when she was 13 and had an abortion. Chalk-white and shocked, mommy confirmed the boy's revelation. No friends or family knew about the abortion, and the mother had long since forgotten it. But here was her "only" child quoting what her aborted child told him. Sadly, the schism that subsequently developed between the parents over this affair led to a divorce.

Again and again, detailed revelations such as this, absolutely impossible for the individual to know, are seen and later externally verified: descriptions of the accident scene, hospital room or family secrets. Obviously the dynamics of the human spirit defy what can be proven scientifically, or even what can be defined by our reason and sensory faculties.

The near-death phenomenon, both the experience and its aftereffects, reveals more about life than it does death. It reveals an aliveness and a power above and beyond anything we can presently fathom.

Questions

1. In your own words name and describe the four types of NDEs as narrated by Dr. Atwater.
2. Describe the effects an NDE had on the lives of Ernest Hemingway, Jeanne Eppley, Arthur Yensen, and Hung Hsiu-ch'uan. Do you consider these generally to be positive effects? Why or why not?
3. Review the list of "psychological aftereffects" of the NDE. Which of these do you consider most beneficial and why?

---

6 Dr. Kenneth Ring, *Interpretations of the NDE*

Kenneth Ring, Ph.D., was the first to accept Raymond Moody's challenge to scientists back in 1972 to apply scholarly investigation to the near-death experience. Ring, a professor of psychology at the University of Connecticut, and cofounder and past president of the International Association for Near-Death Studies (IANDS), published his findings in 1980 under the title *Life at Death*. He has since published several other books on the near-death experience, each further unfolding his unique interpretation of what the NDE means.

Dr. Ring was the first researcher to perform statistical research on the near-death experiencers themselves. His findings confirmed several of the hypotheses that Raymond Moody had put forth in his 1972 bestseller, *Life After Life*. For example, Dr. Ring discovered that the prior religious background of those who experienced near-death was not statistically related to the occurrence of the NDE itself. In other words, atheists were just as likely to have an NDE as devout believers. He also confirmed that having an NDE leads to profound lifestyle changes in the experiencers, as well as changes to their belief systems. After having an NDE, a person is less likely to take harmful drugs or drink to excess, and tends to be more tolerant and loving of others. Interestingly, while an increase in spirituality is noted among near-death experiencers, churchgoing actually decreases. There tends to be a general distrust of all organized religions, but at the same time, experiencers are often more open to the practice of prayer and meditation, and to the idea of reincarnation.

Dr. Ring mentions three general interpretations of the NDE: the biological, where the NDE is strictly an experience produced by a dying brain; the psychological, where the NDE is a kind of dream, welling up from our unconsciousness and intended to comfort us as we are dying; and the transcendental, a more straightforwardly religious interpretation, where the experience is seen to be exactly what its experiencers say it is—the survival of the soul after death in the presence of God. Dr. Ring holds to the transcendental view, but goes on to say that the reason why the NDE is more common in our own day is because we as a human species are on the verge of a new breakthrough in consciousness. The testimonies of near-death experiencers are finding wide audiences around the world, he asserts, because the human mind is at a point in its evolutionary development where it is able to understand this deeper view of reality. The Light, or God, is sending us messages of hope and transformation, via NDErs, at a particularly violent time in our history. But it is up to us, Dr. Ring cautions, to take these messages seriously, and to begin to change both ourselves and our society in response to them.

Parameters and Interpretations of the NDE

Among the first questions usually asked about this phenomenon is, how often does it actually occur? If one were to take one hundred consecutive cases of patients who clinically died, how many of the survivors would relate NDEs?

Early research (Ring, 1980; Sabom, 1982) suggested that the answer might be about 40%, and this estimate has also been supported by the results of a Gallup poll (Gallup, 1982), which was based on a much larger and more representative sample of people who had been close to death. The body of research on near-death experiences is consistent in showing that most people remember nothing as a result of a near-death crisis, but that a very high percentage of those who claim to have some conscious recall report experiences that conform, at least in part, to the prototypic NDE we've already considered. A scattered number will report idiosyncratic experiences that usually seem to be hallucinatory in character; likewise, a tiny fraction of all cases appear to be negative experiences.

If one extrapolates from Gallup's sample base to the population from which it was designed to be representative (160 million adult Americans), it is possible to estimate how many people living in the United States have already had an NDE—about 8 million. This number has astonished many people (including some researchers) and should be carefully noted since it plays a key role in the thesis to be advanced later in this article.

Another question that is often asked is, does the way one nearly dies affect the experience? Investigators have examined a diverse array of conditions associated with the onset of death: combat situations, attempted rape and murder, electrocutions, near-fatal falls, near drownings, vehicular crashes, freezings, hangings, as well as a great range of strictly medical and surgical conditions. Overall, the pattern seems quite clear-cut: by whatever means a person comes close to death, once the NDE begins to unfold, it is essentially invariant and has the form described earlier. In addition, research on suicide-related NDEs (Greyson, 1981; Ring & Franklin, 1981–1982) has shown that these experiences likewise tend to conform to the prototypic pattern. In short, so far as is now known, situations covering a wide gamut of near-death conditions appear to have a negligible effect on the experience itself.

If situational variables do not significantly influence the experience, what about personal characteristics? Are certain people more likely to have such an experience because of social background, personality, prior beliefs, or even prior knowledge of near-death experiences? Once again, the research to date is consistent in finding that individual and social factors appear to play a minimal role. Demographic variables such as gender, race, social class, or education, for example, have been shown not to be connected with NDE incidence and form. Similarly, it is evident that there is no particular kind of person—defined by psychological attributes—who is especially likely to have a near-death experience. It might be thought that people who have a preexisting or strong religious orientation or who already believe in some form of postmortem existence would be more prone than others. But this is not so. Atheists and agnostics are no less likely to recount prototypic near-death experiences

than religious people, though their interpretation of the experience is apt to be different. Finally, prior knowledge does not seem to increase the probability of having one.

Thus, despite persistent inquiry and recently renewed interest into the question, we are obliged to conclude that the near-death experience seems to "select" its recipients in a random manner. At any rate, if there is any type of person who is an especially good candidate, we have not yet succeeded in identifying the characteristics.

When we come to the question—and it is an all-important one—of *universality,* we must admit that this is an area of research that is still lamentably underdeveloped. Nevertheless, we do at least have a fair amount of data from various cultures that afford us some tentative answers concerning the extent to which the NDE is a culture-free phenomenon.

We already have enough information to assert confidently that in England and in continental Europe near-death experiences take the same form as in the United States (Giovetti, 1982; Grey, 1985; Hampe, 1979). This is hardly surprising since these countries share a Judaeo-Christian heritage. In the IANDS archives and in a few scattered articles (Counts, 1983; Green, 1984; Pasricha & Stevenson), there are fragmentary data from a diverse number of cultures whose traditional beliefs are quite different from those of the west. Included here are cases from India, Japan, South America, Melanesia, and Micronesia, among others. In general, these cases show some obvious parallels to the classic pattern, but often involve elements that deviate in specific ways, especially in the deeper stages where more archetypal imagery comes into play. At this point, then, the prudent conclusion must be that, in western cultures, our data are simply too fragmentary to permit any firm judgment concerning the universality of the prototypic NDE model.

Nevertheless, from the body of cross-cultural data that we do have, it seems plausible to infer that despite some degree of cultural variation, there may be certain universal constants such as the out-of-body experience, the passage through a realm of darkness toward a brilliantly illuminated area, and the encounter with "celestial" beings. Only further research, however, can substantiate this hypothesis as well as settle the question of the universality of the prototypic near-death experience as a thanatological phenomenon.

Finally, we must address the issue of the general interpretation of the NDE. As many considerations of this formidable matter have already established (Grey, 1985; Greyson & Flynn, 1984; Grosso, 1981; Moody, 1975; Ring, 1980; Sabom, 1982), there exist a plethora of theories and a minimum of consensus about them. The interested reader is advised to consult the literature in near-death studies for the specifics of the theory, over which debate continues to be heated. These theories tend to fall into three broad classes: biological, psychological, and transcendental, though many interpretations do not confine themselves to a single perspective. The biological theories tend to be reductionistic and anti-survival in tone whereas those with transcendental emphases tend to be empirically untestable but compatible with a survivalistic interpretation. Naturally the psychological theories are intermediate in most respects.

We must emphasize that a decade of research on the near-death experience has utterly failed to produce any kind of generally accepted interpretation, even among those who have spent years carefully examining it. Moreover, I have recently tried to show (Ring, 1984) that the surrounding interpretative issues are even more complex than many theorists have apparently appreciated. At the present time, then, the question of how such an experience can be explained—or, indeed, whether it even can be—remains shrouded in a cloud of obscurity and contentiousness. The irony is that this entire question may well prove to be entirely irrelevant to the issue of its importance to humanity at large.

The larger significance of the near-death experience turns not so much on either the phenomenology or the parameters of the experience but on its *transformative* effects. For it is precisely these effects that afford us a means of merging it with certain broad evolutionary currents that seem to be propelling humanity toward the next stage of its collective development. To understand the basis of this linkage, we must now explore the ways in which a near-death experience tends to change the lives, conduct, and character of those who survive it.

Transformative Effects of NDEs

The most recent work in near-death studies (Bauer, 1985; Flynn, 1986; Grey, 1985; Ring, 1984) has been increasingly focused on the aftereffects of the NDE, and it is concordant in revealing a very provocative set of findings. First, it appears that just as the near-death experience itself seems to adhere to a common pattern of transcendental elements, so also there seems to be a consistent pattern of transformative aftereffects. Second, this pattern of changes tends to be so highly positive and specific in its effects that it is possible to interpret it as indicative of *a generalized awakening of higher human potential.* To see how this could be so, and to lay the group work for its possible evolutionary significance, let us now review the findings of my own study of aftereffects, described in my book *Heading Toward Omega* (Ring, 1984).

This investigation, whose findings rest on the statistical analysis of specially designed questionnaires as well as qualitative data from personal interviews, examined three broad categories of aftereffects: (1) changes in self-concept and personal values; (2) changes in religious or spiritual orientation; and (3) changes in psychic awareness. Wherever possible, the self-reports of respondents were compared to assessments provided by individuals such as close friends or family members who had known the experiencer well both before and after his or her near-death experience. For most statistical analyses, data from appropriate control groups were also available for comparative purposes. What, then, is the psychological portrait that can be drawn from this study?

First, in the realm of personal values, people emerge from this experience with a heightened *appreciation of life,* which often takes the form not only of a greater responsiveness to its natural beauty but also of a pronounced tendency to be focused intently on the present moment. Concern over past grievances and worries about future problems tend to diminish. As a result, these people are able to be more

fully present to life now, in the moment, so that an enhanced attentiveness to their environment and a freshness of perception follow naturally. They also possess a greater appreciation of themselves in the sense that they have *greater feelings of self-worth* generally. In most cases, it is not that they show signs of ego inflation, but rather that they are able to come to a kind of acceptance of themselves as they are, which they will sometimes attribute to the tremendous sense of affirmation they received "from the Light."

Perhaps one of the most evident changes that follows a near-death experience is an *increased concern for the welfare of others.* This is a very broad and important domain with many different aspects to it. Here I will only be able to briefly summarize its principal modes of expression—increased tolerant compassion for others, and especially an increased ability to express love. Indeed, after a near-death experience, people tend to emphasize the importance of sharing love as the primary value in life. In addition, they seem to feel a stronger desire to help others and claim to have more insight into human problems and more understanding of other human beings. Finally, they seem to demonstrate an unconditional acceptance of others, possibly because they have been able to accept themselves in this way. In a sense, one might characterize all these changes as exemplifying a *greater appreciation of others* and, as such, it may represent still another facet of what appears to be a general appreciation factor that the near-death experience itself serves to intensify.

As there is an overall increase in the aforementioned values, in other values there is a clear and consistent decline. For example, the importance placed on material things, on success for its own sake, and on the need to make a good impression on others, all diminish after individuals undergo a near-death experience. In general, people-oriented values rise while concern over material success plummets.

Finally, one more change in the realm of personal values should be noted. These people tend to seek a deeper understanding of life, especially its spiritual or religious aspects. They tend to become involved in a search for increased self-understanding as well, and appear more inclined to join organizations or engage in reading or other activities that will be conducive to achieving these ends.

Incidentally, with respect to these value changes—as well as to other categories of aftereffects—it appears that these self-reports may well reflect changes in behavior. Though we clearly need more corroborative evidence than is available in *Heading Toward Omega,* statements by close friends and family members tend to provide support for the behavioral changes these people describe in themselves.

Moving to the area of religious and spiritual changes, it will come as no surprise to learn that there are far-reaching aftereffects here, too. In general, however, such changes tend to follow a particular form to which the term *universalistic* might most appropriately be applied. In characterizing this universalistic orientation, it will be helpful to distinguish a number of different components that together make up the model spiritual world-view of those who have experienced a near-death crisis.

First, there is a tendency to describe themselves as more spiritual, not necessarily more religious. By this they appear to signify that they have experienced a deep inward change in their spiritual awareness, but not one that made them more outwardly religious in their behavior. They claim to feel, for example, much closer to God than they had before, but the formal, more external aspects of religious worship often appear to have weakened in importance. They are also more likely to express an unconditional belief in "life after death" for everyone and to endorse the conviction that not only will there be some form of post-mortem existence, but that "the Light" will be there for everyone at death, regardless of one's beliefs (or lack of them) about what happens at death.

Interestingly—and this is a finding also suggested by my earlier research in *Life at Death* (Ring, 1980) as well as Gallup's (1982) survey—a greater openness to the idea of reincarnation is often expressed. It is not that they find themselves ready to subscribe to a formal belief in reincarnation, but rather that it is a doctrine that makes more sense to them than it did prior to their near-death experience. My impression is that this increased receptivity to reincarnational ideas is part of a more general friendliness to and acquaintance with Eastern religions and with some of the more esoteric and mystical variants of Christianity and Judaism.

Finally, the near-death experience draws people to a belief in the idea known to students of comparative religion as "the transcendent unity of religions," the notion that underlying all the world's greatest religious traditions there is a single and shared transcendent vision of the Divine. In espousing this view, people will sometimes aver or imply that they came to this realization directly through their own near-death experiences. Similarly, they are more inclined than others to admit to a desire for a form of universal spirituality that by embracing everyone would exclude no one. This is not a naive hope or wish that the multitudinous and incredibly diverse religious traditions throughout the world might somehow melt into a single "universal religion," but only that individuals of different and seemingly divisive religious faiths might one day truly realize their unity with one another.

The last domain of aftereffects explored in *Heading Toward Omega* dealt with changes in psychic awareness. Not only my findings but those of others (Greyson, 1983; Kohr, 1983) tend to support the hypothesis that the near-death experience serves to trigger an increase in psychic sensitivity and development—that following their experience they become aware of many more psychic phenomena than had previously been the case. For example, they claim to have had more telepathic and clairvoyant experiences, more precognitive experiences (especially in dreams), greater awareness of synchronicities, more out-of-body experiences, and a generally increased susceptibility to what parapsychologists call "psi-conducive states of consciousness" (that is, psychological states which seem to facilitate the occurrence of psychic phenomena). Although the data on apparent increases in psychic awareness lend themselves to various interpretations, it does seem clear that a heightened sensitivity to psychic phenomena follows a near-death experience (which, of course,

may well include subjectively convincing paranormal features in its own right).

Having now reviewed the findings on some of the major aftereffects of near-death experiences, we must seek a coherent framework to place them in so that their implicit patterning may be brought into relief. I believe it is possible and plausible to regard the near-death experience as playing a critical *catalytic* role in personal development. Specifically, it seems to serve as a catalyst to promote the *spiritual awakening and growth* of the individual because of its power to thrust one into a transcendental state of consciousness whose impact is to trigger a release of a universal "inner programming" of higher human potentials. There may be in each of us a latent spiritual core that is set to manifest in a particular form if only it can be activated by a powerful enough stimulus. In the near-death experience it appears that the stimulus is the Light, and the similarity and consistency of the spiritual changes following a near-death experience point to what may be a common "spiritual DNA" of the human species. In these people, the pattern of changes in the consciousness and conduct bears a marked similarity to what Bucke (1969) long ago claimed for his examples of "cosmic consciousness" and to which the modern psychiatrist, Stanley Dean (1975), has more recently called to our attention. A near-death experience certainly tends to stimulate a *radical spiritual transformation* in the life of the individual, which affects his self-concept, his relations to others, his view of the world and his world-view, as well as his mode of psychological and psychic functioning. But how does any of this—profound as these changes may be—speak to the weighty issues of human evolution and planetary transformation?

Implications of the Near-Death Experience for Human Evolution and Planetary Transformation

I believe only a very partial understanding of the significance of the near-death experience can be attained from a strictly psychological perspective, i.e., one that concentrates on the *individual's* experience and its effects upon him. A more complete appreciation is available, however, if we shift the level of analysis from the individual plane to the sociological, where the meaning of the transformative pattern will be more apparent. We must look at the near-death experience from this broader perspective in order to discern the possible deeper significance for humanity at large.

Recall, first of all, that it has already been projected that perhaps as many as *8 million* adult Americans have experienced this phenomenon—and we know that American children also report such experiences (Bush, 1983; Gabbard & Twemlow, 1984; Morse, 1983; Morse, Connor, & Tyler, 1985). Although we do not have even a crude estimate of how many people in the whole world may have had this experience, it certainly does not seem unreasonable to assume that additional millions outside the United States must also have had them. But the point is not simply that many millions will know this experience for themselves but also *how the NDE will transform them afterward*. We have already examined how people's lives and consciousness are affected and what values come to

guide their behavior. To begin to appreciate the possible planetary impact of these changes, we must imagine these same effects occurring in millions of lives throughout the world, regardless of race, religion, nationality, or culture.

From various studies of transcendental experiences (Bucke, 1969; Dean, 1975; Hardy, 1979; Hardy, 1982; Grof, 1985; James, 1958), we know that the radical spiritual transformation which often follows a near-death experience is by no means unique to that experience alone. Rather, as Grof (1985) has recently implied, transcendental experiences, however they may come about, tend to induce similar patterns of spiritual change in individuals who undergo them. In short, the near-death experience is only *one* means to catalyze a spiritual transformation, but many others, which seem to reflect the same underlying spiritual archetype, have unquestionably been triggered by something of other than a near-death crisis.

Is there any way to estimate the extent of such transcendental experiences in general? Probably not with any real hope for acceptable accuracy, but we do have at least a basis for a rough sort of guess for English-speaking countries. In national surveys in the United States, England, and Canada, for example, up to *one third* of those polled admit that they have had some kind of powerful spiritual experience (Hay, 1982). Of course, from these data only, it is impossible to claim that such experiences necessarily induce the kind of transformative pattern I have previously delineated. Nevertheless, it does seem warranted to infer that many more people must undergo these transformations by means other than a near-death experience.

Thus, if these other transformations are added to the presumed millions of near-death experiences, we immediately see that we are dealing with a far more pervasive phenomenon than one might have first assumed.

A third consideration in this argument pertains not simply to the number of people in the world who may have experienced a major transformative awakening, however it may have been occasioned, but to the rate of increase in such transformations. In the case of near-death experiences, of course, it is mainly modern resuscitation technology that is responsible for creating such a large pool of survivors. Before the advent of cardiopulmonary resuscitation, for example, most would have died; now many not only are saved but go on to live drastically changed lives because of their close encounter with death. With resuscitation technology likely to improve and to spread in use around the globe, it appears inevitable that many more millions will undergo and survive near-death experiences and thus be transformed according to this archetypal pattern.

Similarly, although there are not, as I have indicated, any systematic studies of the incidence of transcendental experiences in general, various students of higher consciousness (Ferguson, 1980; Grof, 1985; Russell, 1983; White, 1981) have speculated that such experiences are widespread, at least in the western world, and that their number may be growing exponentially.

Such intriguing possibilities fit neatly with the next observation needed to complete the foundation for my argument based on recent theories concerning the spread of behavioral properties throughout a population. I am thinking here particularly of the theory of the young English biologist, Rupert Sheldrake, whose book, *A New Science of Life* (1981), has fanned widespread interest and controversy in scientific circles ever since its publication. In his book, Sheldrake propounds a hypothesis of what he calls "formative causation," which states that the characteristic forms and behavior of physical, chemical, and biological systems are determined by invisible organizing fields—*morphogenetic fields,* in Sheldrake's phrase. Although I cannot review here the author's evidence in support of his hypothesis, Sheldrake's basic idea is that once such fields do become established through some initial behavior, that behavior is then facilitated in others through a process called *morphic resonance.* Thus, for example, once an *evolutionary variant* occurs in a species, it is likely to spread throughout the entire species.

Sheldrake's ideas are similar to (but certainly not identical with) the theme of the popular "hundredth monkey effect," whose empirical authenticity now appears entirely without foundation, but whose appeal as a framework for conceiving social contagion phenomena is almost irresistible. This seemingly apocryphal tale describes how a new behavior, potato washing by monkeys, spread to all monkeys on a certain Japanese island as well as to monkeys on adjacent islands when an imaginary "hundredth monkey" indulged in the new ritual. In principle, once the hundredth monkey engaged in this new behavior, that was all that was needed to create a strong enough field for morphic resonance to occur, thus turning innovation into custom. In this case, the hundredth monkey presumably established the critical mass necessary to transform the eating habits of the entire colony. What is the relevance of all this to the near-death experience and to the issues of the evolution of consciousness and planetary transformation? There is a possible connection stemming from the following observation, which has previously been made by a number of others besides myself. We do not know the limits of Sheldrake's hypothesis. If it is correct—and it is at present the subject of much excited interest and experimental work—it is distinctly possible that it may also apply to states of consciousness as well. This extrapolation has, in fact, been made by science writer Peter Russell (1983) whose commentary will make explicit the connection between our concerns here and Sheldrake's work. According to Russell:

> Applying Sheldrake's theory to the development of higher states of consciousness, we might predict that the more individuals begin to raise their own levels of consciousness, the stronger the morphogenetic field for higher states would become, and the easier it would be for others to move in that direction. Society would gather momentum toward enlightenment. Since the rate of growth would not be dependent on the achievements of those who had gone before, we would enter a phase of super-exponential growth. Ultimately, this could lead to a chain reaction, in which everyone suddenly started making the transition to a higher level of consciousness. (Russell, 1983, p. 129)

Although Russell's own formulation may seem somewhat hyperbolic and simplistic, it does have the virtue of suggesting both a hopeful and larger vision of the inherent potential of the near-death experience and of other similar transcendental experiences. If we now consider the high base rate of all transcendental experiences generally throughout the world, the likelihood of their increasing incidence, and the possible mechanism by which the effects of such states may spread across a population, we may finally discern the possible global significance of the near-death experience.

May it be that this high rate of transcendental experience *collectively represents an evolutionary thrust toward higher consciousness for humanity at large?* Could it be that the near-death experience is itself an *evolutionary mechanism* that has the effect of jump-stepping individuals into the next stage of human development by unlocking previously dormant spiritual potentials? Indeed, are we seeing in these people, as they mutate from their former personalities into more loving and compassionate individuals, the prototype of a new, more spiritually advanced strain of the human species striving to come into being? Do these people represent the "early maturers" of a new breed of humanity emerging in our time—an evolutionary bridge to the next shore in our progression as a species, a "missing link" in our midst?

These are heady and provocative questions, but they are not entirely speculative ones. Many thinkers before me have dreamed and written of the coming to earth of a higher humanity and have attempted to describe the attributes of such people. Although these visions of a higher humanity are subjective, the transformations I have outlined in this article have happened to real people, and they are among us now. And we can at least ask: How well do these visions of a new humanity match the characteristics of these people?

For one representative portrait of this new humanity, let me draw on the views of the well-known author, John White (1981), who has helped to popularize the term *Homo noeticus* in this connection. In reading his description, bear in mind that it was not intended as a characterization of someone who had experienced a near-death crisis, and that it is similar in many ways to accounts provided by other evolutionary thinkers who have addressed the same issue:

> Homo noeticus is the name I give to the emerging form of humanity. "Noetics" is a term meaning the study of consciousness, and that activity is a primary characteristic of members of the new breed. Because of their deepened awareness and self-understanding, they do not allow the traditionally imposed forms, controls, and institutions of society to be barriers to their full devel-opment. Their changed psychology is based on expression of feeling, not sup-pression. Their motivation is cooperative and loving, not competitive and aggressive. Their logic is multi-level/integrated/simultaneous, not linear/sequential/either-or. Their sense of identity is embracing-collective, not isolated individual. Their psychic abilities are used for benevolent and ethical purposes, not harmful and immoral ones. The conventional ways of society don't satisfy them. The search for new ways of living and new institutions concerns them. They seek a culture founded in higher consciousness, a culture whose institutions are based

> on love and wisdom, a culture that fulfills the perennial philosophy. (White, 1981, p. 14)

Although this is an idealized description, the transformative process that the near-death experience tends to set into motion certainly appears to lead to the development of individuals who approximate the ideal type White posits as the prototype of the new humanity.

Even if my own ideas about the seeding of a new humanity through the spread of near-death experiences and other transcendental experiences are found to have some plausibility, their implications for planetary transformation admittedly allow for a variety of short-term scenarios. I am not one who foresees the emergence of a new, cooperative planetary culture as a necessary consequence of the kind of evolutionary shift in consciousness I detect. Rather, I see that shift as a potential of the human species that is beginning to manifest, but whether it takes hold and transforms the earth depends on many factors; not least is the extent to which many of us consciously align with these trends and seek to awaken. Clearly, nothing in the collective human potential emerging from the spawning grounds of transcendental experiences precludes the possibility of our planet's self-destructing. Nothing is assured or inevitable. No one living in the last years of the twentieth century—unarguably the most horrific in history—could deny for a moment that our prospects for surviving intact into the next millennium are shrouded in black uncertainty.

At the same time, human beings live in hope as well as fear and this recent curious phenomenon—the near-death experience—seems to be holding out a powerful message of hope to humanity that even, and perhaps especially, in its darkest moments, the Light comes to show us the way onward. It is up to each of us whether we shall have the courage and the wisdom to follow where it beckons.

Questions

1. List the various transformative effects of NDEs as Ring explains them, and analyze, using your own beliefs and values, whether you think these effects are beneficial or not.

2. What are the foundations of Dr. Ring's argument that the NDE is part of a larger, evolutionary development in human consciousness?

3. What, according to Dr. Ring, is *homo noeticus,* and what is its relationship to the NDE?

Small Group Exercises

1. In your small group, role-play an NDE as described above. Assign the roles of doctor, nurse, patient, departed loved ones, and a being of light. Play out all the elements of the NDE, including a life review, and the decision to return back to the suffering body. Consider filming the role-play to show to the rest of the class. Afterwards, discuss how it felt to play each part.

2. Find out whether anyone in your group has had an NDE, or knows someone who has had one. Discuss this experience in the group.

3. Discuss the religious problems associated with NDEs, such as:
   a. If they are genuine spiritual experiences, then why do people of different religions see different sorts of "heavens"?
   b. If they are merely functions of a dying brain, then is there any life after death?
   c. If only believers go to heaven, why do atheists have more NDEs than theists?
   d. If NDEs lead some people to believe that all religions are equal, that God accepts all into heaven, and that reincarnation is likely, are they (as some conservative Christians claim) an invention of the devil?

Practical Learning Component

1. Visit a local chapter of the International Association of Near-Death Studies (IANDS). This organization sponsors support groups around the world. Attend one of these groups and ask questions of the members about their experiences and how their beliefs and attitudes have changed since their NDE.

2. Find someone in your family or local community who has had an NDE. Ask this person to explain the experience, and what it has meant to them since then.

3. Interview a specialist in brain research (for example, a neurosurgeon or behavioral psychologist) about the possibility that the NDE is merely the function of a dying brain. Find out whether they believe all the components of a full NDE can be explained exclusively in terms of brain structures and chemistry.

Chapter 8

Preparing for Death

Cowards die many times before their deaths,
The valiant never taste of death but once.
—WILLIAM SHAKESPEARE

It seems fitting to conclude this introduction to the study of death with a section on how to prepare oneself, or how to help a loved one prepare, for dying and death. Considerations under this topic range from the practical (Do I have a living will? What sort of funeral arrangements are needed? How will my loved one's pain be managed?) to the spiritual (How can my dying loved one's spiritual needs best be met? What possible meaning does my dying have? Have I made my peace with God?) In this section our contributors will be asking and answering these and other related questions.

Thanatologist Charles Corr identifies four primary life areas that come into play when someone is dealing with a terminal illness.[47] These are:

- *Physical/Material:* identifying bodily needs and minimizing physical discomfort and distress in ways consistent with the values of the patient and the patient's family; working with the patient's financial and vocational issues
- *Psychological:* minimizing emotional distress (fear, anxiety, depression, etc.) and maximizing feelings of security, esteem, and empowerment
- *Social:* sustaining and enhancing significant personal relationships; putting closure on work relationships and friendships, and making sure the needs of those left behind will be taken care of
- *Spiritual:* identifying and developing or affirming those sources of spiritual strength and meaning which are important to the dying person

At the physical level, there is a long list of concerns that can preoccupy both the dying and the dying's friends and family members as the time of death approaches. In the case of sudden death, it is not possible to deal with these concerns directly. Death from an accident or an unexpected heart attack can deeply afflict those left behind who are sometimes left without a will for the estate, without life insurance, without a source of income, even—in the case of small children—without parental care. But when someone is facing the prospect of a prolonged terminal illness, these concerns can be addressed in a timely fashion.

Concerns associated with one's physical and material interests may change as the patient progresses through the dying process. Hospice often works with people around these issues and in many cases will take the initiative in seeing that they are properly handled. Shortly after hospice contracts with the patient to help orchestrate the patient's dying process, it will likely organize a strategy session with the patient, the patient's caregivers, and the patient's close family and friends. At this meeting a hospice facilitator, usually a social worker, will help all concerned brainstorm through a series of questions related to the tasks that lie ahead in the dying process. These questions might include the following:

- Is there a living will (a binding statement that explains the wishes of the dying regarding medical care should they not be able to speak for themselves)? Has a copy of this will been filed with the patient's physicians and hospital?
- Who will act as a proxy (or a durable power of attorney) regarding healthcare decisions should the dying not be able to speak for himself or herself? Is this person in agreement with the stipulations in the living will?
- Is there a will for the estate? Are all life insurance policies up-to-date and accessible? Are there any outstanding debts that should be addressed?
- Would the patient prefer to die at home, in a hospital, or in an outpatient clinic of some kind (institutional hospice, nursing home, etc.)?
- How does the patient wish his or her pain to be managed? Are there any ethical or religious objections to the use of narcotics as a pain management strategy? What special comfort needs are there?
- What are the wishes of the patient regarding the disposal of his or her body (cremation or burial)? Are there any special wishes for the funeral and/or burial ceremonies?

LIVING WILLS

While the living will was originally proposed in 1967, it had no legally binding force until 1990, the year the U.S. Congress passed the Patient Self-Determination Act (PSDA). The PSDA requires providers of Medicare and Medicaid services to

- inform their patients that they have the right to participate in and direct their own healthcare decisions;
- the right to accept or refuse medical or surgical treatment;
- the right to prepare an advance directive;
- the right to information on the provider's policies that govern the utilization of these rights.

The act also prohibits institutions from discriminating against a patient who does not have an advance directive. The PSDA further requires institutions to document patient information and provide ongoing community education on advance directives.[48]

The living will, sometimes called a "natural death directive," is one of a pair of documents—the other is the "durable power of attorney for health care"—which collectively are known as "advance directives." The living will indicates, in a legally binding way, the wishes of the dying patient regarding health care, while the durable power of attorney is a formal agreement on who will be act as the decision-maker for all healthcare matters should the patient be unable to speak on his or her own behalf. These documents are called "advance directives" because they determine what the patient's wishes regarding health care *in advance* of needing that care, and they act as *directives* to the physicians who administrate that care. In more concrete terms, advance directives formalize the right that all competent adults have regarding whether or not they would like to decline life support when it is clear that death is imminent or when a coma becomes permanent.

The living will comes in a variety of forms, some very simple and straightforward, others very detailed and complex. The format of a living will varies from state to state as each jurisdiction draws up its own living will contract in consultation with the local governing body of the American Medical Association. But all living wills, which are only in effect when their owners are terminal, grant the right to stipulate to medical personnel exactly what is to be done, or not done, when one is terminally ill and in a life-threatening situation. Living wills provide patients some degree of autonomy over what will be done to their bodies as they are dying. Often a terminally ill patient with a living will has a small sign placed near his or her bed with "DNR" ("do not resuscitate") written in bold letters. But a living will can also specify, among other things, the patient's wishes regarding pain management, palliative surgical procedures, nutrition, and hydration.

There are some problems associated with living wills as they are implemented in today's fast-paced, highly technical medical environments. Even though a patient may have a living will on file at the hospital, for example, it is not always the case that an attending physician is made aware of this fact. The living will may have been placed on file years before it was needed, and subsequently forgotten. Or even when a physician is aware of a living will—that is, of the wish of the patient not to receive resuscitation efforts should he or she go into cardiac arrest—it remains up to that physician to make the decision whether the patient is in a life-threatening condition. Sometimes the course of a patient's illness is such that the distinction between terminal and nonterminal is not at all clear, in which case doctors are obligated to ignore the living will and apply resuscitation.

There may also be issues of self-esteem that come into play in determining whether a doctor follows the wishes of the patient as outlined in a living will. Doctors are routinely evaluated on how often, and how soon, patients under their care die. Decisions of promotion and tenure are sometimes key on these statistics. Therefore it may be in the doctor's own best interests to keep the patient alive as long as possible. Additionally the doctor may have religious or ethical values that conflict with the wishes in a living will. Although doctors are required to remove themselves from a case in which there is conflict of interest, they may not always do so.

MANAGING PAIN

The most common complaint of people suffering from terminal illness is that of the pain their illness causes in their body. Pain during terminal illness or injury can come from a variety of sources: the injury itself (for example, a severe burn), cancerous tumors, high fever, gastrointestinal complications, a diminished oxygen supply, etc. Pain can also stem from psychosomatic sources that have no real physical component. It is therefore imperative that pain be addressed in any protocol for terminally ill patients.

The effective management of pain is the hallmark of all hospice care,[49] and a primary aim of all palliative or nontherapeutic treatment. There are two general types of pain: *acute pain,* which is the kind of pain associated with injury and which tends to be intermittent and temporary; and *chronic pain,* which is the kind of pain associated with illness and which tends to be persistent and long-lasting. While acute pain can be accompanied by fear and anxiety, the physical and emotional consequences of chronic pain are often much more severe. With chronic pain can come:[50]

- sleep disturbances
- loss of appetite
- constipation and other gastrointestinal disturbances
- the inability to work
- weight loss
- excessive irritability
- relational problems
- diminished sexual interest
- depression

While acute pain is often remedied by simply removing or minimizing the source—through surgery, for example, or through nerve-blocking medication—chronic pain is not as easily dealt with. Ordinarily a "stepwise approach" is used to treat chronic pain. This approach consists of four sequential steps:

- assessment of the pain
- determination of the treatment
- patient feedback and adjustment of the treatment
- control of side effects

The first step is the accurate assessment of the pain itself. Questions are asked, such as, how intense is the pain? Where in the body does the pain occur? How often does the pain occur and how long are the intervals of pain? Such an assessment should also include a psychological profile of the patient to determine any possible psychosomatic influence (where the mind produces pain not associated with the illness or injury) upon the experience of pain.

The second step is the determination of what sort of pain treatment is best prescribed for the patient. There are four recognized levels of pain, each of which requires a unique pain treatment process:[51]

- *mild pain,* which is treated with non-opioid analgesics (like acetaminophen)
- *moderate pain,* which is treated with weak opioids (like codeine)
- *severe pain,* which is treated with potent opioids (like morphine)
- and *intractable pain,* which requires more invasive therapy (like total sedation)

This second step includes selecting the drug or combination of drugs that will be used to combat the pain, and how these drugs will be administered. Pain medication can be administered through intermittent injections or oral medications (non-opioid and weak opioid analgesics), continuously through an intravenous or intraspinal drip (weak opioids), or through a patient-controlled device on an as-needed basis (potent opioids). Possible drug allergies and side effects need to be taken into consideration in this stage of the process. Unless the pain is severe, a non-opioid analgesic will likely be suggested at first.

Death and Dying Fact

Types of Pain Medication

Over-the-counter pain medicine
- *acetaminophen*
- *nonsteroidal anti-inflammatory drugs, or NSAIDs. Aspirin, ibuprofen, and naproxen are all NSAIDs*

(Continued)

(*Continued*)

Prescription pain medicine

- *anticonvulsants, which can relieve chronic nerve pain. Examples include pheny-toin and carbamazepine*
- *antidepressants, which may relieve certain kinds of chronic pain. Common anti-depressants include amitriptyline, trazodone, and imipramine*
- *capsaicin, which can relieve skin pain caused by shingles, nerve problems, and other causes*
- *corticosteroids, which can relieve pain from inflammation*
- *narcotics, which are the most effective for moderate to severe pain. Common narcotics include morphine, codeine, meperidine, and oxycodone*
- *sumatriptan and naratriptan, which can relieve the pain of a migraine headache*
- *tramadol, which is used mainly for chronic pain*

The third step is gathering feedback from the patient as to what level of pain he or she is experiencing, and in response to that, adjusting the prescribed pain protocol if needed. If the milder, non-opioid analgesics are not effective in reducing pain to a tolerable level, then an opioid drug would be introduced into the protocol at this point. Codeine is the most commonly prescribed weak opioid, while morphine is the most commonly prescribed strong opioid. Despite its reputation as a dangerous street drug, heroine is also routinely used to relieve pain in the terminally ill. Morphine is usually administered to the patient through an intravenous device that patients can control themselves. These devices shunt morphine into the blood in regular doses at regular intervals, but can also deliver a "bolus" of morphine—an additional, between intervals dosage—if the patient is feeling extraordinary pain. Both the intervals of medication and the extra bolus can be controlled by the patient.

The fourth and final step in pain management is the control of side effects that result from the pain medication itself. While there is no longer much worry about terminal patients becoming addicted to an opioid like codeine or morphine, there are physical discomforts that come with the use of all the opioid analgesics, both strong and weak. In combination with the pain and complications associated with the terminal disease or injury, these side effects can be quite devastating. Such side effects can include:

- constipation
- drowsiness, dizziness, and sedation
- nausea and vomiting
- skin irritations
- mild to moderate respiratory depression
- severe respiratory depression
- dysphoria, confusion, hallucinations
- urinary retention

Controlling side effects like these can be as simple as making changes to the diet or applying an oxygen tube to the nostrils. But more severe side effects may need to be medicated.

The technology of pain management is advancing as fast as the technology of other
areas of medicine. As studies of the human brain progress, scientists are learning more
and more about how the brain processes pain. We now know that pain does not occur
in the painful limb or internal organ. It occurs in the brain as certain centers in our
cerebral cortex "channel" the neural transmissions from injured parts of the body
toward complex brain mechanisms. These mechanisms then turn the neural transmissions into what we feel as a searing sensation of pain. From these studies have come the
development of "analgesic cocktails," mixtures of drug compounds that when working
together more effectively moderate these pain centers in the brain.

Today medical personnel not only work to manage physical pain, they also try to
alleviate other forms of pain as well. Hospice speaks of treating a patient's "whole" or
"total" pain, which includes not only physical sensations of discomfort but also psychological, social, and spiritual discomfort. Integral to any holistically minded pain-
management protocol is the use of such medications as antidepressants, anxiety
blockers, muscle relaxants, and sleeping aids. In some hospitals there is also experi-
mentation with such alternative therapies as hypnosis, acupuncture, guided imagery,
aromatherapy, yoga, and meditation.

THE SPIRITUALITY OF DYING

What role do spiritual or religious beliefs play in your perception of death? If you were
given a terminal diagnosis, what would you want to accomplish before your passing?
Would there be friends to whom you would want to say goodbye; a fractured relationship you would like to heal? What do you see as your mark on this earth and would
you feel that you had done all you could to leave that mark? What do you anticipate
will happen to you, if anything, at the death of your body?

With these questions we move beyond the realm of physical concerns to embrace the
psychological, social, and spiritual aspects of the dying process. Some see such aspects
from a faith-based perspective. They believe that death is the end of the physical, but not
the spiritual, life. Some feel that how we spend our time on earth will determine where
we spend eternity—heaven or hell—while others believe that we will be sent back to
earth for another chance to learn life's lessons. Others view the dying process from the
perspective of science rather than faith. For them death is primarily a biological process
that signals the complete end of existence. Death is part of the natural cycle of birth, life,
death, and decay, and as a part of nature we have no choice but to submit ourselves to
this process. Numerous questions emerge from this wide divergence in perspective. How
does one's metaphysical perspective on death, one's "spirituality," affect the way one
approaches death? How does that perspective support coping with the loss that death

brings? What special spiritual needs are there in someone who has no particular religious perspective on death? Is it necessary to believe in an afterlife of some kind in order to come to terms with the end of this life?

These questions demonstrate just how important a role spirituality plays in helping patients cope with terminal illness. For years, the medical and scientific community held that spirituality and medicine had little or no bearing upon each other. Recently, however, this relationship has been looked at in a new light. A 1990 Gallup poll indicated that religion, as one form of spirituality, plays a central role in the lives of many Americans. The same poll revealed that 95 percent of Americans believe in God or some kind of "higher power," 82 percent believe in a heavenly afterlife, 56 percent pray on a daily basis, and 40 percent attend worship services on a weekly basis.[52] Other studies and surveys have confirmed this finding as well. When asked whether people believed in the power of personal prayer to heal, 82 percent of those surveyed reported yes. 73 percent believed that praying for someone else could help that person, and 78 percent believed that God can intervene as the result of personal prayer (a 2004 survey by the National Center for Health Statistics).

Many patients not only have strong spiritual beliefs, they also want their physicians to talk to them about spiritual issues. In one study, 64 percent of the patients surveyed wanted their doctor to join them in prayer. In another study, 63 percent thought that doctors should talk to their patients about spirituality although only 10 percent reported that this actually happened. The majority of patients surveyed perceived their spirituality as an integral part of who they are, and wanted recognition of their spirituality to be integrated into their medical care.[53]

Sixty-one of the 125 medical schools in the United States now include a "spirituality and medicine" component in their curricula. Physicians and medical schools increasingly are recognizing that that they do not have all the answers and that there is more to medicine than scientific technique. However, spirituality remains not well integrated into traditional forms of medical care.

The definition of spirituality varies widely according to individuals and cultures. In a broad sense, spirituality can be understood as a set of beliefs and practices which lends transcendent meaning to life. While spirituality is most often expressed through a formal religion, it can also be a very private thing, highly individualized and esoteric. Transcendent meaning may have many sources: a divine creator, nature, a benevolent energy or force, human goodness, creative energy, or family and community. Catholic theologian Michael Downey defines spirituality as "an awareness that there are levels of reality not immediately apparent," noting that spirituality is primarily a "quest for personal integration in the face of forces of fragmentation and depersonalization."[54]

Terminal illness is a powerful life event of potential fragmentation and depersonalization. It causes most people who experience it to question who they are, the meaning and purpose of their lives. It can sever an otherwise intimate relationship with the divine. If viewed as being without justification, the suffering associated with dying can leave the victim feeling lost, abandoned, bitter. In his classic memoir, *Man's Search for Meaning,* Viktor Frankl wrote, "Man is not destroyed by suffering; he is destroyed by suffering without meaning."[55] When Frankl wrote about the experiences of concentration camp survivors, he noted the importance of finding meaning in the midst of the suffering. Most of those he befriended in the camps perished. But the few who survived the ordeal were the ones who were able, despite the immense suffering, to attribute some sort of transcendent meaning to their plight. For many patients facing terminal illness, the only way for them to make their way through the long days and nights of uncertainty, pain, loss of autonomy, and aloneness is to view their fate from a spiritual perspective. Spirituality is, for many in such a condition, the means by which one's dying days are not filled with grief and remorse, but are rather a time of renewal, growth, even hope. It is an integral part of the dying process and an important part of the developmental task of transcendence.

In the following readings, you will be introduced to a variety of topics that reference the relationship of spirituality and the dying process. We begin with a practical discussion of the two types of advance directives: living wills and durable powers of attorney. This article includes a frank discussion of the drawbacks to living wills, and what precautions can be taken to minimize their inherent risks. Included in the reading is an actual living will declaration. This document is legally viable, and can be copied by the student and used as his or her own living will.

There follows a detailed discussion of pain management from a leading figure in the field of psychological coping mechanisms. We then turn to an article that outlines three unique spiritual needs of the dying: the need for meaning, to die appropriately, and to find hope. This article leads naturally into a discussion on the various tasks of spiritual integration that befall someone facing terminal illness. Next we hear from a pair of hospice nurses who talk to us about the "final gifts" the dying can impart to us as they move from this world to the next. Finally, it seems fitting that we close our study on death with a final word from the pioneer of death studies, Dr. Elisabeth Kübler-Ross, who shares with us from her autobiography her hard-won pearls of wisdom culled from a lifetime devoted to helping the dying die in peace.

---

1 Elaine Landau, *Advance Directives for Health Care*

Popular author Elaine Landau worked as a newspaper reporter, an editor, and a librarian before becoming a full-time writer. She has written over two hundred nonfiction books on such varied subjects as surrogate mothers, terrorism, ancient civilizations, and AIDS. Ms. Landau holds a B.A. in journalism from New York University, and an M.A. in library sciences. She lives with her family in Miami.

In the following article, taken from her 1993 book, *The Right to Die,* Ms. Landau discusses what are collectively called "advance directives for healthcare." Generally, these directives come in two forms, living wills and durable powers of attorney. The living will refers to a document that a patient may sign before entering the hospital. It records the patient's wishes with respect to specific forms of life-prolonging treatment, should the patient be diagnosed as terminal. The living will is an enforceable contract between the patient and his or her attending physicians, and can prevent the application of such "heroic measures" as cardiac defibrillation and mechanical respiration. The durable power of attorney places the same decisions in the hands of a family member or close friend who is to act on the patient's behalf should he or she go into a coma, or for other reasons be unable to communicate. It is presumed that the appointed proxy will be familiar with the patient's wishes in such situations. Like the living will, the power given to the proxy by a durable power of attorney is enforceable by law. The attending physicians must abide by the proxy's instructions once the patient has been diagnosed as terminal and is unable to speak on his or her own behalf.

At age eighty-five, Estelle Browning of Dunedin, Florida, had seen enough hopelessly ill friends to know that she did not want her life prolonged by machines if she were unable to speak for herself. To make sure that never occurred, Ms. Browning filled out a document known as a living will, clearly spelling out her health care wishes. In precisely listing the medical procedures she didn't want, Mrs. Browning rejected the use of a feeding tube. She wrote, "I do not desire that nutrition and hydration be provided by gastric tube or intravenously." Once the documents were in order, the elderly woman breathed a sigh of relief. She told her friends, "Thank God, I can go in peace when my time comes."

But Estelle Browning wasn't able to do that after all. In 1986, the following year, she suffered a cerebral hemorrhage, resulting in permanent brain damage. Although her doctors saved her life, friends who saw Ms. Browning afterwards realized that she was just a shadow of her former self, exhibiting only fleeting signs of consciousness. The physicians inserted a feeding tube into Ms. Browning's abdomen, and

when her condition stabilized, they transferred her to a nursing home for long-term care.

Although in her living will Estelle Browning asked not to have a feeding tube, the health care facility claimed that her request could not be honored due to a state regulation requiring nursing homes to feed all patients. In addition, Florida law did not recognize a patient's right to refuse food and water.

Mrs. Browning was forced to remain as she was even though she had tried to take precautions against this. The annual cost of her care was over $36,000, and outside of the small percentage paid by Medicare, the money was systematically withdrawn from her personal assets. Estelle Browning did not have a large family to come to her aid. She was a widow, and her only child had been killed on the battleship *Arizona* when Japan attacked Pearl Harbor during World War II. But, fortunately, a second cousin agreed to act as her court-appointed guardian in a legal effort to have Mrs. Browning's feeding tube removed in accordance with her wishes.

However, a court dispute arose over the interpretation of the term "imminent death." Mrs. Browning's living will specified that heroic measures should be stopped once death was imminent—a condition which her guardian felt had been met. Yet a Florida court determined that Estelle Browning's death was not imminent, since she could be sustained indefinitely by the feeding tube. The case was slated to be heard later by Florida's Supreme Court, but meanwhile Estelle Browning was left in a medical and legal no man's land.

State laws on living wills differ significantly, and in some areas, such as Florida, safeguards originally designed to protect the individual sometimes contradict a patient's final wishes or what may actually be in his or her best interests. Mrs. Browning's attorney, George Felos, expressed the essence of his client's plight: "The standard should not be whether she [Mrs. Browning] could live on the feeding tube, but how long she would live without it."

As time passed, Estelle Browning's condition deteriorated. Despite medical efforts to keep her alive, she died in July 1991, nearly five years after she initially lost consciousness. Two months after her death, Florida's Supreme Court ruled that living will provisions must be honored by health care facilities throughout the state. While the verdict brought welcome relief to other Florida patients in similar predicaments, it came too late for Estelle Browning.

Although Mrs. Browning's living will did not protect her as she had hoped it would, these documents have been extremely useful to countless other Americans. Since the 1980s, increasing numbers of individuals have expressed the desire to exert some degree of control over their medical treatment if they become unable to make decisions. To ensure that their feelings are known, they complete advance health care directives while they are still competent. An advance directive may be a living will, a durable power of attorney for health care, or a combination of both. These choices are discussed below.

Living Wills

A living will, sometimes referred to as an "instruction directive," specifies an individual's wishes or instructions for health care in advance. Generally, living wills give directions regarding life-prolonging treatments and conditions under which the person would or would not want these treatments carried out. "Life-prolonging" treatments generally include artificial breathing, feeding through tubes, surgical procedures, dialysis, restarting the heart, medications (other than those for comfort), and other treatments.

The first living wills tended to be nonspecific, but were thought sufficient to convey an individual's future health care wishes. A typical one might have been similar to the sample below:

"Should I be in an incurable or irreversible mental or physical condition with no reasonable expectation of recovery, I direct my physician to withhold or withdraw treatment that merely prolongs my dying. I further direct that my treatment be limited to measures to keep me comfortable and to relieve pain."

In practice, these wills often proved problematic for doctors and health care facilities. Accurately discerning a patient's wishes in a crisis was difficult when health care professionals had to decipher such vague terms as "terminally ill," "life-prolonging," and similar wording which frequently surfaced in these documents.

Ambiguous phrases, open to various interpretations, left doctors without a clear notion of which measures were to be stopped, started, or maintained. In numerous instances across the country, physicians continued life supports simply because they feared the courts might not support their interpretation of the patient's instructions. The situation was worsened by the fact that various states often define the general terms used in living wills differently. This is particularly true in instances where a patient is being kept alive through a feeding tube. In states in which artificial feeding is considered a "life-sustaining procedure," the measure can be withdrawn. But in other areas where tubal feeding is not deemed heroic or life-extending, feeding cannot be stopped.

These factors make it especially important when writing a living will to specify which treatments are to be withheld or performed and under what circumstances. It is best to clearly state whether cardiac resuscitation, mechanical respiration, or artificial feeding should be resorted to and, if so, under what conditions. It is also possible to specify if a particular treatment should be tried and discontinued if there is no improvement.

Yet even under the best circumstances, living will problems may arise when the unexpected occurs. For example, a person might have his or her living will state that artificial feeding is not to be instituted if there is no chance of recovery, but may fail to say whether he or she wants antibiotics (a life-extending measure) used to combat pneumonia under the same conditions. In other instances, such as the Browning case previously described, living will specifications may conflict with state laws. If the law further states that life supports may only be withdrawn if the person is terminally ill, these measures will be applied to a comatose person even though that may not be what that person wanted.

Another difficulty with living wills is that it is impossible for anyone to know how he or she will feel once illness becomes a reality. What if at the last minute a patient changes his or her mind, but because the illness makes the patient intermittently delusional, the medical staff adheres to the original terms of the patient's living will?

Despite the flaws and inherent complications of living wills, many medical experts believe a living will at least affords an individual a measure of input. Different forms may be used to create a living will, but all these documents basically have the same intent. A person can either use the form provided by Choice In Dying (see sample), a form devised by the state in which the person resides, or a similar format of one's choice. Once the living will has been completed, it is best to take the following further precautions:

1. A living will should be signed in front of two witnesses and a notary. Copies

should be given to responsible family members, the individual's clergyman, lawyer, or any other person who might be called upon to help interpret the individual's wishes.

2. The individual should discuss the living will with his or her physician. It is important that the doctor understand and support the person's wishes and agree to follow the directives in a medical emergency. If the doctor strongly disagrees with the patient's views in these matters, it might be wise to consider changing physicians. In any case, the physician should not be designated in a living will as a decision maker. The doctor cannot act as proxy and treat the patient at the same time.

3. A living will should be kept in a place where family members or other appropriate people can easily find it. It is not advisable to keep a living will in a safe-deposit box since the ill person may be the only one with access to the key.

4. Living wills should be signed again and dated every two to four years. A living will that has been recently reviewed is more likely to be honored by a physician or judge if there is a controversy.

Through the years, living wills have gained increasing acceptance. In December 1991, a new law went into effect requiring all federally funded hospitals, nursing homes, and hospices to inform incoming patients of the laws in their state regarding living wills and other advance directives for health care. They are then supposed to help the patient draw up one if he or she wishes to do so.

In California, some health care facilities even offer information on living wills in ten different languages.

Durable Power of Attorney

Still another advance directive for health care which can be used in connection with or in place of a living will is a durable power of attorney. Also known as a proxy directive, this document appoints someone to make health care decisions for an individual when that person is no longer able to act on his or her own behalf. A durable power of attorney differs from the standard power of attorney often used in business dealings, in that it does not lapse after a specified period of time or when the person granting it becomes incompetent.

The proxy chosen, usually a friend or family member, should be thoroughly familiar with the person's health care wishes. Ideally, the proxy would make the same health care decisions that the ill individual would make if able to. In selecting a durable power of attorney, it is important to remember that if there's a conflict, a judge is more likely to be persuaded by an impartial friend than a relative who also happens to be the incapacitated person's heir. It is also advisable to designate a back-up person for the task in case the first proxy is unavailable at the time of an emergency.

Perhaps the main advantage to having a durable power of attorney is that the proxy can assist in interpreting the patient's probable wishes if a situation arises that has not been covered in the ill person's living will. The proxy can evaluate various

Living Will Declaration

INSTRUCTIONS

Consult this column for help and guidance.

To My Family, Doctors, and All Those Concerned with My Care

This declaration sets forth your directions regarding medical treatment.

I,_____, being of sound mind, make this statement as a directive to be followed if I become unable to participate in decisions regarding my medical care.

If I should be in an incurable or irreversible mental or physical condition with no reasonable expectation of recovery. I direct my attending physician to withhold or withdraw treatment that merely prolongs my dying. I further direct that treatment be limited to measures to keep me comfortable and to relieve pain.

You have the right to refuse treatment you do not want, and you may request the care you do want.

These directions express my legal right to refuse treatment. Therefore I expect my family. doctors, and everyone concerned with my care to regard themselves as legally and morally bound to act in accord with my wishes, and in so doing to be free of any legal liability for having followed my directions.

You may list specific treatment you do not want. For example:
Cardiac resuscitation
Mechanical respiration
Artificial feeding/ fluids by tube Otherwise, your general statement, top right, will stand for your wishes.

I especially do not want:_____
_____
_____
_____
_____
_____
_____
_____
_____
_____

You may want to add instructions for care you do want—for example, pain medication; or that you prefer to die at home if possible.

Other instructions/comments: :_____
_____
_____
_____
_____
_____
_____
_____
_____

If you want, you can name someone to see that your wishes are carried out, but you do not have to do this.

Proxy Designation Clause: Should I become unable to communicate my instructions as stated above, I designate the following person to act in my behalf:
Name _____
Address _____
If the person I have named above is unable to act on my behalf, I authorize the following person to do so:
Name _____
Address _____

Sign and date here in the presence of two adult witnesses, who should also sign.

Signed:_____ Date: _____
Witness:_____ Witness:_____
Address:_____ Address:_____

Keep the signed original with your personal papers at home. Give signed copies to doctors, family, and proxy. Review your Declaration from time to time; initial and date it to show it still expresses your intent.

Courtesy of Choice In Dying

treatment alternatives with the fullest information possible.

Since there are no national laws or guidelines regulating the implementation of advance health care directives, their value and effectiveness continue to vary from state to state. Nevertheless, in an age of growing awareness about medical practices, many people feel that these documents are a positive step in the right direction.

Questions

1. What sort of problems with living wills does Ms. Landau describe?
2. What precautions does Ms. Landau suggest taking to ensure that one's living will is both enforceable and available to physicians?
3. If you were diagnosed with a terminal illness, and decided to appoint a durable power of attorney, whom would you appoint, and why?

---

2 Patricia Weenolsen, *Power over Pain*

Patricia Weenolsen, Ph.D., is a psychologist who specializes in life-span development as well as issues pertaining to death and dying. Her first book, *Transcendence over the Life Span,* was hailed as a classic in its field. The selection you are about to read is from her 1996 book, *The Art of Dying,* which has also received critical acclaim. Rabbi Harold Kushner, author of the best-selling *When Bad Things Happen to Good People,* said of *The Art of Dying,* "Along with our caring presence, this book may be the finest gift we can give someone facing the last stage of life."

In the following passage, Dr. Weenolsen discusses what is perhaps the most fear-invoking part of the dying process for most people: pain. Make no mistake, there is normally a great deal of pain involved in dying. It is the very rare person who dies peacefully in her sleep. Rather, and contrary to the quick, clean deaths of Hollywood, dying is often slow and nearly always painful. In former times, and still today in many places around the world, not much was/is done to control the pain of dying. But with the marvels of modern medicine, we are able to a large degree minimize, if not eliminate altogether, the pain and discomfort of dying. The problem, as Dr. Weenolsen points out, is that not all doctors are up to speed on the latest pain control techniques. And some who are up to speed still fail to implement them because they fear turning their patients into "drug addicts." But the author is convinced that any means that reduces a dying person's physical and emotional pain is good, so long as the patient benefits. In the following essay you will learn of the latest in pain control techniques, and what steps dying patients can take to control their own symptoms.

Why Is Pain Undertreated?

There are numerous reasons for the undertreatment of pain, including communication problems, ethical and legal issues, and "the system."

Communication

Some patients suffer in silence, determined to be staunch and brave; they may even try to conceal their pain. This attitude is a relic of earlier centuries when there wasn't much for pain relief beyond whiskey and laudanum. Patients weren't kept alive (and in pain) by extraordinary medical technology. The first life-threatening illness killed them off at age forty, and they didn't have to endure today's serial multiplicity of illnesses and treatments.

Some patients are too embarrassed to complain. What's hurting you is in a place that's either intimate or "dirty." You were scolded for having problems in those places as a child. Besides, you may feel that if you're labeled a complainer, the medical staff will get angry and withhold painkillers. Then, too, you fear you're not using the "right" vocabulary, that there are buzz words you don't know.

Many patients believe in the myths I've outlined above. They say they're satisfied with pain relief even when it's inadequate, often not realizing that more relief is possible. They need to educate themselves and become aware of treatment options and of potential side effects. They must learn to (1) *listen* to their bodies, and (2) *take action* by communicating to family and medical professionals.

But communication is a two-way responsibility. Some patients are not heard. Medical schools do not adequately train physicians in pain assessment and management. And many medical personnel also believe these very same myths concerning addiction, tolerance, side effects, and the rest—as do family members and caregivers! They may also believe they can't relieve the pain unless they know the cause. Not true!

In a series of courageous articles, Margo McCaffery, R.N., and her colleagues have alerted nurses to the many factors affecting their pain-control decisions, including gender, lifestyle, age (women, adolescents, and elderly undertreated), and whether the patient may be exaggerating.

Ethical and Legal Issues

Physicians suffer "opioidphobia"; they fear disciplinary action for overprescribing narcotics; they fear being blamed for a patient's death. To be on the safe side, they *under*prescribe.

Some states severely restrict the use of narcotics, even for pain relief. What are the regulations in your state?

The System

One in seven people in this country suffers from "chronic debilitating pain." But in these days of cost-cutting, insurance companies and Medicare are increasingly reluctant to finance additional pain relief, especially newer, nontraditional forms. So, some patients cannot afford them. The federal government is denying and capping patients' pain medications at the same time another federal agency, AHCPR [Agency for Healthcare Policy and Research], is pushing for more aggressive pain treatment. Patients and caregivers need to fight for the financing of adequate pain relief.

While the AHCPR survey . . . concluded that pain could be controlled in 90 percent of patients, there seems to be an underlying expectation, especially by some euthanasia opponents, that all pain can be eliminated or at least satisfactorily minimized. There is no proof that this is so. One recent study investigated a group of over four thousand patients "in advanced stages of one or more of nine illnesses," and who were estimated to be six months from death. In spite of supportive interventions, family members reported "moderate to severe pain at least half the time" in 50 percent of conscious patients who died in the hospital. Some pain, such as that of thoracic outlet syndrome, causalgia, trigeminal neuralgia, reflex sympathetic dystrophy, and other conditions, is more difficult to manage, although not impossibly so.

Much suffering can be relieved, but not all.

The Emerging Revolution in Pain Relief

Thanks in large part to hospice, founded by Dr. Cecily Saunders in Great Britain in 1969, the emphasis on pain control has grown in recent years.

Now pain relief is moving in a newer direction still, from a humane concern for the suffering of the dying to a recognition that pain is actually unhealthy. Pain is stressful; it can inhibit improvement or recovery, limit physical activity, decrease appetite, interrupt sleep needed to fight the disease, raise blood pressure (implicated in strokes and heart attacks), increase anxiety over future pain, thereby increasing pain, and cause depression that alters the immune system; it may result in suicide, and may even promote tumor growth. Pain can damage the nerve cells—permanently, if it is chronic—resulting in increased pain from future

injuries. Pain used to be thought secondary to disease: heal the disease and the pain will go away. Now pain is recognized as an ailment in itself with negative consequences. According to Ada Jacox, R.N., Ph.D., and her co-authors, "Patients in pain are reluctant to cough, to breathe deeply, or to move, for fear of exacerbating the pain. And immobility contributes to complications, such as pneumonia, thrombosis, and ileus." Pain can interfere with normal functioning, relationships, thinking, and work.

The medical community used to believe that pain relief could be harmful. The current thinking is that pain itself is harmful. As Jane Cowles points out, if your pain is treated you "heal faster, have fewer medical complications, spend less time in the hospital . . . enjoy a better quality of . . . life." Proper treatment of pain also can lower medical costs.

Typically, pain medication has been scheduled every four to six hours, or ordered PRN (as needed); this meant the patient had to feel pain first, suffer for perhaps an hour or two until the busy nurse could get to him, and then wait for the medicine to take effect. The current goal is to *preempt* pain, either by giving relief earlier than needed or by using a continuous method of delivery. Anesthesiologists may even inject a local anesthetic into the surgical wound site or epidurally before the patients leaves the OR.

Your timing may be more clever than you realize. Alarmed by increasing demands for "death with dignity," including both passive and active euthanasia (by, for example, the Hemlock Society, and physicians Jack Kevorkian and Timothy Quill), many antieuthanasists are now calling for better treatment of pain. They reason that fewer patients will want to end their lives if their pain is relieved. In my view, they often dismiss or forget the psychological suffering. What all of this means to you is that you are dying at a time in history that promises better pain relief than ever.

The Basic Pain-Relief Information You Need

As you know, different kinds of pain and suffering have their own modes of relief. Some modes can interact, or neutralize or weaken each other. Many physical ailments listed below are the result of treatment rather than disease; the solutions depend on the cause. Your physician, nurse, anesthetist, and pharmacist can give you the information you need to help you make choices.

You need to be able to talk with them intelligently, to ask the right questions, and to understand the answers. That's a tall order. Obtaining the right information is, unfortunately, your responsibility—not fair, in that you may feel too ill to do so, but all is not lost. To the extent that your pain is and has been chronic over a period of time, you're already familiar with some analgesics. Further, you may also have experienced *acute* pain such as that of childbirth, surgery, or the physical trauma of an accident—all of which are distinguished from the pain of life-threatening illness, in that acute pain is usually temporary. Should your pain become extreme and/or *intractable*, you may need methods you haven't used before.

The following is a broad outline of available pain relief. It differs from other outlines you may have seen in that it includes not only traditional, allopathic medications, but also so-called alternative treatments, those for which I feel there is enough scientific evidence about their effectiveness to try them (some disagree). Margo McCaffery, however, advises you to relieve pain with medication first, and then add alternative methods.

This is by no means a comprehensive list. I offer it as a basic survey chart to demonstrate the wide variety of frequently used methods available to you, depending on your medical condition, your preferences, and your doctor's advice. This should both comfort you and increase your knowledge. I have not included naturopathic or herbal remedies, which may relieve some symptoms. Always consult your physician, and remember that there is often controversy.

Symptom-Treatment Chart

Mild Pain: Aspirin, acetaminophen (Tylenol), nonsteroidal anti-inflammatory drugs (NSAIDs such as ibuprofen), topical applications (capsaicin—from chili peppers!), salicylate menthol (Ben-Gay), biofeedback, appropriate stretching and physical reconditioning, relaxation exercises, music, imagery.

Moderate Pain: See above. Codeine and other opioid analgesics, some combined with NSAIDs (Percodan, Darvon), appropriate adjuvants—such as antidepressants, anxiolytics, anticonvulsants, and corticosteroids—

TENS units, physical therapy, meditation, support groups, biofeedback, acupuncture, hypnosis, massage.

Severe/Intractable Pain: See above. Opioids (narcotics including morphine, methadone, oxymorphone, levorphanol, fentanyl, Demerol, Dilaudid), PCA (patient-controlled analgesia), implanted pumps, nerve blocks, trigger-point injections, radiation, surgery. Amphetamines may reduce sedation from the above.

For years, novelist Reynolds Price suffered intractable pain from a spinal tumor that had been partially resected and treated with radiation. He rated the pain an 11 or 12 on a scale of 10. Then, through biofeedback, he found freedom—not from the pain itself, which still "roars" continually, but from awareness of it. In an average sixteen-hour day, he's aware of it for perhaps a total of fifteen minutes. Hypnosis and self-hypnosis also helped.

Constipation: Laxatives, stool softeners, enemas, suppositories, fiber, psyllium (Metamucil).

Nausea/Vomiting: Antiemetics (Dramamine), THC from marijuana (cannabis), Marinol, Compazine, Phenergan, and others.

Cannabis relieves the severe nausea of patients treated with chemotheraphy in AIDS and cancer. (It also relieves eye pressure in glaucoma patients as well as muscular sclerosis spasms.) Even though cannabis is illegal (without a doctor's prescription), underground sources exist for those with evidence of medical conditions. For example, the San Francisco Cannabis Buyer's Club has 3,200 members; laws against them are "low priority" for enforcement, by resolution of the city's board of supervisors.

Anorexia (poor appetite): Corticosteroids, *moderate* alcohol intake before meals, favorite foods, allowing patient to eat when hungry rather than on schedule, cannabis.

Diarrhea: Antidiarrheal medications (Pepto-Bismol, Lomotil, Immodium), fiber, surgery if necessary.

Inflammation: NSAIDs, steroids.

Cough: Expectorants and suppressants (Robitussin), codeine, hydrocordone.

Hiccups: Haldol, Thorazine, surgery.

Dry Mouth: Artificial saliva, ice chips, lemon drops.

Mouth Pain: Prescribed medicated lozenges, mouthwash, and topical agents.

Itching: Antihistamines, cortisone creams, and others.

Depression: Close supportive relations with family, friends, and groups; psychological and/or pastoral counseling; cognitive behavioral therapy; acupuncture; antidepressants such as tricyclics (Elavil, Tofranil), MAO inhibitors (Nardil), Prozac.

Anxiety: Anti-anxiety agents such as Librium, Valium, Equanil, and Xanax, counseling.

Insomnia: Antihistamines, Dalmane, Nembutal, Seconal.

Dyspnea (breathing difficulties): bronchodilators, morphine.

The goal of pain relief during the final months is to relieve your pain without making you too sleepy, so you can "live" your dying, interact with family and friends, make decisions, engage in limited activities, and gradually close your circle.

Coping with Pain

Pain is a subjective experience, not an objective one. Just as there are easily observable differences among people's physiques, so it is logical to presume *physiological* differences among pain thresholds. Your pain is your own, no one else's. Recognize this and ask for relief when you need it, not when someone else says you do.

A doctor I adored told me a week after my surgery, "You shouldn't be feeling so much pain." He was wrong; he subsequently discovered an unsuspected complication.

The following methods will help you cope with and control your pain:

1. Pain and suffering take different forms. Raise your awareness of the various areas of your body. *Where and how does it hurt?* Is it a stabbing, burning, aching, gnawing, shooting, crushing, tingling, throbbing, sharp, steady, tender, pricking, pulling, tight, hot, or grinding sensation?

2. *Communicate* with your nurse, physician, or other caregiver. Tell them what hurts, how badly, and what the pain is like. How else are they to know?

3. Be prepared to *describe* it on a scale of 0 to 5 or 0 to 10. People tend to pick a lower number, just as they undermedicate themselves. The advice I am about to give you is philosophical, not medical. Pick a higher number, particularly if you feel you are undertreated. If you're feeling pain at 6, choose 7. But don't choose 8, because you really don't want overmedication's possible side effects.

4. Ask to see the AHCPR policy guidelines for aggressive pain management (see the Notes and Resources for this). They call for (1) a collaborative interdisciplinary approach to the care of patients with cancer pain (apply to your own)—this team may include the *patient* (my emphasis), family, surgeon, nurse, psychologist, anesthesiologist, general practitioner, and pharmacist; (2) an individual plan of management; (3) continued assessment of pain; (4) use of both drug and nondrug therapies; and (5) institutional support for these policies. "A patient's report of pain should determine pain control," says Jacox.

5. Demand your *Patient's Bill of Rights*— to a pain history, assessment, measurement, plan adequate timing, and control—and to explanations of how much pain to expect from all treatments, as well as side effects and alternatives. You have a right to answers, to be believed, to secure a second opinion, to refuse treatment, to view records, and to receive "compassionate and sympathetic care."

6. Set specific pain relief goals with your doctor and nurses—for example, your goal may be to be able to walk, and you figure lowering your pain to 2 (on a scale of 1 to 10) will help.

7. Consider the pain clinics and therapy groups discussed in Chapter 11. They often use alternative approaches such as behavior modification, support, meditation, and visualization. These work for some who never thought they would, but not for others. "They'll just tell me to love my pain," said Maddie, but to her surprise the

clinic proved effective. Many of us know from experience that some pains we get rid of; others we work with.

Bill Moyers was talking with psychologist Jon Kabat-Zinn, who leads one of the most lauded stress-reduction through meditation groups. Moyers quoted a friend as not wanting to relax into his pain: "I don't want any [pain]. . . . "

"Lots of luck," responded Kabat-Zinn.

8. Keep a *comfort-assessment journal* with the date and time of entry, how you're feeling, and the medication or exercise and results. Your nurse may be able to help you set this up.

9. Reject myths and remember realities. Don't worry about addiction or tolerance. Most pain relief is by mouth, but for severe pain, if your doctor agrees, a slow, continuous method of pain relief may be best, via a patch, implanted pump, or the like. Patients who control their own pain relief often undermedicate themselves, waiting too long to take those pills or press that button. But don't worry, you can't overdose on the pump; built-in regulators and adjustment mechanisms increase or decrease the amount. You'll actually need less, because the greater frequency of delivery lowers both pain and anxiety over pain.

10. "The squeaky wheel gets the grease." Unless you've decided to suffer bravely, *complain,* and have all your relatives do the same. If that doesn't work, change hospitals and physicians. (Many years ago I worked in a hospital where a woman screamed down the halls for weeks, while my friend, the nursing supervisor, assured me, "She doesn't feel a thing." She really believed that.)

11. Depending on where you are on your life-threatening illness trajectory, consider hospice. (See Chapter 14.)

12. In many ways the psychological pain and suffering during the dying process is far worse than the physical, but you must relieve the physical first. Unresolved relationships and conflicts greatly magnify suffering. Much of the rest of this book is aimed at relieving psychological pain.

The Spiritual Uses of Pain

Not all suffering can be relieved. So a review of the possible spiritual uses of pain may be helpful to some of you, although, to be honest, I'd rather not have to go through this spiritual lesson.

Pain arouses compassion in others, which, if they act upon it, may be the salvation of their souls.

Pain, if it doesn't shrink our minds, makes us pause and evaluate our lives, selves, and relationships. It gives us the time and justification to do so.

Pain may open us to others, and them to us, bringing us closer to one another.

Finally, pain snips at the threads that bind us to this life—snip, snip, and we are less and less attached, bits of us floating skyward like a bouquet of balloons, released one at a time, until they are too far away for us to see them pop in the increasingly rarefied atmosphere.

Questions

1. List the primary reasons why, according to Dr. Weenolsen, pain is often undertreated.

2. List five side effects common with taking pain medication, and for each suggest two ways the side effect can be minimized. From Dr. Weenolsen's list of ways to cope with pain, identify the three that make the most sense to you and rewrite them in your own words.

3. Rewrite in your own words the "spiritual uses of pain," and describe an example from your own life when something painful taught you a valuable spiritual lesson.

---

3 Kenneth J. Doka, *The Spiritual Needs of the Dying*

Dr. Kenneth J. Doka is a professor of gerontology at the Graduate School of The College of New Rochelle where he has taught since 1981, and concurrently served since 1993 as a senior consultant to the Hospice Foundation of America. A prolific author, Dr. Doka's books include *Living with Grief: Children, Adolescents, and Loss; Disenfranchised Grief; Living with Life-Threatening Illness; Children Mourning, Mourning Children; Death and Spirituality; Caregiving and Loss: Family Needs, Professional Responses; AIDS, Fear and Society;* and *Aging and Developmental Disabilities.* In addition, he has published over sixty articles and book chapters. Dr. Doka is editor of *Omega: The Journal for Death and Dying* and *Journeys: A Newsletter for the Bereaved.*

Dr. Doka was elected president of the Association for Death Education and Counseling in 1993. In 1995, he was elected to the Board of Directors of the International Work Group on Dying, Death and Bereavement and served as chair from 1997 to 1999. The Association for Death Education and Counseling presented him with an award for Outstanding Contributions in the Field of Death Education in 1998. In 2000, Dr. Doka received the Scott and White Award for Outstanding Contributions to Thanatology and Hospice, and in 2001 his alma mater, Concordia College, named him recipient of their first Distinguished Alumni Award. Dr. Doka has keynoted conferences throughout North America as well as Europe and Australia. He participates in the annual Hospice Foundation of America Teleconference, hosted by Cokie Roberts, and has appeared on *Nightline.* In addition he has served as a consultant to medical, nursing, funeral service, and hospice organizations as well as businesses and educational and social service agencies. Dr. Doka is also an ordained Lutheran minister.

In the following article, taken from Dr. Doka's 1993 book, *Death and Spirituality,* three spiritual tasks are identified as essential for the dying person to accomplish: to understand the meaning of one's death; to die in an appropriate way; and to find hope for what lies beyond death. The aim in accomplishing these, as Dr. Doka states, is the attainment of a sense of "spiritual wholeness" before the end of one's life.

It has become a truism to describe contemporary American culture as secular. Yet the term "secularization" often has very ambiguous, different, and even conflicting meanings. To many, secularization is essentially a social process whereby religious symbols and doctrines lack social significance and societal decisions are made on a rational and pragmatic rather than on a theological or spiritual basis. Such definition does not deny the potency of both religion and spirituality on an individual level. Gallup polls affirm that vast majorities of Americans both believe in God and consider religion and spirituality important in their lives. This is clearly evident when one faces the crisis of dying, a crisis when scientific explanations are largely silent.

Individuals, of course, differ in the extent that religion plays a part in their lives. These differences continue even throughout the dying process. As Pattison noted, dying persons will use belief systems as they have used throughout life—constructively, destructively, or not at all. To some individuals, belief systems can be a source of comfort and support; to others, it will be a cause for anxiety. Pattison even notes that individuals who seem to find religion in terminal illness often show a basic continuity, for these "foxhole" religionists are likely to be individuals who seek out and grasp each new treatment, diet, or drug.

Counselors are increasingly recognizing the value in exploring religious and spiritual themes with the dying; for dying is not only a medical and personal crisis, it is a spiritual one as well. Though individuals may adhere to different religious beliefs and explanations, *or even the lack of them,* dying *focuses one on questions* such as the meaning of life, the purpose of one's own existence, and the reason for death, that have an inherently spiritual quality. Thus as individuals struggle with dying, spiritual and religious themes are likely to emerge. In fact, often these spiritual interpretations are, to paraphrase Freud, "a royal road into the unconscious."

While this chapter will emphasize religious and spiritual themes in the terminal phase of disease, it is important to recognize the presence of these themes throughout the illness. Even at the point of diagnosis, persons may interpret the disease in a spiritual or religious sense. For example, one person may define AIDS as a punishment from God. That interpretation is likely to have very different reverberations throughout the illness than those from someone who sees the disease as a result from an unfortunate exposure to a virus.

It is not unusual for a person's interpretation of the disease to have religious and spiritual dimensions. Every disease has a component of mystery. Why does one smoker get lung cancer and another not? Why does a disease manifest itself at any given time? Why, in fact, do we die? None of these questions yield to totally satisfactory scientific and rational explanations.

Hence in exploring someone's interpretation of disease, it is essential to be sensitive to these religious or spiritual dimensions. Often because religious or spiritual explanations are not socially validated, individuals may be reluctant to share them or even be fully aware of them. There is a need then for counselors to probe such issues in a permissive and nonjudgmental atmosphere.

Religions or spiritual themes may also be intertwined with affective responses evident in the living-dying interval. Numerous observers have noted that persons with a life-threatening or terminal disease often exhibit emotions such as anger, guilt, bargaining, resignation, hope and anxiety. All of these responses may be tied to spiritual concerns. Anger may not only be directed against significant others but also comically—against nature, the universe, faith, or God. And such anger can be combined with both guilt and fear that anger toward the deity or other transcendental power is both wrong and dangerous. One person, for example, was both angry at God for her disease, but also was fearful that God would continue to punish her for that anger. In counseling, the woman has been able to reinterpret her anger as a form of prayer, and with that reaffirmation of both her relationship to God (e.g., she had the freedom to communicate such anger) and his power. A comment by Easson helped. In describing the anger of a thirteen-year-old boy with leukemia, he noted the child's comment that "if God is God, He will understand my anger, if He does not under my anger, He is not God." This allowed the woman to see her anger as an aspect of faith.

Similarly bargaining may be directed toward God leading to a sense of hope or resignation if the bargain is perceived as accepted and a sense of anger, guilt and fear if perceived as denied. One man with leukemia gave up hope at the time of his first relapse. In his mind he had made a "bargain" with God at the time of his first hospitalization. At that time he had hoped for the health to participate in a family event. When a relapse soon followed, he now believed that God had fulfilled his part of the deal—the man was now resigned to dying. Such bargains do not have to be theistic in nature. One woman once had made a deal with "the universe" to give something back if she achieved a desired success. In her own intensely spiritual frame of reference, her illness was a manifestation of her selfishness and

unwillingness to part with her time (sessions. She had not fulfilled her p her illness was the result.

It is important then for counselors to recognize that *any* response to life-threatening illness can be intertwined with religious themes. Throughout the illness, these religious or spiritual interpretations should be explored as they can facilitate or complicate a person's response to illness.

Religious and spiritual values may also influence treatment decisions. Extreme examples of this may be found when adherence to particular beliefs precludes certain medical procedures such as blood transfusions or even causes patients to reject any conventional medical therapies. But even in other cases, religious and philosophical perspectives may certainly be part of treatment decisions. For example, persons may decline treatments because of personal perspectives on quality of life or because they perceive a value to life or an obligation to God or fellow humans. Perspectives in euthanasia may be profoundly influenced by religious and spiritual values.

While religious and spiritual themes are often found throughout the struggle with life-threatening illness, they are often especially critical in the terminal phase. For beyond the medical, social, and psychological needs of dying individuals, there are spiritual needs as well. The terminally ill patient recognizes Becker's paradox that humans are aware of finitude yet have a sense of transcendence. It is this paradox that underlies the three spiritual needs of dying persons: 1) the search for meaning of life, 2) to die appropriately, and 3) to find hope that extends beyond the grave.

1. The Search for Meaning of Life

One major crisis precipitated by dying is a search for the meaning of one's life. Theoreticians of various disciplines have long recognized that we are creatures who create and share meaning. This purposiveness extends to self as well. In the prologue of the play *Ross,* a biography of Lawrence of Arabia, various characters posthumously assess Lawrence's life. As the spotlight descends on one Arab chieftain, he defiantly exclaims "that history will sigh and say 'this was a man!'" It is a statement that in one way or another we wish to make: that our life had purpose, significance, and meaning. Developmental psychologists and sociologists, such as Erikson, Butler, and Marshall, assert that the knowledge of impending death creates a crisis in which one reviews life in order to integrate one's goals, values and experience. This awareness of finitude can be a consequence of either old age or serious illness. Even very young children, and their families, will review the child's life to find that sense of purpose.

The failure to find meaning can create a deep sense of spiritual pain. Individuals may feel that their lives changed or meant nothing. This has implications for caregivers. One of the most important things that caregivers can do for the dying persons is to provide time for that personal reflection. While the caregiver can help dying persons find significance in their lives, things they have done, events they have witnesses, history that they have experienced all provide fruitful areas of exploration. Counselors may use varied techniques to facilitate this process. Reviewing life and family histories, viewing family or period photographs and mementos or sharing family humor and stories can facilitate this process. Films, music, books, or art that evoke earlier periods or phases of life can encourage reminiscence and life review.

Religious beliefs of philosophical and spiritual systems can be very important here. They can give one's life a sense of cosmic significance. And, they can provide a sense of forgiveness—to oneself and to others—for acts of commission and omission and for dreams not accomplished.

2. To Die Appropriately

People not only need assurance that they have lived meaningfully, they must die meaningfully as well. First, people want to die in ways consistent with their own self-identity. For example, a group of elderly women have established a call system to each other. Each woman has a set of multiple keys to each other's apartment. "This," one woman assured, "was so we don't die stinking up the apartment and nobody has to break down any doors." To these old-world women, cleanliness and orderliness are key virtues. The thought of leaving dirt and disorder even at the moment of demise is painful. They wish to die congruent with the ways in which they lived.

Dying appropriately also means dying comprehendingly. It means being able to understand and interpret one's death. If one suffers, it means having a framework to explain suffering. Pope John Paul noted that our secular and comfort-oriented society lacks a theology of pain. This suggests that caregivers need to explore with patients their beliefs about pain and death.

To die appropriately is difficult in a technological world. The fantasy of a quick death surrounded by loving relatives contrasts starkly with the reality of dying by chronic disease, alone, and institutionalized. It is little wonder that people fear not so much the fact of death as the process of dying. Caregivers can be helpful here in a number of ways. First, by empathetic listening, they allow the dying space to interpret their deaths. Second, whatever control can be left to the dying aids in their construction of their deaths. The opportunity to discuss one's death with relatives, either near the time of death or earlier, permits occasion to prepare to die as one lived. This allows specifying modes of treatment, ritual requests, special bequests, or simply educating families in the details that accompany death.

3. To Find Hope That Extends Beyond the Grave

Another spiritual need is transcendental. We seek assurance in some way that our life, or what we left, will continue. Perhaps the popularity of Moody's *Life After Life* is that it recasts traditional images of the afterlife in a quasiscientific framework.

Religion and other belief systems are one way to provide critical reassurance of immortality. Religious rituals may affirm a sense of continuity even beyond death.

Yet Lifton and Olson's typology remind that there are other things that help as well. Actions of caregivers are important too. The presence of personal artifacts and dignified treatment of the terminally ill reaffirm personhood and suggest significance. Institutional policies that encourage intergenerational visiting provide subtle reminders of one's biological legacy.

Summary

Yet while there seems some recognition of these spiritual needs, it remains unclear as to how well these needs are being met. Observers have recognized a variety of obstacles to religious or spiritual wholeness. Some of these obstacles may be structural. Lack of access to clergy, a lack of privacy, or a reluctance of caregivers to explore religious and spiritual issues can inhibit any attempt to address their spiritual concerns.

The lack of structure may also be an inhibitor. Within the Christian tradition, there is an absence of recognized ritual that mandates the presence of clergy and focuses on spiritual issues such as reconciliation and closure. Such a ritual has never been particularly significant in Protestant liturgy or theology. In the Roman Catholic tradition, the sacrament of extreme unction, or popularly "last rites," has changed its meaning significantly since 1974. Retitled (or restored to the title of) "anointing of the sick," it now emphasizes a holistic notion of healing that is rooted in a context of prayer and counseling. While much is gained by this change, it ends the notion of a sacramental rite of passage into death. Death becomes simply a medical event where clergy have no defined role. There then is an absence of any structure of ritual that focuses on addressing these spiritual needs.

Other failure may be failures of personnel. Clergy or clinicians may be unable to facilitate this process. There may be a number of reasons for this. Clergy may be intolerant of other beliefs or seek to proselytize. They may fail to be understanding. They may hide behind prayer or ritual. Intellectually or emotionally they may have little to offer dying persons. Other caregivers may not be religious, may not have explored their own spiritual beliefs, or are hesitant to explore beliefs of others.

Finally, dying persons may be unable to meet their own spiritual needs. They may lack conviction in their own beliefs, fail to appreciate or explore their own spiritual needs, or be consumed by dysfunctional elements of their own belief system.

Clergy and clinicians can facilitate spiritual wholeness in a number of ways. First, in their own conversations with dying persons, they can provide individuals with opportunities to explore these concerns in a nonthreatening and nonjudgmental atmosphere. These are times to listen and explore the individual's perspective. Should some of these beliefs have dysfunctional elements, counselors can explore the ways that these issues can be addressed within the belief structure. For example, in one case, a man was consumed with religious guilt. Exploration of his own beliefs allowed

him to address how that guilt could be expiated.

Varied rituals may facilitate this process. Rituals such as confession or communion can prove a visible sign of forgiveness. As DeArments notes, prayer can be a powerful way to express emotion or approach intimate reflection without the patient feeling exposed or vulnerable. It can also be useful to explore faith stories or "paricopes" with individuals. By asking persons to relate faith stories that they believe speak to their situations, one can assess significant issues and themes in their own spiritual journeys. Sometimes one can help individuals reframe these faith stories to serve as additional support. For example, many individuals in the Judaic-Christian tradition interpret Job as fatalistically responding to loss. "The Lord giveth and taketh." Another way to view that story, though, is as a long intense struggle of Job as he experiences loss. The latter is often more helpful to people in struggle and is quite faithful to text. In those cases in which the counselor cannot utilize such rituals or beliefs, they are still able to assist in locating empathic clergy or layperson of the person's own faith. This also reminds one that faith communities—the churches, congregations, and temples—that individuals may belong to can be helpful resources.

In recent years, there has been increasing recognition that dying persons not only have medical needs but psychological and social needs as well. Recognition of spiritual needs, too, will allow individuals to approach death as they have approached life—wholly.

Questions

1. Identify and describe various ways in which the dying can satisfy their need to "search for the meaning of one's life."

2. What does Dr. Doka mean when he says that the dying have a need "to die appropriately"?

3. What are some of the ways a pastor or clinician can "facilitate spiritual wholeness" for the dying person?

---

4 David Kessler, *Spirituality and Death*

David Kessler is a consultant and lecturer in the growing home healthcare industry. He is founder and president of the Progressive Home Health Care Agency, an award-winning provider of hospice care for the dying in the Los Angeles area. He also has been associated with the work of hospice for decades, has consulted with Mother Teresa in Calcutta, India, and served as an advisor during the dying processes of actor Michael Landon and billionaire Armand Hammer.

His work has been written about in *The New York Times* and in *Life* magazine. He has acted as advisor to former President and Mrs. Clinton on hospice issues, and has served on the National Education and Health Care Advisory Committee. In recent years he has collaborated with Dr. Elisabeth Kübler-Ross on a series of books about the spirituality of dying.

Mr. Kessler here discusses his experiences with patients who, in their final weeks and days of life, found a deeper sense of spirituality. He outlines five stages of spiritual growth seen in dying patients: reconciliation, expression, responsibility, forgiveness, acceptance, and gratitude. Together they form a helpful "checklist" for the sort of personal development that can only happen in those final moments of life.

The quest for spirituality is a search for a place of peace and safety. Many people begin looking for this place during the final chapters of their lives. They may do so through religion, on their own, or both. Whatever approach one chooses, it should be honored and supported, even if you think it is "incorrect." This last exploration is a rite of passage for the soul. It is also a right of the dying to be honored.

Ronald and Shirley had been married for forty-five years. Now both in their mid-sixties, they had spent most of their lives together. When I visited them shortly after Ronald's retirement, they talked about spending more time going to church, taking trips, planting a vegetable garden in the backyard, and getting into shape. But things began to go wrong with their happy retirement plans almost immediately. Only a little exercise or activity left Ronald breathless and tired, so he went to the doctor for a checkup—his first in twenty years.

Unfortunately, the news was bad. Ronald had coronary artery disease and would have to undergo triple bypass surgery within the next few weeks. Shirley told me that although she was frightened by the prospect of surgery and terrified that her beloved husband might die, there was a "little gift" in the bad news. "It's made me realize more than ever that our time is limited," she explained as we sat together in the waiting room during the surgery. "It's gotten us to look back on life, talk about some things we never talked about before, and forgive each other for things we did. We've been able to forgive ourselves, accept life just as it is, and be grateful for all that has happened. Ron said that he realized that his life could end anytime and he wanted to get rid of all the grudges he was carrying. He wanted to forgive people."

"I didn't know Ronald was religious," I said.

"He wanted to get his house in order. He wanted to enjoy life and be at peace inside," she replied.

Fortunately, Ronald sailed through the bypass without any problems. He was soon up and around, more energetic than ever. The couple bought a dog and took long walks; they planted their garden and did volunteer work through their church. They traveled to Yosemite and Yellowstone and other parks, enjoying nature and life. And they continued to seek spirituality through their religion. "Not in a silly way," Shirley said. "But in the sense that we wanted to get rid of our anger and resentment."

Several years passed. Life was good for Ronald and Shirley. I called them one evening to make plans to get together over the upcoming weekend. Ronald said that they were eating dinner and he would call back soon. Fifteen or twenty minutes later he got up from the table and asked Shirley if he could get her anything. She smiled and said, "No thanks, I'm fine." He walked into the kitchen, set down a dish, and had a massive heart attack. He died instantly.

Shirley went into the kitchen a minute or two later. "I knew when I opened the door and saw him on the floor that he was dead. I called 911, then I lay down on the floor next to him. I felt his soul in my heart. I felt that he was okay and at peace. I lay there with tears coming out of my eyes, telling him how excited I felt when we first met. I caressed his face and said how grateful I was to have met him. Even now, when I think of Ronald dying in the kitchen, it comforts me to know that he'd examined his life and found peace, for the most part. And that's where he died, in peace."

Others have found comfort by following less traditional paths. Walter and Marion had been married for thirty-seven years. He was a novelist, she was an accountant; together they raised three boys in a small community outside of Santa Cruz, California. They lived in the same house for thirty years, and Marion worked at the same accounting firm in San Jose for fifteen years. Walter worked at home.

One day, after coughing up blood, Walter went to the doctor. The diagnosis was quickly made: He had a tumor in his lung. The surgery was performed a week later. It went well, and the doctor felt that all the cancerous tissue had been removed. However, Walter knew that a recurrence was always possible.

For the first time in his life, Walter wasn't sure what to do. He wasn't even sure that there was anything to do: He already ate a healthful diet, and he jogged along the beach every evening. But he didn't want to simply wait for the cancer to come back.

A friend of his, the editor of several of his books, suggested that he consult with a woman who did spiritual counseling. This took Walter by surprise. A spiritual counselor?" he asked. "What does she do? Is she a psychologist, a social worker, a minister? Does she look into crystal balls? Do I have to burn incense and talk to spirits?"

"It's nothing like that," the editor replied. "She has no degrees, she's nondenominational. She just counsels from a spiritual viewpoint."

Curious, Walter made an appointment with the spiritual counselor. They discussed his condition, and he told her about his life. She asked him questions he had not thought about: Do you know why you are here? Do you know what you would like to do in your remaining time, however long that may be? What do you want to leave behind? "You've spent your entire life looking outside of yourself," she explained. "Now it's time to look inward."

All this struck a chord in Walter, who asked her for a list of books to read and questions to consider. He asked her to show him how to meditate.

As the weeks passed, Walter became more involved in his daily meditations and spiritual readings. He turned the two hours he used to devote every morning to reading the latest newspapers and magazines and the hour he had spent watching the news every night over to meditation and spiritual readings.

Marion, however, became increasingly upset. Finally she said: "Walter, this is not

you. You don't read the papers, you don't watch the news. You're changing your life. It's like you're withdrawing from your old way of life. Don't you have enough to worry about without getting into all this spiritual stuff, thinking about the bogeyman? You have a serious disease, so we don't have time for this hocus-pocus."

"Why don't you try some of it with me?" Walter asked.

Marion was disdainful. "I only believe in what I can see and touch."

Despite his wife's strong objections, Walter continued to explore spirituality. In time, it became a way of life for him. Outwardly, his life remained pretty much the same. Inwardly, he let go of some of the financial and status concerns that had occupied his mind for much of his life. Overall, he felt much calmer and accepting. When he shared this with Marion, she said: "Good. Now that you got where you're going, you can stop with the counselor, stop with the books, stop with the meditation, stop with all this strange stuff. I want you to go back to the way you were. I'm worried about what our friends and family will think."

"This is my life now," he replied. "It helps me cope with what's going on. I don't mean for it to be threatening. It doesn't contradict our religion. I don't want to leave you out of it. I would like you to join me in any part of it you like. And I don't care what our friends think. I'm on a different playing field now, what matters is how I feel. I hope this can be a way for us to become closer, not separate us."

As time passed, Marion had many more discussions with Walter and their sons about his growing spirituality. The sons immediately understood what their father was doing. Eventually, Marion began to see that it was helping her husband. A year later she shared with me, "I'm glad he has it now. At first I thought it would be a one-time thing, which was okay. But it upset me that he stayed with it, because the cancer had already changed our lives and I didn't want any more changes. But Walter is a happier, more peaceful man, and that's all that matters to me."

Like Walter, many people facing life-threatening illnesses often examine their lives as they prepare to move from a place of body and spirit to the realm of spirit alone. They set aside the concerns of money, status, beauty, and possessions that have beset them during their lifetimes. Perhaps it's more correct to say that these things simply do not matter anymore as they reach out to grasp love, forgiveness, and peace.

We spend most of our lives looking outward until time, illness, and age force us to turn inward. We begin to examine our true natures, our souls, our spirits. Seeking spirituality as life draws to a close, reviewing life and asking questions about what comes next, is not a new concept. Human beings have probably been doing this since they became aware that everyone dies. Primal questions arise as we feel our time drawing to a close: Where do I go from here? Have I accomplished all that I was supposed to? Am I still whole and intact, despite my disease-ravaged body? Will I continue in one form or another? How do I find peace, the only thing that really matters now? Who am I really? Am I more than just a physical body? Do I have a spirit that will live on?

I believe so. In his book *Your Sacred Self,* Dr. Wayne Dyer says, "we are not human beings having a spiritual experience, we are spiritual beings having a human experience." Spirit is that part of you that will last forever, the unique thing that is you and will continue to live on after your body has ceased to function. When you look at someone who has just died, you can instantly tell that whatever it is that gives us the energy of life has left that body. That energy, that life force is the spirit or the soul. For some, spirit is the essence of who we are, for others it is God, and as their lifetimes draw to a close, people begin to explore the spirit that lasts forever.

Birth is not a beginning, it is merely a continuation, and death is not an ending, it is also a continuation. Your body came and your body will go, merely the suit of clothes you wear in this lifetime, but spirit is indestructible, for it is energy. As Einstein pointed out, energy can neither be created nor destroyed: It was, it is, and it always will be.

The word "spirituality" means different things to different people. For some, it is the recognition of a higher power or their deeper selves. For many, it means getting in touch with God. For others, spirituality is simply the act of loving. It is not *what* we love, such as flowers or ice cream, but the *act* of loving, the feeling of loving. Being spiritual means trying to react to the everyday challenges of life in a loving and peaceful way. It is easy to be spiritual sitting on a mountaintop where no one can insult you, steal your money, or cut you off in traffic. Finding peace in a world where people die, crime goes unpunished, co-workers annoy you, and goals seem out of reach is a different matter.

The Five Stages of Spiritual Reconciliation

Our belief systems shape our lives. We believe that if we are educated, we will get a good job. If we accumulate money, we will be safe from hunger. If we eat right and exercise often, we will be healthy. We believe that pills will work, that medical technology will keep disease at bay, and that doctors will save us. Inevitably, our beliefs fade as we realize that we will not live forever, no matter how smart, rich, or healthy we may be, no matter how good our doctors are. As the end approaches, we realize that we must leave behind families, friends, money, possessions, status, technology, and society itself. At that point it is natural to feel the desire to believe that there is rhyme and reason to the world, that everything happens for the best, and that our lives have had meaning. As we must let go of everything we have known, faith allows us to escape the fear that all is random and meaningless.

We find our comfort and faith in the love and peace that is spirituality. It gives meaning and order to life, especially as one is leaving this life. Neither philosophy nor technology can give us these precious gifts. When all else must leave us, spirituality and faith remain.

Elisabeth Kübler-Ross has described the five steps we go through as we face death: denial, anger, bargaining, depression, and acceptance. There is a similar approach to spirituality. Upon developing a genuine desire to explore their spiritual selves,

people go through five stages of spiritual reconciliation: expression, responsibility, forgiveness, acceptance, and gratitude.

Expression—Many people have trouble accepting the demise of their physical selves because they're blocked by anger. Being human, we all make judgments, we all hate, we all blame others, we all become furious, and we all behave in petty ways. Sometimes we're justified in doing so; more often we're not. As far as healing is concerned, it doesn't matter. For healing to take place, we must overcome our taboos and express our feelings. You've been taught not to say that you're jealous of your sister because you think your mother loved her more than you. You shudder to say that you hate your father for the way he treated you.

We fear that we will be punished if we express our "ugly" feelings but in fact the opposite is true. We are rewarded for releasing our anger by making ourselves ready for peace. You don't have to tell your father or sister that you hate them. You can say it to a trusted friend, you can whisper it into the air, or you can scream it into your pillow. Once you do, the angry thoughts begin to dissipate. The hate that held you hostage disappears. You can also tell God why you're upset, if that's the case. Anger toward God is a problem for many. I've worked with people from various faiths, and I've found that they often need permission to become angry with God. How could He have allowed Mom to suffer so horribly and die so young? How could He have allowed Dad to be cheated out of his life savings? How can He now allow me to suffer so much, then die, leaving behind a widow and three young children? How can He be so cruel and callous? Many of us feel that it's absolutely taboo to admit to being angry with God, but until we admit to our feelings, we cannot heal. I've had people express their anger verbally, I've even had them express their anger by hitting the bed with a baseball bat. God understands that you need to express and release your feelings in order to love.

We may also be blocked by our negative feelings toward our diseases. In her book *A Return to Love,* Marianne Williamson describes the technique of writing your disease a letter and many people I work with say it's a powerful technique. Exercises like this help us admit to and confront our buried feelings. They also help us get in touch with our deeper, spiritual selves. People I have cared for have written "Dear Cancer" letters, "Dear Leukemia" letters, and "Dear AIDS" letters. In these letters, they talk about their anger at their diseases, they share their feelings about what has happened. Some ask their diseases to leave, others ask that they live together in harmony.

Responsibility—People have often said that facing a life-challenging illness has improved the quality of their lives. Specifically, it helped them take responsibility for their actions, thoughts and lives. They know that they're not to blame for their diseases and that dying does not mean that they have somehow failed. They also understand that they have played a role in all that has happened to them in life.

Harvey, suddenly faced with pancreatic cancer and given only a short time to live, gained a new understanding of responsibility.

"I used to blame everyone else for my problems," he said. "I'd say that my ex-wife ruined our marriage, my lousy business partner was only out for himself, my friends betrayed me. But now I look back on all the bad things that ever happened to me and realize that they all had one common denominator: me! I was involved in all of them. Sure, my wife quit trying to make our marriage work and my partner was a selfish crook and my friends didn't always see things my way, but I chose them. And you know what? It's not just *their* fault. I made mistakes in the marriage; I wasn't the best business partner or friend. *I* have to take responsibility for my life. I don't want to live as a victim, and I certainly don't want to die as one."

Harvey learned that he is not to blame for the misdeeds of others, but that he bears responsibility for all that has happened to *him*.

Forgiveness—In the end, our diseases stop spreading, our hearts no longer beat, and our minds cease thinking. So do our fights, grudges, and judgments end. Whether we like it or not, our part of the quarrel will be over, for we will no longer be here. The dying understand this intuitively, which is why they often have a meeting with forgiveness. To forgive does not mean to accept bad behavior. When we forgive, we release ourselves from the binds of hates and hurts. When I forgive you for cheating on me fifteen years ago, I'm not saying that it's all right to hurt people. I am saying, however, that I understand that you made a mistake, I've made mistakes, and we all make mistakes. I'm no longer going to define you or our entire relationship by that one mistake.

Unforgiveness is an open wound. We forgive ourselves and others because we want to die whole. I am constantly struck by how strong a role forgiveness plays. I have seen two sisters who have not spoken for thirty years become best friends again as one of them is faced with death, because they finally forgive one another for something that happened three decades ago. I have seen a mother, a father, and their son come back into one another's lives after the parents had disowned the son for marrying outside his religion. It was not until his father became ill that they realized their time together was limited and that forgiveness was the only thing that could lead to a reconciliation. I am touched by the story of a Hindu man whose son was murdered by Muslims during the religious wars that convulsed India as the nation prepared to become independent from Great Britain in the 1940s. The grieving Hindu man went to see Mahatma Gandhi, who was also a Hindu, asking, "How can I possibly forgive the Muslims? How can I ever find peace again with so much hate in my heart for those who have killed my only son?" Gandhi suggested that the man adopt an orphaned Muslim boy and raise him as his own.

We're afraid that forgiving the people who have hurt us is the same as absolving them of their misdeeds. But we forgive for our own sake, when we realize that holding on to grudges forces us to live in unhappiness. When people are reluctant to forgive, I tell them, maybe it's not up to us to punish. Meanwhile, this is your death. Do you want to die awash in hatred? Our final acts are the ones that will be remembered by our loved ones. Few of

us would choose hatred and revenge as our exit lines. We'd prefer to be remembered for kindness and joy.

Forgiving ourselves is just as much a part of spiritual growth as forgiving others. Most people are very hard on themselves at the end, remembering all the things they've done wrong, whether little or large, and wondering if they can ever be forgiven. I tell them that if they feel that they cannot forgive themselves, they should simply ask their God or Higher Power for help. We can die in unforgiveness; that's an option and some people do die that way. But many choose to make way for inner peace by forgiving.

Acceptance—I remember very well the stout forty-two-year-old banker who grasped his dying father's shoulders as the older man lay in his hospital bed and practically shouted at him: "Dad! Fight it! Fight it! You've been a fighter all your life, you can beat this!" And I remember so many other loved ones sobbing, "How could he die so young?" and "She was such a good person, it's unfair that she should have to die."

We live in a fix-it society with the technology to repair many broken things at our fingertips. We forget that we've all been deliberately designed to "end" one day. When that ending happens, there's nothing to fix. Optimism and a fighting spirit are good things, but at a certain point optimism becomes denial. It's important that patients be willing to fight when fighting is appropriate, but we will all face that moment in life when it is time to stop fighting, to stop treating death as the enemy. This is not giving up. It's accepting what is happening, riding the horse in the direction it's going. Once the final death process has started it cannot be stopped, any more than a woman in labor can be prevented from delivering her child.

We don't have to like what we accept. We think that to accept something is to somehow make it good or desirable. However, I think we can own our feelings, and accept what is happening. I believe individuals on their deathbed can honestly say: "I don't want to die," yet accept that they are dying.

Accepting that life is complete is perhaps the most difficult of the steps toward spirituality. We find it especially hard to accept death when it's "premature." People will say "he was so young" or "she never got to retire" or "there were so many things that he never got to do," as if those lives had been incomplete. From our vantage point, it often seems so. It's hard for us to accept that a five-year-old who dies from leukemia or a thirty-year-old felled by breast cancer has had a complete life. It's only when the deceased is eighty or ninety years old that we allow ourselves the peaceful feeling that they had a complete life.

Every life is complete. The only two requirements for a life to be complete are birth and death. People may say that life isn't complete without a family, or a career, or a certain number of years, but whether we like it or not, birth and death define a life. An eighteen-year-old with cystic fibrosis married a seventeen-year-old who also had the disease. Before she died a year later, she felt that she had had a complete life. A twelve-year-old boy with cancer said he wouldn't miss old age; he'd never planned on it. A forty-four-year-old man with AIDS said: "Many people with this disease die in their twenties. I accept that I've had many years of life." There may be things we wish had happened—more time, more opportunities, and more experiences. But their absence doesn't mean that a life was incomplete.

Gratitude—Having expressed one's feelings, taken responsibility for all that has occurred, forgiven oneself and others, and accepted what is now occurring, the person on a spiritual journey becomes profoundly grateful for his or her life, for both the good times and the bad.

Grateful for the bad times? Yes. Many women who were dumped by philandering husbands are grateful for the good times they had, for the children they produced together. A woman who had been cheated out of ten thousand dollars early in her business career was grateful, "for I learned a good lesson early on that only cost me ten thousand dollars, while most of my friends didn't learn it until much later and were hit a lot harder." Forty-two-year-old Mark, who lost his eyesight in an accident at age fifteen and was now dying of lymphoma, told me he remembered the colors. His favorite was blue. "Some are born blind. They have never seen blue. I am so thankful; I can still see it in my mind." And Eric's mother, who knew that she would soon bury her thirty-two-year-old son, his body shriveled and ravaged by AIDS, prayed to God, thanking Him for giving her such a beautiful boy and thirty-two years together.

Expression, responsibility, forgiveness, acceptance, and gratitude, all leading to reconciliation: These are the steps I've seen countless people take on the road to spirituality. And the peace they attain is medicine for their souls.

Questions

1. What are some of the different ways "spirituality" can be defined, according to Mr. Kessler? How would you define "spirituality"? How is "spirituality" different from "religion"?

2. Rewrite the five stages of spiritual reconciliation mentioned by Mr. Kessler, and identify the one stage you would have the hardest time with. Explain why.

3. What do you think is the best way to approach someone you love who is dying and wants to take up a spiritual practice that goes against your own religious beliefs? Explain your answer.

---

5 Maggie Callanan and Patricia Kelley, *Final Gifts*

Both Maggie Callanan and Patricia Kelley work as hospice nurses. Hospice nurses are trained in the various techniques of palliative medicine, which treat the effects of the disease but not the cause. Palliative medicine is designed to increase the comfort level of the patient once it has been realized that aggressive medical intervention is no longer feasible. Palliative treatment usually involves pain management medication and surgical protocols, but can also involve the use of antidepressants and other psychologically beneficial forms of medicine.

As hospice caregivers, nurses Callanan and Kelley came to discover that very often with dying patients, there are moments of genuine lucidity and profound insight as death approaches. They call this state "Nearing Death Awareness," a heightened experience of consciousness—despite the painkillers, despite the debilitating illness—that is somewhere on the border between life and death. Sometimes dying patients in their final moments are able realize the deep meaning of life, but they struggle to find a way to express this to loved ones. Sometimes these patients have hallucinatory visions—angels, rainbows, brilliant colors and lights, etc.—but are afraid to speak of their visions for fear of ridicule. Sometimes they face death with uncertainty and fear, and want to find some way to overcome those negative emotions.

In their best-selling book *Final Gifts,* Callanan and Kelley share their experiences with patients at this late stage in their lives, the stage of Nearing Death Awareness. What they tell us is that very often dying patients will try to communicate their needs, reveal their feelings, impart their wisdom, and even choreograph their final moments before they die. The nurses caution us that the best way to be with someone who is dying, therefore, is not to go in filled with your own needs, but to strive to listen to what the dying person wants to express. They offer the following list of practical suggestions:

- pay attention to everything the dying person says, however strange
- know that there is significance in any form of communication, however vague or garbled
- watch for key signs: a glassy-eyed stare, inappropriate smiles or gestures, waving at someone who is not there, efforts to get out of bed
- respond with open-ended inquires like, "Can you tell me what's happening?"
- don't push the conversation, but let the dying person control it
- if you don't know what to say, then don't say anything; sometimes the best response is simply to touch the dying person's hand or stroke his or her forehead

The following selection contains stories from *Final Gifts* of dying patients who experience what the authors call Nearing Death Awareness. Though the circumstances are different in each case, the message binding them together seems clear enough: that the dying person has tremendous spiritual needs which are often overlooked by all the focus on the physical side of their suffering. These needs demand to be met before the dying is free to depart in peace.

Andrea

Walking through the front door of Andrea's comfortable suburban home, I introduced myself.

"I have some questions to ask you," she said in a businesslike manner.

Her husband, Tom, stood behind her with a look of calm curiosity, holding the youngest of their three little children; the other two were sprawled out on the kitchen floor, busy with their coloring books.

"I need to know who you are," Andrea said to me as she put on a coffeepot. We sat together at the kitchen table as I briefly told her about my professional background.

"Why do you do this work?" she asked in the same direct, efficient manner. "Isn't it depressing?"

"That's a hard question to answer," I said. "The sadness and tragedy of somebody's dying is always there—I feel it, too. But beyond that is an opportunity for me to help a patient cherish the final chapter of her life, to use this time to resolve issues, say important things, finish unfinished business, and share important moments with people she cares about.

"My job is to keep my patients as comfortable as possible—not just physically—so they can do those things and use this special time the best way they can. I also feel strongly that, like birthing, dying can be an opportunity for the whole family to share positive experiences, rather than only sadness, pain, and loss. That is the challenge of this work, and that's the joy for me."

Andrea was quiet for a few minutes, then smiled and poured me another cup of coffee. I realized that I hadn't finished my "job interview" yet.

"I have uterine cancer, and have been told I'm dying," she said. "I want to know what it's going to be like."

I was amazed at the lack of fear in the eyes of this remarkable twenty-nine-year-old woman. And clearly it was not unusual for this couple to talk so openly with their young children present.

"I have never died," I said, "so I can't tell you from personal experience. But I have cared for dying people for many years now, so I can tell you what I've seen and what they've told me."

"Great!" she said. "I'd like to hear about that!"

I started by telling her of the physical changes that were common with her disease: loss of appetite, with resulting weight loss, weakness, some pain, and possibly some mild nausea.

I explained how we would try to control the various discomforts she might develop, using diet changes and medications. I explained she probably would experience increasing sleepiness and dreaminess—perhaps some confusion toward the end—leading to a brief coma before she died. She probably would die of liver failure, but with proper symptom control we would be able to keep her comfortable.

"Okay, that's what's going to happen to my body," she said. "But what's going to happen to *me*?"

She was curious and amazed when I told her about Nearing Death Awareness—that other patients had talked of being with someone who had died already, getting ready to leave, seeing where they were going, and knowing when it would happen. I told her they also showed us they were not powerless in this process, and were often able to tell us what they needed to die peacefully, and even choose the actual time they died.

I assured Andrea that in all my experience, with rare exception, I hadn't seen painful or frightening deaths. She seemed surprised and relieved.

I gave Andrea a copy of Dr. Raymond Moody's book, *Life After Life,* which describes near-death experiences, suggesting that she might get additional information from it.

I explained that although she might have near-death experiences, as she got closer to dying her experiences probably would be different from these, possibly much slower and more gradual, and she might be able to share them with the people around her as they actually happened. She was very excited about this.

The conversation had taken two hours and the day was quickly disappearing.

"I was *supposed* to tell you about the hospice program and how it could be of help to you!" I said. We laughed.

"You've told me what I really needed to know," she said. "When will you come back?"

On my next visit, Andrea greeted me at the door; she was excited.

"Tom and I read the book together," she said. "It was so helpful; we read parts of it to the kids. If that's what dying is like, I think I can do it!"

I was touched by her remark—"I think I can do it!" Not "I want to," but "If I have to, I think I can!" This information clearly helped Andrea feel less frightened and powerless about dying.

"I'm fascinated," she said. 'This information has really helped me. So I want to help you any way I can, so you can help others. I tell you what, if any of these things happen to me, I *promise* to tell you all about it. Okay?" So we had a pact early in our relationship.

Being involved with Andrea, Tom, and their young children was a delight. Their openness, desire for honesty, and ability to work out difficulties as a family amazed me. I applauded them for involving the children in all that was done or discussed, as I knew it would play a major role in how well they would deal with this tragedy now, and the process of grieving later.

"We've always included them," Andrea said. "We believe honesty is the best policy with kids. But, even if we didn't, how could we have a private conversation with three kids under the age of seven underfoot?" She laughed.

I asked how the kids had reacted to the book.

"They thought it was neat," Andrea said. "Lisa said it sounded like magic!"

One day I arrived to find Andrea in tears, silently sitting on the living-room floor, surrounded by three grocery bags—one for each child.

"These are the kids' baby books," she said. "I never had time to put them together properly."

"Look at my beautiful babies!" she said, handing me some pictures. "How I *hate* having to leave them! I'm afraid they'll forget me, so I want each one to have something special to remember me by. Would you help me? It's too hard for Tom to do."

I sat on the floor with her. Together we cried, shared the tissues, and started working on three little books, each titled "Mommy and Me." I felt drained by sadness but filled with admiration for this beautiful young mother.

Three weeks later, I happened to be driving through Andrea's neighborhood. Her routine visit wasn't scheduled, but my day had ended early; having some extra time I decided to stop by. Andrea met me at the door, looking very pale but pleased to see me.

"What a surprise!" she said. "I was just thinking about you. Come on in!"

She started to sway as if dizzy.

"I'm going to be sick," she mumbled.

I grabbed her arm as she stumbled past me to the bathroom. I shouted for Tom to come quickly as Andrea fainted in my arms. Awkwardly we lowered her to the floor. She was hemorrhaging.

Tom was panic-stricken.

"Don't tell me this is it!" he said. "Isn't there anything we can do?"

"They may be able to reverse this with aggressive treatment in the hospital," I said. "Or we can keep her comfortable here at home. But if she loses too much blood, she'll die very soon. Andrea said she didn't want any more treatment for the cancer, but what do you think she'd want us to do in this situation?"

"It's too sudden!" he said. "She's not ready yet—and neither are we." He started sobbing. "There are things she wants to finish for the kids. And she'd just started helping me figure out the family finances. If it's possible to buy a little more time—I think we need it—she'd want us to try."

We called the ambulance. Andrea was admitted to the hospital Intensive Care Unit, where she responded to treatments and blood transfusions, finally regaining consciousness. I was allowed in to see her.

"Andrea, I'm so glad you're feeling better," I said. "We all had quite a scare!"

She reached for my hand and held it very tightly.

Remembering the look on her face before she became unconscious, I suspected Andrea had experiences we couldn't see, and felt sure she'd share those with me if she could.

"Did anything happen?" I asked. I could see her struggle to put her thoughts into words. It's impossible to describe the look in her eyes as she stared intently at me. Awe? Wonder? Amazement?

"Did something good happen?" I asked.

"Yes," she murmured. "Oh yes!"

"Can you tell me anything about it—even just a word?" I asked.

"I can't," she whispered. "I just can't!" She slowly shook her head.

"Don't worry," I said. "It's okay—maybe later. I'm just so glad you're back and it was a good experience for you."

Andrea never was able to describe what happened to her that day, but there was a peace and tranquility about her that was felt by all around her.

"Andrea puts on a brave front to protect others from her pain and fears," Tom said a few weeks later. 'That's her way of making it easy for them. Every now and then she'll let me hold her and we cry about what's happening to us, but not too often."

"She won't say anything, but I know she's hurt about the way my father has acted," he continued. "The two of them became pretty close after her parents died. I think she and Pop really love each other. He's not much of a talker, but they got along great, anyway."

"After he retired and my mother died, he'd come by every day to help Andrea with the kids. But that was *before* she got sick."

"When we told him about her cancer, he flew into a rage, shouting at both of us. We were speechless and it really upset the children.

"Give him time," Andrea told me. "He needs to work this out on his own. He's just too upset right now." There was an angry edge in Tom's voice.

"Well, time turned into weeks and things didn't get better," he said. "Pop stopped by occasionally, but didn't stay long and was gruff and abrupt. I came home from work after one of his visits and found Andrea in tears. "I feel like he's angry at *me* because I might die and leave you stuck to raise these kids alone," she sobbed. "Does he think I would *choose* this to happen?"

"Let me tell you," Tom said, "I could've killed him on the spot! I grabbed that phone so fast and called him. "Damn it," I shouted, "we've got enough going on without putting up with you, too!"—and slammed the phone down. We haven't seen him since. It's so unlike him. How can he be so cruel?"

Judging from the description of Pop's behavior before Andrea's diagnosis, I suggested that perhaps his father actually loved Andrea so much he couldn't deal with losing her—or face the changes that were happening.

"You and Andrea have met our social worker," I said. "I feel certain he could help with this problem. I truly think Pop's suffering a lot of emotional pain himself right now."

"You're right!" Tom said. "The social worker has been real helpful. Maybe he could talk to Pop. I'd rather not deal with him myself."

Our social worker visited Pop and reported that he was so devastated about Andrea's illness that he was overwhelmed by rage, grief, and fear. "How can something like this happen?" he'd said. "I don't know what to say! I don't know what to do! Andrea acts so brave. I'm afraid I'll lose control and break down every time I look at her. I love her so much; she's the daughter I never had. Then I look at those babies and I just can't bear it—she's such a good mother—what will become of them? How can Tom possibly manage all this and support his family, too?"

The social worker visited regularly and was able to help Pop begin to recognize his feelings and confront his fears. But we all felt a sense of urgency for this reconciliation to take place, as Andrea was now deteriorating rapidly.

She'd been able to finish the financial work she'd started with Tom and the books she lovingly made for each of her children. She had hired a woman to care for the kids while Tom was working. And as though knowing that her work was done, she seemed to just "let go."

Andrea was in bed all the time now, so I suggested a hospital bed might be easier.

"We don't want one," Tom said. "There won't be room for me and the kids in a hospital bed!"

Too weak to participate in any of her care, Andrea slept most of the time and had increasing periods of restlessness and confusion. But a clear and insistent phrase in her incoherent ramblings was "We *must* go to the park." I asked Tom what that might mean. I was concerned that her restlessness indicated that something was making her uncomfortable.

"She and Pop used to take the kids to the park all the time," he said. "It's Pop she's waiting for—I'm certain! She's suffered long enough; I'm going to get him and bring him here right now, whether he's ready to come now or not!"

Eyes blurred with tears, Pop could barely navigate the stairs of his son's home. When he saw Andrea, he exploded into sobs, cradling her in his arms.

"I'm here, sweetheart, I'm here," he said. "I'm so sorry. Please forgive me. I love you so much! I'll never stay away again. I'll come every day. I promise!" Andrea's eyelids fluttered as she barely whispered, "Pop."

"Could I stay here tonight?" Pop asked.

"Yes, we'd like that," Tom said.

Andrea died peacefully that evening, in their king-sized bed, surrounded by Tom, her children, and Pop.

Moments after I arrived, Tom told me that, as Andrea was dying, their daughter Lisa—who must have remembered the descriptions of leaving the body as part of Near-Death Experiences described in the book they'd read—looked up to the ceiling and, waving, called out, "Bye, Mom. We love you! Have a good magic trip and don't forget to save us front-row seats in Heaven!"

Theresa

Theresa, twenty-two, was dying of bone cancer. She was the younger of two children, abandoned by their father when she was five. Though he lived nearby, the father had had little contact with his son and daughter over the years, and had contributed nothing toward their upbringing. Theresa lived with her mother, who took care of her; her brother, who lived nearby, visited frequently and did what he could to help.

During my first visit, Theresa and her mother described the father as "that man," not "my father," or "my ex-husband." I asked if Theresa wanted to see him. She said that since they had no relationship she didn't feel any need to do so.

Theresa's biggest problems were pain and weight loss. As often happens with young people, whose metabolisms run faster than those of older people, Theresa's pain required fairly large doses of pain medicine. We tried other pain-relieving techniques also: Theresa found meditation and music particularly helpful, and we instituted a regular schedule for those.

The weight loss was difficult for her mother to see. Theresa was five feet seven, and had always been slim. But now she ate very little and refused all dietary supplements. As she became weaker and spent more time in bed, her mother had to turn her from side to side every few hours to prevent bedsores.

Four months after admission into our program Theresa was dying. Her pain became increasingly severe; the dosage of her pain medicines had risen accordingly. We thought her physical pain was controlled, but still she moaned. We asked what the matter was, but couldn't get an answer; her speech was difficult to understand. Several times her mother asked me how Theresa could still be alive.

But one day, mixed in among a jumble of words, she said, "Dad."

We wondered if she wanted to see her father. We asked her, but her response was unintelligible, a few words lost in another moan. Her mother felt it was worth a try. She telephoned the father and explained what was happening.

That afternoon Theresa's brother picked up the father and brought him to the apartment.

He went into the bedroom, sat beside Theresa, held her hand, and told her he was there. He said no more. He looked shaken and upset, but also stiff and uncomfortable. After a few minutes he stood.

"I can't take this," he said, leaving the room and saying an awkward farewell.

But Theresa's moaning stopped, her agitation eased, and she died quietly a few hours later. No one can say that her estranged father's visit was what Theresa

needed for a peaceful death. But the only circumstance making that day different from those preceding it was his presence. Her mother and brother feel that in some way Theresa needed something from her father, and that after his visit she was able to let go and die.

Theresa realized very late that she needed to see her father; her weakened condition kept her from being able to communicate intelligibly. Any delay in getting her father to come arose from our difficulty in understanding her; finding and bringing her father to see her was easy. Sometimes it can be hard to find the important person, which can lead to much frustration.

Sheila

In a thick brogue Sheila's nephew described her background during my first visit.

"She had great promise," he said. "But with so little in the way of opportunity for such a girl in the old country, her family pooled their meager resources and sent her to America. The poor little thing was an innocent wisp of a girl. Traveling alone at eighteen, she sailed to this country in steerage: they were packed in like animals. It's a wonder she survived the trip."

Like so many Irish girls of her generation, Sheila immigrated to America, worked as a maid, sent money home, and lived a lonely life—until she met a boy and fell in love. The love didn't last, but the daughter born of it did, and Sheila found herself out on the street, struggling to keep herself and her infant daughter, Maureen, alive.

"Those were hard days," the nephew said. "Until Sheila met Mr. O'Malley, a farmer. He's years older, but a hard-working man, and has provided well for her all these years. He's never had any use for Maureen, though, because she's illegitimate. He sent her to boarding school when she was seven, and allowed her home to visit only twice a year."

"Where is Maureen now?" I asked.

"Maureen turned out to be a good-for-nothing, and no one knows her whereabouts," he said. "It's like a knife in poor Sheila's heart, but she never mentions her name. It's like she's dead!"

Despite their fifty-five-year marriage, Sheila always referred to her husband as "Mr. O'Malley" or "himself." He was a man of few words and gruff by nature, but surprisingly active and strong for a man in his eighties, doing the daily chores around their farm. Their relationship did not seem to be a warm and affectionate one, but rather one of quiet dependency, or perhaps comfortable tolerance. What care Mr. O'Malley was unable to give Sheila was provided by the live-in help he'd hired.

Sheila was dying at home of uterine cancer. As her condition deteriorated, she became more and more depressed and quiet—often refusing to eat, instead just staring off into space sadly.

"I want this to be done," she'd say, but lingered on as if waiting for something.

"Sheila, it seems like you're waiting for something," I said. "Is it Maureen?"

Sheila's eyes filled with tears. She waved her hand as though pushing the conversation away, rolled onto her side, and closed her eyes.

She battled one complication after another: in her weakened condition, she seemed likely to die with each problem. But she hung on, and the hospice team members discussed their sense that Sheila was waiting to see someone before she died—probably Maureen.

The chaplain, the social worker, and I visited one day, hoping that together we could discuss our concern with Mr. O'Malley. Was there some way to determine Maureen's whereabouts and notify her that her mother was dying and needed to see her?

"There'll be no such talk in this house!" Mr. O'Malley shouted, becoming irate. "That girl's been nothing but heartache and trouble since the day she was born. I won't hear of it!" he roared, waving his cane around as he stormed out the back door.

But within the week Sheila's cousin Eileen timidly called the chaplain to report that some months before Maureen had sent her a letter postmarked in Florida with her return address. In the letter Maureen asked how her mother was, explaining that she had written many times and never received an answer. She went on to say that she knew she had caused her mother great sorrow, but was now in an alcoholic-treatment program and was trying to pick up the pieces of her life. She wanted her mother to be given the message that she loved her and was sorry for having caused so much trouble.

Eileen knew Sheila relied on Mr. O'Malley to read the mail to her and suspected he had hidden Maureen's letters. She felt guilty for not giving Maureen's message to Sheila, but was afraid to deal with Mr. O'Malley's wrath. "He's a fierce man, that one!" she said.

Eileen told the chaplain about Maureen's harsh upbringing and of Sheila's timidity in the face of her husband's domineering personality. The last thread between Sheila and her daughter was broken when, after running away from school, Maureen became a hippie, and came home to ask for money. Her stepfather threw her out, threatening to call the police if she ever returned.

"Sheila's heart was broken," Eileen said, sadly. "She never saw Maureen again, nor did she mention her name. That was almost twenty years ago. We heard she'd married and had two children, but divorced and lost custody of them because of her drinking."

The next day, I went with the chaplain as he confronted Mr. O'Malley with this information. He became angry and defensive.

"It's a husband's job to protect his wife!" he stormed. In a gentle, kind way, the chaplain then explained to Sheila what had happened. She defiantly looked her husband straight in the eye.

"O'Malley, you're the devil himself!" she said. With that he threw a handful of letters on her bed and stormed out. They were all from Maureen. The chaplain read them as tears rolled down Sheila's thin cheeks.

"Bring her to me!" she pleaded.

Needing to maintain his lifetime pattern of control over others, Mr. O'Malley refused to pay for Maureen's airplane ticket, or allow her to sleep in his home, but other relatives chipped in for the ticket and provided her with a place to stay.

Sheila was too weak to get out of bed, sleeping most of the time, but on the day her daughter arrived, she was alert and bright with anticipation. Maureen indeed showed the signs of many years of self-abuse, but there wasn't a dry eye in the room when Maureen rushed into her mother's arms. They wept silently, holding each other for what seemed like hours. Mr. O'Malley spent the day in the barn with his animals.

Maureen spent as much time with her mother as Mr. O'Malley would permit; each day he seemed to allow a little more. She bathed her mother, massaged her feet with lotion, and gently brushed her long white hair. She sat for hours, patiently spoon-feeding the dying woman puddings and applesauce. It was a close and tender time for both of them.

Finally one day Mr. O'Malley announced, "You can stay here tonight if you wish." Maureen sat by her mother's bed all that night, humming the songs she remembered Sheila singing to her when she was a small child. Sheila peacefully drifted off to sleep, quietly slipped into a coma, and died at dawn with Maureen holding her hand.

The hospice chaplain took up a collection so Maureen could buy a nice dress for her mother's funeral. Despite her sorrow, Maureen looked younger and healthier than she had, when she arrived only three weeks before.

Another theme that recurs is reconciliation with a supreme being. Those who belong to a religious congregation often want the support, prayers, and blessings of that community as they prepare for death. But the same need may occur in people not committed to an organized religion, in those who disavow the spiritual, and in those who have lost whatever faith they once might have had.

Arthur

Arthur had had cancer for years, but had responded well to treatment. Now the cancer was active again and he was dying slowly in his small, neat apartment. He lived alone and had no relatives; his wife had died five years before. He had married her soon after his first wife left him—an event that began his drift away from the Episcopal faith in which he'd been raised. It had been decades since he'd set foot in a church.

"God and I have a good relationship," he'd say. "We don't need any go-between."

Arthur kept his condition to himself; he didn't want to burden his friends by asking for help, and resisted offers of assistance, from friends or professionals. He contacted the hospice because his doctor had suggested a nursing home, and the manager of his apartment building had explained how hospice helps to keep people at home. He was wary that we too would push him toward an institution, but once he knew us better, he was pleased to see any of the hospice staff.

"I like you people," he'd say. "You come and check on me, show me how to feel better, and then you go away and leave me alone!"

As he got sicker, we urged him to let us arrange for someone to be with him, especially at night. He refused until he became so weak that we thought it was no longer safe for him to be alone, and persuaded him to have a nurse stay at night.

By now Arthur had a partial bowel obstruction that caused pain, which we relieved with injections every few hours. He could tolerate little more than sips of water or dietary supplements, and often vomited. Even so, he insisted that he wanted to be at home, with as little attention as possible.

One afternoon the hospice doctor visited to check Arthur's condition. As she was getting ready to leave, he said, "Would you pray with me, please?"

The doctor held Arthur's hand and said a prayer, then asked if he needed anything else.

"Would it be too much trouble to have a priest come to see me?" Arthur asked.

"Of course not," she said. "Do you want to see one tonight?"

"No, not tonight," Arthur said. "Tomorrow would be fine."

The next morning I brought an Episcopal priest with me. A friendly man in his early thirties, he greeted Arthur warmly. I checked Arthur's vital signs, then left, telling him I'd complete my nursing visit later that day. When I returned he thanked me for bringing the clergyman by.

"He stayed for an hour or so, and I really enjoyed it," Arthur said. "I can't believe how much better I feel. We talked, he said the prayers of absolution, and he anointed me with oil. It's strange; nothing has really changed, but I feel much easier."

That evening the priest returned, bringing Arthur communion. Afterward they prayed together, then talked for a while, sipping whiskeys. Arthur died quietly in his sleep early the next morning.

His condition had led us to expect Arthur to die for more than two weeks. The day before he died, there were no significant physical changes; the only difference was his interaction with the clergyman. We think Arthur died that night because the priest had helped him become reconciled to a church with which he had once had strong ties.

Arthur's request was straightforward—he simply asked to see a priest. When the request is not as clear it may take onlookers longer to understand, and this can lead to great frustration or anguish for the one dying.

Gus

As strange as it may seem to others, those of us who work with dying people become accustomed to the physical changes that are so often distressing to see. The profound weight loss experienced by many dying people can be a very upsetting symptom for family and friends. But as we get to know these patients they become beautiful in our eyes, despite their frail and chiseled appearance.

My immediate reaction when Gus answered the door for my first visit was that I had the wrong apartment. Here was a tall, handsome, well-nourished man in his early fifties, certainly not thin or frail-looking. Except for the molded neck brace that held his head rigid, he looked healthy.

"How about a beer?" he said. "It's almost noon! I never drink before noon! But, damn, I don't get up until eleven-thirty!" He laughed heartily.

I was beginning to realize that Gus had a strong will and enjoyed being a tease. He especially delighted in using rough language.

Gus's cancer was dangerously near the spinal cord in his neck. Considering his medical report, I was amazed to see that he was so functional.

"I'm on sick leave from the precinct," Gus said. "The captain is pushing me to go on disability leave, but no ways I can still work. By the way, my ex-wife wants you to call her. She just lives two blocks away."

His ex-wife, Kim, asked to meet me at the local fast-food restaurant.

"I divorced Gus six years ago," she said. "I love the man, but I couldn't take it. He was crazy about being a Marine and just couldn't get enough combat. He requested assignment to Vietnam THREE times! Can you believe that? And I was left alone with the kids. While he was there, he was exposed to Agent Orange, and we suspect that's how he got the cancers.

"After his last tour, I had my little boy," she said, her eyes filling with tears. "He died from birth defects when he was only three months old. Gus dealt with that by partying and drinking more. He quit the Marines and joined the police, asking to work in the worst precinct in the city as an undercover cop. That was the last straw. I was just plain worn out—always living on the edge of danger and crisis. I had my kids to think about. But we live real close and the kids see him regularly.

"Then he got the cancer," she said. "The treatments were hard on him, but he's a tough guy and insisted on as much as he could possibly have done. The doctor says he's terminal now, but he won't believe it! I go over every day to check on him; I need to help him through this for the kids—they're too young to be losing their dad. I guess I'm doing it a little bit for me, too. I do love him, I just can't live with him. I don't know how we're going to get through this. But however we do, it will be his way, I can tell you that!"

Gus continued to be his strong, independent, and colorful self for a few weeks, enjoying his beer and playing cards with his buddies. Then the cancer grew into his spinal cord and he quickly became paralyzed, bedridden, and confused. Private-duty nurses were put in to help Kim and his family take care of him. He was comfortable, but it was clear that he was dying quickly.

I received an urgent call from the nurse on duty.

"Please get out here fast," she said. "Everything seemed to be going okay but now he's very confused and anxious, and we're losing it."

"No, I bet we're finally getting it," I thought to myself. I had wondered how long Gus would be able to keep up the tough-guy facade. I felt there must be times he felt frightened—even if he wouldn't talk about it or allow his fear to show.

The scene was chaotic. Gus was crying out in anguish; his speech was so disjointed it was hard to make any sense of it. But in his confused language were the words "villages," "babies," "napalm," "burning"—and the tragic words "I did it, I did it!" In the middle of this swirling jumble was the sentence "I need religious integrity!"

Gus had been clear on my first visit that he was raised in a churchgoing family, but religion had not been important to him in his adult life. However he did enjoy a few visits from the hospice chaplain, so I called him.

"Can you come quickly?" I asked. "I think you are the one who can fix this."

Kim, the children, and Gus's parents and brothers were all there when the chaplain arrived. We sat together in the kitchen so the chaplain could talk with Gus privately. Minutes passed; and slowly the cries stopped. The house became peaceful. The chaplain called the family into the bedroom.

For a few moments, Gus became very clear. He looked around at each of us, then at the chaplain, seemingly surprised at this gathering.

"Am I dying?" he asked the chaplain, who was holding his hand.

"Yes, Gus, barring a miracle, we think you are," he answered gently.

Gus looked the clergyman straight in the eye and thought for a long moment.

"Aw, shit!" he said.

The family spent the next few hours with Gus, caressing him and reminiscing about happier times together, as he quietly slipped into a coma and died.

Perhaps this story doesn't sound like a triumph, but for Gus to have died experiencing the anguish of the unspeakable things he had done in Vietnam would have been a tragedy. His only request for help easily could have been missed, buried as it was in a jumble of confused cries. It would have been easier to sedate him until the cries stopped. But whose needs would have been met—those of the observers, who were having to deal with the discomfort of watching Gus's anguish, or Gus, who needed to be forgiven so he could die peacefully?

Questions

1. Which of the five stories did you find most interesting, and why?

2. Write out three "life lessons" one can learn from these stories. Explain how these 'life lessons' can be applied to your own life, and to the lives of your loved ones.

3. Write out a list of the reconciliation issues you would want to work on if you knew you were dying. Whom would you want to see, and what would you want to say to them? What in your past would you want to ask forgiveness for? What final words would you most want to say to those you love?

---

6 Thomas Attig, *Relearning Our World*

Thomas Attig received his bachelor's degree in philosophy from Northwestern University in 1967 and his M.A. and Ph.D. in philosophy from Washington University in St. Louis. He taught philosophy at Bowling Green State University for twenty-four years, serving as department chair for eleven years and leading efforts to establish the world's first Ph.D. in applied philosophy in 1987. Tom left as professor emeritus in philosophy in 1995 to become an independent applied philosopher. A past president of the Association for Death Education and Counseling, he also served as vice-chair of the board of directors of the International Work Group on Death, Dying, and Bereavement.

Dr. Attig has written two well-received books on the subject of grief and bereavement: *The Heart of Grief: Death and the Search for Lasting Love* and *How We Grieve: Relearning Our World,* both with Oxford University Press, in addition to numerous articles and reviews on grief and loss, care of the dying, suicide intervention, death education, expert witnessing in wrongful death cases, the ethics of interactions with the dying, and the nature of applied philosophy. Attig is also active as a speaker and conference leader, having offered programs across the United States and Canada, and in England, Australia, Israel, and Germany, as well as numerous talks and workshops for nurses, physicians, funeral directors, clinical psychologists, social service providers, gerontologists, hospice workers, bereavement coordinators, clergy, educators, civic organizations, and the general public.

This passage, taken from the concluding chapter of *How We Grieve*, narrates Attig's grief-coping emphasis on the idea of "relearning our world" after a loved one has died. Dr. Attig states that death need not sever our relationship to the departed; instead, we can find new ways of relating to him or her which respect both the relationship and the reality of their no longer being present. The death of a loved one can radically change the world we live in. But, as Attig asserts, if we actively learn to adapt to this new world, we can go a long way toward overcoming the more devastating effects of our grief.

Advantages of the Idea of Relearning Our Relationships with the Deceased

The Idea Provides Understanding

Those of us who desire it can find a dynamic, life-affirming, life-promoting, enriching, and, most often, loving connection with those who have died. We can reintegrate our relationships with the deceased into a new personal wholeness in all the ways that I discussed in Chapter 5: We can incorporate caring about the deceased as a person in his or her own right, and caring about what the deceased cared about, into our newly coherent daily lives. We can reinterpret and reshape our life stories as we revert to, appreciate the values of, reinterpret the meanings of, accept the influence of, and take inspiration from the stories of, those we have cared about and loved. As we maintain our relationships, we can derive meaning and purpose from an abiding self-transcending connection.

This understanding allows us to reinterpret several aspects of our experiences as survivors. Part of what we do when we relearn the world is learn how to sustain a loving connection with the dead or disentangle ourselves from the destructive negative legacies of our unhappy but still binding relationships. We must relinquish our concrete loving of the presence of those we have cared about and replace it with abstract loving in separation; our yearning and searching reflect the pain of letting go of the physical attachment. That we must experience this pain does not mean that we must let go entirely of all attachment to the deceased. Finding a way to love without physical presence can help us move from dwelling in this pain to carrying it as a far less pervasive aspect of our lives. We must overcome the emotionally crippling effects of dependence, possessiveness, and other dysfunctional aspects of our relationships if we are to progress as we grieve and make the transition to loving in separation (or, in some cases, to disentangle altogether).

When we are bereaved, we may fear both letting go of those who have died and losing ourselves in the past if we do not let go. Completely severing our relationships with the dead is unnecessary, though the fixity of, for example, dependence or possessiveness is undesirable. As we come to understand the life-affirming potential of loving in separation, we can overcome our fear of morbidity, and our common, and often fervent, desire to remain linked to the dead can be validated.

The Idea Promotes Respect for Individuality

No two of our relationships are identical. We communicate in distinct ways; cooperate and interact distinctively in daily life; share unique memories, present experiences, hopes, and aspirations; interweave our life histories in idiosyncratic ways; develop personal understandings of ourselves and others; realize values and find meanings unique to the relationships; experience ambivalence; and accumulate personal unfinished business. In all of these ways, and in others, the deceased, when alive, found distinctive places in our daily life patterns, personal life histories, and sense of connectedness. Respect for our individuality when we grieve requires that others appreciate the significance of each of these aspects of our relationship with the deceased as it is affected by the death.

No two of us relearn our relationship with the deceased by meeting identical challenges. Reintegration of our relationships within our present living, in understanding of our individual autobiographies, and in our new patterns of self-transcending connection demands different things of each of us. Each of us takes a distinctive course, and, as we do so, the deceased finds a unique place in each of our lives as our losses and grieving transform them.

The Idea Addresses Our Helplessness

As I first noted in Chapter 2, extreme grief can cripple and even paralyze us. In it we experience the futility of our desire to have the person we loved (or, for that matter, hated) returned in living presence. Dwelling in extreme grief makes us helpless and powerless. Still, some of us remain in extreme grief in part out of fear that if we let go of the desire for the deceased's physical return, that will end our loving. It is possible to interact meaningfully with the deceased in their absence, love them, have and hold them dear, without dwelling in extreme grief. Understanding this can help us overcome the fear of relinquishing our desire for the return of the deceased that can hold us in the emotion grief and free us actively to relearn ourselves and our worlds.

We can continue to "have" what we have "lost," that is, a continuing, albeit transformed, love for the deceased. We have not truly lost our years of living with the deceased or our memories. Nor have we lost the influences, the inspirations, the values, and the meanings embodied in their lives. We can actively incorporate these into new patterns of living that include transformed but abiding relationships with those we have cared about and loved. This understanding can motivate and support our return to dynamic, life-affirming living in which the gift of the life of the deceased continues to give and to be appreciated by us.

The Idea Provides Guidance for Caregivers

As caregivers, we can be with the bereaved as they experience and express the anguish of letting go of the concrete reality of the dead. We can listen patiently and understandingly to the pain at the loss of presence, offer comfort and support and give it when it is welcomed. But we need not, and indeed should not, encourage complete letting go of the deceased. We can reassure the bereaved that the desire for a continuing relationship with the deceased is normal and not necessarily, or even usually, morbid. We can support and nurture their potential for continued, albeit transformed, loving of the deceased by sharing memories and stories of our own as they are available.

We can support and encourage others as they grieve to remember and explore the narrative of the life now ended for its sustaining value and meaning. Here we can encourage retelling of the stories of the lives lived and treasured. Retelling makes the lives real and freshens and enlivens memory. We can encourage retelling during the funeral period. We can encourage grieving persons to establish times and places to revisit the story, such as birthdays, anniversaries, or holidays, in a quiet place at home, at a place of worship, or at a graveside. We can encourage them to keep a diary or journal as a means of accumulating a fuller record of cherished memories. We can support them as they record their and others' memories on audio or videotape, or we can encourage them to write pieces about their most unforgettable experiences with the deceased.

We can promote and encourage grieving persons to fill in details of the lives as they may be available from diverse sources. When the death is anticipated, we can encourage life review with those who are dying before death comes. We can encourage those who grieve to invite others to share details of the stories during visitation, at funerals or memorial services, or later. Many who grieve long for the reassurance this provides that others, too, cared for the deceased. We can encourage them to seek out and informally interview persons to draw from them aspects of the lives of the deceased that they may not know, as Colleen did. We can encourage them to solicit letters or stories from others, as Kathryn did, or to engage in the equivalent of genealogical research. We can encourage them to establish occasions for sharing the story, for example, at anniversary, birthday, or holiday gatherings.

We can encourage those who grieve to continue to explore the diverse aesthetic, ethical, and religious meanings, influences, and inspirations embodied in the stories of the lives now ended. We can encourage them to extend diary writing or journal keeping beyond simple record keeping to include reflections on why the lives of the deceased are so memorable, what they cherish in them, or how they are better for having known the deceased. In an aesthetic way of caring, we can encourage them to appreciate the interest of the story, the joys, delight, laughter, tears, and fascination it arouses in them and its provocative, curious, mysterious, and perhaps even tragic aspects.

Caring in an ethical framework, we can encourage those who grieve to appreciate the moral dimension and significance of the stories. We can explore with them ways of meeting any responsibilities they feel they now have because they knew the deceased. We can support them as they mull over how to find ways of going on that reflect commitments inspired by, values instilled by, or promises and covenants entered into with the deceased. We can support them as they find new resolve and give new direction to their lives in ways that the deceased inspired.

Last, to demonstrate our caring in a religious context, we can encourage those who grieve to appreciate the spiritual and religious dimensions of the stories now ended, including the transcendence of others, the wonder and awe of standing before the independent reality of the deceased, and the challenges that the deceased's separate lives continue to present to those who survive them. We can encourage them to reflect on the abiding meaning of the lives now ended, which are not canceled by death. We can invite them to consider how they may continue in dialogue with the deceased, how they may continue to be affected by the gift of knowing them. We can support them as they struggle to forgive the deceased for their limitations and fallibility. We can encourage prayers of grace, in which they express gratitude for the privilege of knowing and being a part of the stories; prayers of confession, in which they seek self-forgiveness for what they perceive to be failings in interaction with the deceased; and prayers of supplication, in which they seek to arouse a renewal of hope, motivation, resolve, and rededication in terms of a continuing loving relationship with the deceased.

As caregivers, we can help those who grieve to discern ways in which they can continue to care about what those who died cared about. We can support them in sustaining dynamic, nonobsessive loving connectedness with the deceased by living in terms of those cares. We can also support them as they attempt to disentangle themselves from any destructive, fixating, and dysfunctional connections that may remain. We can use concrete objects and mementos to help them make the transition from concrete relation in presence to abstract relation in absence. We can relieve their guilt over

new involvements in projects or relationships by urging them to explore whether the deceased's love for them included a desire that they continue to live fully and to flourish. We can help survivors discern what has not been lost of the value and meaning of the lives of those who have died and continue to treasure the gifts of the lives of the deceased that are still theirs. We can motivate them actively to relearn their worlds and to let go of extreme grief emotion by bringing this end into view—the goal of recovering the fruits of the lives now ended.

Questions

1. Describe what Dr. Attig means by the idea of "relearning our relationships with the deceased." Offer a critical assessment of this idea.

2. How does this idea of "relearning our relationships with the deceased" help us when we want to offer care and comfort to someone in grief?

3. Describe three or four practical ways in which one can "relearn our relationship with the deceased" following a tragic death.

---

7 Elisabeth Kübler-Ross, *On Life and Living*

We have introduced you before the Dr. Elisabeth Kübler-Ross, the pioneer of death studies in America whose writings became the catalyst for major, positive changes in the way the American medical establishment treats dying patients. It seems fitting here, at the end of the book, to give Dr. Kübler-Ross the final word. We have chosen a passage from her autobiographical book, *The Wheel of Life*. Dr. Kübler-Ross had suffered a series of debilitating strokes, and in 1997, at the age of 71, she began writing out her final thoughts about life.

Dr. Kübler-Ross devoted her entire professional career to the study of death and its significance for the living of life, and discovered many new and lasting insights. In more recent years, Dr. Kübler-Ross devoted her attention to more spiritual themes, especially the kind of awakening of consciousness some experience as they approach death, a mental state that Maggie Callanan and Patricia Kelley describe in their book, *Final Gifts,* as "nearing death awareness." Dr. Kübler-Ross herself was convinced that every individual life has a great purpose, that our sense of satisfaction with life is dependent on finding that purpose, and that "there are no accidents." She also believed that we will find clues as we make our way through life that can keep us on the right path, and that we have spiritual guides—she called them "my spooks"!—who remind us of our true calling in life. In the passage that follows, you will read of Dr. Kübler-Ross's summary of these insights as she outlines, her philosophy of life and death.

It is just like me to have already planned what will happen. My family and friends will arrive from all parts of the world, wend their way through the desert until they come upon a tiny white sign planted in a dirt road that says *Elisabeth,* and then drive until they reach the Indian tepee and the Swiss flag that stands high above my Scottsdale home. Some will be grieving. Others will know how relieved and happy I finally am. They will eat, trade stories, laugh, cry and at some point release dozens of helium-filled balloons that look like E.T. into the blue sky. Of course, I will be dead.

But why not throw a going-away party? Why not celebrate? At seventy-one years old, I can say that I have truly lived. After starting out as a "two-pound nothing" who was not expected to survive, I spent most of my life battling the Goliath-sized forces of ignorance and fear. Anyone familiar with my work knows that I believe death can be one of life's greatest experiences. Anyone who knows me personally can testify to how impatiently I have been awaiting the transition from the pain and struggle of this world to an existence of complete and overwhelming love.

It has not come easily, this final lesson of patience. For the past two years, I have—thanks to a series of strokes—been totally dependent on others for the most

basic care. Every day is spent struggling to get from bed to a chair to the bathroom and then back again. My only wish has been to leave my body, like a butterfly shedding its cocoon, and finally merge with the great light. My spooks have reiterated the importance of making time my friend. I know that the day that will end my life in this form, in this body, will be the day when I have learned that kind of acceptance.

The only benefit of making such a slow approach to life's final passage has been the time it offers for contemplation. I suppose it is appropriate that after counseling so many dying patients I should have time to reflect on death now that the one I face is my own. There is a poetry to it, a slight tension, like a pause in a courtroom drama where the defendant is given the chance to confess. Fortunately, I have nothing new to admit. My death will come to me like a warm embrace. As I have long said, life in a physical body is a very short span of one's total existence.

When we have passed the tests we were sent to Earth to learn, we are allowed to graduate. We are allowed to shed our body, which imprisons our soul the way a cocoon encloses the future butterfly, and when the time is right we can let go of it. Then we will be free of pain, free of fears and free of worries . . . free as a beautiful butterfly returning home to God. . . which is a place where we are never alone, where we continue to grow and to sing and to dance, where we are with those we loved, and where we are surrounded with more love than we can ever imagine.

Thankfully, I have reached a level where I no longer have to come back to learn any more lessons, but sadly I am not comfortable with the world I am departing for the last time. The whole planet is in trouble. This is a very tenuous time in history. Earth has been abused for too long without regard for any serious consequences. Mankind has wreaked havoc with the bounty of God's garden. Weapons, greed, materialism, destructiveness. They have become the catechism of life, the mantra of generations whose meditations on the meaning of life have gone dangerously awry.

I believe Earth will soon correct these misdeeds. Because of what mankind has done, there will be tremendous earthquakes, floods, volcanic eruptions and other natural disasters on a scale never before witnessed. Because of what mankind has forgotten, there will be enormous casualties suffered. I know this. My spooks have told me to expect upheavals and seizures of biblical proportions. How else can people be awakened? What other way is there to teach respect for nature and the necessity of spirituality?

Just as my eyes have seen the future, my heart goes out to those who are left behind. Do not be afraid. There is no cause for it, if you remember that death does not exist. Instead know your own self and view life as a challenge where the hardest choices are the highest ones, the ones that will resonate with righteousness

and provide the strength and insight of Him, the Highest of the High. *The greatest gift God has given us is free choice.* There are no accidents. Everything in life happens for a positive reason. *Should you shield the canyons from the windstorms, you would never see the beauty of their carvings.*

As I pass from this world to the next, I know that heaven or hell is determined by the way people live their lives in the present. *The sole purpose of life is to grow. The ultimate lesson is learning how to love and be loved unconditionally.* There are millions of people on Earth who are starving. There are millions who are homeless. There are millions who have AIDS. There are millions of people who have been abused. There are millions of people who struggle with disabilities. Every day someone new cries out for understanding and compassion. Listen to the sound. Hear the call as if it was beautiful music. I can assure you that the greatest rewards in your whole life will come from opening your heart to those in need. The greatest blessings always come from helping.

I truly believe that my truth is a universal one—above all religions, economics, race and color—shared by the common experience of life.

All people come from the same source and return to the same source.

We must all learn to love and be loved unconditionally.

All the hardships that come to you in life, all the tribulations and nightmares, all the things you see as punishments from God, are in reality like gifts. They are an opportunity to grow, which is the sole purpose of life.

You cannot heal the world without healing yourself first.

If you are ready for spiritual experiences and you are not afraid, you will have them yourself. You do not need a guru or a Baba to tell you how to do it.

All of us, when we were born from the source, which I call God, were endowed with a facet of divinity. That is what gives us knowledge of our immortality.

You should live until you die.

No one dies alone.

Everyone is loved beyond comprehension. Everyone is blessed and guided.

It is very important that you do only what you love to do. You may be poor, you may go hungry, you may live in a shabby place, but you will totally live. And at the end of your days, you will bless your life because you have done what you came here to do.

The hardest lesson to learn is unconditional love.

Dying is nothing to fear. It can be the most wonderful experience of your life. It all depends on how you have lived.

Death is but a transition from this life to another existence where there is no more pain and anguish.

Everything is bearable when there is love.

My wish is that you try to give more people more love.

The only thing that lives forever is love.

Questions

1. Write out three statements from Dr. Kübler-Ross's philosophy of "life and living," and describe in your own words what they mean to you.

2. Put the following sentence into your own words, and illustrate it with an example from your own life: "Should you shield the canyons from the windstorms, you would never see the beauty of their carvings."

3. Do you find yourself mostly agreeing, or mostly disagreeing with Dr. Kübler-Ross's philosophy of "life and living"? Identify three statements with which you agree or disagree most, and explain your reasoning.

Small Group Exercises

1. In your small group, discuss the factors that most make you afraid of dying. Suggest practical ways in which these fears could be minimized.

2. Discuss in the group your views on pain medication for the terminally ill. Work on such questions as:
   a. Would you be worried about the patient becoming addicted to the pain medicine?
   b. Would you be opposed to the patient using an illegal substance like cannabis or heroine if it helped with the pain of the illness?
   c. If you were the patient, would you want more or less pain medication than you actually needed, and why?

3. Identify the essential spiritual tasks each of you would want to accomplish if you were suddenly to learn that you had only three months to live. Describe in detail exactly how you would accomplish each task. Use the following questions as guides for discussion:
   a. Whom would you want at your bedside in your final days?
   b. To whom would you want to offer forgiveness?
   c. From whom would you want to ask forgiveness?
   d. What special possessions would you give away, and to whom would you give them?
   e. What final words would you like to say to your loved ones?
   f. How would you like to make your peace with God (if appropriate)?

Practical Learning Component

1. Ask the chair of the ethics committee at your local hospital if you can sit in on one or more of their monthly meetings. Here medical personnel, hospital staff, and local pastors and ethicists gather to discuss cases in which, among other things, end-of-life decisions have to be made.

2. Interview an oncologist at your local hospital on the issue of pain management for terminal cancer patients. Ask about the types of medicines used, problems associated with each, and what new forms of pain treatment are now available. Ask the doctor his or her opinion on alternative forms of pain management (acupuncture, meditation, guided imagery, etc.).

3. Interview several hospice nurses and chaplains about "nearing death awareness." Ask whether they have seen examples of it. Undoubtedly they will have many stories to tell about their experiences with it.

Copyright Acknowledgments

—✦—

Glossary of End-of-Life Terms

Active Euthanasia: deliberate action (usually lethal injection) to end the life of a terminally ill patient.

Advance Directive: legal term for a written statement from the terminal patient to his or her doctor that life-support equipment is not to be used when it will only delay inevitable death.

Assisted Suicide: providing the means by which a person can take his or her own life.

Bioethics: the study of the moral problems that face modern medicine and other biological sciences.

Brain Death: complete cessation of cognitive activity in the brain. The body can be kept alive using life-support equipment, but recovery is a medical impossibility.

Competency: the ability of the patient to communicate actively with the physician, and to understand the implications of his or her condition and the consequences of the medical procedures involved.

CPR: cardiopulmonary resuscitation; nonsurgical massage of the heart which has stopped to try to get it working again.

DNR: do not resuscitate; an order on the patient's medical chart advising health professionals that heroic measures should not be used to attempt to save the patient's life.

Durable Power of Attorney for Health Care: an advance directive by which the patient nominates another person to make healthcare decisions in the event he or she becomes incompetent and is unable to make those decisions.

Euthanasia: a "good" (i.e. happy, painless, dignified) death. *Eu* is a Greek prefix and means "good" or "well"; it elevates the quality of any substantive it is attached to. *Thanatos,* the root of euthanasia, is the Greek word for "death."

Health Care Proxy: a combination of a living will and a durable power of attorney.

Heroic Measures: medical procedures which are thought likely to be futile due to the terminal nature of the patient's condition.

Hopelessly Ill: patient will die from the illness despite medical intervention, but the condition is not immediately life-threatening.

363

Hospice: a formal program of palliative and pastoral/psychological care for dying patients in the final months and weeks of life. This care can be given either in the home or in special institutions designed for the purpose.

Incompetency: the lack of the above ability.

Informed Consent: permission given by the patient to the physician to carry out a medical procedure after he or she is made fully aware of the potential benefits and risks of the procedure.

Involuntary Euthanasia: the hastening of death without the patient's request.

Living Will: popular name for an advanced directive.

Mercy Killing: term loosely applied to all forms of euthanasia.

Nearing Death Awareness: theory put forward by hospice nurses Maggie Callanan and Patricia Kelley that as people near their death, they experience a heightened sense of awareness in which they are able to communicate more effectively the meaning of their lives, and what they wish for their loved ones after they are gone.

Negotiated Death: a formal agreement between family and physicians that life support to an incompetent person in a terminal condition is best withdrawn.

Palliative Care: medical measures given to the patient to increase his or her comfort level, but not to treat the illness.

Passive Euthanasia: the deliberate disconnection of life-support equipment, or the cessation of any life-sustaining medical treatment, permitting the natural death of a terminally ill patient.

Persistent Vegetative State: severely brain-damaged person in a permanent coma from which they are not expected to recover, usually on life support.

Right to Die: popular term that reflects the belief that end-of-life decisions ought to be a matter of individual choice.

Right to Life: popular term that reflects the belief that end-of-life decisions are not a matter of individual choice, but are best left to nature or the divine will.

Rule Ethics: obedience to moral standards as dictated by religious or philosophical belief.

Situation Ethics: obedience to moral standards as dictated by the prevailing sociocultural conventions, and the peculiarities of the situation concerned.

Slippery Slope Argument: holds that sanctioning certain practices for which there is general acceptance, like voluntary euthanasia for the terminally ill, may lead some to attempt related practices that are unacceptable, like involuntary euthanasia or euthanasia for the nonterminally ill.

Terminally Ill: patient will die from the illness despite medical intervention.

Voluntary Euthanasia: the hastening of death at the request of the patient.

Endnotes

1. S. Nuland, *How We Die: Reflections on Life's Final Chapter* (New York: Knopf, 1994), 255.
2. R. Dumont and D. Foss, *American View of Death: Acceptance or Denial?* (Cambridge: Schenkman, 1972), 2.
3. M. Leming and G. Dickinson, *Understanding Dying, Death & Bereavement* (Orlando: Harcourt, Brace & Co., 1998), 4.
4. Ibid.
5. F. M. Bordewich, "Mortal Fears: Courses in 'Death Education' Get Mixed Reviews," *Atlantic Monthly* 261 (1988): 30–34.
6. Kevin Browne and Amanda Pennell, "The Effects of Video Violence on Young Offenders" (London: Home Office Research and Statistics Directorate, 1998).
7. The Government's Home Office Report on Video Violence, January 1998.
8. *The Sun,* 29 May 1999.
9. *The London Times,* 27 November 1999.
10. Robert Fulton and Greg Owen, "Death and Society in Twentieth Century America," *Omega: Journal of Death and Dying* 18, no. 4 (1988): 379–95.
11. Stacey McArthur, "A Culture in Denial," *Indianapolis Star,* October 5, 1997.
12. David Stannard, *The Puritan Way of Death: A Study in Religion, Culture and Social Change* (New York: Oxford University Press, 1977), 17.
13. Octavio Paz, *The Labyrinth of Solitude: Life and Thought in Mexico* (New York: Grove Press, 1961), 60.
14. Herman Feifel, "Psychology and Death: Meaningful Rediscovery," *American Psychologist* 45 (1990): 537–43.
15. Patrick Vernon Dean, "Is Death Education a 'Nasty Little Secret'? A Call to Break the Alleged Silence," in *The Path Ahead: Readings in Death and Dying,* ed. L. A. DeSpelder and A. L. Strickland (New York: Mayfield Publishing, 1995), 325.
16. Marie de Hennezel, *Intimate Death: How the Dying Teach Us How to Live,* trans. C. B. Janeway (New York: Knopf, 1997), xi.
17. Elisabeth Kübler-Ross, *On Death and Dying* (New York: Macmillan Publishing, 1969), 19.

[18] Sherwin Nuland, *How We Die: Reflections on Life's Final Chapter* (New York: Vintage Books, 1995), inside cover.

[19] Ibid., 268.

[20] N. T. Wright, *Jesus' Resurrection and Christian Origins* (Minneapolis: Augusburg Fortress Press, 2003), 27.

[21] Ian Stevenson, *Children Who Remember Past Lives* (New York: McFarland & Co., 1999), 27, 49.

[22] *San Francisco Examiner,* 26 August 1923.

[23] Cf. Lynne Ann DeSpelder and Albert Lee Strickland, *The Last Dance: Encountering Death and Dying* (Mountain View, Calif.: Mayfield Press, 1999), 155.

[24] Adapted from Naomi Naierman and Jo Turner, "Demystifying Hospice," *AAPA* [American Academy of Physician Assistants] *News,* 15 July 1997, 7.

[25] All statistics contained in this writing come from *In Harm's Way: Suicide in America,* published by the National Institute of Mental Health, Washington D.C. (NIH Publication No. 01–4594).

[26] www.save.org

[27] Edwin Schneidman, *Deaths of Man* (New York: Quadrangle Books, 1973), 81; cited in Lynne Ann DeSpelder and Albert Lee Strickland, *The Last Dance* (Mountain View, Calif.: Mayfield Press, 1999), 427.

[28] Adapted from Trevor Hazell, "Defining Suicide and Attempted Suicide," presented at a conference sponsored by the Hunter Institute of Mental Health, November, 1998.

[29] Ludwig Edelstein, *The Hippocratic Oath: Text, Translation, and Interpretation* (Baltimore: Johns Hopkins Press, 1943).

[30] Manual of the Center to Advance Palliative Care, New York, 2001.

[31] Jacob Neusner, *The Mishnah: A New Translation* (New Haven: Yale University Press, 1988), 207.

[32] *The Code of Maimonides*, book 14, ch. 4, paragraph 5; New Haven, Yale University Press, 1982.

[33] *Islamic Code of Medical Ethics,* First International Congress on Islamic Medicine (1981), 10.

[34] Mahatmah Gandhi, *All Men Are Brothers: Autobiographical Reflections* (New York: Continuum, 1980), 84.

[35] Raymond Moody, *Life After Life* (New York: Bantam Books, 1975), 183.

[36] This list is compiled from the "elements" as they are described in Moody's books *Life After Life* and *The Light Beyond.*

[37] Maurice Rawlings, *Beyond Death's Door* (Nashville: Nelson Publishers, 1978).

[38] Moody, *Life After Life,* 24.

[39] For a summary of this research, see Ian Stevenson and Bruce Greyson, "Near-Death Experiences: Relevance to the Question of Survival After Death," in *The Near-Death Experience: A Reader,* ed. Lee W. Bailey and Jenny Yates, (New York: Routledge, 1996), pp. 201–2.

[40] Kenneth Ring, *Life at Death* (New York: William Morrow, 1980); Michael Sabom, *Recollections at Death: A Medical Investigation* (New York: Harper and Row, 1982).

[41] Adapted from Atwater, P. M. H., *The Complete Idiot's Guide to Near-Death Experiences* (New York: Alpha Books, 2000).

42 Cf. Susan Blackmore, "Near-Death Experiences: In or Out of the Body?", in *The Near-Death Experience: A Reader,* ed. Lee W. Bailey and Jenny Yates (New York: Routledge, 1996), 285–97.

43 Cf. Kenneth Ring and Sharon Cooper, *Mindsight* (Boston: William James Center, 2000).

44 K. Osis and E. Haraldsson, *At the Hour of Death* (New York: Avon Books, 1977), 7.

45 Carol Zaleski, *Otherworldly Journeys: Accounts of Near-Death Experiences in Medieval and Modern Times* (New York: Oxford University Press, 1987), 182.

46 Carol Zaleski, "Evaluating Near-Death Testimony," in *The Near-Death Experience: A Reader,* ed. Lee W. Bailey and Jenny Yates (New York: Routledge, 1996), 334.

47 Charles Corr, "A Task-Based Approach to Coping with Dying," in *Omega: Journal of Death and Dying* 24 (1991–1992): 81–94.

48 Elizabeth Leibold McCloskey, "The Patient Self-Determination Act," *Kennedy Institute of Ethics Journal* 1, no. 2 (1991): 163–69.

49 Michael Levy, "Pain Control Research in the Terminally Ill," *Omega: Journal of Death and Dying* 18, no. 4 (1987–1988): 265–79.

50 Lynne Anne DeSpelder and Albert Lee Strickland, *The Last Dance: Encountering Death and Dying,* 5th ed. (London: Mayfield Publishing Company, 1999), p. 181.

51 World Health Organization, *Cancer Pain Relief and Palliative Care: Report of WHO Expert Committee,* 3rd ed. (Geneva: World Health Organization, 1996).

52 Richard Ostling, "In So Many Gods We Trust," *Time,* July 28, 1996.

53 Christina Puchalski, "Spirituality, Healing and Cancer," (lecture given as part of the "Insights into Cancer" lecture series, sponsored by the Ted Mann Cancer Research Center, July 2000).

54 Michael Downey, *Understanding Christian Spirituality* (Boston: Paulist Press, 1997), 12.

55 Viktor Frankl, *Man's Search for Meaning* (New York: Pocket Books, 1997), 47.